Attachment and Neurobiology

Preconception to Young Adulthood

Attachment and Neurobiology

Preconception to Young Adulthood

E. Gail Horton, Ph.D.

Florida Atlantic University

SAN DIEGO

Bassim Hamadeh, CEO and Publisher
Amy Smith, Senior Project Editor
Casey Hands, Production Editor
Emely Villavicencio, Senior Graphic Designer
Stephanie Kohl, Licensing Coordinator
Natalie Piccotti, Director of Marketing
Kassie Graves, Vice President of Editorial
Jamie Giganti, Director of Academic Publishing

cognella® | ACADEMIC PUBLISHING
3970 Sorrento Valley Blvd., Ste. 500, San Diego, CA 92121

Brief Contents

Detailed Contents

Preface

Background

I became interested in neurobiology a number of years ago when I was engaged in research on spirituality among individuals in treatment for substance use disorder. One of our studies (Diaz, et al., 2011) had found some counterintuitive results in which individuals who scored relatively high on self-reported existential purpose and meaning in life scored relatively lower on depressive symptoms (which we had expected). However, we also found that those who scored relatively high on the belief in the presence of God in their lives scored relatively high on depressive symptoms (which we did not expect). We eventually began to think that these results may have been associated with the tendency of individuals who had serious problems in their day-to-day relationships to look to their relationship with God for comfort. This idea suggested that these individuals were suffering from attachment issues stemming from insecure relationships with their early caregivers, a situation that is not uncommon among individuals with substance use issues. Therefore, we began to explore associations between spirituality and attachment among individuals in treatment for addiction issues (Diaz, Horton & Malloy, 2014; Horton, Diaz, Weiner & Malloy, 2012; Horton, Luna & Malloy, 2015; Horton, Luna & Malloy, 2016; Luna, Horton & Malloy, 2016; Luna, Horton, Newman & Malloy, 2015).

Once our research led us to the literature on attachment, it was just a short step to the literature on neurobiology because, as that literature makes abundantly clear, attachment and neurobiology are very closely interrelated. Indeed, it is primarily through the attachment relationship that babies' brains are, quite literally, built (Schore, 1994). Furthermore, the neural foundations that are laid in their first months of life tend to influence everything that comes afterwards—thoughts, relationships, behaviors, and both mental and physical health.

Although most social work programs include some information on attachment in their classes, the study of neurobiology has only recently become a subject of interest. The brain has long been an object of study among neuropsychologists and among some medical practitioners, but social work and other mental health academic programs have not traditionally included neurobiology in their course work. For many years, social work researchers have bemoaned social work's lack of interest in and knowledge of biology in general and neurobiology in particular (Saleeby, 1992). This lack of interest by social workers is understandable to some extent since we are interested in helping people overcome their difficulties and in achieving social justice. For us, the term "micro" means practice with individuals, not studying something too small to see except when magnified under an electron microscope. Until recently neurobiologists have appeared to most of us to be more interested in how many times a rat blinks its eyes or in the action of esoteric and mysteriously named neurochemicals than it is in the practical and messy work of combating problems like child abuse, depression or addiction. We may have been happy when they found a medication that relieved our clients' symptoms, but we weren't so interested in how that medication actually does what it does or what neural processes necessitated its administration.

In recent years, there has been a move toward viewing neurobiology not from the microscopic, cellular, electrochemical perspective but instead from an *interpersonal* perspective. Believing that human beings are inherently social animals with brains that are built specifically for relationship, researchers are interested in how human behavior and psychopathology are produced and governed by the brain. Siegel (2012b) explains that from the Interpersonal Neurobiology (IPNB) perspective, neurobiology includes three elements: mind, brain, and relationship. He defines *mind* as "an embodied and relational process that regulates the flow of energy and information" (p. 2). The brain, on the other hand, is the physiological structure located both in our heads and throughout our bodies through which the mind flows. The brain's structure is determined by both our genetic inheritance and by our experiences, especially our experiences within our interpersonal relationships. That is, "both our internal neural functions and our shared communicative processes give rise to the process defined here as mind" (p. 5).

With this shift in perspective, neurobiology has become something that makes sense to those of us who are interested in what makes our clients do the seemingly completely crazy things so many of them do and in what we can do to help them improve their lives. After all, neurobiology is the very foundation of all human behavior; without a brain, we don't behave. Therefore, it is essential that social workers develop a basic understanding of the brain functions associated with and affecting social interaction so that we can optimize our prevention and intervention efforts. The purpose of this book, then, is to introduce interpersonal neurobiology and attachment to mental health workers and students in a way that will help them understand how the brain develops across time in the social context into which it is born and lives.

Organization

If you will allow me in the pages to come, I will guide you through a review of brain anatomy specific to social functioning. I will also provide a summary of attachment theory and its effect on brain development and functioning, and explore how attachment and neurobiology influence behavior during the formative years between conception and young adulthood when the brain finally matures. The book is divided into three sections. First is a section containing five chapters that provide (1) an introduction to the most basic components of the brain, (2) an explanation of the major nervous systems and divisions of the brain, (3) an introduction to basic brain systems, (4) a detailed exploration of the systems that make up the social brain, and (5) a discussion of the importance of neural integration to healthy emotion, behavioral and social functioning.

Section II contains three chapters devoted to attachment. Chapter 6 provides a summary of attachment theory and explains the neurological foundations of attachment. Chapter 7 discusses how attachment is related to relational functioning and psychopathology, and Chapter 8 is devoted to the clinical implications of the information included in the previous chapters.

Section III consists of eleven chapters devoted to brain development and attachment as they influence functioning in the developmental stages from preconception to young adulthood. Chapters 9 through 12 address pre- and postnatal development to about age three and developmental challenges that individuals face in these stages. Chapters 13 through 16 look at neurobiology and attachment and the challenges associated with them in early and middle childhood. Then, in Chapters 17, 18 and 19, I present the development of adolescents and young adults and some of the most troubling aspects of behavior during these life stages.

To help the reader visualize how neurobiology and attachment influence behavior, I have provided a series of case studies in which I introduce four children—Sophia Rodriguez, Jet and Luke Wolverton, and Macy Oster—as they transition through the developmental stages. These cases are entirely fictional, loosely based on my own clinical experience working with children and adolescents, on anecdotes provided to me by several clinician friends, and on cases presented in the literature reviewed during preparation of the manuscript. The events depicted in the case studies come directly from my imagination and are not based on any events actually experienced by my past clients. In addition to the case studies, I have provided questions in the margins of some of the chapters that can be used for class discussion or personal reflection.

I must caution the reader that, although I have ended the book at young adulthood, it should not be presumed that neural development stops at that time or that attachment is no longer important as an individual ages. On the contrary, the brain continues to change in response to the environment, and social interaction remains important up until the very moment of death. I stopped at the young adulthood developmental stage because the fundamental structure of the brain, including the prefrontal cortex (which is the last part of the brain to mature), is in place by then. In addition, the attachment styles forged during infancy and childhood tend to be relatively stable in adulthood. Thus, neurological and relational functioning during the middle and late adulthood stages are built on the foundations laid down in the stages that I have included here.

Lastly, I recognize a real deficiency in this book related to how attachment and neurobiology vary among different groups. For example, I do not go into how individuals from different racial, ethnic and cultural groups may have profoundly different life experiences that influence their brain development, attachment experiences, and psychological and behavioral outcomes. The same goes for variations in the experiences of individuals with different gender identities and sexual orientations. Unfortunately, space limitations simply did not allow me to go into these differences even though they are of great importance to our understanding why individuals behave the way they do.

A Final Word

Writing this book has been a real labor of love. I am passionate about the profound foundational influence of attachment on neurobiology and human behavior because I have experienced its effects not just in the therapeutic relationships I have had with clients but with my students in the classroom, young therapists who I supervise as they are just starting out in their careers, and even in my relationships with my friends and family. It is my fervent hope that after reading this book you, too, will recognize how important it is to notice how very old emotional and behavioral patterns can affect the present moment. If you have questions or concerns about any of the information included in this book, please feel free to contact me.

—E. Gail Horton
Boca Raton, FL
ehorton2@fau.edu

Acknowledgments

There are a number of people who I would like to thank for their support during the writing of this book. First, I would like to thank my great friend and colleague, Naelys Luna, who conducted the research with me that led to my initial interest in neurobiology and attachment. Her unfailing support, kind attention, and sense of humor have lifted me up and kept me going when times got hard. I am also grateful to my friend and colleague, Sara Dochterman, for her encouragement, support, and advice throughout this process, and for introducing me to Michael Shea whose knowledge and resources concerning embryology, intersubjectivity and polyvagal theory helped me enormously. I would also like to thank my friend Helen Trainor for her efforts in editing the manuscript; her keen insights and eye for detail made me see things I had not thought of. Lastly, I would like to thank Michael Cardinale for his helpful remarks concerning parts of the manuscript. If I have forgotten anyone, please forgive me; the writing of this book was such a long process, and I have such a short memory. Thank you!

The Brain: Its Structure, Systems, and Relationship with Social Connectedness

Introduction

This section of the book focuses on the brain. First, we should have a basic understanding of where your brain comes from and what makes it take its characteristic shape. Well, in the simplest terms, the brain is constructed from the genetic contributions of a sperm and an egg that, when combined, produce a genetic sequence (the human genome) that when expressed during the earliest stages of fetal development lays the foundations for the basic structure of the human body, including the brain. However, all brains are also unique. Although every cell in the body has exactly the same genetic content, genes are responsible for only about 50 percent of our psychological and behavioral functions (Littrell, 2015). What accounts for the other 50 percent? The *environment*! The term epigenesis refers to gene expression that is influenced by proteins that are produced in response to environmental stimuli.

Scientists argued for many years about which was most important to survival, nature or nurture. We have more recently come to recognize that both are essential. Nature provides the genetic contribution to our development. Without the information that genes provide, we would not be able to develop into a human being. But nurture, in the form of a well-functioning environment, completes the process. The term *environment* includes both a physical environment (a particular house, street, community with particular weather patterns and food availability, for example) as well as social relationships, especially those social relationships that support growth and development. Thus, nurture—the social and environmental resources that are available to us—is an important epigenetic contribution to our development. The dynamic interaction between nature and nurture builds and rebuilds your brain from conception to old age and death, and it is this interaction that we look at throughout the chapters of this book. Let me explain in more detail what we know about genetic and epigenetic processes that structure the brain.

Brain Development as a Genetic Process

The brain begins to form very early in the fetal development process. After a sperm (with half of the DNA required for development into a human being) and an egg (with the other half of the DNA) merge, the new cell with the complete set of DNA provided from both parents floats down into the uterus, dividing and dividing and dividing as it drifts and finally attaches to the uterine wall. The cells that result from those early divisions are all clustered into a single, undifferentiated blob, called "stem cells."

An amazing thing happens to this blob of stem cells after about two weeks: the cells begin to migrate and to differentiate. DNA contains the instructions for building certain proteins that will determine various cell functions as development of the fetus progresses. For this to happen, some of the genes in the differentiating cells are "packed away" (Littrell, 2015, p. 29) or silenced so that those particular attributes are not expressed. Other genes are allowed to express, so the little toe doesn't look like an eyeball. Some of the cells in that blob suddenly begin to form an indentation that becomes a tube inside the blob. This is the beginning of the brain and spinal column. Others cells begin to form the heart and respond to an electrical stimulus that causes them to beat rhythmically. Still others begin to divide into little protrusions that later become arms and legs and so on for all the various and sundry parts of the body and brain.

These genetic contributions to brain development mean that all human beings will have parts of the brain devoted to, for example, vision, hearing, language, memory, emotion, judgment, and social interaction in specific and expected areas. Genes are also associated with a predisposition toward psychological issues such as addiction and depression as well as antisocial behaviors. Nonetheless, research is showing more and more clearly that our genes are not entirely responsible for how we turn out. That is, we are not at the mercy of our genes. Because each individual is born into a specific environment, the brain has mechanisms by which it can prepare itself for whatever environment it is born into. That environment then shapes it so that the probability of survival is maximized. This mechanism, called *epigenetics* is discussed next.

Brain Development as an Epigenetic Process

While we are not yet sure about the exact percentages that genetics and epigenetics contribute to development, Combs-Orme (2013) argues that "DNA does not predict destiny. It rather assembles a set of potentialities to be activated (or not) by experience and environment" (p. 27). Epigenesis is a biochemical process that occurs during cell division throughout an organism's life span from shortly after conception all the way to his or her death. This process, called *methylation*, block proteins from attaching to a gene and thus keeps the gene from expressing. We know through studies with twins (identical twins have identical genes) that over time twins become less identical than they are at birth. For example, even though both may carry within their DNA a gene that is strongly associated with the development of breast cancer, one may develop the cancer while the other doesn't. Even though both may carry genes that predispose them to addiction, neither may become addicts, or perhaps one does while the other doesn't.

It is abundantly clear that genes, while important, are not the whole story. The uterine environment, and the environment that an individual is born into and develops within, contributes equally to his or her physical and psychological development.

Thus, while epigenetic changes do not affect the genetic composition of the individual's DNA (Wade & Archer, 2006), they do affect the ultimate attributes and qualities exhibited by the person as he or she goes through life and may even affect subsequent generations. Indeed, Hackett et al. (2013) suggest that methylation acts something like a memory that is passed down from one generation to the next. For example, several studies were conducted to explore the possible effects of stress on babies whose mothers were in their second or third trimester and developed PTSD associated with the World Trade Center attacks in 2001. One study found that these children had alterations in their stress hormones that increased their reactivity to loud noises and new stimuli (Yehuda et al., 2005), while another found differential expression of 16 genes among those mothers who developed PTSD compared to mothers who didn't develop the disorder (Yehuda et al., 2009). This same research team was able to identify epigenetic changes on a specific gene among victims of the Holocaust and their children (Yehuda et al., 2016). Moreover, research on animals has shown that increased stress reactions can be passed down *three* generations (Franklin et al., 2010).

Poverty, racism and discrimination are major causes of stress-related epigenetic changes that result in poorer outcomes for individuals who live their lives in a social environment where these factors are present. According Combs-Orme (2013), "poverty is the number-one threat to the expression of genetic potential" (p. 27). He points out that children who grow up in disadvantaged circumstances associated with a lack of financial and other resources do worse in every area of achievement—including physical and mental health, cognitive, intellectual and social functioning and school achievement—than their peers who do not live in poverty. These children tend to show up at the schoolroom door with deficits that get worse with each passing school year. Later in life, they generally earn less than their peers who had more advantages early in life, and they tend to have more medical problems, die sooner and contribute less to society.

This state of affairs is clearly an issue of social justice. Since social justice is a central tenet of the social work profession (National Association of Social Workers, 2017), it would natural for social workers to find ways to address this issue. These outcomes do not have a genetic source but are instead due to environmental factors that can be changed by continuing to work to reduce macro factors such as chronic and unrelenting racism, discrimination, victimization, and oppression. In addition, social workers could educate individuals and groups about poverty-related poor diet, also advocate for affordable housing to reduce crowded living conditions and for the clean-up of polluted environments where the poor often live. These epigenetic factors, some of which have likely been passed down for generations, are related to the high levels of reactivity to stress, low birth weight and infant mortality, and school failure and dropout that we see in this population.

Structure of the First Section

The important thing to remember here is that the dynamic interaction between genes and the environment affects how the brain is built and how it functions. In the chapters contained in this first section, readers will learn how the brain and its fundamental components and systems are arranged and how they function to support and influence human behavior. Researchers and practitioners who take the interpersonal neurobiology perspective (IPNB) (e.g., Badenoch, 2008; Cozolino, 2014; Fishbane, 2013; Siegel, 2012a) hold that the brain is a *complex* system that is totally integrated with the body. From this perspective, the brain is made up of differentiated, specialized parts that are linked together into a functioning whole. It includes the brain, of course, but also includes all of the nerve cells and the networks through which they are linked throughout the entire body, including large, dense clusters of neurons (i.e., brain cells) in the heart and in the gut. Indeed, Siegel (2003) cautions that the body and brain are so completely intertwined that the brain should be thought of as the "brain-body" (p. 13). Therefore, in Chapters 1 and 2, I describe the structure of the brain in terms of individual specialized cells as well as the networks that form the nervous systems.

The brain is a physical structure consisting of billions of individual cells linked together into networks and systems, and it is through these networks and systems that the *mind* emerges. What is the difference between the brain and the mind? From the IPNB perspective, the mind is "a process that regulates the flow of energy and information" (Siegel, 2012b, p. 1–1) through the brain and body. That is, electrical and chemical energy flow through the brain's networks producing information (mental representations) that is perceived as thoughts, feelings, memories, sensations, and so on, or that cause actions within the body, such as movement, heart beats, breathing, release of hormones. This is an *emergent* and *self-organizing* system. That is, the mind both emerges from this flow of energy information and at the same time constructs and regulates it. The brain provides the mind a place to manifest, while the mind directs and manages the circuits, networks and systems through which the mind runs as it encounters the environment in which it lives. It has taken millions upon millions of years for this complex system to emerge as it is in the modern human. Therefore, in Chapter 3, I discuss how the brain and mind have developed into their present form through evolution from the primitive structures and systems transmitted to us by genes and influenced by environmental pressures.

To complicate matters further, human beings are social animals, and our environment includes not just the physical elements in which we live, but also our relationships with other human beings. Therefore, in Chapter 4, I discuss the development of the social brain. From the IPNB perspective (Siegel, 2012b), the flow of energy and information (i.e., the mind) occurs not just *within* ourselves but also *between* us and others. Human beings are profoundly social animals, having developed through evolution a complex social engagement system with a *shared* neural network that allows us to understand and respond

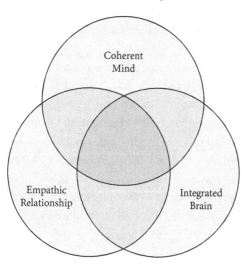

FIGURE I.1 **An illustration of the facets of Interpersonal Neurobiology**

Adapted from Daniel J. Siegel, "An Interpersonal Neurobiology Approach to Psychotherapy," Psychiatric Annals, vol. 36, no. 4, pp. 250. Copyright © 2006 by Slack, Inc.

appropriately to each other (Cozolino, 2014). Figure I.1 is a visual representation of the IPNB "triangle of well-being" (Siegel, 2012b, p. 4–1) in which brain, mind and relationship can be seen as separate but linked elements making up a single system. The physical brain supports both mind and relationship; the mind regulates both the brain and relationships; relationships influence both mind and brain. When the elements are functioning as a well-integrated whole, physical, psychological and relational well-being ensues. Siegel (2012b) explains:

> The functional connection of differentiated individuals to one another permits compassionate and empathic communication and rewarding relationships to be created. Healthy relationships thrive with integrative communication in which differences are honored and compassionate connection is cultivated. A coherent inner mental life arises from such embodied and relational integration. An integrated mind is a resilient and healthy mind. And so we could state that health emerges with integration in the triangle. We could also reframe this as health emerges from a balanced and coordinated brain, empathic relationships, and a coherent and resilient mind. (p. 4–4)

Therefore, in the final chapter in this first section, I will discuss nine pathways to integration necessary for optimal functioning.

CHAPTER 1

Neurobiology Basics

LEARNING OBJECTIVES

After completing this chapter, readers should understand:
- What the most basic structural and functional components of the brain are.
- How specialized cells allow information to flow through the brain.
- Which neurochemicals are responsible for mood and behavior.
- How the environment affects brain functioning.

KEY IDEAS

1. The brain is a complex system of interconnected neurons and neural networks.
2. Information is transmitted through the brain via neurochemicals, including amino acids, peptides, dopamine, serotonin, and stress hormones.
3. The brain is a self-organizing system that changes itself in response to environmental factors.

Introduction

Social workers and other mental health professionals take a biopsychosocial-spiritual perspective of human behavior. We believe that human behavior is influenced by the interactions among a wide range of factors, including genes and growth-inducing proteins; genes and the environment; the developing embryo and its intrauterine environment; the infant and his or her primary and other caretakers; the individual and his or her peer-group; and the individual and his or her community (French, 2008). The brain is a major biological feature that is affected by its environment and that is fundamental to our psychological and social functioning. It is therefore essential that mental health practitioners have a basic understanding of how the brain works so that we can formulate effective treatments and policies to address mental health problems.

In this first chapter, I will introduce the most basic elements that comprise the brain—neurons and neurotransmitters—and discuss how the brain uses the environment to structure itself.

Basic Brain Elements

The brain is an incredibly, indeed an almost unimaginably, complex system. The parts of the brain located inside the skull consist of one hundred billion specialized cells called neurons. Each neuron is directly connected to an average of ten thousand other neurons. That many cells with that many direct connections means that there are about one million billion connections within a person's brain. And this number doesn't include the supportive cells called glia that surround the neurons and provide physical support, nutrition and other services to the neurons, nor does it include any of the neurons located in the rest of the body!

Neurons and Glial Cells

Glial cells outnumber neurons by about ten to one. There are three different types of glial cells. One type, called astrocytes because they are shaped like stars, holds the neurons in place, provides them with nutrients, and cleans up their waste. Another type, called oligodendrocytes, produces myelin, a fatty substance that is important to the speedy and efficient flow of information through the brain and the firing of individual neurons and networks. A final type of glial cells, microglia, is an immune cell, present only in the brain, that destroys invading bacteria and viruses.

In contrast, a neuron is a highly specialized cell that sends and receives electrical and chemical information. Although scientists assumed for many years that the brain was incapable of generating new neurons, relatively recent research makes it clear that 5,000 to 10,000 new brain cells are created every day of a healthy adult's life (Aimone, Deng, & Gage, 2010).

Like any other cell, a neuron has a cell body that contains all of the normal cellular material such as cytoplasm, nucleus, and DNA. Neurons connect with other neurons through extensions called axons (which send impulses) and dendrites (which receive impulses). Information moves through the brain when a neuron shoots an electrical impulse (called an *action potential*) down an axon to its end, at which point there is a tiny gap (called a synapse) between it and the receiving dendrite. When the electrical impulse gets to the terminal end of the axon, it causes the terminal to release a neurochemical (called a neurotransmitter because it transmits information) into the synapse. This chemical floats across the gap and bumps into receptors on the dendrite. The receptor then converts the chemical into electricity and shoots it up to its cell body, which then sends it on to another neuron in the same manner.

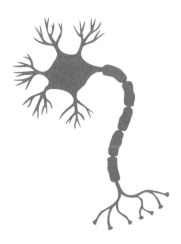

FIGURE 1.1   **Neurons**

Source: https://pixabay.com/vectors/nerve-cell-neuron-brain-neurons-3759541/.

Neural Networks

Each neuron is directly connected across synapses to an average of ten thousand other neurons. When a single neuron is stimulated, it sets off a whole string of neurons when it fires that together form a neural network. For example, imagine that you have just seen a rose. The light reflecting off the rose enters your eye, hits your retina and sets off electro-chemical action potential in neurons that carry the information to the visual cortex at the back of the brain. The next time you see a rose, that same set of neurons will fire, a phenomenon resulting in the well-known expression *neurons that fire together wire together* first introduced by Hebb (1949).

Thus, the brain is structured in such a way that neurons work together as small clusters of connected cells which may be then connected into larger groups that form whole brain regions (like those responsible for seeing or hearing). These groups may then connect into even larger groups (like the left and right hemispheres of the brain) with a multitude of differentiated but connected functions. As will be discussed in Chapter 2, we have specialized cell groups in the left side of the brain that are connected to specialized cell groups in the right side; we have groups in the front of the brain connected to the middle and the back of the brain; and we have the brain in the skull connected to the brain in the body. Thus, we are connected left to right, front to back, and top to bottom.

Neurotransmitters

Neurotransmitters are chemicals that are manufactured in the brain and that make it possible for energy and information to flow from one neuron to another and from one neural system to another. They can be classified into three distinct groups: amino acids, peptides, and monoamines.

Amino Acids

Two amino acids are of particular importance to brain functioning—glutamate and GABA (gamma-aminobutyric acid). These chemicals are the two most common neurotransmitters in the brain (Littrell, 2015). GABA is widespread throughout the brain, and where it is present, neurons are *less* likely to fire. This ensures that only relatively strong stimuli will activate them, thus avoiding needless activation by the constant stream of irrelevant stimuli coming from the environment. Alcohol and some of the most popular sedatives, many of which are associated with addiction, work by enhancing the inhibitory effects of GABA and dulling our senses.

Glutamate, on the other hand, makes it *more* likely that a neuron will fire. It, too, is scattered throughout the brain, and disturbances in the release of glutamate in the brain can result in over-stimulation of brain systems that we see in diseases like epilepsy, Parkinson's, and Alzheimer's. When these two neurotransmitters are properly balanced, the brain can send and receive information efficiently and effectively.

Peptides

Although many different peptides affect many brain systems, of particular interest to our study of human behavior in social environments are the opioid peptides: endorphins, oxytocin, and vasopressin. According to Cozolino (2014), these neuropeptides affect our experiences of pleasure and pain (physical, psychological and social) and are important to a wide range of feelings and behaviors, including our sexuality and attachment systems, pain management and responses to stress as well as to digestion and immune functioning.

Endorphins

The term *endorphin* is a contraction of the words *endogenous* and *morphine*. Endogenous means that something is produced internally. Morphine (like other opiates such as heroin) is an opiate medication used to block pain receptors in the brain. Thus, endorphin is an internally generated opiate that helps to manage the stress associated with physical or psychological pain. In addition, morphine and other opiates can cause euphoria, and so endorphin is also associated with pleasure. Endorphin receptors are found in multiple locations in the cerebral cortex, the limbic system and the hindbrain. Even though there are three types of endorphins, they will not be differentiated in this text but will be referred to simply as endorphins, regardless of type.

Endorphins affect our physiological response to stress, our breathing and the functioning of our digestive tract and immune system (Le Merrer, Becker, Befort, & Kieffer, 2015). They are released by the hypothalamus under three circumstances. First, they help to manage physical or psychological pain. For example, they are released during childbirth and also in response to loss, separation or social isolation. Second, they are released in response to positive social interaction such as touch and sexual pleasure and are associated with mother-child attachment. Last, they are released in times of extreme stress, causing dissociation and a freeze response (Lanius, 2014).

Oxytocin and Vasopressin

Oxytocin and vasopressin are two other peptides that, like endorphins, are associated with sexual activity, birthing, and attachment behaviors (Cozolino, 2014; Littrell, 2015). In addition, both are involved in the regulation and maintenance of social relationships. Oxytocin and vasopressin originate in the hypothalamus and make their way through the limbic system and up into the cortex. Oxytocin is also produced in the heart, with increased levels being associated with both receiving care and providing care to someone else (McCraty, 2015b). Women have more oxytocin receptors than men have, and men have more vasopressin receptors than women have.

According to Lanius (2014), oxytocin and vasopressin have opposite effects on social behavior. While oxytocin appears to prompt decreased levels of arousal related to social connection, vasopressin tends to prompt avoidance of social connection by increasing arousal and prompting aggressive defensive behaviors. Vasopressin is related to an increase in displays of aggression in animal models, including both playful fighting (Cheng & Delville, 2009) and active maternal aggression in response to threat to her baby (Nephew, Byrnes & Bridges, 2010).

In contrast to vasopressin, oxytocin is involved in all things nurturing and calming. In addition, it is involved in the pleasure associated with exploration. Often called the *trust hormone*, oxytocin is the "physiological mechanism for healing the body and the soul" (Lanius, 2014, p. 116). It is known to increase the pain threshold and reduce blood pressure and stress hormones. It is present in a woman's bloodstream during vaginal stimulation, copulation and orgasm and then later during labor. It is also stimulated by breast-feeding and seems to increase bonding and maternal caregiving behaviors. Positive touch such as hugging, cuddling and massage produces oxytocin, providing a sense of well-being and safety that is correlated with good mental and physical health. In addition, oxytocin release is related to emotional sounds, in particular, the cry of a baby who has been separated from his or her mother.

Why not, then, give everyone in the world oxytocin so that we could all just get along? Unfortunately, it's not that simple. Fishbane (2013) points out that recent research shows that oxytocin's calming, love-promoting effects increase "parochial altruism" (p. 113) when administered to males. That is, instead of increasing feelings of love for everybody, it increases them only for one's own group, resulting in ethnocentrism, exclusion of members of the out-group and favoritism toward the in-group. This makes some evolutionary sense in that, if long ago primitive man had strong, oxytocin-driven feelings of empathy and love for his family and tribe, he would probably have actively protected them against invaders. However, in today's world, more oxytocin could result in more of the divisions we already see between cultures, races, ethnicities, countries and even sports fans.

Interdependence of Endorphins and Oxytocin/Vasopressin

Lanius (2014) explains that the endorphins regulate production of oxytocin and vasopressin. Under normal circumstances, when opioids are released into the system, oxytocin and/or vasopressin is also released. However, in situations in which an individual faces severe trauma or neglect, it appears that endorphins inhibit the release of both oxytocin and vasopressin, inhibiting both the ability to seek out and connect with others and the ability to react to a threat defensively. Mental health professionals should be aware of the effects of this collapse of the oxytocin and vasopressin systems since disruptions in these systems appear to be related to a host of problems that we attempt to address in many of our clients, including PTSD, depression, substance abuse and borderline personality disorder as well as dissociative, somatization and attention disorders. In addition, a number of physical problems are also associated with low levels of these neurohormones, such as irritable bowel syndrome, chronic pelvic pain, interstitial cystitis, and hyperemesis gravidarum (Lanius, 2014).

Monoamines

Monoamines govern our energy and activity levels and our feelings of well-being (Cozolino, 2014). Some of the neurotransmitters most closely associated with the psychopathologies that social workers often treat are the monoamines dopamine, serotonin and the stress hormones cortisol, epinephrine, and norepinephrine (Littrell, 2015). These substances actually work in concert with GABA and glutamate to either create or inhibit arousal as they regulate our energy and activity levels and our sense of wellbeing.

Dopamine

Dopamine is a neurochemical that is associated with movement, learning, and motivation. When dopamine is present in our brains, we are able to move around in our world with relative ease. In its absence, we develop diseases like Parkinson's in which there is a gradual "freezing" of muscles that eventually leads to death.

In the past, dopamine was thought to be associated with pleasure because it is released in the reward center of the brain of animals that were engaged in pleasant activities, such as eating tasty food, having sex, or ingesting drugs of abuse. However, more recent research shows that the release of dopamine is not so much about pleasure itself but about *seeking* pleasure (Kringelbach & Berridge, 2015). As Littrell (2015) puts it, dopamine "is the neurotransmitter of 'wanting,' rather than the neurotransmitter of 'liking'" (p. 42). I can, for example, really like vanilla ice cream, but unless the thought of that pleasure stimulates the release of dopamine in my brain, I won't actually get up and go down to the vending machine and deposit money.

Serotonin

Serotonin is manufactured primarily (90%) in the intestines, while a small proportion of it (10%) is manufactured in the brainstem. However, serotonin receptors are found in a number of important brain regions, affecting memory and learning, aggression and sociality. In the gut, it is responsible for the motility of the intestines, moving food through the gastrointestinal tract. It also influences appetite and sleep, both of which are problematic in individuals with depressive and anxiety disorders. Low serotonin levels are, in fact, associated with depression, withdrawal, isolation, and increased vulnerability to negative life events. It is also associated with anxiety disorders, including PTSD and panic disorder, and appears to prompt withdrawal from dangerous and stressful situations (Cozolino, 2014).

Among humans, adequate production of serotonin is associated with feelings of contentment, and prompts empathy and prosocial behavior. It also is associated with vulnerability to depression, anxiety, and aggression that may be brought about through epigenetic changes resulting from stressful experiences. These changes result in too little serotonin being released into synapses. Therefore, treatment for this problem is often to prescribe serotonin reuptake inhibitors (SSRIs). These medications interfere with the normal functioning of neurons to allow the serotonin to remain in the synapse longer than it would naturally, thus elevating mood (Cozolino, 2014).

Although researchers recognize that the serotonin produced in the intestines influences mood and emotional stability, the mechanism(s) for this relationship is not yet clearly understood. However, recent research using rodents has shown that the lack of healthy postnatal gut bacteria was causally related to immune and endocrine system deficits and exaggerated stress responses (Clark et al., 2013). Other research has suggested that gut bacteria may be influencing the brain via the vagus nerve (discussed below) and that administering certain beneficial probiotic bacteria orally may help to relieve symptoms of anxiety and depression (Bravo et al., 2011).

Stress Hormones

Littrell (2015) also talks about the stress hormones cortisol, epinephrine (adrenalin) and norepinephrine (noradrenalin). Produced by the adrenal glands located on the top of the kidneys, epinephrine and norepinephrine are released very quickly into the system during times of danger and set the body up for fight or flight. When danger is perceived, the heart rate and blood pressure level increase, digestive activity is reduced, breathing gets faster, the palms may sweat, and so on. When that danger has passed, the levels of these neurotransmitters should fall back into the normal range fairly quickly. For example, if you are cruising down the interstate and someone suddenly veers over into your lane, epinephrine and norepinephrine will surge into your system, your heart rate will jump, your breathing will become fast, your eyes will be wide open, and you will slam on the brakes or run off the road. When you stop and are safe, your breathing and heart rate will return to normal within a few moments. Crisis averted, you can relax again.

Littrell (2015) notes, however, that cortisol, although released at the same time as epinephrine and norepinephrine, takes longer to get into the system and then stays there longer. This is not a problem when there is only occasional danger and the system has an opportunity to recover before the next stressful event. In fact, cortisol is necessary for simple day-to-day functioning such as getting up in the morning and going to work or school. However, when there is chronic stress, there can be serious problems. Let's imagine that your boss is an unhappy person and micromanages everybody. When he catches even a small mistake, he yells and threatens to fire you. You need the job; you bought a house back during the housing bubble that you can't really afford; your twins are going to college next year; and you cannot do without this income, so you can't just quit. As a result, your stress system perceives danger over and over again every day increasing the level of cortisol floating around your system. Your blood pressure is probably high, you feel anxious all the time, and you have difficulty sleeping. Now further imagine that you are out driving down the interstate and someone veers into your lane, causing adrenaline to surge into your system and your heart rate to go up. But unlike a person who faces only occasional stress, you are not able to return to a more normal resting state once the crisis is averted because of all of the cortisol already in your system. Instead, your level of epinephrine remains high in response to your cortisol level. Unsurprisingly, excessive cortisol is implicated in a host of physical and mental health problems, including endocrine, cardiovascular and immune functioning, obesity, hypertension and bone loss as well as neurogenesis in the parts of the brain associated with memory and learning, and impaired functioning in the executive center of the brain (Fishbane, 2013).

Interestingly, oxytocin counteracts the effects of cortisol (Fishbane, 2013). Thus, social support during times of stress, a friendly touch, a smile, or words of encouragement from family and friends can activate our "calm and connection system" (p. 33) and reduce the negative impact of cortisol on our physical and mental health.

Neuroplasticity

Because the brain has trillions of possible connections and interconnections, it can reorganize itself in response to the environment. This ability to change in response to the environment is called neuroplasticity. Neuroplasticity is what makes it possible for us to learn. Because we have such an incredibly complex system of connections between neurons and neural networks, we have the ability to accommodate all that the environment can throw at us over our life spans and to update the information from our internal and external environments so that we can maximize the probability of survival.

As will be discussed in greater detail in Chapter 3, the brain begins to develop approximately two weeks after conception when undifferentiated cells begin to form a tube that will eventually become the brain. During gestation, a developing fetus generates about 250,000 new neurons per minute, and when babies come into the world, they have almost all of the neurons that they will ever have (Rakic, 2006)—about 100 billion!

Many of those neurons are connected with each other even before the baby is born, but through a rapid growth process called synaptogenesis, or blooming, the neurons reach out to each other during the first three years of life and produce trillions of connections. In fact, during this blooming time, the brain grows to about 80% of its adult volume (Nowakowski, 2006) and produces about twice as many synaptic connections as it will need. This is apparently nature's way of making sure that the brain has enough connections for basic structures such as vision or language to function but also so that it can accommodate whatever it finds in the environment. Then at about age four or five, apoptosis, or pruning, begins to happen.

In this process, connections between synapses that have not been utilized during the blooming process die off so that the brain can process information efficiently (Huttenlocher, 2006).

The synaptic connections that are formed during blooming become the neural pathways that process information and allow us to form memories, learn, and make our way through the world. Pathways that are used frequently become both strong and fast. The strengthening of synapses is called long-term potentiation (LTP). What happens in LTP is that a neuron fires and sends a signal down its axon causing a neurotransmitter to be released into the synapse between it and a receiving dendrite. With repeated activation, the receiving dendrite actually increases the number of receptors it has available to receive the neurotransmitter in the synapse, thus becoming more sensitive. This strengthening can be very quick. For example, it has been shown that when cocaine is used even once, cells within the brain's reward and motivation system develop more cocaine receptors (Heshmati, 2009). With repeated use, the changes in receptors become permanent, a process that is believed to be associated with, and helps to explain the persistence of, addiction.

In addition to individual synapses getting stronger with use, the networks that they are part of also become faster through a process called myelination. Frequently used networks develop a covering of a fatty substance over their axons called myelin. This covering acts to insulate the axons and allow the pathway to function very quickly and efficiently, making them as much as 3,000 times faster than non-myelinated pathways (Siegel, 2012a). Myelinated neural pathways appear lighter than other areas of the brain and are therefore called white matter while parts that have not been myelinated are called gray matter. Synapses that are part of the myelinated pathways are unlikely to be pruned because these neural pathways are important for the individual's survival and functioning.

Summary

In this chapter, I have introduced the most basic components of the brain, neurons and glial cells, and have explained how neurochemicals act to allow energy and information to flow through the brain and the body. In addition, I have explained the concept of neuroplasticity, i.e., the ability of the brain to structure itself in response to the environment through long-term potentiation and myelination. In the next chapter, you will learn about the structure and functioning of the two main nervous systems, the central and peripheral systems, and the functions of the two brain hemispheres.

CHAPTER 2

Divisions of the Enskulled and Embodied Brain

LEARNING OBJECTIVES

After completing this chapter, readers should be able to identify:
- The parts and functions of the Peripheral Nervous System.
- The parts and functions of the Central Nervous System.
- The functions of the left and right hemispheres of the brain.

KEY IDEAS

1. The billions of neurons that make up the brain are organized into two systems: the Central Nervous System (the enskulled brain and the spinal cord) and the Peripheral Nervous System (all the other nerves in the body).
2. These two systems are further divided into multiple interconnected subsystems.
3. The human brain has emerged through evolution in three stages:
   - The hind brain, sometimes called the lizard brain because it first emerged in reptiles
   - The middle brain and its limbic (emotional) system which emerged with mammals
   - The cortex, which emerged with primates and developed into our sophisticated abilities to think, reason, and self-reflect.
4. The brain is divided lengthwise into two interconnected halves, the right and left hemispheres, each with its own specialized functions.

Introduction

As discussed in Chapter 1, the brain is located not just in the head but throughout the body in what Siegel (2003) characterizes as the "brain-body" (p. 13). The nervous system is divided broadly into two branches, which are each divided into multiple subsystems that regulate the functioning of the physical body and the mind. They control a host of processes that keep us alive, including heartbeat and breathing, hormone production, sexuality, hunger, thirst, management of emotions, and on and on. Figure 2.1 is a chart of the human nervous system, the primary branches of which are the Central Nervous System (CNS) and the Peripheral Nervous System (PNS).

The CNS consists of the brain inside the skull (including the retina at the back of the eye) and the nerves within the spinal column. The PNS consists of all the nerves outside of spinal column going out to (and back from) our heart, lungs, gut, extremities and even to our face

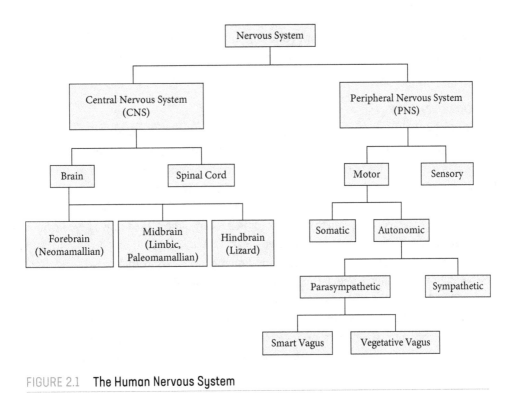

FIGURE 2.1   **The Human Nervous System**

and ears. Both systems include components of the brain and spinal cord, but they have very different functions as discussed below.

The nerves of the CNS located in the enskulled brain are divided into interconnected regions with specific functions, such as vision, hearing, language and so on. In addition, the enskulled brain is divided from front to back into two hemispheres that have distinct and separate functions but that work together to provide optimal functioning. In this chapter, I will discuss the parts and functions of the PNS first and then those of the CNS. Last, I will discuss how the left and right hemispheres function both separately and together.

Peripheral Nervous System and the Embodied Brain

The PNS consists of two subsystems: the somatic system and the autonomic system. These systems are in turn divided into subsystems. The somatic system is divided into the sensory and the motor systems, while the autonomic system is divided into the sympathetic, the parasympathetic, and the vagal systems. Activity in the somatic system is generally conscious and under our own control. In contrast, activity in the autonomic system is generally non-conscious and involuntary.

Somatic System

The somatic nervous system allows us to sense what is going on in our external and internal environments and to move in response. The sensory system provides information from both the external world (our five senses) and our internal world (bodily sensations, balance, etc.), and brings the information to the enskulled brain where it is processed. That information is then used by the motor system to guide movement. This movement is volitional; it is conscious movement in response to a sensation. For example, I am thirsty (an internal sensation), so I reach for a glass of water (voluntary movement). It starts to rain (external information), so I go inside (voluntary movement).

Autonomic System

In contrast to the somatic system, the autonomic system (ANS) is not under our voluntary control. Proper functioning of the ANS is important to the survival of each individual and of the species in general for two reasons. First, it controls the endocrine and immune systems that promote survival of the individual. The endocrine system works through a collection of glands (e.g., pituitary, adrenal, pancreas, ovaries, testes, etc.) that secrete hormones that are carried through the blood stream to organs and tissues throughout the body. These hormones affect our hunger, thirst, digestion, sex drive, heart rate, metabolism and growth as well as sleep, mood and other functions. The immune system protects us from infection and disease.

Second, human beings are social animals, and the ANS facilitates and regulates social interactions. Traditionally, the ANS has been described as having two circuits—the sympathetic and the parasympathetic systems. Newer thinking, however, suggests that there is a third circuit in the ANS—the vagus system (pronounced like the Vegas in Las Vegas) (Porges, 2011). These three systems and their interactions are described briefly below and in more detail in Chapter 5.

The Parasympathetic System

According to Porges' (2011) polyvagal theory, evolution built the parasympathetic system first. It was present in ancient, now extinct, invertebrates similar to our present-day starfish, sea urchins and jellyfish. It served as the earliest defense system, allowing the animal to freeze in response to a threat, reducing its need for oxygen and food, and letting it sink to the bottom of the ocean until the threat had passed. The system was conserved in later amphibians, fish, and reptiles, and it is present in mammals (including humans) as what is known as the dorsal vagal complex (also called the vegetative vagus). It consists of a group of nerves that extend from the hindbrain at the bottom of the skull all the way down through the digestive tract to the intestines and colon. It controls functions of visceral organs underneath the diaphragm, such as the liver, pancreas and digestive tract. When activated, it has a calming influence on us, putting us to sleep at night, and letting us rest, digest, recuperate and grow. In addition, it continues to provide us with an immobilization response to threat, and its healthy functioning is essential to our immune response and even to our mental health.

The Sympathetic System

As vertebrates became more complex, they retained the useful functions of the parasympathetic system (visceral functions and immobilization response) but added new functions with the sympathetic system. The development of this system gave animals a second defense system involving mobilization. The sympathetic system is about excitation and defensive action; in the presence of threat, it shifts blood flow away from activities that are not directly needed for survival (e.g., digestion) and moves it to parts of the body that will allow the individual to either stay and fight or turn and run away (fight/flight). Heart rate and respiration are increased, and the muscles are made ready to act (Porges, 2011). Thus, the sympathetic system is thought of as being "the gas pedal" while the parasympathetic system is "the brakes."

The Vagal System

As discussed above, the ancient parasympathetic vegetative vagus and the sympathetic nervous system provided (and continue to provide) animals with two defense systems—immobilization and mobilization. However, with the evolution of mammals, things got more complex. When animals began to form social units, there was a need for a nervous system that would allow them to live safely in groups, cooperating with rather than killing each other. The system that developed is the ventral vagal complex (also called the smart vagus).

Porges (2011) explains that before we had the technology that allows us to see the structure of nerves clearly, scientists thought that the vagus was a single nerve. Although we still often refer to it in the singular, we now realize that the vagus is actually a tube through which a number of different nerve fibers run, all originating in slightly different locations in the hindbrain. Thus, the ancient vegetative vagus originates in one area of the brain stem while the newer smart vagus originates in another area nearby. The vegetative vagus innervates the visceral organs found beneath the diaphragm in the lower abdomen, while the smart vagus innervates the visceral organs above the diaphragm, including the heart and the bronchi. Importantly, the smart vagus also innervates the throat, face, head and inner ear.

The primary purpose of the smart vagus is to facilitate social interaction. It accomplishes this in two ways: (1) it communicates social signals that allow others to know when it is safe/not safe to approach, and (2) it inhibits the sympathetic system so that we can cooperate and settle differences among us without the fight/flight/freeze responses getting in the way. That is, whereas the sympathetic system and the vegetative vagus act rather like on/off switches on your TV, the smart vagus acts like the volume control; it modulates your excitement during social interaction so that you don't automatically lash out, run or withdraw, and provides some conscious control over your actions and interactions (Porges, 2011; Rosenberg, 2017).

Porges (2011) cautions that, although the smart vagus developed so that social animals could stay in groups together safely, sometimes those social signals are not able to alleviate the danger an individual faces. Remember that in the autonomic system, the vegetative vagus (immobilization response) developed first, followed by the sympathetic system and finally by the smart vagus. In times of threat (real or perceived), they work in reverse. We will generally use the smart vagus to try to defuse the situation first. If using the smart vagus doesn't defuse the situation, the sympathetic system will go into fight/flight mode. If we can't fight or run, though, the vegetative vagus may take over and make us freeze. It is important to remember that the autonomic system is not under conscious control; in the presence of life threat, the body takes over. More will be said about this in Chapter 5.

The Gut Brain

Closely associated with the vegetative vagus system and the sympathetic spinal nerves is a dense network of neurons embedded in the gastrointestinal tract that comprises the enteric nervous system, or the gut brain (Mayer, 2011). Interestingly, the gut brain is organized in such a way that it can actually function completely independently from the enskulled brain, so that should the enskulled brain stop functioning, the gut brain can continue to work—as long as the rest of the body can be kept alive. The gut brain is connected to the enskulled brain via the vegetative vagus, which acts as a two-way street, conducting information to and from the gut and the enskulled brain. For example, my gut can send feelings of hunger to my enskulled brain that prompt me to think about where I want to eat lunch. When I get to the restaurant, what I see and smell may prompt my stomach and intestines to get ready for digestion.

The gut brain is not just about eating, digesting and eliminating food, however. Have you ever had a "gut feeling" about something? That feeling is your gut brain sending (via the vagus nerve) information that it has received from the environment to the enskulled brain where it can be acted on consciously (Mayer, 2011). Mayer puts it this way:

> Intuitive decision making can be defined as the rapid assessment of the probability of a favourable or unfavourable outcome of a planned behavior in a situation of uncertain outcomes, which is dependent on previous experiences rather than on serial processes of inductive or deductive reasoning. (p. 461)

The gut brain is thus an ancient rapid response system, acting below the level of consciousness to send messages to the newer conscious brain so that it can then determine the best response.

The gut brain has recently become a subject of great research interest because of findings concerning what is called the microbiota-gut-brain axis. The human intestinal tract is inhabited by 100 trillion beneficial bacteria, a veritable world in our guts called the microbiome. Evrensel and Ceylan (2015) note that there are ten times more bacteria in our intestinal tracts than there are cells in the human body and 150 times the number of genes as there are in the human genome. Indeed, a huge community lives inside each of us! In a symbiotic relationship with these bacteria, we eat food that keeps them alive, and they in turn break down the food so that our intestinal tracts can absorb it and send it out to our bodies as fuel to make us physically healthy. These researchers also point out that advances in medicine and hygiene have allowed us to reduce disease and live longer, and yet these same advances are also having detrimental effects on our gut microbiota. Antibiotics, vaccines, and antimicrobial disinfectants may all change our gut bacteria, resulting in serious health issues such as irritable bowel syndrome, autoimmune and allergy reactions, and obesity and diabetes.

Furthermore, it appears that our microbiome is also involved in our mental health as well as our physical health. About 90% of the serotonin (the neurochemical associated with depression) produced in the body is actually made in the gut (Evrensel & Ceylan, 2015). Though most of the research in this area has been based on animal studies, growing evidence indicates that the gut microbiota influence levels of stress, anxiety, and depression in humans and may also be associated with autism and PTSD (Mayer & Hsiao, 2017). Other research has reported associations between disturbances in gut bacteria and alcoholism, chronic fatigue syndrome, fibromyalgia, restless leg syndrome, and schizophrenia (Galland, 2014). Research on the microbiome is still in its infancy, and the mechanism(s) for its influence on brain functioning and mental health are not yet completely determined. However, this is an area of research that should produce valuable tools for medical and mental health professional to use in the treatment of some of the most troubling problems our clients face.

The Heart-Brain

Also closely associated with the vagal system is another dense network of neurons located around the heart that sends and receives messages from the enskulled brain (Ardell, 2004;

Brack, 2015; McCraty, 2015b). McCraty (2015b) holds that "this heart-brain's neural circuitry enables it to act independently of the cranial brain to learn, remember, make decisions and even feel and sense" (p. 5). Remember that the vagal nerve is primarily parasympathetic: Its purpose is to put the brakes on the sympathetic system, to rein in the fight/flight/freeze responses so that the body can relax, digest, grow, recuperate, and sustain relationships with others. When the vagal nerve has good, or high, vagal tone, it means that it is able to manage an individual's heart rate, a reliable measure of the individual's ability to regulate his or her emotions and behavior.

According to McCraty (2015b), the heart's nerve network communicates with the rest of the body and with the enskulled brain by four means: the vagal nerve, hormones, pulse waves, and electromagnetic fields. The heart sends information through the vagal nerve and through nerves in the spinal column to the brain stem and limbic system and then on up to the cortex. Information comes down to the heart through the same pathways. There are actually more nerves going from the heart to the brain than from the brain to the heart.

The rhythm of the heartbeat matches the pattern of hormone release (McCraty 2015b). Hormones released by the heart can reduce the amount of stress hormones released by our stress response system, helping to control the fight/flight/freeze responses. In addition, the heart produces oxytocin, the "calm and connect" hormone associated with feelings of trust, love and well-being, at approximately the same level as the enskulled brain itself does. Therefore, the heart-brain is, according to McCraty, important to an individual's ability to regulate his or her emotions and behavior.

Moreover, those emotions can be conveyed to others through the heart's ability to generate an electromagnetic field around the body. McCraty (2015b) explains that when the heart beats, it produces pressure waves in the arteries (pulse waves) that push oxygen into the body's cells. At the same time, this action causes the arteries to generate an electrical charge that generates an electrical field around the heart in all directions and can be detected up to several feet away from a person. It is thought that this field may allow "energetic communication" (p. 39) between individuals just below the level of consciousness and may influence empathy, intuition, and the development of attraction/repulsion between individuals.

Central Nervous System and the Triune Brain

As mentioned above, the CNS consists of the enskulled brain and the spinal cord. As Cozolino (2014) puts it, the contemporary human brain is "a brain within a brain within a brain, each successive layer devoting itself to increasingly complex functions and abilities" (p. 17). The brain has developed its current structures over millions of years of evolution, new parts evolving in response to the survival needs of species as they have arisen through time. This process has resulted in very primitive neurological structures serving as the base for the development of more complex structures, which have then been used as the base for even more complex structures.

The enskulled brain is usually divided conceptually into three sections. First is the brain stem, which is the most ancient and primitive part of the brain, developing first among the reptiles and conserved as higher animals evolved. Second is the limbic system (the paleomammalian brain), which developed around the lizard brain and added emotional capabilities to its functions. Third is the cerebral cortex (the neomammalian brain) which came on the scene as primates evolved, adding more and more sophisticated thinking, reasoning and self-reflection capabilities that eventually culminated in today's human brain.

Hindbrain

The hindbrain is frequently referred to as the reptilian brain (or, affectionately, as the lizard brain) because of it ancient origins among reptiles. In humans, it contains several components important to both individual survival and social engagement: the brain stem, the thalamus and the cerebellum.

Brain Stem

The brain stem is located at the very bottom of the skull, arising out of the spinal cord and connecting the enskulled brain to the rest of the body. It is the most ancient part of the brain and is responsible for the basic bodily functions that keep us alive, such as breathing and heart rate, reflex actions and basic states of arousal (e.g., awake, sleepy, asleep). A number of nerves associated with social functioning and stress management also originate in this part of the brain.

Thalamus

Just above the brain stem is the thalamus, a structure that acts as a relay station for information that is coming into the body through four of our five senses, routing the information to various other parts of the brain for processing. The only sense that does not pass through the thalamus is smell, which is handled by the olfactory lobe located just behind the nose.

Cerebellum

Located behind the brain stem and just below the occipital lobe, the cerebellum is also extremely ancient. It is a complex brain structure that coordinates movement, muscle tone, and balance. In addition, this area is also associated with the storing of motor learning as well as preverbal and procedural memory. Researchers currently studying the cerebellum suspect that the cerebellum's functions include much more than motor functions since it is closely connected with the parts of the brain responsible for imagining and planning movements (Wolfe, 2010).

The Limbic System

The limbic system evolved after the brain stem and is generally associated with our emotions as well as with learning and memory. It is the next step up from the pure survival functions of the hindbrain. It consists of a number of interconnected regions that work together to influence memory and learning, reward and motivation, and emotions. The limbic system includes the amygdala, the hypothalamus and the hippocampus, all of which are deep in the center of the brain just above the brain stem. In addition, it includes the anterior cingulate and the anterior insula (Siegel, 2012b), both of which interface closely with the prefrontal cortex. Lastly, it includes our reward system, which has dense connections to both the prefrontal cortex and the brain stem.

Amygdala

The amygdala is present and active in humans as early as the sixth month of pregnancy (Cozolino, 2014). Babies come into the world with a fully functioning amygdala. Its main job is to keep us alive by appraising situations as they arise in the environment for either possible danger or possible benefit. The amygdala is particularly sensitive to facial cues, providing us with an instant, intuitive sense of safety/threat concerning others. It is often characterized in the literature as being the *fear center* of the brain because of its role in triggering the fight/flight/freeze responses to danger. But it is also activated by positive stimuli, suggesting that its activation has more to do with appraising the emotional intensity of a stimulus than its potential for danger (Keltner, Oakley & Jenkins, 2014).

The amygdala keeps a record of intense positive and negative stimuli, forming memories that will be triggered the next time the same type of stimulus comes along. Those memories, however, are unconscious and expressed not in words, but in emotions, bodily sensations, images and assumptions. When triggered, they result in an emotional response. It is these memories that individuals access in panic attacks and phobias (Wolfe, 2010). In Chapter 3, we will learn more about the memories encoded by the amygdala and how they differ from memories encoded by the hippocampus (discussed below). For now, the memories stored by the amygdala are central to organizing the emotional and somatic elements of our experiences, especially those that are associated with threats to survival (Cozolino, 2014).

The amygdala is a relatively primitive structure that sets into motion automatic and very rapid reactions to danger encountered in the environment by triggering the fight/flight/freeze response through the sympathetic nervous system. This is a good thing since we need to protect ourselves from real and present dangers that threaten us. However, the amygdala is also responsible for fear that arises from something that is just imagined (Cozolino, 2014). That is, if you *think* that something bad is going to happen (even though that fear may have no basis in reality), the amygdala will react in the same way that it would to a real danger, starting a cascade of neurological responses that results in the fight/flight/freeze responses. This process seems to be what happens in generalized anxiety disorder and PTSD. An old memory put into place by the amygdala is triggered by something in the current environment, causing the amygdala to set off the fight/flight/freeze response now. This is clearly not helpful since it is a response to something that doesn't exist anywhere except in our imaginations.

Hypothalamus

According to Fisher (2014), one of the primary functions of the hypothalamus is bodily homeostasis. Homeostasis refers to the balance that arises in biological systems as they adjust to changing conditions. This process is similar to that of a thermostat that turns on the air conditioning when it gets too warm in the room and turns it off again when it cools off. For example, when our blood sugar gets too low, the hypothalamus sends a signal for hormones to be released that make us feel hungry; when we've eaten some food, it releases other hormones that tell us we're full. But the hypothalamus is also an important part of our stress system, or the hypothalamic-pituitary-adrenal (HPA) system. When the amygdala perceives possible danger, it sends a signal to the hypothalamus. The hypothalamus then sends a message to the pituitary gland (that lies just behind the bridge of the nose) which secretes a hormone that is sent through the blood stream to activate the adrenal glands (that lie on top of the kidneys). The adrenal glands then secrete stress hormones (cortisol, epinephrine and norepinephrine) that trigger arousal and vigilance as well as the physical and emotional sensations of anxiety and fear. This is the fight/flight system; when it is activated, we are primed to either attack or run away. Because of its capacity to influence heart rate and respiration, it is also intimately connected with the vagal system (discussed below).

Hippocampus

According to LeDoux (2002), the hippocampus, located deep in the center of the brain and closely connected to the amygdala, stores long-term, factual memory about the world and our experiences in it. Hippocampal memory is often called episodic because it consists of whole episodes of things that have happened, from their beginning to their end. It also is responsible for what is often called autobiographical memory, that is, memory about the places we have been, the experiences we have had, the people and things we have known. Autobiographical memory forms our sense of identity and provides a context within which to experience our on-going lives (Cozolino 2014).

While memories stored by the more primitive amygdala are experienced as images, visceral sensations and emotions, memories stored by the later developing hippocampus tend to be experienced in words. Moreover, in contrast to the amygdala (which is fully functional at birth), the hippocampus does not begin to function until about the same time that we begin to talk, around the age of eighteen months to two years.

Both the amygdala and the hippocampus are essential to survival in that they each provide a way for us to learn about our environment and what we can and can't do in it. The learning provided by the amygdala is unconscious while the learning provided by the hippocampus is conscious. For example, if a large dog attacked you at the age of two, later in life you may have no conscious memory of the attack yet still be afraid of large dogs. That is amygdala memory at work. If, however, your family tells the story again and again that you were attacked by a large dog when you were two years old, you may tell that story again later in life as a way of explaining why you are afraid of large dogs. This is hippocampal memory at work. The amygdala memory is experienced viscerally as fear; the hippocampal memory is experienced cognitively as a story. Because the hippocampus has access to conscious memories, it can actually modulate the often hair-trigger responses of the amygdala. The need for balance between the amygdala and the hippocampus will be explored in greater detail in Chapter 3.

Cingulate Cortex

According to Cozolino (2014), the cingulate cortex developed during the same evolutionary time that maternal behaviors, nursing of young, and social communications involving sound emerged. Thus, it is older than the prefrontal cortex but younger than the limbic system or the even older lizard brain. It appears to act as an interface between those ancient systems and the newer cortical regions associated with complex thinking.

The cingulate cortex is divided into two sections: the posterior cingulate (toward the back of the brain) and the anterior cingulate (toward the front of the brain). Though information about the functions of posterior cingulate is still very sparse, it appears to be associated with internal thoughts about self (particularly about autobiographical memory) and with attention to the changes in the environment that signal a need for a change in behavior (Leech, Braga & Sharp, 2012). It is also important to decisions concerning what behavior is appropriate to a given situation (and errors in behavior) and the processing of emotions associated with social interaction (Cozolino, 2014).

In contrast to the posterior cingulate, the anterior cingulate has been the focus of a lot of research. Holroyd and Umemoto (2016) suggest that this part of the brain coordinates a wide range of neural systems responsible for "learning the value of tasks, selecting tasks based on those learned values, and motivating task execution, which it affects by applying control over the activity of action-production systems" (p. 421). Very closely linked to higher levels of the brain (the prefrontal cortex, discussed below), it is involved in decision-making (based on reward expectation) and in maintaining the focus needed to complete whatever has been decided. In addition, it is involved in determining differences in expected outcomes and actual outcomes and spurring behavioral responses to the differences it finds (Lavin et al., 2013). Thus, the anterior cingulate may be responsible for "a spectrum of personality traits that include persistence, reward sensitivity, cognitive control, and anxiety, and many others" (Holroyd & Umemoto, 2016, p. 425). Moreover, dysfunction in this area of the brain may be associated with a wide variety of mental health disorders, including depression, ADHD, schizophrenia, substance abuse, obsessive-compulsive disorder, and Parkinson's.

Researchers (e.g., Cozolino, 2014 and Lavin et al., 2013) have pointed out that there is, apparently, a strong social component to this region's activity related to the integration of social information and empathy that guides decision-making. Through its ability to integrate bottom-up (emotional) information and top-down (attentional) processes, the anterior cingulate is crucial to social communication, cooperation, and empathy. It is probable that this area also directs the shifting of attention and motor responses associated with the expression of emotion (Wallin, 2007). Closely linked to the part of the brain associated with the perception of pain (the parietal cortex, discussed below), the anterior cingulate is involved in the emotional expression of both physical pain and social rejection (Fuchs, Peng, Boyette-Davis, Uhelski, 2014), as well as pain experienced when observing a loved one's pain (Lavin et al., 2013).

Activity in the anterior cingulate has been noticed in conjunction with complex functions associated with social information processing, allocation of attention and behavior, awareness and regulation of emotions, and memory for the past and the future. In sum, Cozolino (2014) says that the "anterior cingulate appears to be involved in simultaneously monitoring personal, environmental, and interpersonal information, and allocating attention to whatever is most salient" (p. 103). He suggests that while the posterior cingulate and the anterior cingulate have distinctly different functions, together they enhance the survival of both self and others.

Insula Cortex

Similar to the anterior cingulate, the insula cortex integrates the ancient lower brain system with the more recently developed cortex. However, whereas the anterior cingulate processes information about self and others and links that information to thought and behavior, the insula processes information about our internal physical and emotional sensation (called *interoception*), allowing us to be conscious of what is going on inside ourselves and also to recognize that we are separate from others. As Cozolino (2014) puts it, "the insula, which is a step closer to bodily experience than the anterior cingulate, is more specific to the processing of pain in the self and others" (p. 236).

The insula is activated during numerous bodily processes such as when we encounter disgusting tastes and smells, or when we are nauseated or feel pain. It is also activated during the processing of social information and emotional self-states. It is this region that apparently makes us want to laugh when others laugh or cry when others cry. Like the anterior cingulate, it is associated with empathy but more specifically with empathy for the very real pain that we experience within our own bodies when witnessing pain being suffered by a loved one. It is also activated when we are rejected socially or when we witness the social rejection of someone we care about.

Interdependence of the Anterior Cingulate and the Insula

Researchers (e.g., Cozolino, 2014; Siegel, 2012a) agree that the anterior cingulate and the insula are separate brain regions with distinctly separate functions but that they are highly interdependent. Together they are involved in the integrative processing of thoughts and sensations, the awareness of our own emotions as well as the emotional states and intentions of others, and the choosing of appropriate behaviors in reaction to whatever is going on around us. Cozolino (2014) suggests that these two regions work together as a "saliency network" (p. 240) that decides which internal and external stimuli should be used to promote our emotional and behavioral responses to interpersonal events.

The Cerebral Cortex

The cerebral cortex was the last major addition to evolve in the brain. Scientists who have studied the cerebral cortex (e.g., Kandel, Schwartz & Jessel, 2000; Siegel, 2012b) describe it as being the outermost part of the brain, consisting of six horizontal layers of cells that are folded into the characteristic wrinkled texture that we generally think of when picturing the brain. The cortex is associated with numerous essential functions such as perception, memory, language, thought, awareness, attention, and consciousness. The rear parts of the cortex are mainly responsible for processing signals from the external environment (our five senses) while the front parts process information located inside the brain itself that it uses to inform behavior.

Structure of the Cortex

The cell layers in the cortex form a *hierarchical structure* referred to by Roman numerals I, II, III, IV, V and VI. Layers I, II and III convey information from the subcortical regions and the body (sensations and emotions), or *bottom-up* processing. In contrast, *top-down* processing happens in layers VI, V and IV using information within the cortex itself. Goleman (2013) explains that the bottom-up circuitry is extremely ancient in evolutionary terms and generally conveys information concerning basic survival mechanisms. This information is usually involuntary, automatic, and impulsive and is conveyed very quickly through emotion and images. The top-down circuitry, on the other hand, was developed much more recently by evolutionary standards. It acts more slowly and analytically and is conveyed through thought with words. It allows us to consciously manage our impulses and feelings, to set goals and make plans, and to reflect on our actions and memories.

Top-down processing can cause us trouble, however, because our past experiences always color our present perceptions. The invariant representations accessed through autoassociation in the cortex can be activated by distorted or fragmented stimuli. When this happens, the prediction that your brain makes about what is going to happen next and what you should do will be based on inaccurate, outdated information. For example, if I was sexually abused by my uncle when I was four years old while Beethoven's Fifth Symphony was playing in the background, I may feel terrified by and enraged at my loving husband when we go to the symphony years later. I cannot hear the music without its being filtered through my memories of

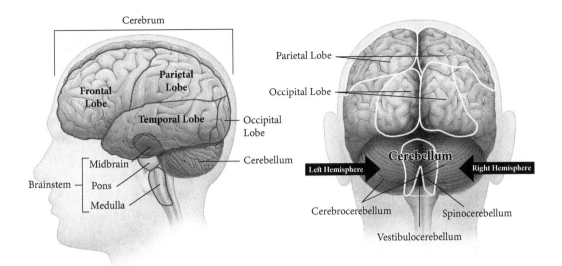

FIGURE 2.2   **Major Divisions of the Brain**

Source: https://pixabay.com/vectors/brain-human-anatomy-organ-medicine-148131/.

abuse—whether I want it to be or not. Hawkins (2005) cautions that our brains do not base predictions on what our senses actually perceive but on what our memories tell us about those perceptions, and to a great extent, those memories actually determine what we perceive.

Major Divisions of the Cortex

The cortex is divided into four major sections called "lobes": occipital, temporal, parietal, and frontal (See Figure 2.2).

Occipital Lobe

The brain region located at the back of the skull behind the eyes is known as the occipital lobe. It is responsible for color recognition, depth perception, reading, and other processing of visual information.

Parietal Lobe

Across the top of the skull between the frontal and occipital lobes is the parietal lobe. Sometimes called the "association cortex" (Fisher, 2014, p. 54), its main function is to process information sent to it from all the senses except smell (which is processed by the olfactory bulb just behind the nose). Parts of the parietal lobe are particularly important because they harbor certain neurons that give us the capacity to imitate others' behaviors and to have empathy for others (Fabbri-Destro & Rizzolatti, 2008).

Temporal Lobes

Located along the sides of the skull are the temporal lobes. These lobes are responsible for auditory processing, speech and writing, language comprehension and arithmetic as well as music and rhythm, prosody (rhythm and intonation of language), and face recognition and memory.

Although much of the cortex is involved in processing stimuli that come from the external environment (vision, touch, hearing, etc.), three cortical areas deserve special attention in the context of human behavior in the social environment: the prefrontal cortex, the cingulate cortex, and the insula cortex.

Frontal Lobe

The front-most region of the brain (located from just above the eyes to about a third of the way to the back of the skull) is divided into two sections—the motor cortex and the prefrontal cortex. The motor cortex is responsible for voluntary movement, while the prefrontal cortex has a wide range of functions that are of particular importance to human behavior.

The *prefrontal cortex* is located at the very top of the limbic system. Siegel, Siegel and Shah (2010) suggests that this placement allows it to act as an interface between the lower parts of the brain that are relaying information from the body and the senses and the upper parts of the brain that integrate information from all parts of the brain and body. This interface allows us to have complex thoughts, plans and goals. These authors describe the prefrontal cortex as having several essential functions: (1) giving meaning, value and the emotional valence (salience) to incoming stimuli; (2) providing regulation of our responses to our own emotions; (3) promoting social cognition in which we are able to perceive the mental state of someone else; and (4) promoting the ability to reflect on the past, relate it to the present, and imagine a future.

The prefrontal cortex can be divided into two basic sections: side and middle. The side part, the *dorso-lateral prefrontal cortex (DLPFC)*, is the part of the brain that is responsible for conscious awareness and attention, through which we manage the complex cognitive processes involved in learning, reasoning, and comprehension (Siegel, Siegel, & Shah, 2010; Wallin, 2007). It also holds our working (or short-term) memory, which allows us to temporarily store information and hold it in the "chalkboard of our mind" (Siegel et al., 2010, p.10) while we manipulate and manage it (e.g., remembering what someone has just said in a conversation or multiplying something in your head).

The middle section of the prefrontal cortex is called the *orbitomedial prefrontal cortex (OMPFC)*. This section of the brain is associated with a number of important functions (see Table 2.1).

TABLE 2.1   Functions of the OMPFC

1. **Bodily regulation** through the balancing of the sympathetic and parasympathetic (vagal) nervous systems;
2. **Attuned communication** in which our own state of mind resonates with another's state of mind during social interaction;
3. **Emotional balance** resulting from the ability of this region to control responses to both negative and positive emotions and modulate behaviors associated with them;
4. **Response flexibility** that allows us to be creative in our emotional and behavioral reactions to changing or unexpected circumstances rather than responding reflexively and automatically;
5. **Extinction of fear** through this region's direct connection with the amygdala that can preclude fright/flight/ freeze responses;
6. **Empathy** arising from our ability to take another's perspective and respond to it appropriately;
7. **Insight** through the ability to reflect on our own past and imagine the future;
8. **Morality**, which entails being able to recognize and respond to the greater good for others when solving problems; and
9. **Intuition**, which arises when we are able to recognize messages being sent to us by the clusters of neurons around the heart and intestines.

Source: Siegel, D. Siegel, M. W., & Shah, A. V. (2010). Brain, Mind and Behavior. In D. Wedding and M. L. Stuber (Eds.), *Behavior and Medicine* (5th ed.) (pp. 3–21). Cambridge, MA: Hogrefe Publishing.

These functions allow us to understand ourselves and our relationships (Siegel et al., 2010; Wallin, 2007). The OMPFC is located in an area of the brain that lets it integrate the flow of energy and information between the embodied brain, the brain stem, the limbic system and entire cortex. Therefore, it is considered to be the mediator of attachment processes, regulation of emotion, and interpersonal social communication (Wallin, 2007). While the DLPFC specializes in cognitive intelligence, the OMPFC specializes in emotional intelligence. It is particularly important to our ability to manage our emotions and cooperate with others, functions that will be discussed in detail in Chapter 4. Wallin emphasizes that psychotherapists should be very conscious of the need to activate the OMPFC during therapy:

> The clinical implication of this (largely) missing linkage between dorsolateral and limbic regions is that simply thinking aloud about difficult emotions with our patients—particularly, traumatized patients—may be useful ... but insufficient. We need, in addition, to activate the middle prefrontal cortex by helping these patients attend to their internal experience, especially bodily experience including in particular, perhaps, the breath. (p. 81)

Wallin is suggesting that mindfulness interventions in which the client is encouraged to become grounded in the present moment rather than being stuck in the painful past or feared future can help the person modulate intolerable emotions. He argues that the cortex is, in essence, "an organ of memory and prediction" (p. 75). That is, the cortex is structured to notice repeated patterns in the information we are receiving from our internal and external environments (bottom-up input) and send it down to the memory systems to be stored. It can then use those memories when new sensory information comes in (top-down processing) to predict both what we can expect to happen in the immediate and the more distant future.

The processes involved in how memories are encoded and consolidated will be discussed in the next chapter. However, it is important to understand first how the brain developed through evolution to become the organ that makes human beings different from all other animals.

Hemispheric Specialization

In addition to the regions of the brain described above, the brain is divided longitudinally into two hemispheres, left and right. Some generalizations can be made about the functions of each, but it is their working together that optimizes functioning. Although human beings can often function adequately when damage has occurred to one or the other side of the brain, for optimal functioning, both sides of the brain need to be working well with communication between them. Even though in a given individual, one side may be dominant, integration and balance are necessary for healthy functioning. McGilchrist (2009) summarizes this arrangement:

> What is offered by the right hemisphere to the left hemisphere is offered back again and taken up into a synthesis involving both hemispheres. This must be true of the processes of creativity, of the understanding of works of art, of the

development of the religious sense. In each there is a progress from an intuitive apprehension of whatever it may be, via a more formal process of enrichment through conscious, detailed analytic understanding, to a new, enhanced intuitive understanding of this whole, now transformed by the process that it has undergone. (p. 206)

Thus, without this kind of right, left, right processing, we would have a greatly diminished capacity to maneuver through our world and thrive. Without hemispheric integration, there is a lack of understanding of pattern, nuance and of relationships between individual things within the context of place and moment. We would have memories of facts devoid of the personal and emotional context that guide good decision making. We would have no jokes, no irony, no sarcasm. There would be no empathy because we would not understand what someone is trying to tell us through their words, gestures, vocal intonation, and posture. Balancing left and right brain functions, then, is fundamental to the development and maintenance of psychological health.

Moreover, therapists would be pretty much out of business since there would be no putting of feelings into words, the means by which our clients gain an understanding of how their past is being acted out in the present. Indeed, one of our major functions as mental health practitioners is to help clients who are driven by unconscious (right brain) emotions to put those emotions into (left brain) words. Conversely, we help clients who overly intellectualize their problems (left brain) to go down into their bodies and feel their emotions (right brain).

According to Cozolino (2014), for about the first year and a half to two years of life, babies' brains are growing primarily on the right side. They learn about the world by encountering and interacting with their physical and relational environments. They learn to crawl and walk and begin to develop hand-eye coordination. They begin to develop a sense of their bodies in space and to differentiate themselves from others. In addition, as we will discuss in Chapter 7 in detail, they become attached to their caregivers with deep and long lasting emotional bonds, a process that leads to the ability to regulate their emotional and bodily states.

During the second year of life, the corpus callosum develops. The corpus callosum is a large bundle of nerves that runs from the front to the back of the brain beneath the cingulate and separates it into two halves. According to McGilchrist (2009), the purpose of this structure is not so much to facilitate connection between the two sides of the brain but to allow each to inhibit the other. Evolutionary pressures apparently demanded that, rather than developing two whole heads with brains inside, animals should develop two autonomous systems in one brain. They needed to be able to communicate with each other, but they also needed to be able to do their own thing without the other interfering.

Around the age of two, the right hemisphere stops growing and the left hemisphere begins a growth spurt, the two sides taking on distinctly different functions in a process called lateralization. For reasons that remain unclear, functions on the right side of the brain are responsible for the left side of the body and functions on the left side of the brain are responsible for the right side of the body (contralateralization). Alternating between growth spurts on the left and the right sides, the brain begins to develop the ability to speak and understand language and over time, develops rationality and logic.

We see two hemispheres among animals as far back in the evolutionary family tree as early vertebrates. This feature developed most likely in response to the need for two different and mutually exclusive kinds of attention. That is, having two differentiated hemispheres allows us to have two very different but equally important versions of the world (McGilchrist, 2009). Rogers (2000) noted that animals need the narrow, focused attention associated with the left hemisphere in order to get particular needs met. For example, the left hemisphere allows a bird to identify a specific dot on the ground as food while the right hemisphere remains vigilant and flexible for whatever else is going on. As McGilchrist (2009) puts it, hemispheric specialization allows for both *breadth and flexibility* (right) and *focus and grasp* (left):

> If it is the right hemisphere that is vigilant for whatever it is that exists 'out there', it alone can bring us something other than what we already know (possibility). The left hemisphere deals with what it knows and therefore prioritizes the expected (predictability). (p. 40)

Cozolino (2014) points out that these are very different and useful ways of apprehending the world for higher-level information processing. The left brain functions to promote conscious coping and problem solving while the right brain organizes a sense of the emotional and bodily self and appraises the environment for safety (approach/avoid). The two together maximize our chances of survival.

According to McGilchrist (2009), information from the environment is delivered first (through the thalamus and the amygdala) to the right side of the brain. That information is perceived as an entirety, not as a group of parts. However, the details of the whole are important, too, and so the right brain sends the information through the corpus callosum to the left brain where it is broken down into component parts (abstracted), categorized, classified, manipulated, understood, and perhaps put into words. Still, in order for us to be able to utilize that information to the fullest, it must be sent back over to the right brain where it will be reintegrated and placed into context. McGilchrist provides this example:

> The right hemisphere takes whatever is said within its entire context. It is specialised (sic) in pragmatics, the art of contextual understanding of meaning, and in using metaphor. It is the right hemisphere which processes the non-literal aspects of language. ... This is why the left hemisphere is not good at understanding the higher level meaning of utterances such as 'it's a bit hot in here today' (while the right hemisphere understands 'please open the window', the left hemisphere assumes this is just helpful supply of meteorological data). (p. 49)

Table 2.2 shows how the functions of the two halves of the brain differ. The details of those functions are discussed next.

TABLE 2.2   Hemispheric Specialization

LEFT HEMISPHERE	RIGHT HEMISPHERE
Focus and grasp	Breadth and flexibility
Knowing	Experiencing
Known	New
Predictability	Possibility
Division	Integration
Part	Whole
Abstraction	Context
Categories	Individuals
Impersonal	Personal
Non-living	Living
Cognitive empathy	Affective empathy
Superficial social emotions	Primary process emotions
Logic	Emotionality
Optimism	Depression
Explicit	Implicit
What	How
Control	Care
Medium	Message
Books	Life
Prose	Poetry

Source: McGilchrist, I. (2009). *The master and his emissary: The divided brain and the making of the western world.* New Haven, CT: Yale University Press.

Right Brain Functions

Most of the work done in the right hemisphere is below the level of consciousness. The right brain is relational and emotional, and it is here that we recognize faces of people we know and where we manage and express our emotions (affect regulation). Attachment, empathy and love are located on this side of the brain. It does not use words but instead thinks in images, feelings, and expectations, and it is here that we understand metaphor (that is, something beyond the words that are being spoken). However, PTSD flashbacks come from here, too.

The right brain processes visual and spatial information allowing us to send and receive non-verbal communication (eye contact, facial expressions, tone of voice, gestures, etc.). The right brain also houses an integrated map of the entire body as well as "the felt reality of our own story—our wordless autobiography as felt in and by our bodies" (Badenoch, 2008, p. 19). The right side becomes active when there is something novel in the environment. It is also here that we process music and that babies process their mother's prosody (vocal intonation, the lilting, musical language that mothers use in baby talk). This side of the brain looks at the world in context. That is, we comprehend the world as a whole on this side rather than as a group of parts (forest vs. trees).

Left Brain Functions

The left brain is all about organizing things into categories and sequences; it understands the pieces rather than the whole (trees/forest). We also experience our sense of consciousness in this hemisphere. Siegel and Hartzell (2003) say that the left brain is where logic, linearity, language and literalness lie. Cozolino (2010) explains that the left brain is responsible for language, reading, writing and math develop, and it is on the left side that we learn and recall facts we have learned. The left brain figures out logical explanations for the images and emotions that the right brain experiences. While the left brain sees nothing but black and white, the right brain sees many shades of gray.

Summary

In this chapter, I have described the components and functions of the human nervous system. In the PNS, there are two subsystems, the somatic system and the autonomic system (ANS). Special emphasis was placed on the origins and functions of the subsystems of the ANS because they are so important to both mental health and social interaction, as will become apparent in later chapters. The evolutionary underpinnings of the triune brain—hind, limbic, and cerebral cortex—was also described and the individual parts identified. Finally, the left and right hemispheres were compared and contrasted, and the importance of integration of the two for optimal mental health was emphasized. In the next chapter, I will discuss the influence of genes and epigenetic processes on the development and functioning of all these interconnected systems.

CHAPTER 3

Basic Brain Systems

LEARNING OBJECTIVES

After completing this chapter, readers should understand:

- Different kinds of memory and how memories are formed.
- What emotions are and how they influence behavior.
- Which parts of the brain and which neurochemicals are involved in reward and motivation.
- Which parts of the brain and which neurochemicals are involved in the regulation of stress.

KEY IDEAS

1. Memories are representations of events that are encoded into sections of the brain as electrochemical energy and information and are essential to all learning.
2. Right-brain, implicit memories are not available for conscious recall, while left-brain, explicit memories are available for conscious recall in the form of words.
3. The limbic system controls the basic emotions (e.g., fear, pleasure, anger) and survival-related drives (e.g., hunger, sex, dominance, maternal care).
4. The brain's reward system is evolution's way of getting us to be interested in and seek out the things that are most important to survival.
5. The stress regulation system constantly scans the environment for signs of danger and regulates our arousal level to meet it and recover from it.

Introduction

In this chapter, I introduce four neurological systems that control human behavior—memory, emotion, reward, and stress regulation. Each of these systems is extremely ancient, having developed in response to evolutionary survival demands. The memory system, which is controlled by the amygdala and the hippocampus, makes it possible for us to learn. Thus, we can seek out things that have been beneficial to our survival in the past and avoid those things we remember are dangerous. Emotions are electrochemical responses to things that are happening in the environment or to memories of things that have happened. This electrochemical activity is located in the limbic area of the brain and causes the physical sensations that allow us to recognize emotions and to respond to them. Emotions are a survival mechanism. We tend to seek out those things that bring us pleasure and result in positive emotions, while we tend to avoid those things that cause us distress and result in negative emotions. Conserving what has aided survival in more primitive animals, nature provides us with a system that brings us pleasure and associates positive emotions when we engage in activities that promote survival—the reward system. Nature also provides us with a system—the stress regulation system—that prompts uncomfortable emotions and causes us to fight, run, or freeze in times of danger.

Although these neurological systems are highly interconnected, they are distinct systems. Therefore, I will address each one separately in the sections below.

Memory Systems

LeDoux (2002) has characterized memory as:

> A marvelous device, a means of transporting ourselves to earlier times. We can go back a moment, or most of a life. But as we all know, it's not perfect, and is certainly not literal. It's a reconstruction of facts and experiences on the basis of the way they are stored, not as they actually occurred. (p. 97)

Wallin (2007) explains that memories have two defining characteristics: autoassociation and invariant representation. The term *autoassociation* means that if any part of the network holding the memory is triggered, the entire network is triggered. Thus, for example, if you hear part of something familiar, say, "Mary had a little …," not only can you finish the phrase, but you probably can't stop yourself from doing so. *Invariant representation* (Hawkins, 2005) refers to the brain's functional storing of experience into neuronal patterns (memories) that allow us to predict the future when the pattern is triggered by a relatively similar experience in the present. For example, imagine your mother's face. You have probably seen it thousands of times in various settings and from different angles. If you were to see her right now partially obscured from the side, you would most likely still recognize her because you have an invariant representation of her face in your brain that doesn't change just because her position does. The same process means that when I say the word "mountain," a representation of that geographical feature will pop into your mind. It also lets us understand a word that someone says to us even though they may be speaking it with, say, a French accent. This is a very valuable function since, without it, we would have to figure out what we are seeing, hearing, or experiencing from scratch every time, causing the brain to go into gridlock and confusion.

Following is a discussion of how memories are formed, stored and accessed and of how the two distinct but interrelated types of memory—implicit and explicit— influence healthy functioning.

Memory Formation and Access

As discussed in the previous chapter, when we experience internal thoughts/feelings or external events/sensations, clusters of neurons fire in electrochemical action that establishes pathways that interconnect with other pathways in networks all across the brain. This firing of neural pathways is call encoding. An interesting thing happens to neurons when firing occurs; their receptors become stronger, making it more likely that the next time a stimulus similar to the one that caused the original firing occurs, it will go down the same pathway. This phenomenon is called long-term potentiation (see Chapter 1 for a review of this term), and it is fundamental to the encoding and access of memory and thus to all learning.

Of course, the brain can't create an actual physical event in the brain. Rather, it creates a *representation* of the event in the form of electrochemical energy and information. After the representation (sensation, thought, action, event, etc.) has been encoded once, anytime we encounter a similar stimulus, the same set of neurons fires again. The more often a network is triggered, the stronger it gets. In addition, neural pathways are linked with each other through association networks (i.e., portions of the cortex devoted to the processing and integration of information and sensory input) all across the brain so that retrieval of a single memory representation may activate many different parts of the network. As Siegel (2012a) puts it, the brain is "an anticipation machine" (p. 53). It uses representations it has established in the past to predict what is going to happen in the future. All new information is sent through the existing networks, effectively filtering everything we perceive and influencing our expectations of and interactions with the world.

Some researchers suggest that when a representation is encoded into memory, it includes two separate elements, a *verbatim* element, in which exact details of what happened are encoded, and a *gist* element, in which the underlying meaning of what happened is encoded (Brainerd et al., 2008). Although over time, the details in the verbatim element tend to fade, the gist tends to linger so that when, at a later time, an attempt is made to reconstruct a memory, the brain must rely only on the gist of the event. This can result in distortion and incorporation of information not related to the event at all.

When we think of memory, we tend to think of the things that have happened sometime in the past, information we have memorized for an exam, our loved one's birthday, the name of that person we met last week, where did I leave my phone, and so on. However, memory is much more than the words and pictures in our heads that we consciously call up when we try to remember something. There are, in fact, two different memory systems—explicit and implicit—and both are involved in learning processes.

According to which system encoded them, memories will be either explicit or implicit. That is, they either will be accompanied by an internal sensation that you are recalling something that happened in the past (conscious recall), or you will not be aware that what you are remembering happened in the past (nonconscious recall). Next is a discussion of the differences between the two memory systems and how memories in the systems are formed and accessed.

Implicit Memory

According to LeDoux (2002), implicit memory is an ancient system found among all mammals and most vertebrates. It works below the level of consciousness because the parts of the brain associated with consciousness did not develop until later in evolution. Implicit memory derived from ancient survival needs, like "perceiving stimuli, controlling precise movements, maintaining balance, regulating circadian rhythm, detecting friend and foe, finding food, and so on" (p. 117).

Implicit memory is the only kind of memory we have from the time we are born until about the age of two (at which time the hippocampus matures sufficiently to support the encoding of explicit memory). Remember that when we come into the world, we have billions and billions of neurons waiting to encode whatever experiences come our way—hearing mom's voice, feeling her touch, smelling her skin, tasting the delicious milk she feeds us, the temperature of the room, the color of the sky outside. However, it will also encode the sound of mom screaming at us and hitting us when we cry, or lying in bed helpless, wet, and hungry when she doesn't come. Since this information is encoded into the right brain and is thus not available for conscious recall, it will be accessed in the form of images, emotions, bodily sensations, expectation and behavioral impulses. When an implicit memory is triggered, we will be aware that we are feeling and doing things, but we will not be aware that they are memories. The implicit memory system consists of two kinds of memory: procedural (skills) and conditioning.

Procedural

Think about the first time you rode a bicycle. More than likely, when you read that last sentence, almost immediately you remembered details of that experience—where you were, who was with you, the color of the bike, the fear of falling, and perhaps the handlebars wobbling wildly as you tried to get your balance.

Now, think about the experience of retrieving that memory. You were aware as you remembered the first time you rode a bicycle that this was a memory, weren't you? It felt like it was something that happened sometime in the past. However, if you go outside and hop on a bicycle right now, you will probably just pedal on down the street, aware simply of the reality of riding the bike. It won't feel like you are accessing any memories of how to ride the bike; you'll just ride it. However, you are in fact accessing memories associated with riding bicycles, or you would be wobbling and falling all over again. This is an example of procedural memory. In addition to riding bikes or driving a familiar route to work or school without thinking about it, procedural memory influences many of the traits that make us who we are. These traits can be so automatic that they may feel innate and unchangeable. Characteristics such as the way we walk, our gestures, posture, facial expressions and vocal intonation, even the way we think, are all created out of our procedural memory.

Conditioning

Remember Pavlov's dogs? They hear a bell, followed immediately by food, which makes them salivate. Over time, they hear a bell and immediately salivate because they have learned that food is on the way. This is classical conditioning, or learning through association. This kind of memory can be seen very clearly in fear conditioning. If, for example, a big German shepherd dog bit you in early childhood, when you see a little chihuahua later in life, you may go into a fight/flight or freeze mode even though that tiny little dog couldn't possibly hurt a fully-grown adult and even though you have no conscious recollection of having been bitten earlier.

Early life experiences such as that mentioned above can influence our emotions and behaviors through a process called *priming*. We tend to remember those things that have had big emotional impacts, that have happened relatively recently, or that have happened repeatedly. For example, you can be primed to fear dogs as in the example above. Now, imagine that you have recently seen the word "green." If someone then gives you a list of items, such as sand, house, dog and grass, and asks you to choose one of them, you will be more likely to choose "grass" than the others *even if you were not aware that you had seen the word "green"* because you have been *primed* to choose it. Advertisers know this and use it to their advantage when selling something. Think of all the ads you see on TV in which there are happy, smiling, loving people enjoying each other's company enormously while a voice is telling you that side effects of the particular drug they are trying to sell include things like seizures, loss of memory, and death. Humans are so suggestible!

Similarly, imagine that your father told you again and again how disappointed he was in you throughout your childhood. When you grow up and have a child of your own and the child does something like, say, throwing his spaghetti on the floor, you may unconsciously slip back into your childhood state of mind and repeat to your child what was said to you by your own father. You were *primed* to say it.

When experiences are repeated again and again, we begin to generalize them into assumptions concerning ourselves and our relationship with the world, forming what are called mental models or schema. Since the brain's job as an anticipation machine is to figure out what is going on in the world so that we have a chance of surviving it, those generalized experiences are placed into implicit memory. From there, they will color our expectations without our being aware of it, causing us to do, say, feel, and even imagine things that are not necessarily appropriate responses to something that is happening years later.

For example, if mom ignores or maybe even hurts me when I cry, I learn that crying either doesn't help me get my needs met, or that asking to get my needs met results in a world of hurt. This information is encoded into implicit memory. If it happens once or only a few times, the memory may simply be discarded over time. However, if these early interactions are the primary way in which my mom relates to me, the memories will be generalized into mental models that will be eventually be consolidated into permanent memory (discussed below). Because these memories do not feel like memories, the expectations and assumptions of my mental models become *the lens through which I see my world*. Those memories will be triggered later (maybe even for the rest of my life) anytime I have needs that must be met, and I won't know that they are memories. They will be remembered through images, emotions, feelings, and behavioral impulses and experienced as happening in the present. Because we have no sense that our own memories are causing us to feel and act as we do, we are likely to blame something or someone in the environment as causing the problem. These memories will simply be felt as a reluctance to ask for help, an assumption that people can't be trusted, or a tendency to abuse your own baby.

The good news is that it's not just bad memories that are encoded in the right side of the brain. For example, babies have heard their mothers' voices while they were still in the womb, and they remember them and seek them out after coming into the world. Babies also experience the delightful effects of oxytocin and endorphins when their mothers cuddle them and speak lovingly to them. These memories will also be present on the right side of the brain since the left side is not yet working. Yet, these memories, just like the bad memories mentioned above, cannot be accessed consciously, nor will they have words associated with them; they may simply be felt as a sense of trust in someone you just met, an assumption that people at your new job will like you, or a strong desire to cuddle your own baby.

Explicit Memory

While the amygdala encodes memory into the right brain, the hippocampus encodes memory into the left brain. While the amygdala matures in the third trimester of gestation and is active at birth, the hippocampus does not become active in a baby's brain until around 18 months or two years of age, about the time that a child begins to talk. At this age, when the thalamus receives information of some sort, it will send it to the amygdala as usual, but also will send it to the prefrontal cortex into what is called working memory. If the prefrontal cortex deems the information to be relatively important (by scanning the entire brain for related information), it will send it to the hippocampus to be encoded into long-term memory.

Working Memory

Siegel (2012b) explains that for the hippocampus to be activated, the individual must have directed his or her attention to the stimulus, focused on it to some degree, and be conscious of it. Then the stimulus is placed very briefly (one quarter to a half a second) into sensory memory. Because the brain has to sift through the billions of bits of information it receives on a moment-to-moment basis, only a tiny fraction of those bits are sent to a section of the prefrontal cortex that is devoted to working memory.

One purpose of working memory is to allow the brain to manipulate information. For example, what if you need to make an important decision, say, whether to take that job offer requiring you to move to Michigan in January for really good money or to take that job offer in Hawaii starting next week for less money? Your working memory will hold these factors in consciousness for you while you search your memory to determine how important location, time, money, needs and preferences are to you. This is a really handy function.

Similarly, imagine if you are driving to school or work and see a parking space close to the front door, but the cars on either side are parked really close to the white lines. You have to decide whether your car can fit into that space without scraping the other cars, so your working memory takes what the brain knows about space, what it knows about how big your car is, and decides whether you can get away with it. It's really nice not to have to rely on trial and error, isn't it?

Another function of working memory is taking something from the past and applying it to the present so that you can figure out what to do in the future. This is the "time travel" feature of explicit memory. For example, imagine that you went to a Thai restaurant for the first time a month or so ago. Because you generally like spicy food, you ordered a green curry chicken dish and asked for it to be hot. When it arrived and you took the first bite, your mouth exploded into flames, your eyes and nose started running wildly, your friends burst out laughing at you, and the waiter was nowhere to be found. The next time you go to a Thai restaurant, as you read the menu, your memory obligingly reminds you of your previous pain and humiliation, and after consideration, you order beef with broccoli, mild, please. It's pretty handy to be able to use the past to predict the future. Thank you, working memory!

Long-Term Memory

One of the problems with working memory is that it is short; there's only about a 30-second window before that information simply evaporates. For example, someone leaves you a phone number on your voice mail, but you don't have anything to write with. You walk all over the house trying to find a pencil and paper while repeating the phone number aloud over and over again. If you hadn't refreshed your working memory by saying the number aloud, your brain would just let it disappear. However, if over the next few days, you dial that number several times, the hippocampus will find a place to put it (a neural network) so that it can be retrieved when needed. This is called long-term memory.

When the hippocampus places information into long-term memory, it will remain available for recall for some period of time but not forever. For example, imagine that you are a student cramming for your Research Methods midterm. You read the notes that you took in class over and over, repeating them to yourself and your study partners until you can access the information pretty well. You take the exam the next morning, you remember most of the information, and get a passing grade. Three months later, a professor in a different class asks you about independent variables, and you remember that you studied it, but you can't access the details. Remember from Chapter 1 that the more often a neural pathway is used, the stronger it gets. If the pathway isn't used much, it tends to get lost among all the other pathways that are being created, and eventually you can't find it at all. For memories to become permanent, they have to go through a process of consolidation (a process discussed in detail below).

The part of the hippocampus that encodes memory is situated in the left side of the brain where we experience both consciousness and language. Memories encoded there can be accessed consciously, are accompanied by the sensation that "I am recalling something from the past," and can have words associated with them. Siegel (2012a) explains that explicit memories allow us to travel through time, "to have a sense of the recollection of the self at a particular time in the past, awareness of the self in the lived present, and projections of the self into the imagined future...." (p. 58). There are two kinds of explicit memories: semantic (facts) and episodic ("chunks" of time that make up parts of one's life, sometimes called "autobiographical").

Semantic memory includes those things that you *know* but have not necessarily experienced, like the date when Columbus sailed the ocean blue, the capital of the state or country in which you were born, or your professor's name. Episodic memory includes those things that you have experienced at a particular time and place, like, "I drove with my friend Rachel to our 1:00 class last Thursday and learned that there are two types of memory. Then we had lunch at the food court."

Episodic memory requires that the brain be sophisticated enough to include both space and time. Since babies are born with very primitive brains, it takes a couple of years for them to develop these capabilities; however, as the brain develops, it allows an individual to have a sense of self as being located in the world in relation to other things (a three-dimensional sense of *where* I am) and also a sense of being located in time (a fourth-dimensional sense of *when* I am). In addition, it allows the person to place events into sequence (where, when, and *in what order*). For example, semantic memory contains the fact that I went to Maine last summer and ate lobster. Episodic memory, however, includes a rich sense of entering the restaurant, being taken to a table, ordering the lobster, eating it, and driving back to the hotel. The episode becomes part of my autobiography, my personal knowledge about who I am that I can communicate to others.

Impact of Context on Memory

To complicate matters even further, explicit memory is to some extent "context dependent" (Siegel, 2012a, p. 65). That is, the ability to recall something is easier when conditions are similar to those that existed when the memory was encoded. Imagine again that you are cramming for your Research Methods exam. This time, envision yourself alone, stretched comfortably out on your bed in your relatively dark bedroom, having drunk six lattes during the long night before the exam. Now, imagine the next day when you have to take the exam. You leave the house late because you were exhausted, you overslept, and you don't have time to stop by Starbuck's for your usual morning latte. You join 35 other students in a brightly lit classroom, and you're anxious about your performance. Because the context this morning is profoundly different from the context in which you studied last night, retrieving that needed information may not be easy. The associations that the brain makes include the context in which the original event (cramming) occurred, and without all those associations to help guide it, the brain may lose its way to the answers you need.

Impact of Emotions on Memory

The encoding of explicit memories can also be influenced by our emotions. As mentioned above, the laying down of explicit memory requires that there be focused, conscious attention to the stimulus. This is, however, something of a "three-bears" kind of situation. Look at these three different examples:

1. A six-year-old girl walking home from school overhears someone passing her on the street, saying, "He told me to get in the car." This means nothing to her, and she walks on down the street, forgetting it immediately. In this scenario, the stimulus was very weak, and the information didn't even make it into working memory.
2. A six-year-old girl is walking down the street and a large man grabs her and tells her to get in the car. She is found days later, beaten, raped and terrified, but she can't tell anyone what happened to her. In this scenario, the girl's sympathetic system activated in response to the danger, releasing the fight/flight neurochemical cortisol. Large amounts of cortisol in the system can shut the hippocampus down, making it impossible to encode a memory of the event.
3. A six-year-old girl is walking home from school when her dad pulls up beside her and tells her to hop in. The next day, she tells her friends that her dad picked her up and took her home. In this scenario she has an explicit memory that can be retrieved because it had enough, but not too much, energy to be placed into long-term memory; the emotional value of the stimulus was just right for conscious retrieval.

It is important to realize, though, that just because the fictional little girl mentioned above is not able to tell people what happened to her because she can't retrieve an explicit memory of it doesn't mean that there is no memory of it. Even though the hippocampus wasn't working, the amygdala was, and the amygdala is the part of the brain that encodes fear memories. It places them in the right side of the brain in implicit memory. It is possible, therefore, that this poor little girl will be plagued by implicit intrusive images, emotions, bodily sensation and behaviors, symptoms associated with post-traumatic stress disorder, for some time to come and perhaps permanently.

Accuracy

Another important issue with explicit memory is that it may not be accurate. It may feel accurate, but there are two problems with the assumption that one's memory of an event actually reflects what happened. One problem has to do with the way memory is linked and integrated.

As discussed above, the brain links and integrates newly formed representations with older memories in cortex-wide association networks. Siegel (2012a) states that

> The reconstruction process may be profoundly influenced by the present environment, the questioning context itself, and other factors, such as current emotions and our perception of the expectations of those listening to the response. Memory is not a static thing, but an active set of processes. … not merely the reactivation of an old [representation]; it is the construction of a new neural net profile with features of the old [representation] and elements of memory from other experiences, as well as influences from the present. (p. 51)

It is important to understand that new information is always filtered through our older mental models contained in our implicit networks (the lens through which we perceive the world). Therefore, non-conscious implicit information may become part of the new explicit memory without our being conscious of it in any way. Then when we recall the memory next time, it may include the old mental model but feel like it is exactly what we experienced.

A second problem concerning explicit memory accuracy is even more basic. We can put into explicit memory only those events of which we have become consciously aware. Awareness itself, however, is influenced by what is happening in that moment and what has come before. Siegel (2010) has suggested awareness arises out of two streams of information that move through the brain simultaneously. Figure 3.1 shows how this works. Recalling that the cortex is composed of a very thin layer of neurons only six cells deep (layers I-VI in the figure), we access stimuli from our external (the world) and internal (our bodies) environments through our five senses (see Chapter 2, and the section on the structure of the cerebral cortex). This is what Siegel calls *bottom-up* information because it comes through subcortical structures into the cortex through layers VI, V and IV. At the same time, the cortex is scanning its memory networks (both implicit and explicit) for associations between this new information and anything like it we have encountered before (layers I, II, and III). This is called *top-down* information. Siegel suggests that awareness occurs when these two streams of information—bottom-up (not-yet-learned) information and top-down (already learned) information—merge. When there

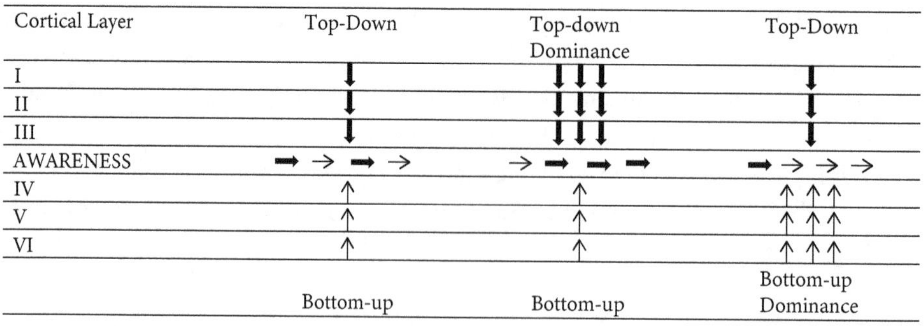

Cortical Layer	Top-Down	Top-down Dominance	Top-Down
I			
II			
III			
AWARENESS			
IV			
V			
VI			
	Bottom-up	Bottom-up	Bottom-up Dominance

FIGURE 3.1 **Bottom-Up and Top-Down Processing and Awareness**

Daniel J. Siegel, "A Schematic of the Six-Layered Cortical Column and the Bottom-Up and Top-Down Flow of Information," The Mindful Therapist: A Clinician's Guide to Mindsight and Neural Integration, pp. 105. Copyright © 2010 by W. W. Norton & Company, Inc.

are no deficits in mental processing (biological or psychopathological), the two streams should be fairly equally balanced. However, psychopathology can occur when the top-down information outweighs the bottom-up (top-down dominant) or bottom-up outweighs top-down.

In top-down dominance, senses coming from the subcortex are overwhelmed by expectations, assumptions, and habitual thought patterns dictated by prior learning and memory. When this happens, new information gets ignored, and old reactions and responses take over. For example, imagine that a therapist at a substance abuse treatment center is meeting a client for the first time. Having read the intake summary, she is aware that the client had been physically abused by his alcoholic mother until he was removed from the home and placed with his aunt when he was two years old. The client comes into her office and sits in a chair, crossing his arms tightly across his chest and staring at her with an extremely angry expression. Trying to engage him, she asks several general, polite questions. He refuses to answer her and after about ten minutes demands to see her supervisor. He then tells the supervisor that he wants a new therapist because this one has been rude to him and threatened him.

This client has no conscious memory of the abuse he suffered in infancy since he was removed from the home before his hippocampus was fully active and encoding explicit memory. However, his senses perceived (bottom-up) something about the therapist (perhaps the color of her hair, the soap she used that morning, her position of authority) that brought up (top-down) an implicit, pre-verbal, non-conscious memory of his mother, which he experienced as fear, helplessness, and rage. Since the top-down memory was experienced as something happening in the present rather than as something that happened in the past, he couldn't recognize it has having come from his terrible experiences with his mother but instead blamed the therapist for them. This irrational reaction by a client, by the way, is called transference. When the client recalls his session with the therapist later, his memory of the therapist will be distorted by the implicit fear, helplessness, and rage that he unknowingly incorporated into it; he will swear that she was rude and threatening even though she was nothing but polite.

In bottom-up dominance, sense perception is not usually associated with any memories. For example, the first time a baby tastes her mother's milk, she is tasting sweetness for the very first time. Since there are no memories of taste yet in her brain, her awareness is not influenced by any associations from prior experience. Obviously, pure bottom-up experiences do not happen very often, and the next time this baby nurses, the memory of that first sip of mother's milk will be there along with any experiences associated with that taste, such as her mother's soft skin and voice, or the smell of her body. It is possible to increase bottom-up input so that a better balance can be achieved in someone who is dominated by top-down processing and its associated psychopathologies.

Take again the example of the angry substance disorder client mentioned above, but this time imagine the therapist's reaction to her client. As it happens, this therapist had an alcoholic father who was violent and verbally abusive to her throughout her childhood. She is now being threatened and verbally assaulted by this client. Like her client, she is overwhelmed by her top-down processing, and after the client storms out to complain to her supervisor, she bursts into tears (just like she used to do with her father). This reaction to her client is what is meant by countertransference. The difference here is that, while the client is completely taken over by his memories, this therapist recognizes that her response is inappropriate. She has done her own personal work and can recognize when implicit memories are triggered.

She calms herself by sitting quietly in her office for a few minutes and paying attention to her breathing, a common meditation technique known to promote relaxation and stress reduction (Siegel, 2010). Consciously turning her attention to her breathing enhances the flow of bottom-up information, thus bringing her from the past (her implicit memories of her father) into the present. Calm and centered, she goes to her supervisor to discuss the case.

It should be noted that clients can sometimes recall deeply buried memories at some point later in life, perhaps after therapy, a phenomenon called *delayed recall*. Siegel (2012a) points out that since a memory can be affected by other memories with which it is associated throughout the explicit and implicit memory networks, and since it can be changed every time it is retrieved, it is very possible that delayed recall will be less than accurate. In addition, he points out that when we tell someone about something that has happened to us, we can be influenced unconsciously be whomever we are telling it to (especially during childhood, but also later in life). Memory is vulnerable to suggestion (as advertisers know very well and use to their benefit, and as practitioners who use hypnosis can demonstrate), and the possibility of inadvertently implanting false memories is something of which mental health practitioners need to be aware.

Formation of Long-Term Memory

For something to become a permanent part of memory, whether implicit or explicit, it will need to go through a process called cortical consolidation. Although researchers have not yet identified exactly what goes into the process of memory consolidation, it appears that long-term memories are first stored in the association cortex. The association cortex consists of areas of the cerebral cortex that surround the major lobes of the brain—occipital, parietal, temporal, frontal—and provide linkage between these disparate systems. It allows us to recognize objects, sounds, and sensations, to remember them in context, and think about how they help or hurt us. It supports complex mental processes and behaviors. For example, the association cortex around the parts of the brain that process visual stimuli can communicate with the association cortex around the parts of the brain that process language. Therefore, I can recognize my friend's face and understand that she is saying something to me. Without the connections between the two systems, I would see a person whose mouth is moving, and I would hear sounds. However, I wouldn't connect the two. Memories are also stored in the association cortex and linked to other mental representations stored throughout the brain. New information is coming into the association cortex all the time, and some of that information will be related to information that has already been processed and consolidated, perhaps during sleep and dreaming (Born, 2010). Therefore, the brain is constantly rearranging itself to accommodate this new information.

Because it is such a complex process, cortical consolidation can sometimes take long periods of time (weeks to years) (Siegel, 2012b). For example, using scenarios from the sections above as examples, cramming for an exam may work for the short term, but if you want to retain what you learn, you need to give your brain time to make the associations so that it can find that information easily when it is needed. As for the traumatized little girl, it is likely that her experience will be consolidated into her implicit network. Her memories may color her sense of efficacy, her self-confidence, her self-esteem, and her sense of whom she feels safe/unsafe with both in the days and weeks following the trauma and perhaps for the rest of her life, and she may not know why. Badenoch (2008) puts it this way: "Sadly, one axiom that proves true most of the time is that the greater the early wounding, the more power these implicit memories exert in the present, until there is some kind of integrative healing experience" (p. 26). The offices of mental health practitioners are filled with people whose moods and behaviors are being influenced by their consolidated nonconscious memories. Helping them to become aware of the nature of their memories and where they came from can go a long way toward helping them to heal.

The Limbic System: Emotions

The limbic system is a complex system of nerves and networks in the brain involving several areas just below the cortex and concerned with instinct and mood. It controls the basic emotions (e.g., fear, pleasure, anger) and survival-related drives (e.g., hunger, sex, dominance, maternal care). Wallin (2007) explains that the limbic system "is where the internal and external worlds meet" (p. 71) so that when things happen out in the world (external), our limbic system (internal) processes them so that we both sense them internally and manifest them in ways that are recognizable to others (external) as emotional responses. Understanding emotional responses is obviously essential for mental health practitioners because, according to McGilchrist (2009),

> the irreducible core of experience: they [emotions] are not there merely to help out with cognition. Feeling is not just an add-on, a flavoured coating for thought: it is at the heart of our being, and reason emanates from that central core of the emotions, in an attempt to limit and direct *them*, rather than the other way about. Feeling came, and comes, first, and reason emerged from it. (p. 185)

Damasio (2018) further explains the importance of emotion to human functioning and behavior:

> Feelings are *for* life regulation, providers of information concerning basic homeostasis or the social conditions of our lives. Feelings tell us about risks, dangers, on-going crises that need to be averted. On the nice side of the coin, they can inform us about opportunities. They can guide us toward behaviors that will improve our overall homeostasis and, in the process, make us better human beings, more responsible for our own future and the future of others. (p. 139)

The subject of emotions is not simple for two reasons. First, although many researchers refer to the limbic system when discussing emotion, it should be understood that there is no well-defined center of emotion. Instead there are numerous, complex and interconnected emotional systems in diverse parts of the brain that, when aroused, elicit changes in emotional states and the physical manifestations of those states (Panksepp, 2009). Although some neuroscientists (e.g., LeDoux, 1995) suggest that the term "limbic system" should be abandoned, it is both a convenient term and one that continues to be used by neuroscientists (e.g., Damasio, 2010; Panksepp, 2009; Siegel, 2012a).

Second, the terminology concerning emotions can be confusing. At times, the terms *emotions, feelings, affect,* and *mood* seem to be used almost interchangeably. Damasio (2018) defines emotions as "action programs activated by confrontation with numerous and sometimes complex situations" (pp. 7–8). He explains that emotions are the product of a continuous two-way energetic loop between the brain and the body (Damasio, 2010). Emotion is a complex, automatic, nonconscious neurochemical reaction to an emotionally relevant stimulus that causes predictable changes in the body, readying it for action of some sort (e.g., fight, run, laugh, cry, etc.). These bodily changes manifest both as observable (e.g., facial expressions, tone of voice, posture, behavior) and as hidden reactions (e.g., changes in heart and breathing rates, relaxation or tensing of muscles, release of glucose into the bloodstream). Closing the brain-body loop, these bodily changes are then consciously sensed by the brain, providing the individual with the feelings (bodily sensations) characteristic of the emotion.

Panksepp (2010) suggested that the term affect is synonymous with the more commonly used term *feeling,* both defined as "the subjective experienced aspects of emotion" (p. 534). It is often used in mental health practice settings to refer to the conscious experience of emotion and its expression (e.g., inappropriate, blunted, or flat affect). Affect has two dimensions—*valence* and *arousal* (Montgomery, 2013). Valence concerns how positive/pleasant or negative/unpleasant the emotion is, while arousal concerns how intense the emotion is, how much energy it elicits, how calm or exciting it is. Davidson (2000) suggests that individuals have an affective *style* that they use consistently in their reaction to and regulation of their emotions, including levels of arousal and valance as well as features of their expression of specific emotions. While emotions are continuously changing in response to changing thoughts and events, the experience of the emotion and its bodily manifestations over a relatively prolonged period of time is called mood.

To put these terms into context, imagine for a moment that a client is standing at the door to your office. She is tense, her heart rate is up, her palms are sweating, and her hands are trembling. These are all bodily sensations (i.e., *feelings*) that indicate some level of fear (i.e., an *emotion*). You notice her shakiness, and her tight body posture, and when you ask her how she's doing today, she says, "I *feel* really anxious." When you write your note for the session, you say that your client presented with a highly aroused *affect.* Because you have been seeing her for several months and know that this affect is not at all unusual for her, you recognize that she is presenting with a *mood* disorder—anxiety.

Evolution and the Structure of the Limbic System

Emotions evolved in humans as part of their evolutionary heritage. They are essential to survival (Damasio, 2010; Panksepp & Watt, 2011) and to the regulation of social interaction (Damasio, 2018). Damasio notes that the positive emotions that we feel as pleasurable are generally relaxing and associated with low levels of stress, while the negative emotions that are uncomfortable and distressing are associated with a host of physical problems.

Panksepp (2009) emphasized in his discussion of emotion that the human brain includes extremely ancient systems inherited from animals lower on the evolutionary tree that inform and interact with more recently developed systems. That is, our emotions are produced by activity in the ancient brain circuits that we have in common with early vertebrates (the lizard brain) as well as in circuits that developed among the mammals that came along before humans (the paleomammalian brain) (see Chapter 2 for information on the hind brain and limbic system). These earlier circuits that developed through the ages hold "ancestral memories, successful solutions to living encoded in genetically dictated brain systems" (p. 6) that are now connected to more recently developed parts of the human brain (the neomammalian brain), including the ability for language and cognition. Thus human emotions have ancient origins. However, we have more control over our emotional responses and more ways of expressing them than earlier animals did.

Along these same lines, Damasio (2018) argues that humans have emotions because emotions helped earlier animals—all the way back to single-cell organisms—to get the resources they needed to sustain their lives and to avoid things/situations that could hurt or kill them. We have the same primordial drives (e.g., hunger, thirst), motivations (e.g., lust, love, play), and emotive responses (e.g., sadness, happiness, fear) that our ancient ancestors did along with others that we have developed all on our own (e.g., jealousy, admiration, contempt).

How do emotions do what they do? According to Damasio (2018)

> Emotive responses originate in specific brain systems—sometimes in a specific region—responsible for commanding the varied components of the response: the chemical molecules that must be secreted, the movements of the face, limbs, or whole body that are parts of a particular emotion, be it fear, anger or joy. (p. 110)

The more primitive brain systems are located in the deep middle areas of the brain, the most important regions being the hypothalamus, amygdala, and nucleus accumbens (Damasio, 2018). These older brain regions are nested in the more recently developed forebrain, including the anterior insula and anterior cingulate and the orbitofrontal cortex, ventromedial prefrontal cortex, and dorsolateral prefrontal cortex (Davidson, 2000). Connections among these regions allow us to be conscious of our emotions, to think about them, to put them into words, to moderate them, and perhaps even to promote the ability to create art, music and poetry (Panksepp, 2010). These regions are also connected to the hippocampus and thus allow memory to trigger emotion. Emotion, in turn, affects both what the brain remembers how it remembers it.

Neurobiological Processes: Primary, Secondary and Tertiary Appraisal

According to Damasio (2010), in the creation and expression of emotion, the body and the brain interact together continuously in a two-way loop in which a change in one causes a change in the other. It starts when the brain receives emotionally relevant information either from the environment through our sense organs (exteroception) or through our own bodily sensations (interoception). This information goes through a three-stage appraisal process (discussed below) that activates emotion-triggering areas of the brain (e.g., the amygdala for fear or parts of the prefrontal cortex for compassion). When a region is triggered, a cascade of reactions occurs in the body, such as changes in heart rate, muscle tone, hormone release. These changes in the body are accompanied by sensations (i.e., feelings) which, in turn, inform the brain that an emotion is being felt. This awareness, in turn, stimulates memories, thoughts, and plans for action. As LeDoux (1995) puts it, a feeling emerges as we become aware that our brain has determined that something important is present and we are reacting to it. ... [and] we do things to cope with or capitalize on the event that is causing us to be emotionally aroused. Emotional actions ... occur when emotions motivate us to do things. (p. 206)

Primary Appraisal

Keltner et al. (2014) explain that the first stage of the neurobiologicial process is an initial, primary appraisal of a stimulus to evaluate it for cues as to its level of risk or safety, life threat or benefit. Porges (2011) calls this process neuroception and emphasizes that it is automatic, instinctive, and unconscious. Neuroception causes changes in our physiological state in order to prepare us to approach or avoid what has been perceived. Neuroception results in a core affect of positivity or negativity (that is, a primitive evaluation of the stimulus as being either good or bad). Primary appraisal processes result in Panksepp's (2009) prime emotions discussed below. They serve as internal sensations that indicate the areas in our lives in which we feel comfortable or uncomfortable, and because they are connected to our memory systems, control learning through conditioning.

Porges (2011) points out that neuroception may not be accurate in that it may detect risk where there is none or assume safety where there is risk. Interestingly, the evaluation of whatever is being sensed will be stronger for negative appraisals than for positive, suggesting that the amygdala (and its danger appraisal function) is responsible for primary appraisal (Keltner, 2014). This negativity bias makes evolutionary sense, since it would make us pay close attention to something that might hurt or kill us. As Keltner puts it, "we only die once" (p. 166), while we can do pleasurable, fun things repeatedly and still survive.

Secondary Appraisal

After the initial, automatic appraisal of a stimulus, a secondary appraisal occurs based on our memories and thoughts (Keltner et al., 2014). Because the ancient limbic system has dense connections, the association cortex (with its ability to access and organize memories) and the prefrontal cortex (with its ability to make reasoned decisions based on memory, expectation, culture, and experience) allow us to modulate those prime emotions rather than just react to them. Thus, the exact same event experienced by two different people can mean two very different things. Imagine two people sitting in a car at a stop light when a car pulls up behind them and hits their bumper. One person is outraged that this idiot hit them and opens the car door to go get the other driver's insurance information; the other person is terrified that they are about to be robbed and quickly tries to lock the door.

Tertiary Appraisal

The limbic system is also connected with the part of the cortex responsible for language, which allows tertiary appraisal of events. Language allows us to label our emotions and to share them with others. Moreover, as Siegel and Bryson (2011) suggest, we can "name it to tame it" (p. 151), meaning that when we label an emotion, it becomes less charged. For example, in the addictions field, it is common for people new to recovery to be told to HALT before giving in to a craving to use. What this means is that they should check their bodies to see if they are

Hungry, Angry, Lonely, or Tired. Individuals with substance use issues tend to address any unwanted, uncomfortable emotion/feeling by using their drug of choice. If they can just pause long enough to label what they are actually feeling, they may not relapse.

It is important to understand that emotions happen whether we want them to or not, and whether we can name them or not (Damasio, 2010). Some people may not have a name for what they are feeling, especially young children but also adolescents and adults who come for therapy. It is not uncommon when treating adolescents, for example, to see intense frustration resulting from the fact that they were never taught how to name their feelings. What might look like intense emotion based on their actual feelings might instead be intense frustration based on their inability to even name what they are feeling.

In addition, some people may not be able to recognize that the physical sensations they are experiencing have anything to do with their own emotions and may accuse the people around them of having those very same emotions. This is called *projection*. Still others are adept at hiding their emotions from other people and sometimes even from themselves. In all of these cases, however, an emotion is being experienced. It cannot be wished or willed away.

Cozolino (2014) points out that language is a higher, left-brain function that allows us to talk about our emotions with others. Being the social animals that we are, we often recruit someone else to help us manage our emotions. For example, whom do you call when you are sad and need cheering up—a friend, your mom, your therapist perhaps? In the mental health professions, therapists often use "talk therapy" to help hurting people understand where their troubling emotions are coming from and how to manage them.

Therapists also often suggest that clients write about their thoughts and emotions in journaling exercises. Keltner et al. (2014) notes that research has shown that either writing or talking about emotions allows clients who have experienced trauma to understand their emotions and what those emotions imply about what has happened to them. Cozolino (2010) explains that when individuals who have suffered trauma talk about it, parts of their prefrontal cortex actually reduce their amygdala activation (top-down neural modulation). Tronick (2009) suggests that human beings are essentially meaning-making animals; we try to make sense out of things that happen to us, and understanding our emotions helps in that effort. Emotions have meaning and push us toward meaningful action. They "may be the foundational form of … sense making" (p. 93).

Sometimes, our clients have real difficulty making sense of their emotions. It is not uncommon for our clients (and ourselves, for that matter) to lose control of emotions and explode in anger with no idea why they have lost control. The explanation for this common phenomenon lies in the way the brain was structured as it evolved. Remember that in Chapter 1, we learned that the neocortex (the newest part of the brain) was built on top of the limbic area, which in turn was built on top of the hindbrain. In the primary appraisal of any situation, processing of sensory information occurs below consciousness in the oldest parts of the brain. However, in secondary appraisal, that same information is sent up to the neocortex for more sophisticated processing so that instead of reacting automatically (like a lizard), we can moderate our reaction consciously.

Siegel (2004) explains, though, that secondary appraisal occurs in the higher levels of the brain (the prefrontal cortex), what he calls the "high road" (p. 283). Secondary appraisal may, however, be overwhelmed by the primary appraisal occurring in the lower levels (the amygdala)—what he calls the "low road" (p. 283). What can happen is that when right-brain, nonconscious memories are triggered by a situation during primary appraisal, the PFC, which normally would be able to manage fear and anger, can simply go off line. Rationality goes out the window, and we fall back onto old, inadequate, and sometimes wildly inappropriate responses. Loss of control can happen to almost anyone when we are hungry, tired, stressed, or emotionally vulnerable. However, it is more likely that it will happen to someone who has unresolved trauma or grief (like many of our clients). In these cases, our clients may take the low road almost instantly and behave in ways that harm themselves or others. In addition, they also stay in that state longer and recover from it more slowly than individuals who are more psychologically healthy.

Categories of Emotions

It is widely accepted that there are emotions that people all around the world are able to reliably recognize through facial expressions, including sadness, anger, fear, disgust, surprise, happiness. Panksepp (2009) argued that humans have at least seven basic emotional systems, or what he calls "emotional primes" (p. 9): SEEKING/Desire, RAGE/Anger, LUST/Sexual, CARE/Nurturance, GRIEF/Separation (originally termed PANIC/GRIEF), and PLAY, each involving distinct emotional circuitry. (Please note that capitalization of these words was Panksepp's idea, in an effort to make sure that the reader recognizes that they refer to brain *systems* rather than to discrete categorical emotions.) His terminology is included here because he is the first researcher to place emotions into categories that are based on the inner workings of the brain.

According to Panksepp (2009), the SEEKING/Desire system provides us with a sense of curiosity and anticipation, resulting in the motivation to act in an effort to get our needs and/or wants met. The RAGE/Anger system is activated in the face of competition for resources or when the individual is either restrained or frustrated. The FEAR/Anxiety system helps us to avoid pain and destruction/death. The RAGE and FEAR systems work together as our fight/flight system. The LUST/Sexual system is the sex drive, while CARE/Nurturance is the system that prompts maternal and nurturing behaviors. The GRIEF/Separation system is activated during real or perceived abandonment (especially during childhood) and may be the "gateway to depression" (Panksepp, 2010, p. 541), while the PLAY system is activated among the young of all mammals as an instinct that prompts joyful, rough and tumble physical social interaction. The play activities help children learn social rules and work out what they can and cannot do with others.

Panksepp and Watt (2011) have suggested that the SEEKING/Desire system is the "granddaddy" (p. 391) of all the other emotional primes. That is, SEEKING/Desire is the urge "to find, to consume, and at times to hoard the fruits of the world" (Panksepp, 2009, p. 9). It is the most primordial and fundamental urge to go out and find what you need to survive rather than simply float in the ooze and hope that food bumps into you.

After SEEKING/Desire developed, the emotional primes that are triggered in the lizard brain developed, namely FEAR/Anxiety, RAGE/Anger, and LUST/Sexual, followed finally by those higher order primes found among the mammals, the social primes (CARE/Nurturance, GRIEF/Separation, and PLAY). All of these later emotions, however, were (and still are) influenced by the SEEKING system. That is, it makes us seek safety when afraid, seek justice when wronged or when our resources are threatened, seek a mate to satisfy our sexual urges, seek ways to keep our children safe and happy, seek our loved ones when they or we are separated, and seek out others to play with (Panksepp & Watt, 2011).

Panksepp and Watt (2011) went on to explain that among humans, it is relatively seldom that these emotional primes manifest in their "pure" form (p. 388). The neocortex is so densely connected with the limbic areas that these primes are almost always diluted to some degree by higher cognitive appraisals and attributions. The prefrontal cortex, for example, has the ability to reduce the intensity of these instinct-driven emotions. Therefore, RAGE can be toned down to just irritated, FEAR can be modulated to worried, LUST can manifest as flirting, and so on. In addition, these primes are often combined. For example,

> Jealousy may coalesce and derive its nuanced affect from concatenations of mild FEARful, PANICked, LUSTy feelings. … [It] may emerge when one begins to PANIC that they will no longer have anyone to CARE for them (or share LUST with them), making them less happy/PLAYful, all of which promotes demanding SEEKING of reunion, commonly contaminated by RAGEful displays. (p. 391)

Although he did not attempt to place each of the traditionally accepted categorical emotions under one of his primes, Panksepp (2009) did suggest that loneliness, sadness, shame, and guilt may be rooted in GRIEF/Separation responses. In addition, he disagreed with the notion that certain affects like disgust and hunger should be counted among the basic emotions, stating that they are more "sensory and homeostatic affects, not emotional ones" (p. 17).

Damasio (2018) further differentiates some emotions into two identifiable groups—*background emotions* and *social emotions*. The background emotions include enthusiasm and discouragement. These emotions can be triggered by specific life circumstances but may also sneak in when we are sick or tired. They are similar to moods in that they color an individual's experience, often unconsciously. However, they tend to be more fleeting than moods and can be recognized easily when attention is turned to them. Social emotions, on the other hand, have apparently arisen due to our social nature. These emotions occur in social situations and include the negative feelings associated with embarrassment, shame, guilt, contempt, jealousy, and envy as well as the positive feelings associated with compassion, pride, and admiration.

Cultural Influences

Recent research has suggested that the expression of emotion is influenced by culture and that not all cultures identify facial expressions the same way (Gendron, Roberson, van der Vyver, & Barrett, 2014). Damasio (2018) points out that the social emotions are influenced largely by the culture individuals are raised in. In particular, while compassion is fundamental to the health of a society, if it is not actively rewarded by society, people are less likely to act compassionately. If people get nothing for giving to the poor but get admiration and respect for acquiring and spending wealth on selfish interests, what do you think they are going to do? Of course, mental health practitioners are, by and large, compassionate people, or we wouldn't be doing what we do. However, it might be wise to recognize that some of our clients may never have received compassion from their family and never learned that showing compassion can actually feel good. Thus, we may have to both model compassion and reward it when we see it in those clients.

Hemispheric Differences in Emotions

Cozolino (2014) explains that the right hemisphere has traditionally been considered the emotional side of the brain while the left hemisphere has been associated with rationality. He suggests that our positive and negative emotions developed in response to evolutionary pressures and that our negative emotions (e.g., anger, fear) developed first in response to the need to survive (fight/flight). Positive emotions (e.g., humor, social affiliation, aesthetic responses) came later in response to the development of social interaction. Since the right side of the brain is more primitive than the left, it tends to process negative emotions (fear/anxiety, sadness/depression, shame/guilt) and to prompt defensiveness and withdrawal behaviors. In contrast, the left side tends to process positive emotions (happiness/joy, surprise, laughter) and prompt approach behaviors. Cozolino also points out that because the right brain developed among animals before the left brain and because the right side is dominant in infancy when we begin to develop our most fundamental understanding of self, our brains have a negativity bias in which we may actually be predisposed to developing shame, guilt and depression.

McGilchrist (2009), however, posits that that the idea that the left side processes positive emotions while the right processes negative emotions doesn't hold up entirely. He points out that anger (a negative emotion) and associated aggression is activated in the left brain, while many pleasurable experiences are activated in the right.

> It seems to me a possibility that those emotions which are related to bonding and empathy, whether we call them "positive" or "negative," are preferentially treated by the right hemisphere. ... By the same token, those to do with competition, rivalry and individual self-belief, positive or negative, would be preferentially treated by the left hemisphere (p. 63).

When the right side of the brain is damaged, the left is vulnerable to uncontrolled positivity and optimism even in the face of clear danger. In contrast, when the left side of the brain is damaged, the right is vulnerable to extreme depression. McGilchrist points out that, although the right brain has rightly been associated with emotion and image, and the left with rationality and language, neither has a monopoly on those functions, and they work together to obtain balance. As Cozolino (2014) also affirms, we need integration of the left and the right sides of the brain to function optimally.

The Reward System

Rewards are pleasurable. We like them. However, they are more than just pleasurable; they are related to our survival both as individuals and as a species. As Kringelbach and Berridge (2015) emphasize, "All animals including humans have to survive and procreate, and reward is the common currency that makes this happen. Pleasure can be thought of as evolution's boldest trick for sustaining and nourishing interest in the things most important to survival" (p. 131). When we learn that something provides us pleasure, we tend to be motivated to repeat whatever behavior has provided the reward. Researchers have recognized that reward and motivation are different and are controlled by different circuits in the brain.

Berridge and Robinson (2016), for example, argue that rewards are about "liking" something while motivation is about "wanting" something. They place quotation marks around the words "liking" and "wanting" when discussing these systems to differentiate neurological processes from cognitive processes. That is, "wanting" and "liking" do not need conscious thought processes to trigger them. They argue that *"liking"* involves the *hedonic impact* of something that we consume and that brings pleasure or relief (e.g., eating tasty food, having great sex, ingesting drugs of addiction). In contrast, "wanting" involves *incentive salience,* that is, something provides enough pleasure/relief that one is willing to work for it (go to the restaurant and order food, approach someone to have sex with, drive to the street corner where drugs are sold).

The incentive salience system involves the *mesolimbic dopamine system* deep inside the middle of the brain's emotional system. It connects the ventral tegmentum, a part of the brain located close to the brain stem, to the nucleus accumbens, a part of the brain located close to the forebrain. It then projects up into the OMPFC and other parts of the prefrontal cortex that mediate behavior (see Chapter 2). The system is triggered by reward cues coming from the "liking" system, resulting in the release of dopamine into the "wanting" system. How much dopamine is released into the system depends on how much of a reward the brain's association networks predict there will be when we get our reward. It also depends on how hungry for the reward we are (you haven't eaten all day, it's been a long time since you've had sex, or you're feeling really bad because you're in withdrawal). How much dopamine is released can also be influenced by how stressed or excited you are or how intoxicated you are (Berridge & Robinson, 2016).

According to Berridge and Robinson (2016), the "liking" system consists of a number of "pleasure generating hot spots" (p. 672) in the nucleus accumbens, OMPFC, insula and ventral palladium. These hot spots are activated by endorphins, endocannabinoids (yes, we make our own cannabis as well as our own morphine!) and orexin, a neurochemical that is released when we are hungry and enhances our pleasure response to food.

It is important to understand that although these two systems work together to get us the resources we need and enjoy, they can also get us into a lot of trouble. For example, addiction is a "wanting" system that has gotten out of control. For many people, drugs of abuse are highly pleasurable. A person may indeed not want to use drugs ever again because they have caused them so much trouble. They may not even like them anymore because they no longer give them the high that they found so pleasurable. But if the incentive salience system has been triggered by a reminder of the original pleasure (e.g., seeing drug paraphernalia, hearing a song, being with friends who used to use with them, the smell of their favorite beverage), the "wanting" response will be triggered anyway, and they may be hit with strong cravings or even relapse. Indeed, the "wanting" system in addicts becomes *hyper*sensitive to drug-related cues, and this sensitization may never go away (Berridge & Robinson, 2016).

The Stress Regulation System

Fear, one of the most unpleasant emotions that humans feel, is essential for short-term survival. When the amygdala's neuroception of a stimulus reveals danger (real or imagined), a cascade of reactions is set off in the body to activate fight/flight or freeze responses. The amygdala acts so quickly that it can pair a stimulus with a fear response well before an individual has conscious awareness of the danger. It is this action that causes *conditioned fear*. An example of conditioned fear is the reaction of a rat when it sees a blinking red light in its cage when the blinking is followed immediately with a painful electrical shock. The rat will exhibit fear whenever it sees a red light blink. Similarly, if an infant is abused by, say, a red-headed woman, it may be hard or even impossible for him or her to trust a red-headed therapist later in life.

The cascade of reactions caused by the appraisal of danger happens in the hypothalamic-pituitary-adrenal (HPA) system. The appraisal of danger starts in the hypothalamus, which sends a message to the pituitary gland, which releases hormones into the blood stream that are carried down to the adrenal glands located on top of the kidneys. The adrenal glands then release epinephrine and cortisol into the blood stream. These hormones signal the body either to freeze in place, collapse in a faint or dissociate, or they get the body ready to fight or run away. When the danger is over (or when the prefrontal cortex calms the amygdala), the system should return to a normal resting state fairly quickly. If you have ever watched a TV show in which an animal, say, a gazelle, is being attacked, it mobilizes extremely quickly in its flight from the predator. If the predator gives up, the gazelle stops, shakes off, and starts eating grass again. The stress hormones have been cleaned out of the blood, and life on the savannah goes on.

However, it is a different story if stress goes on and on, such as when a child lives in an abusive home or is the victim of a natural disaster that has uprooted his or her life. Indeed, in modern life there is daily stress for many people from simply trying to make ends meet and dealing with the fear that they may be evicted. In these circumstances, cortisol remains in the blood stream because the adrenal glands continue to release it in response to the on-going stress. The immune response is thus suppressed, opening the individual to increased risk of disease. In addition, chronically high levels of cortisol can cause the death of cells in the hippocampus, affecting memory and learning.

Interestingly, some individuals react to chronic stress by reducing rather than increasing the amount of cortisol produced, in what is sometimes called *adrenal burnout*. Schuder (2005) notes, for example, that although high levels of cortisol may be produced in the initial reaction to stress, when the stress doesn't abate over a long period of time, the adrenal gland may simply not be able to keep up with the demand. Many studies have revealed low levels of cortisol among individuals with PTSD, as have many individuals with alcohol or drug addiction. Vaillancourt, Clinton, McDougall, Schmidt, and Hymel (2010) note, however, that research is needed to determine what factors, or combination of factors, determine why some individuals under-produce cortisol while others produce cortisol at high levels.

Summary

This chapter has introduced several brain systems that are important for the healthy functioning and survival of the individual. In response to ancient evolutionary pressures, the human brain developed a system that allows us to learn from things that happen to us so that we can go after those things that benefit us and avoid those things that may hurt us. The implicit memories that are encoded into the right side of the brain do not have the sensations associated with them that the explicit memories encoded into the left side have. Therefore, we may not be consciously aware that they are memories at all.

Memories may trigger emotions. Emotions are electrochemical responses to things that are happening in the present or that have happened in the past. They cause physical sensations in our bodies that we express either consciously or unconsciously in ways that can be perceived by others. They are essential to survival, first, because they prompt us to approach things that may benefit us (through the reward and motivation systems) or avoid things that may hurt us (through the HPA system). In addition, they help us to survive by letting others know what we are feeling so that they can either approach and help us or avoid us and keep themselves safe. More will be said about the advantages that emotions provide in social interactions in the next chapter.

Helping clients to identify and manage their memories and emotions is one of our primary responsibilities as mental health practitioners. When conditioned fear and other negative emotions are triggered in the right brain, they may cause irrational behavioral responses associated with many mental health issues that practitioners work with. When we are able to address these issues successfully, it can result in increases in both physical and mental health. One of the ways that humans are able to manage emotions is through social interaction, and in the next chapter we will explore the brain systems that are associated with social functioning.

CHAPTER 4

The Social Brain

LEARNING OBJECTIVES

After completing this chapter, readers should understand:
- Which brain structures are involved in initiating and maintaining social relationships.
- Which parts of the brain comprise the social motivation and social engagement systems and how these systems work in human interaction.
- How mirror neurons affect human behavior and relationships.

KEY IDEAS

1. Human beings are fundamentally social animals and have developed brain systems that allow us to live in groups.
2. The motivation system consists of neurochemicals associated with both liking and wanting, thus making social interaction pleasurable.
3. The smart vagus innervates parts of the body that provide social cues and is thus essential to harmonious human interactions.
4. Mirror neurons are part of a shared neural network that is responsible for resonance behaviors and make empathy possible.

Introduction

Earlier in this section I introduced the Interpersonal Neurobiology (IPNB) perspective and discussed various differentiated parts of the brain. In addition, I discussed how some of these parts are organized into systems involved in individual functioning. However, the IPNB perspective makes it clear that human beings are, at the most fundamental level, social animals (Cozolino, 2014; Siegel, 2003). As human beings evolved to be highly social animals, our brains developed complex systems that promote and regulate social interaction within and between individuals. Because the human brain has been built on the foundations provided by more primitive animals, ancient structures still influence our interactions with other humans. However, newer structures are able to reflect on and moderate our reactions to others so that we can live and work together. In this chapter, I will then introduce you to the brain structures and systems that make us the social animals we are. First, I will focus on individuals' cortical and subcortical structures associated with social interaction. Then, I will discuss brain systems that utilize these structures to govern our social behaviors. These systems include those that increase social interaction by making those interactions highly rewarding (social motivation and engagement) as well as those systems that help us to maintain social interactions by regulating our fight/flight/freeze reflexes (stress and fear regulation).

Structures of the Social Brain

The brain structures most influential in social interaction include both cortical (the orbitomedial prefrontal, anterior insula and anterior cingulate cortices) and subcortical structures (amygdala, hippocampus and hypothalamus). Much of the human cortex is devoted to processing sensory information coming to us from the environment (e.g., the occipital lobe, which processes visual stimuli, or the parietal lobe, which processes taste, temperature and touch). However, having arisen out of the limbic system, the cortex is involved with our emotions, too, recognizing them, making sense out of them and regulating them. As Cozolino (2014) puts it, the structures of the social brain "process internal and external information, combine it with past experience, and feed it forward to the prefrontal and parietal lobes for analysis, decision making, and goal-directed action" (p. 43). Let's take a look at these parts of the brain starting at the top (cortical) and going down (subcortical).

Cortical Structures

Orbitomedial Prefrontal Cortex

Cozolino (2014) places the orbitomedial prefrontal cortex (OMPFC) "at the apex of the social brain" (p. 44). It is as strongly connected to the limbic system as it is to the cerebral cortex and thus is equally involved in emotions and thinking/decision making and provides a two-way street between them. That is, the OMPFC processes subcortical, bottom-up sensory and emotional information and integrates it with cortical, top-down consciousness and experience to regulate affect and social interaction. In particular, the OMPFC is responsible for inhibiting fear responses produced by the amygdala by determining whether the danger that the amygdala is reacting to is real or not. In addition, it is involved in planning in response to rewards and punishments. Both of these functions are influenced by early attachment experiences, which will be discussed in the next chapter.

Anterior Cingulate and Anterior Insula

Both the anterior cingulate and anterior insula are key components of a highly complex system that provides us with a sense of self in relationship to others that is used to determine our responses to both internal and external stimuli (Medford & Critchley, 2010). The anterior cingulate is especially important to social communication, cooperation between individuals and groups, and empathy for others' distress. It is a key player in our perception of and response to pain, whether that pain is physical or social.

According to Cozolino (2014), animal research has shown that the anterior cingulate is responsible for the sounds that accompany emotions and that without the anterior cingulate, a mother will not communicate with or respond to her baby. Thus, this part of the brain is clearly of great importance to survival of both the specific individual and the species in general.

Because the anterior cingulate is involved in the allocation of attention, it makes the fluid shifting of attention from the self to the environment, or from one's own needs to those of one's loved ones, possible. Influenced strongly by implicit memories, it turns attention to whatever is most salient in the environment (e.g., my baby crying vs. the TV show I'm watching). It is this part of the brain that also allows us to reflect on ourselves and our behavior and to experience embarrassment when we have made a social mistake.

In contrast to the anterior cingulate, the anterior insula generates our subjective feeling states (i.e., the bodily sensations associated with happiness, sadness, fear, etc.), and because of its connection with the anterior cingulate, we are able to reflect on the emotions we feel. Just as importantly, the close connection between these two parts of the brain allows us to imagine what someone else is feeling by seeing their facial expressions and posture, hearing their tone of voice, etc. Our anterior insula makes us feel their feelings, and our anterior cingulate formulates what our response should be. Lavin et al. (2013) have noted that your anterior cingulate activates when you experience pain, but that both your anterior cingulate and your anterior insula activate when someone you care about experiences pain. Thus, both of these parts of the brain are associated with feelings of empathy. Because the anterior cingulate is highly connected with the OMPFC, we can then make decisions about what should be done to relieve our own suffering and that of others.

Subcortical Structures

The Amygdala

As discussed in Chapter 1, the amygdala is an ancient brain structure devoted to survival, providing us with the most primitive emotions associated with approach and avoidance. When it is activated, the amygdala responds extremely quickly, so quickly that it causes reactions in the body before the individual is consciously aware that there is danger. According to Cozolino (2014), one of the most important things the amygdala does is to act as a social brake, keeping us from approaching someone we don't know (or allowing them to approach us) until we know that it is safe.

The amygdala encodes our earliest memories, those memories that are non-conscious but that color our most basic expectations for safety and relationship—for good or for ill. In concert with the OMPFC and the anterior cingulate, the amygdala influences our decisions and behaviors concerning current situations based on those implicit memories. In addition, the amygdala, in conjunction with the hypothalamus and the pituitary gland, is responsible for the fight/flight response. If connections between the OMPFC and the amygdala are not well developed (as can be the case among individuals who have suffered abuse and neglect or other trauma early in life), emotions may be poorly regulated and, consequently, social relationships may suffer.

The Hippocampus

As discussed in Chapter 2, whereas the amygdala lays down implicit, nonconscious memories, the hippocampus lays down explicit, conscious memories. Furthermore, whereas the amygdala acts extremely quickly (reflexively) in response to a stimulus, the hippocampus acts much more slowly. The hippocampus works in concert with the OMPFC, using conscious memories to make conscious rather than reflexive responses to current situations. Cozolino (2014) explains how the slower hippocampus affects our social interactions negatively, saying,

> By the time we become conscious of others, our brains have already organized ways to think about them. At one extreme, "love at first sight" involves the triggering of positive associations and projects them onto another person. In the opposite case, as in situations of racial prejudice, a person's skin color triggers the faster [amygdala], which unconsciously shapes our experience as based in fear and other negative feelings. (p. 311)

The Hypothalamus

Similar to the amygdala, the hypothalamus is an extremely ancient part of the brain. Among its primary functions is the regulation of body temperature, hunger, thirst, sexual behavior and primitive aggression. In addition, the hypothalamus is the first component of the hypothalamic-pituitary-adrenal (HPA) system, the part of the sympathetic branch of the ANS and is responsible for the fight/flight response to danger. It is included in this section on the social brain because supportive relationships tend to shut the HPA system down effectively and reduce the physical damage caused by chronic stress. In particular, early secure attachment relationships build brains that are less reactive to stress throughout life, a phenomenon that will be discussed in detail in Chapter 4.

The Medial Forebrain Bundle

Running right through the body of the hypothalamus is a loose bundle of nerves called the medial forebrain bundle (MFB). This system includes the ventral tegmental area (VTA) and the nucleus accumbens and is part of the mesolimbic dopamine pathway that stretches up to the OMPFC and comprises our motivation and reward system (discussed below). This part of the brain is activated during any rewarding experience, whether it be eating good food or using drugs of abuse. In addition, its activation during positive social interaction makes relationships rewarding.

The Vagus Nerve

As discussed in Chapter 1, the vagus is a central component of the ANS, and the major conduit between the brain inside the skull and the rest of the body, especially the heart and gut brains. It is not a single nerve, as the name would suggest, but a system of nerves that carries information both to and from the enskulled brain. It carries information from the internal visceral organs up to the anterior insula, allowing us to feel bodily processes happening inside of ourselves as well as emotions triggered by events/things/people in the environment. It also carries information from the enskulled brain back down to the body, allowing us to manage our reactions to those events/things/people. The vagus system is primarily parasympathetic, meaning that its purpose is to put the brakes on the sympathetic system and its reflexive fight/flight arousal responses. Thus, it constitutes what is called the social engagement system (discussed in detail below).

Systems of the Social Brain

In this section, I will discuss two brain systems that are central to the development and maintenance of social relationships. First is a system that makes relating to others feel good so that we seek contact with other human beings, the social motivation system. Second is a system that bypasses the reflexive fight/flight/freeze responses of the ANS so that we can sustain connection with others, the social engagement system. Together, these systems increase our survivability as a social species by letting us cooperate with each other toward shared goals and help each other in times of need.

Social Motivation System

As discussed in Chapter 3, "liking" (reward) triggers "wanting" (motivation). We like food, so we work to get it. We like sex and work to get that, too. However, as social animals, we also "like" and "want" to be with other people, and our reward and motivation systems are activated to promote relationship. Positive social interaction is highly rewarding to us, while social isolation makes us feel terrible. We will work to get the reward of relationship and avoid the pain/fear of being alone.

Cozolino (2014) suggests that motivation for social interaction is mediated by a number of neurochemicals that activate several different regions of the brain. For example, sex hormones in the thalamus affect sexual behaviors; endorphins and oxytocin in the amygdala regulate fear and anxiety; oxytocin and vasopressin in the hypothalamus regulate social approach and avoidance; dopamine in the mesolimbic dopamine pathway influences approach behaviors associated with expected rewards. Cozolino stresses that these neurochemicals are highly interdependent and constantly reinforce each other.

Interestingly, it is suggested that one of the most rewarding human experiences, romantic love, promotes behaviors surprisingly similar to drug addiction (Cozolino, 2014). Cozolino argues that "Love and addiction share a loss of reason, an absence of self-control, and an obsessive longing that must be satisfied" (p. 115), evidence of a highly stimulated mesolimbic dopamine system. Flores (2004) has gone so far as to argue that addiction is a disorder arising from insecure attachment relationships during infancy that result in inadequate self-regulation. As will be discussed in the next chapter, when babies come into the world, they are unable to regulate their bodies in any way and must co-opt the regulation capacity of the brain of at least one adult near them until their brains develop sufficiently to care for themselves. If they don't get consistent sensitive care during infancy, their brains do not develop the capacity to self-regulate. Later in life, Flores argues, they discover that drugs can help them regulate their mood and energy levels.

Addictive drugs do indeed provoke the release of the same neurochemicals that are involved in love—oxytocin, endorphins, and dopamine. However, research shows that although dopamine drives SEEKING/desiring emotions during the early love relationship, the obsessive longing associated with new love tends to give way to attachment and pair bonding over time (Fisher, Xu, Aron, & Brown, 2016). That is, oxytocin and vasopressin, neurochemicals associated with CARING/nurturing emotions, tend to take over from dopamine as the love relationship matures.

It is my belief, however, that there is a glaring difference between addiction and love that researchers have not yet acknowledged. A diagnosis of substance use disorder is based on the negative effects drugs of abuse have on life, including disruption of important relationships (American Psychiatric Association, 2013). Love, on the other hand, is characterized by its positive effects on life, including maintenance and support of important relationships.

As can be seen from the discussion of social motivation above, positive social support is extremely important for both physical and mental health. That is, social engagement is essential for healthy functioning among human beings. Therefore, the next section will focus on the system that promotes social engagement.

Social Engagement System

In Chapter 2, I introduced the elements of the ANS—the sympathetic system and the parasympathetic system (primarily composed of the vegetative and smart vagal systems). In this section, I will go into detail about why the smart vagus developed and how it works to enable social engagement.

Purpose of the Smart Vagus

Mammals, including human beings, evolved to be social animals, many of them forming groups (packs, herds, tribes) to take advantage of the safety provided by numbers and coordinated cooperative action. Mammals don't lay eggs and then just walk or swim away; they bear young who need to be cared for until they are mature enough to care for themselves. As they grow, they are taught where to find food and what they need to do to survive. It takes a lot of adult attention before they can make it on their own; indeed, the human brain isn't completely mature until about age 25.

The need for mammals to find ways to be in groups resulted in changes in the ANS that allowed them to live together safely (Porges, 2011). As discussed in Chapter 2, the earliest threat-management system evolved among early amphibians and included only the parasympathetic vegetative vagus, which caused a freeze response that made them play dead until the threat (hopefully) went away. Later animals evolved the sympathetic system, which gave them fight/flight capabilities in addition to the last-resort freeze response. The smart vagus that developed among mammals was highly adaptive. It took over many of the functions previously managed by the earlier systems and helped them to manage difficult interpersonal situations safely.

With the arrival of the smart vagus, neural regulation of the heart and lungs changed from that found in lower animals (e.g., reptiles and fish) so that the part of the brain that controlled facial muscles also began to control heart rate and breathing. The smart vagus is sometimes called the *vagal brake* because of its ability to manage heart rate and breathing in times of safety (Porges, 2011). Indeed, if the brake is removed, the heart rate will increase by up to 90 beats per minute even in the absence of threat (Porges, 2017). However, when danger is present (whether is real or imagined), the ancient survival systems may take over. That is, the ANS is a hierarchical system. Generally, humans try to manage stress and threat first by using social cues—talking, smiling, submissive gestures, averting eyes, etc. If that doesn't work, though, the sympathetic system will take over and prepare them for fight or flight. If they can't fight or run away, the vegetative vagus may take over and send them into freeze or collapse as a last-resort attempt at self-protection (Porges, 2011).

In addition to the changes in heart and respiration control, mammals used the smart vagus to co-regulate bodily functions via the emotions expressed on our faces, the act of listening and being listened to, eating food together, and other positive social interactions (Porges, 2011). Among humans (and many other primates), social cues developed, including facial expression, vocalizations and intonation, crying, head movements and gestures that tell others that it is (or is not) safe to approach or that help is needed. This reciprocal signaling of safety allowed us to engage in cooperative social interaction and to co-regulate our emotional and physiological responses. Signals that indicate safety turn off the alarm messages coming from the amygdala and shut down the stress response systems (the HPA and the vegetative vagus), thus obviating the need for the fight/flight and freeze responses. Thus, humans do not need to regulate their mental, emotional and physical states on their own; they can use supportive others to soothe themselves and provide them with positive affect, the very essence of sociality.

Thus, mammals developed three ways of handling stress and danger, the smart vagus (for social regulation), the HPA system (for fight/flight responses) and the vegetative vagus (for freeze responses). Both the HPA and vegetative systems are triggered by fear, one causing mobilization and the other causing immobilization. Thus, the fight/flight response can be characterized as mobilization with fear, while the freeze response can be characterized as immobilization with fear. Activation of the smart vagus turns down the volume on the vegetative vagus and the sympathetic system so that excitement and action don't result in fighting or collapse (Porges, 2011).

For example, when the smart vagus acts on the sympathetic system, the volume on the sympathetic system is turned down so that you can experience excitement—play contact sports, roll around on the floor with your happy child, or argue with your lover—without it turning violent. That is, the modulation of excitement provided by the smart vagus allows you to have mobilization without fear. Similarly, when the smart vagus acts on the vegetative vagus, the volume on the vegetative vagus is turned down so that you can be intimate—immobilization without fear. Porges (2011) argues that the smart vagus makes passion possible. That is, the smart vagus allows the individual to be held close without fear and to be sexually aroused and enjoy the visceral experience of copulation. In contrast, unwelcome sexual activity in which the individual is being held against his or her will can cause a massive surge in the vegetative vagus that results in the freeze response or dissociation during which no pleasurable sexual arousal or response is possible.

Sexual responsiveness, however, is not the only pleasurable intimate experience that the smart vagus facilitates. For example, if a stranger approaches a child and tries to put his arms around him, the child will most likely struggle or freeze. If, however, his own mother holds him, he will most likely not just allow it but actively enjoy the contact. Without the smart vagus to manage the sympathetic and vegetative vagal systems, none of these fun and satisfying human interactions would be possible because feelings of safety and trust would not exist (Cozolino, 2014).

The purpose of the smart vagal circuit, then, is to allow us to stay in social interaction even when things get really exciting. We can have fun together; we can solve problems together; we can sit in a meeting with a boss we don't trust or like and put on a happy face; or we can argue with our spouse or our child without clobbering them or dashing off never to be seen again. When the smart vagus is working well, it calms the sympathetic system, which then allows the vegetative vagus to provide the rest/digest/growth functions that keep us healthy.

It is vitally important for mental health practitioners to understand two things concerning the vagal system. First, the smart vagus works only when there is the perception of safety (Porges, 2017). Clients will not feel safe just because there is an absence of danger in your office; feelings of safety require the presence of *signals* of safety. As mentioned in Chapter 3, the human brain has a negativity bias because the amygdala, which scans the environment for signs of danger, would rather be safe than dead. Understanding this is of paramount importance to mental health professionals; it behooves us to be very conscious and intentional about the safety signals we provide our clients through faces, gestures, and voices.

In addition to making sure that clients feel safe with us by providing overt social cues, practitioners should also consider the possible effects of the treatment setting. Porges (2017) explains that low frequency noises are perceived by mammals as signaling the approach of a predator. Therefore, he states that

> This principle of "feeling safe" as the precursor of treatment is not well integrated into educational, medical, and mental health treatment models. In addition, the physical environments in which therapy is delivered are seldom vetted for cues (e.g., low frequency background sounds, street noises, ventilation system sounds, vibrations from elevators and escalators) that would trigger, via neuroception, defensive states of the autonomic nervous system. (p. 24)

The second thing to understand about the vagal system is that it is hierarchical. If efforts to soothe the situation with social signals don't work, the more primitive parts of the system will override the smart vagus and make us fight, run, or collapse whether we want to or not. These are automatic, reflexive responses to environmental stimuli. Thus, if a client has a panic attack, this mobilization (with fear) response has been caused by the ANS, not by any conscious choice made by the client; if someone was raped and didn't try to fight off the attacker, that immobilization (with fear) response was caused by the ANS, not by the victim secretly enjoying the sexual activity. Similarly, when a client in treatment is in a fight/flight or freeze state (very common among people in treatment for mental health issues), we cannot expect the person to behave rationally until he or she feels safe. And remember that what feels safe to you the practitioner may not feel safe to the client.

Structure of the Smart Vagus

According to Rosenberg (2017), the term vagal system is something of a misnomer since the system actually includes eleven other cranial nerves in addition to the vagal nerve itself. All twelve of the cranial nerves (numbered I through XII using Roman numerals) originate in parts of the hindbrain just where it meets the spinal cord. Porges (2011) suggests, however, that five of these nerves (V, VII, IX, X and XI) are of particular importance to social engagement. They control the muscles of the face and head and thus are responsible for the social cues that we send and receive, such as facial expression, eye gaze, vocalization and intonation, and head orientation. By responding to social cues that someone has sent to us, we each determine how much social distance we should keep between, thus co-creating our social experiences. Figure 4.1 shows how the system works.

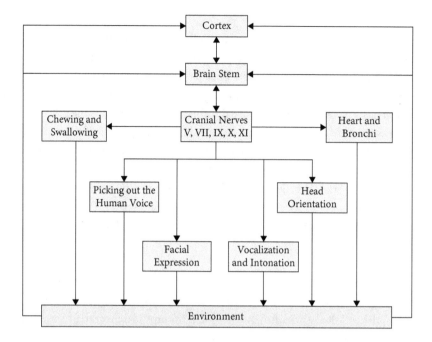

FIGURE 4.1   **The Social Engagement System**

Stephen Porges, Social Engagement System from "Polyvagal Theory: A Primer," Clinical Applications of the Polyvagal Theory: The Emergence of Polyvagal-informed Therapies, pp. 55. Copyright © 2018 by W. W. Norton & Company, Inc.

For example, eye contact, smiling and friendly vocalization can suggest that we can approach someone. Alternatively, wide, staring eyes, clenched teeth, frowning or grimacing and guttural vocalizations may warn us to stay away. A tilt of the head, a sparkle in the eye and a particular vocal intonation can indicate sexual interest, while a mirroring of someone's sad face may indicate that you understand and empathize with them.

As facial expressions change in response to changing emotions, so do heart rate and respiration. Porges (2017) has said that "the social engagement system emerges from a heart-face connection that coordinates the heart with the muscles of the face and head" (p. 27). This heart-face connection facilitates allows us co-regulation of each other's emotions and levels of physiological arousal. When this system is functioning well, it supports the enteric nervous system (the gut brain) and vegetative vagus in the health, restoration, and growth functions that influence both physical and mental health. When the system is not functioning well, however, a host of physical and mental health issues can arise (Porges, 2011).

Although the smart vagus is part of the ANS, it is interconnected with the PFC and therefore is partially under conscious control. For example, we can decide to wink at someone to let them know that we are joking, we can consciously lower our voice to de-escalate an enraged client, or we can sing a lullaby to our baby even though we're so exhausted we want to cry. However, although we can voluntarily form our lips into a smile when we meet someone, we also tend to be able to tell when a smile is genuine and when it is fake; a genuinely happy smile unconsciously engages many more muscles than just the lips. Good actors get paid big money for their ability to access emotional memories that will give their faces the expressions that their roles need to be perceived as real. However, since activation of these nerves is not completely voluntary, it is very difficult to hide our emotions completely. Many a poker player has lost a game because of "tells" that can be read by discerning opponents.

However, because facial expressions (and changes in them) may be subtle, we may not be consciously aware of what a person's face is telling us. For example, we may pick up on a client's facial expression as just a feeling we can't quite put our finger on—a gut feeling. When this happens, our primary limbic appraisal system (non-conscious neuroception) has sent a message to our defense systems (sympathetic and vegetative vagal) saying that all is not right. On the other hand, our spontaneous facial expressions of genuine warmth may provide just the safety signal a client needs to feel comfortable enough to engage with us.

Neurochemicals Serving the Smart Vagus

Recall that the smart vagus came into being so that mammals would have ways of being together that did not involve the more ancient fight/flight or freeze responses to danger. When the HPA system is activated, it releases adrenalin and cortisol into the system. This system was meant to be activated only for short bursts of energy. Once the threat is over, the cortisol should leave the blood stream relatively quickly, and the body should return to a normal resting state. However, if the environment creates an ongoing state of arousal (e.g., war, domestic violence, hostile work environment, abuse/neglect, etc.), cortisol is constantly being released into the blood stream. The presence of cortisol over time damages both the body and the brain, negatively affecting both physical health and psychological functioning. In addition, when the HPA system is activated, interpersonal interactions can quickly turn into aggression and violence, increasing the danger of death and destruction. The smart vagus needed to be able to utilize neurochemicals that would calm the HPA system and yet allow mobilization in the service of social interaction.

Porges (2017) has noted that the freeze response can work very well as a last-resort defensive strategy when fight or flight is not an option. If you have ever seen a cat with a mouse, you have probably seen this defense. A cat's hunting reflexes are activated by movement, and so it may lose interest when its prey just lies there. It may wander off in search of other fun, leaving the mouse to scamper to freedom. Similarly, when a human being is faced with life threat, he or she may faint, an immobilization response that is sometime called a "dorsal dive" (Siegel, 2102b, p. 12–2) because it is the dorsal (vegetative) vagus, most likely facilitated by large releases of endorphin, that causes the shutdown (Lanius, 2014). Unfortunately, in extreme cases the immobilization may be permanent; that is, when someone goes into shock because of a trauma, he or she may actually die, literally having been scared to death. Therefore, the smart vagus needed to be able to utilize neurochemicals that would allow immobilization without the danger of death. Oxytocin and vasopressin came to serve the social engagement system by providing both the needed calming of the HPA and vegetative vagal systems and the rewards associated with social contact.

Oxytocin is associated with all things maternal, including making babies, birthing them, and then caring for them. For example, it is present in a woman's blood stream during sex and orgasm, during labor, and during breast-feeding. In addition, it is present in both mother and baby when the baby is being held and soothed, resulting in high levels of positive affect on both sides. Oxytocin is not, however, just about maternal feelings and behaviors. It is also associated all kinds of positive touch (e.g., massage, snuggling with your honey, petting your dog or cat) (Dunbar, 2010; Walker & McGlone, 2013). No matter how old we are, being with someone we love (family, friend, lover) calms us down during times of stress; babies are soothed by their mother's voice, smell, and touch; we cry on our friend's shoulder when we get a low grade on our exam; our family, friends, and neighbors surround us when a loved one dies. Thank goodness for oxytocin; where would we be without it?

Vasopressin, on the other hand, is the neurochemical that, among males, promotes pair bonding, marital satisfaction, and monogamy. It is present in males during sexual arousal, with large releases occurring during orgasm, and it promotes caring feelings for others (Panksepp, 2012a). In addition, it is also associated with social recognition and memory (Dunbar, 2010) and has been shown to make fathers more attentive to babies' emotional cries (Thijssen et al., 2018).

Vagal Tone

When the smart vagus is working well, it is said to have good *vagal tone*. Vagal tone refers to how well the smart vagus is able to regulate heartbeat and breathing. It can measured by determining how much variability there is in the time between an individual's heartbeats, called heart rate variability (HRV). Although an individual's heartbeat should be generally regular, there should also be some slight variability in the timing between beats. When an individual is stressed (afraid, excited, pressured), the heartbeat is fast and has very little variation; when he or she is in a relatively comfortable and relaxed state, the heartbeat is slower, and there is more variation between beats. McCraty (2015b) puts it this way:

> While too much instability, such as arrhythmias or nervous system chaos, is detrimental to efficient physiological functioning and energy utilization, too little variation indicates age-related system depletion, chronic stress, pathology or inadequate functioning in various levels of self-regulatory control systems. (p. 13)

Therefore, having a high HRV is good news; it means that the smart vagus is doing a good job of supporting emotional and social functioning that allow an individual to self-regulate. If someone is sick, or when his or her cardiac system is not functioning well due to age-related issues, HRV can be expected to be low. The same is true for when the HPA system is chronically activated, such as in situations of abuse, neglect, or trauma.

As can be seen by Table 4.1, higher vagal tone is associated with many emotional and behavioral issues that mental health practitioners address. It is related to better overall functioning and fewer mental health issues in both children and adults. Good vagal tone is the natural out

TABLE 4.1   Mental Health Correlates of Vagal Tone

HIGHER VAGAL TONE	LOWER VAGAL TONE
• Self-regulation of emotion	• Emotional dysregulation
• Self-regulation of behavior	• Impulsivity/acting out
• Social engagement	• Social withdrawal
• Increased attentional capacity	• Distractibility
• Relative calm	• Relative reactivity/irritability
• Higher performance under stress	• Lower performance under stress
• Secure attachment	• Insecure attachment
• Resilience	• Psychopathology

Adapted from: Cozolino, L. (2014). *The neuroscience of human relationships: Attachment and the social brain.* (2nd ed.) (p. 89). New York, NY: W. W. Norton & Co.

come of growing up in a safe and accepting environment that promotes autonomy, curiosity, exploration, and positive emotional states.

As will be discussed in Chapter 6, when children are reasonably well protected and their caregivers are available both physically and emotionally during infancy and toddlerhood, their OMPFC has a chance to make strong connections with the amygdala. This connection enables calming of primary appraisals of danger and sustained higher HRV. If children are not so lucky, the HPA system and/or the vegetative vagus may be chronically activated, resulting in sustained lower HRV and possible chronic anxiety and depression. The good news for mental health practitioners is that it is possible to increase vagal tone (see, for example, Childre & Rozman, 2007; Matto, Strolin-Groltzman, & Ballan, 2014; Porges, 2017; Rosenberg, 2017). Porges (2011; 2017) has reported results of research in which vagal functioning has been significantly increased among clients with depression, anxiety, PTSD, and autism.

Mirror-Resonance System

Cozolino (2014) notes that "our brains are social organs, linked together through multiple channels of rapid, automatic and unconscious communication. ..." (p. 227). This social brain allows us to resonate with others' emotions, that is, to recognize what they are feeling and why they are feeling it and reflect that understanding back. Fredrickson and Siegel (2017) suggest that this resonance allows a beneficial sense of "being seen, feeling felt, ... not just being understood or analyzed but that you exist within someone else's mental life" (p. 211). They further hold that resonance allows us to connect with others in three profoundly important ways: (1) shared positive affective experiences, (2) biobehavioral synchrony, and (3) mutual care and concern. That is, through social interconnectedness, humans produce beneficial neurochemicals in response to vagal activation such as shared positive facial expressions, gestures, etc. that result in empathic concern and compassion, thus promoting physical and mental health. Scientists include the following regions in the resonance circuitry: the amygdala, anterior cingulate and anterior insula, the OMPFC and DLPFC (Cozolino, 2014; Hastings, Miller, Kahnle, & Zahn-Waxler, 2017) and is influenced by the smart vagal system (Porges, 2011).

Although research on mirror neurons has been conducted primarily on animals rather than on humans (because study methods are necessarily invasive), it is highly probable that humans have similar, if not identical, systems (Fabbri-Destro & Rizzolatti, 2008). They were discovered by chance back in the 1990s when neuroscientists noticed that a particular part of a monkey's brain was activated both when it ate a peanut and also when it saw another monkey eat a peanut. The researchers realized that the first monkey's brain was being activated by what another monkey was doing. We now know that mirror neurons become active both when an individual performs a particular motor act and when they see, hear, or even imagine someone else performing a similar act, thus transforming "specific sensory information into a motor format" (Fabbri-Destro & Rizzolatti, 2008, p. 171). It should be noted, however, that mirror neurons fire only for actions that are *intentional*. That is, they don't fire for just any kind of movement or action we happen to perceive but only for those that have some sort of intention behind them. Wallin (2007) notes the importance of this distinction, saying,

Mirror neurons thus appear to simulate in our selves both the observed behavior and the inferred mental states (e.g., feelings) of others. As such, the mirror neuron system has been seen as the neural substrate for empathy, affect attunement, mentalizing, and intersubjectivity. It may even be the foundation for our experiences of the "oneness" we share with other living beings. (p. 77)

Below, I will explain how mirror neurons prompt four interconnected human capabilities—imitation, intersubjectivity, empathy, and compassion.

Imitation

Mirror neurons allow us to imitate others, i.e., mirror their actions. Cozolino (2014) notes that mirroring, called resonance behaviors, probably arose through evolution to support important survival activities such as coordinated hunting and gathering and fighting or fleeing. It can be seen, for example, when a herd of animals stampedes in response to a single animal's startle response. When you find yourself reflexively looking up when you see others looking up or yawning when you see someone else yawns, your mirror-resonance system is to blame. (I apologize if, by writing this, I have made you want to yawn!) In addition, it is working when we experience *emotional contagion*, such as laughing when someone else is laughing even though we don't know what's so funny (Gerdes, Segal, & Harmon, 2014). Unfortunately, we also see it when otherwise reasonable people are taken over by mob mentality.

This ability to imitate is extremely important to us as a species. We can watch someone do something and then immediately do the same thing (simple motor repetition), or we can learn a new skill (mediated by the prefrontal cortex and hippocampus). Can you imagine where would we be if each of us had to figure out on our own how to build a fire, for example? We also learn how to behave by watching how others behave, a fact that many a parent has tried to counteract with the words, "Do as I say, not as I do."

Intersubjectivity

Imitation is only one part of our ability to resonate with others. In the late 1970s, Premack & Woodruff (1978) developed a Theory of Mind (ToM) based on the idea that by picking up on someone's social signals (eye gaze, facial expressions, posture, gestures, and other movements within the environmental context), we sense within our own bodies what that person is feeling. That is, we have an "embodied simulation" (Cozolino, 2014, p. 369) that allows us to develop a theory about what is going on inside that person's head (his or her desires, motivations, intentions, and beliefs). It has been argued, however, that ToM is too narrow a construct to explain the ability to understand what is going on in someone else's mind (Ammaniti & Gallese, 2014; Liljenfors & Lundh, 2015). Instead, it is suggested that this ability is an innate characteristic of all human beings, the neural substrate of which is developed by the 22nd week *in utero* and present in very early infancy, long before a person has the ability to develop a conscious theory about another's behavior. Researchers call this ability intersubjectivity.

Liljenfors and Lundh (2015) describe intersubjectivity as a form of social reciprocity manifested in infant-mother imitation that provides the baby with the nascent ability to engage with another through mutual interaction. They argue that newborns' ability to imitate the facial expressions and movements of their mother indicates that they already have sense of their own body and movement as separate from someone else. They suggest, therefore, that babies are implicitly aware that the other is in some way the same as themselves. Ammaniti and Gallese (2014) note that over the first year or so of life these imitative behaviors lead to a sense of "intercorporeality" (p. 16) that links self and other and the development of what they call "protoconversations" (p. 21). These early nonverbal conversations have structure and rhythm similar to adult conversations and act to introduce babies to the give and take of *mutually regulated* communication. As Stern (2004) puts it, "Two minds create intersubjectivity. But equally, intersubjectivity creates the two minds. The center of gravity has shifted from the intrapsychic to the intersubjective" (p. 78).

Over the first nine to twelve months of life, babies' brains mature sufficiently to recognize implicitly that they have a mind and that their mother does, too. More importantly, they develop a capacity for mentalization in which they begin to recognize that they can know someone else's mind, an ability that will eventually allow them to think about states of mind in general and to see themselves and others as having psychological depth (Wallin, 2007). Allen (2004) argues that mentalization makes our own and others' behaviors understandable to us and that it is the very foundation of self-awareness and sensitivity to others. Bo, Sharp, Fonagy, and Kongerslev (2017) suggest further that the capacity to mentalize is fundamental to the development of "epistemic trust" (p. 175), that is, the ability for an individual to trust the knowledge that someone is passing on to him or her. Without epistemic trust, the individual will have difficulty acquiring societal norms and cultural habits and will have trouble telling if and when someone is lying to them, leading to chronic mistrust of social information. Thus, the central developmental task of Erikson's (1963) first stage (infancy), the development of trust or mistrust in the first year of life, can clearly be seen to relate to the capacity to mentalize. Moreover, mentalization is essential to the attachment process and thus to survival itself (Fonagy, Gergely, Jurist, & Target, 2002), a subject I will discuss in detail in Chapter 6. It is also essential to the development of empathy and compassion, interrelated but distinct concepts that are of the utmost importance to sociality.

Empathy

The terms *empathy* and *compassion* have traditionally been used interchangeably. However, researchers have recently recognized nuances to the terms that deserve clarification. According to Goetz and Simon-Thomas (2017), "empathy is an umbrella term that is used to refer to many related processes in which individuals may come to understand, share, or feel 'moved' by another's emotional or physical state" (p. 6). There may be a genetic component to empathy, either through certain genes' influence on production levels of oxytocin and vasopressin or through other genes' influence on the individual's sensitivity to environmental influences (Hastings et al., 2014). This second factor (i.e., sensitivity to environmental influences) could certainly be the reason that babies who are adequately nurtured tend to develop more empathy than babies who have less warmth and attention (Goetz & Simon-Thomas, 2017).

Goetz and Simon-Thomas (2017) explain that there are two components to empathy, affective empathy (or emotional resonance) and cognitive empathy (appraisal). Affective empathy is thought to arise automatically and reflexively in response to what we are sensing from others and is closely related to imitation and emotional contagion. Cognitive empathy, on the other hand, depends on the individual's ability to mentalize (i.e. think about what someone else is feeling, thinking, wanting or getting ready to do).

While mental health practitioners generally think of empathy as being all warm and fuzzy and good, that is not necessarily always the case. Goetz and Simon-Thomas (2017) note that empathy "can be pan-affective; people perceive, mirror and 'catch' all kinds of emotions, including amusement, pride, anger, or sorrow" (p. 6). That is, while I may "catch" happiness by being around happy people, I may also "catch" anger by being around angry people. In addition, they point out four situations in which my empathy may fail altogether. First, someone else's suffering may be so distressing to me (something called *empathic distress*) that I become so focused on my own discomfort that I become indifferent to their suffering. Second, I may feel someone else's suffering but, if feel helpless to relieve it, I may find ways to turn those feelings off and justify doing nothing to help. Third, if I am envious of the person who is suffering, if I think that he or she is showing pain in order to get something, or if I make a moral judgment that the person deserves to suffer because of who he or she is or what he or she has done, I may actually take pleasure in his or her suffering (i.e., *schadenfreude*). Lastly, my feelings of empathy may be overwhelmed by feelings of disgust or anger at whomever I perceive as being the cause of someone else's suffering. That is, instead of feeling the pain of innocent children killed in war, I may rail against the government that waged it.

Compassion

Goetz and Simon-Thomas (2017) suggest that whereas empathy can be thought of as the recognition and sharing of another's emotional or physical state, compassion can be thought of as an affective state that arises in response to that recognition and sharing. They hold that compassion grows out of empathy. Condon and DeSteno (2017) explain that compassion can be thought of as feeling *for* another rather than feeling *as* another while also feeling an impulse to help relieve their distress.

It appears that empathy may trigger the neural circuitry responsible for our CARE/nurturance emotions and thus may be an innate drive associated with survival of the species (Goetz & Simon-Thomas, 2017). However, it is also more than just a feeling that promotes prosocial behavior; it is apparently an emotion that makes people want to reach beyond themselves in an effort to reduce the harmful effects of the world, promoting cooperation in an effort to help a community thrive (Condon & DeSteno, 2017).

Compassion is more than just feeling what someone else is feeling. We don't have compassion for someone who is happy and satisfied with his or her life, for example. No, we have compassion when we have feelings of concern for someone's distress and want to do something about it. While empathy may be either pleasant or unpleasant according to the visceral sensations prompted by someone else's expressions, compassion can be both pleasant and unpleasant at the same time. That is, I may feel someone's misery as my own, but the motivation to help, as well as the helping itself and the experience of relieving someone's suffering may feel very good.

Goetz and Simon-Thomas (2017) suggest that compassion can also be thought of as a disposition or a personality trait. As explained above, emotions are reactions to the environment. If I am sad again and again and again, I begin to see myself as a sad person; it becomes part of my personality. Goetz and Simon-Thomas note that individuals who score high on measures of compassion show heightened empathic sensitivity and tend to believe that they are going to experience more joy from giving compared to individuals with lower scores. They also note that although higher empathic sensitivity and optimistic anticipation of joy could be genetically determined, those characteristics could have developed in response to warm and nurturing support from parents during infancy and early childhood. That is, the compassion a mother shows her child in the cradle may be internalized and become part of the child's personality.

Cozolino (2014) emphasizes that it is particularly important that mental health practitioners understand that experiencing what our clients are feeling is not enough; our job is to experience what they are feeling *while at the same time maintaining objectivity* so that we can act effectively. That is, if we become fused with our clients, their pain will become our pain, and then both of us will need therapy! Therefore, we must be able to toggle back and forth between our own emotions and bodily sensations and what we imagine our clients are feeling in order to adequately maintain boundaries in the relationship. Without adequate boundaries, it doesn't matter how compassionate we are; we become part of the problem, not part of the solution.

I should caution the reader that, although I have devoted a considerable amount of space in this chapter to empathy and compassion, I do not mean to suggest that other emotions such as fear, anger, surprise, sadness, etc. are less important in the human experience. Indeed, *every* emotion is valid and provides us with important information. If we are in danger, fear tells us to do something to make ourselves safe. If an injustice occurs to ourselves or to someone else, we should get angry about it. Surprise tells us that we should pay attention because something out of the ordinary is happening. If we lose someone or something important to us, we should feel sad because that is what humans feel in those circumstances. I focus on empathy and compassion here simply because empathy is the bedrock of the psychotherapeutic relationship (Watson, 2016) and compassion is such an important part of well-being (our own as well as our clients' and others out in the world) (Davidson, 2012).

Summary

Human beings are profoundly social animals, and our neural structures have developed in ways that are meant to promote harmonious social interaction. Social interaction is inherently rewarding due to the feel-good neurochemicals that connection with important others produces, and so we are motivated to engage with them. The social brain includes elements from all levels of the triune brain (cortex, limbic, and lizard), thus pointing up its ancient evolutionary roots. Social engagement was such a successful adaptation earlier in evolution that an entirely new system, the smart vagus, developed so that individuals could both produce and read social cues. We literally feel another individual's pain or pleasure in our own bodies and thus can empathize with his or her situation. Indeed, social engagement is so important to the survival of individuals and the species that each of us enters the world ready to engage with others and to make them engage with us.

The ability to engage with others is what the parent-child attachment bond is all about, and this amazing connection will be introduced in Section II. However, before moving into the discussion of attachment, I would like to end the neurobiology section of this book by discussing how optimal psychological and behavioral functioning is dependent upon all of the individual parts and interconnected systems working together. Therefore, in the next chapter, I will discuss the IPNB concept of neural integration as it applies to human behavior and mental health.

Neural Integration

CHAPTER 5

LEARNING OBJECTIVES

After completing this chapter, readers should understand:

- Why neural integration is essential to healthy physical and psychological functioning.
- How neural integration and empathy are related.
- The nine pathways to neural integration.

KEY IDEAS

1. Complex systems are made up of differentiated parts that are linked together, each part serving a vital function, which when linked with the others, form a functioning whole.
2. Reciprocal interconnections between differentiated brain regions are inextricably intertwined, actually *requiring* each other for either to function.
3. Neural integration allows energy and information to flow easily through the enskulled and embodied brain from top to bottom and left to right.
4. An unrestricted flow of energy and information through and around the brain and body allows us to make sense of our lives and gives us a stable sense of self that supports mutually satisfying relationships.

Introduction

Up to this point, we have looked at individual parts of the brain and how they work together in systems to accomplish both personal and interpersonal emotional and behavioral functions. Siegel (2003) has said that "the brain as a system is composed of hierarchical layers of component parts that can be analyzed at a number of levels: single neurons, neuronal groups, circuits, systems, regions, and hemispheres" (p. 11). Integration occurs when differentiated neural functions are linked.

To illustrate this idea in non-neurobiological terms, take a moment to imagine that you are getting into your car to go to the grocery store. Your car has a lot of differentiated parts that must work together so that it can carry you where you want to go. You have, for example, an ignition switch that will accept the key that will start the engine. The engine, however, is made of multiple parts such as spark plugs, fuel injector, radiators, and on and on. All of these individual parts have to work together to make the engine run. If the spark plugs are fouled, the engine may run but not smoothly. If, however, the fuel injector is broken, the car won't start at all, and if your radiator overheats, uh oh, there you are on the side of the road with steam pouring out from under the hood.

Complex systems (like human beings, for example) are made up of differentiated parts that are linked together, each part serving a vital function, which when linked with the others, form a functioning whole (Semper, Murillo, & Bernacer, 2016; Siegel, 2012a). If one of those parts is not doing its job well or if it is not linked to the others, the entire system suffers and response to the changing environment is impaired. Moreover, Pessoa (2008) emphasizes that the reciprocal interconnections between brain regions are inextricably intertwined, actually *requiring* each other for either to function. Thus, a clear-cut boundary between, say, emotions and thoughts about emotions cannot be found. Integration, then, is essential to healthy physical and psychological functioning. Taking the IPNB perspective, Siegel (2012a) identifies nine pathways to neural integration that can inform mental health practice.

The Nine Pathways to Integration

According to Siegel (2012a), there are nine pathways to integration: consciousness, vertical, horizontal, narrative, memory, state, interpersonal, temporal, and transpirational. The interpersonal resonance that the mirror-resonance system activates allows an individual to align with the emotional signals being sent by someone else. How well an individual can align with others is dependent on how sensitive he or she is to social cues (Siegel, 2012a). Moreover, the alignment between a mental health practitioner and his or her client is essential to what Siegel calls "feeling felt" (p. 94), emphasizing that "in these transactions, the brain of one person and that of another are influencing each other in a form of 'co-regulation'" (p. 94).

Although not everyone agrees that the functioning of mirror neurons is critical to the development of empathy (see Hickok, 2014), mirror neurons do appear to provide us with a way of experiencing what another person is feeling. It is likely that these neurons are interconnected with other parts of the brain (the anterior cingulate and the anterior insula and others) to produce empathy and compassion (Budell, Jackson, & Rainville, 2010). Moreover, although the terms *empathy* and *compassion* are often used interchangeably, scientists have recently begun to recognize differences between them and to search for differences in their neurobiological processes. Differences in these two related concepts are discussed below.

As I discuss integration and empathy in the sections below I will frequently refer to the "therapist" (or "mental health practitioner") in the examples I provide. However, please understand that integration and empathy are certainly not limited to the therapist-client relationship. I use professional relationships in my examples because I believe that this book is most likely being read by students who want to work in mental health or by practitioners already in the field. It should be understood, however, that neural integration (or the lack of it) influences *all* social relationships in similar ways.

Integration of Consciousness

Human beings are distinctly different from other animals; not only can we be aware of what is going on within and around us, we can also be aware that we are aware. For example, my attention can be snatched up by something happening in the environment (*exogenous attention*); if, say for example, a loud noise happens just outside my window, my amygdala will make sure that I stop what I am doing and get ready to run. However, I also have the ability to purpose-fully choose where I turn my attention (*endogenous attention*). I may have a client who says that she is very sad and tells me a long story about what happened that caused her to be so sad. I have the choice of whether I turn my attention to my client's words or to her facial expres-sions, gestures, and body posture. Or should I pay attention to my own internal responses to what she is saying and how she looks? Is there something underneath her words that needs to be addressed? Do I need to take my feelings into supervision to determine why I have reacted to her feelings and words the way I have?

Siegel (2012a) cautions that we can view the object of attention as the totality of our identity when we do not distinguish awareness from that object of which we are aware. An intense emo-tion becomes who we are, not what we are feeling temporarily at that moment in time. (p. 380). Therefore, a mental health practitioner must understand that integration of consciousness is the ability to move your attention easily between what is going on outside yourself and what is going on inside yourself, to know what thoughts and feelings are yours and what thoughts and feelings belongs to your client. Likewise, for your client, integration of consciousness is the ability to turn attention easily to the internal experience of emotions/feelings and thoughts, to recognize consciously that a thought is simply a thought and not reality.

In addition, a client must be able to turn his or her attention easily to things outside of him-self or herself (the therapist, for example) in order to get the support that needed and to avoid those things that would cause harm. Without integration of consciousness, our awareness of the world and our place in it is impaired.

Vertical Integration

As discussed in Chapter 2, the human brain conserved parts of the neural systems of lower animals as it evolved; the lizard brain became the foundation for the limbic system, and the limbic system became the foundation for the neocortex. In addition, the sympathetic nervous system evolved to provide fight/flight capabilities above and beyond the earlier freeze capa-bilities of the vegetative vagus, and the smart vagus then evolved to control both in the service of social interaction. Thus, vertical integration occurs through multiple linkages between the embodied and enskulled parts of the brain and between the older parts of the neural systems and newer. It allows us to use the "wisdom of the body" (Siegel, 2102a, p. 382) (bottom-up input from the senses and the visceral organs) to inform the conscious, decision-making parts of the brain (top-down input from the PFC and associational cortices) to maximize our abil-ity to survive and thrive.

Badenoch (2008) points out that this vertical integration is of primary importance to mental health practitioners because it allows us to access and manage our own bodies and emotions. Being conscious of what is going on within ourselves allows us to tune in to the signals that our clients are sending us beneath our conscious awareness and helps us to avoid or minimize countertransference. In turn, helping our clients to become vertically integrated allows them to gain access to the wisdom of their bodies and to attune to others and respond to their sig-nals in adaptive rather than maladaptive ways.

Siegel (2006) suggests that encouraging clients to turn their attention to bodily sensations and affective states as well as to notice their thoughts can help them to integrate vertically. Specifically, he suggests that one of the best ways to help clients (and ourselves) to improve vertical integration is through mindfulness practices. He provides instructions on how to use his "Wheel of Awareness" practice (Siegel, 2012a, p. 294) to help clients become conscious of and differentiate between all eight of their senses (the five external sensations, internal sensations, thoughts, emotions, images and memories, and connectedness to others and the broader environment). In my own personal experience, Mindfulness Based Stress Reduction (MBSR) utilizes mindfulness practices that make the individual more aware of both the body and the environment (see https://www.umassmed.edu/cfm/about-us/, http://mbpti.org/programs/mbsr/mbsr-mindfulness-based-stress-reduction-teacher-training/, or https://www.institute-for-mindfulness.org/mbsr/MBSR-Teacher-Training for examples of MBSR training programs). In addition, I have found Insight Dialogue Meditation, with its powerful interpersonal meditation techniques, to be effective in increasing awareness of others' social engagement signals (see https://metta.org/ for more information).

Porges (2017) stresses the importance of strengthening the social engagement system through interventions such as the *Safe and Sound Protocol* (see https://integratedlistening.com/ssp-safe-sound-protocol/ for a full description of the program). He designed this intervention to address auditory hypersensitivity and processing difficulties, and to calm excited physiological states for individuals with auditory sensitivities, anxiety and trauma related disorders, inattention, and social and emotional problems. He also suggests that less formal interventions such as singing, playing a wind instrument, or chanting can also benefit clients with low vagal tone. These activities involve inhaling both deeply and quickly and exhaling much more slowly, thus activating the parasympathetic system and its inhibiting effects on the HPA system.

Horizontal Integration

As discussed in Chapter 2, the brain is divided into two hemispheres, and linkage between the hemispheres can be referred to as horizontal (or bilateral) integration. The two hemispheres have very different functions; the left tends to be logical, abstract, verbal, literal, factual, and categorical, while the right tends to be relational, emotional, nonlinear, contextual, musical, and metaphorical. McGilchrist (2009) has summarized the differences between the hemispheres in the following terms:

> According to the left hemisphere, understanding is built up from the parts; one starts from one certainty, places another next to it, and advances as if building a wall, from the bottom up. It perceives that there is objective evidence of truth for a part outside the context of the whole it goes to constitute. According to the right hemisphere, understanding is derived from the whole, since it is only in the light of the whole that one can truly understand the nature of the parts. ... According to the latter vision, that of the right hemisphere, truth is only ever provisional, but that does not mean that one must "give up the quest or hope of truth itself." (p. 140)

The two sides of the brain allow us to understand the world in two very different ways, both of which are essential—context and detail, the big picture and the bits and pieces that make the picture up, emotion and reason, word and image, language and music. Information about the outside world streams into the right hemisphere where it is screened for danger/safety.

Experiences that it deems important are laid down in implicit memory that becomes part of our understanding of ourselves and our relationship with the world—autobiographical memory that contains both sensual and emotional information. It is then sent over into the left hemisphere where it can be analyzed, measured, categorized and put into words. This information, neatly sliced and diced, is then sent back to the right hemisphere so that it can be reincorporated into a context that now becomes fuller, more focused, more complete.

Without this bouncing back and forth between the hemispheres, something is lost. For example, if we are trying to decide on a career, there are numerous (left brain) logical, rational factors to consider (money, time, location, skills, etc.). But what do we actually want (right brain) to do; what is going to bring us personal satisfaction? Another example: Someone playing blackjack says to the dealer, "Hit me again." If the dealer is using just the left brain, the player may want to duck!

Problems in differentiation and linkage can be caused by both innate and experiential factors, such as genetic anomalies and suboptimal attachment experiences (Siegel, 2012a). When the two hemispheres are not well integrated and one or the other becomes dominant, emotional and behavioral dysregulation is likely. Siegel (2006) emphasizes that human beings are sense-making animals, and it is the left brain that puts our experiences into the words that become the stories of our lives. However, he asks, "What would a life-story be like if the narrating left hemisphere could not easily access the nonverbal autobiographical details of the right side of the brain?" (p. 252). Indeed, individuals who are not integrated horizontally may have very incoherent, confusing and distorted life-stories, something that will be discussed below in the section on narrative integration.

In explaining the effects of poor horizontal integration, Cozolino (2010) suggests that the client who over-intellectualizes and has great difficulty in accessing and expressing emotions has a left brain that is overly dominant. In contrast is the client who is overly emotional, who exhibits magical thinking or who perhaps has auditory hallucination, indications of a right brain that is overly dominant. Moreover, since the left side of the PFC is biased toward positive emotions and the right side toward negative emotions, lack of integration can result in tendencies toward mania or depression. He also suggests that trauma is often the culprit in poorly integrated brains, resulting in inhibited development of the corpus callosum and fewer connecting fibers between the hemispheres among abused or neglected children.

Practitioners tend to address these imbalances in our clients naturally and intuitively. For clients who tend to stay in their heads, we ask them what's going on in their bodies. For clients whose emotions take off like skyrockets, we tend to try to get them express themselves in words rather than in actions, and we may also try to get them to put into words what they are feeling in their bodies. However, Badenoch (2008) cautions that trying to help a client to integrate horizontally may be difficult if the client is not already integrated vertically. She notes that if the client is unable to sense what is going on in the body, "the left hemisphere may receive such little input that the stories it creates are hollow and not reflective of the complexity of their inner worlds" (p. 35). In contrast, sometimes right brain memories of events and bodily sensations may flood a client, making him or her feel extremely confused and vulnerable. In these cases, it is important to get the rational, logical left brain to put words to the situation, thus integrating the left and the right sides (Siegel, 2012b). The important point that Siegel

(2012a) emphasizes is that "Neither side is better than the other. The key to living a creative and fulfilling life is collaboration, not obliteration. Integration across the hemispheres entails respecting differences while cultivating collaborative connections between the two important but distinct ways of knowing" (p. 381).

Memory Integration

Closely associated with horizontal integration is memory integration. In Chapter 3, we discussed the two types of memory—explicit and implicit. Explicit memory is a left-brain function facilitated by the hippocampus; it is factual, can be stated in words, and is accompanied by an internal feeling that is a memory of something that happened in the past. In contrast, implicit memory is a right-brain function facilitated by the amygdala; it is contextual, includes bodily sensations, emotions, and behavioral responses, and is not experienced as being a memory. Instead, it is experienced as sensations, emotions, and behaviors that are happening in the now. This can be very confusing to the person having the experience, and he or she may blame something or someone in the environment for his or her reaction to the memory.

When the two memory systems work together, individuals are able to develop a sense of self across time, an autobiography of who they are and what they can expect from the world. Siegel (2012a) explains that

> Memory integration is the linkage of differentiated implicit memory into the explicit forms of factual and autobiographical memory with which we can exercise intention and choice. This makes our lives more flexible. Memory integration can make the difference between PTSD, with its impairments, and posttraumatic growth. Understanding memory integration helps bring clarity and resolution to overwhelming past events. (p. 383)

Thus, one of the important jobs of a therapist is to help individuals bring the nonconscious memories that are causing them uncomfortable thoughts, feelings, and actions into consciousness where they can be verbalized and made sense of in the context of their lives. In this process, individuals can change the stories of their lives and imagine and work toward a healthier and happier future. Do you see how the different types of integration link with and build on each other? In order for a mental health professional to help an individual with memory integration, the first order of business is to start with helping the person to become conscious. As Siegel (2006) puts it:

> The key to memory integration is the neural reality that focal attention allows the puzzle pieces of implicit memory to enter the spotlight of attention and then be assembled into the framed pictures of semantic and self memories. With such reflective focus, what was once a memory configuration capable of intrusion on a person's life can move into a form of knowing that involves both deep thought and deep sensations of the reality of the past. (p. 253)

Narrative Integration

If individuals are able to integrate the implicit and explicit memories driving dysfunctional thinking, emotions and behaviors, they can develop a new story about who they are. Siegel (2012a) says, "We humans are a storytelling species—one that 'knows we know (Homo sapiens sapiens)'" (p. 383). The narrative that we assemble from our memories helps us to make sense out of our lives and allows us to share ourselves and our histories with others. When we take the time to reflect on our narrative, we may notice patterns that have not served us well. Bringing that to consciousness may then allow us to change those patterns to something more helpful.

Cozolino (2010) explains that during infancy the right side of the brain has developed our capacity to form relationships and to understand and use prosody (voice intonation, rhythm, etc. that convey our emotions). Starting in toddlerhood, the left side of the brain begins to function so that language and grammar begin to develop, and as the two sides begin to function together, we join words and sentences together with emotions. We begin to be able to put our ideas and memories into linear and complex forms, gradually developing a sense of who we are over time, a self in time, space, and relationship.

> As children we are told by others, and gradually begin to tell about ourselves, who we are, what is important to us, and what we are capable of. These self-stories are shaped by culture and co-constructed with parents and peers. (p. 166)

Thus, the stories that we learn about ourselves and tell about ourselves help us to make sense out of our lives. Making sense out of life (telling stories about our experiences) is so important to us that if we don't understand what has happened, we may go so far as to make it up. Imagine, for example, that I am four years old, and my sister is six. My mother is an alcoholic and pays little attention to us. At that age, I don't know what alcoholism is. All I know is that my mother doesn't care about me. The repeated neglect and rejection will be placed into my nonconscious implicit memory system. Because I am a sense-making animal, I try to make sense out of the situation and make up a story that explains it. Having heard her tell friends one time that she would have loved to have had a boy and a girl instead of two girls, I say to myself that if I were just a little boy, she would love me. That story may be the one I tell myself for many, many years, unexamined until I go into therapy. If I have someone who understands memory integration, I may be able to change my narrative into something in which I am not an irredeemable failure.

For some people, however, there is no explanation that they have been able to put together to explain the things that have happened in their lives. This may happen because there are gaps in memory due to trauma. Remember that excessive cortisol in the system can actually shut down the hippocampus. When this happens, there will be no explicit memory of the trauma, only implicit emotions, bodily sensations, assumptions, and expectations with no sense that they are coming from the past. These clients may not have a coherent narrative. In order to tell a coherent story, it is necessary for our implicit and explicit memories to work together, and for them to work together, we need to have well-integrated right and left hemispheres. To have well-integrated right and left hemispheres, we need to have vertical integration.

State Integration

State integration has to do with how we manage our states of mind across time. As our brains react to the environment around it (especially to our relationships), it causes us to have emotions. When we have similar emotions again and again, we tend to begin to see our emotional responses as being who we are—our personality. That is, if I am sad because my alcoholic mother isn't paying any attention to me over and over again, week after week, year after year, I may begin to see myself as *being* a sad person, not as just *having* a sad mood. That is, "these repeated and enduring states of activation of the brain can help define what we see as our personality—the patterns of perception and emotional and behavioral responses that help us denote who we are" (Siegel, 2006, p. 254). Badenoch (2008) notes that, "there is no single self in the objective sense, although increasing integration may bring us a subjective sense of wholeness and unity as our states of mind work in greater harmony" (p. 35). Instead, we are multiple selves with different needs at different times.

For example, Badenoch (2008) suggests that when we are young, we tend to internalize the voices of people who are important to us. I may have the voice of my mother in my head saying to me in a caring way "You should take care of yourself," while I also have her voice belittling me, saying, "Little girls who don't have friends are going to die of loneliness in old age." I may develop "an inner community whose members aren't at peace with one another" (p. 36).

Siegel (2012a) argues that there are two parts to state integration, inter-state and intra-state. Interstate integration is the ability to allow conflicting needs and states to exist. That is, I can allow myself to be alone when I need to and also go out with friends when I want to; I don't rigidly limit myself to one way of being/feeling. Intra-state integration is allowing myself to be fully present in whatever state I am in. That is, if I decide to go out with friends, I join in with the fun; I don't wistfully think about how I really wanted to hang out at home and binge watch *Game of Thrones* all weekend. In other words, state integration is allowing myself to be *how* I am *when* I am. Siegel (2012a) says, "Living a rich and full life entails at least these two aspects of differentiating (inter-state and intra-state) and then linking the many selves that define who we are" (p. 384). As mental health practitioners, we can help our clients increase their level of state integration by doing what we do naturally—accepting our clients' various selves as they appear, facilitating awareness of the inner community of conflicting voices, and helping them change their narrative.

Interpersonal Integration

While state integration has to do with how the individual relates to his or her many selves, interpersonal integration has to do with how well an individual is able to relate to other people. Siegel (2012a) calls this "Moving from 'me' to 'we'" (p. 384). When our various states of mind and being are well-integrated (inter- and intra-state integration), we are aware that we are separate from others (differentiation) but that we have the capacity to link to them (linkage).

Many individuals come into therapy because they are deeply enmeshed with someone, preoccupied with a relationship that is plagued by frequent emotional outbursts and destructive behavioral reactions. Others sabotage their relationships, preferring to be alone rather than risking genuine intimacy. Still others thrash back and forth between clinging to a relationship and driving the other away. In Chapter 4, we learned about the mirror-resonance system. When we understand the signals being sent to us by others and when we resonate with each other, we are interpersonally integrated. It has been suggested that impairment of this integration manifests in psychopathology (Siegel, 2012a). It may be that the relationship that a client has with his or her therapist may open the door to interpersonal integration. In the safety of a sensitive therapist's office, clients may increase vertical and horizontal integration, which lets them integrate memory, narrative, and state. This in turn can lead them to an openness to form healthy relationships outside of therapy and to broaden their connectedness with others. Their increasing ability to regulate their own emotions and behavioral responses lets them turn their attention away from self and begin more accurately reading the social signals that others are sending. This increased mental flexibility would open up the possibility of increased understanding of others' intentions and limitations and perhaps the development of increased empathy both for self and for others.

Temporal Integration

During our infancy and early childhood, our brains develop the capacity to recognize past, present, and future. Parts of our brain allows us to realize that a memory is coming from the past while other parts allow us to imagine what may happen in the future. That is, we have a capacity to "mental time travel" (Siegel, 2006, p. 254), a capacity that other animals probably do not have. This ability is both a blessing and a curse. We can use the past to plan for the future in the present. However, we realize as our brains and bodies mature that there are unexpected twists and turns in life and that nothing is certain, that all things change. We come to know that all living creatures die, including ourselves. We don't like this knowledge. Siegel (2012a) defines temporal integration as "the way we differentiate our longings for certainty, permanence and immortality from—and link them with—the reality of life's uncertainty, transience and mortality. When people deny one or the other side of this temporal slate, rigidity or chaos can ensue" (p. 386).

It is not uncommon, for example, for a mental health practitioner to work with a client who tries to control everyone and everything, desperately striving for certainty. Or the family that sabotages a member who is succeeding in substance abuse treatment, saying (metaphorically) "don't you dare change." Or the client (or perhaps friend or relative) who has multiple surgeries to remove the signs of aging, or who refuses to make out a last will and testament, firmly turning his or her back against mortality. Today's culture (at least in the United States) generally values youth and disparages age. The tendency is never to look at the reality of physical decline and death, not to plan for and come to terms with the inevitable end of life. Temporal integration is about finding purpose and meaning in life while it is being lived, tackling the big existential questions, like, why am I on Earth at this particular time? How can I contribute?

Temporal integration requires that an individual not be mired in ruminations on and regrets about the past or living in terror of what may happen in the future. It requires the self-regulation that comes from vertical, horizontal, memory, narrative, and state integration and the regulation of social interaction that comes from interpersonal integration.

Transpirational Integration

If we are able to achieve temporal integration in which we have accepted that nothing is certain, all things change, and we have only a finite amount of time to live our lives, we may be able to reach what Siegel (2012a) calls transpirational integration. In this domain of integration, there is a well differentiated *me* and *we* that become linked together in a common *one* that is bigger than either. It is a felt sense of connectedness to the self, others, and the universe. Siegel (2006) explains that "the term 'transpiration' denotes how new states of being seem to emerge as a vital sense of life is breathed across each of the domains of integration" (p. 256). This domain is active when people move past their individual differences to enact changes in the world for the greater good of all, recognizing both how fragile life is and how precious each living individual is, and working for the betterment of all beings. Siegel (2012a) makes clear the value of achieving the nine domains of integration, saying that

> health emerges from the integration of our interpersonal and bodily selves. Studies of happiness, health, and wisdom each reveal that positive attributes are associated with helping others and giving back to the world. We achieve a deep sense of meaning and accomplishment when we are devoted to something beyond our personal, individual concerns. Integration creates health and expands our sense of who we are in life, connecting us to others and a wider sense of ourselves. Being compassionate to others, and to ourselves, is a natural outcome of the healthy development of the mind. Kindness and compassion are integration made visible. If we take on the challenge of integration across its many domains, we may just be able to make a meaningful difference in the lives of people here and now, and for future generations. (p. 387)

Summary

The first five chapters of this book were devoted to the structure and functioning of the differentiated and integrated parts and systems of the brain. From the IPNB perspective, healthy physical and mental functioning occurs in, supports, and is supported by, healthy relationships. This is possible when energy and information flow easily through enskulled and embodied brains that are integrated from top to bottom and left to right. Adequate integration allows our memories and our personal stories to be coherent and to make sense to us. We may then have a relatively stable and accepting sense of self that supports our ability to have mutually satisfying relationships. Living a full life connected with others allows us to face our inevitable losses and the decline of age, and gives us a sense of connectedness to something bigger and more complete than life itself.

Because we are fundamentally social animals, there is never a time in our lives that we are not connected to and influenced by others in some way. Our brains are built by genes that other people gave us, and they develop in idiosyncratic ways in response to the environment into which we are born and then live. In the next section, we will learn about the impact our earliest social environment has on the development of our brains, i.e., the attachment relationship we have with our primary caregiver.

Attachment

Introduction

In the introduction to Section I, I explained that the architecture of the brain is determined by both genes and the environment. According to Combs-Orme (2013), three environmental factors are especially influential in epigenetic changes: exposure to toxic chemicals, diet, and the social environment. Exposure to toxic chemicals may disrupt the endocrine system affecting metabolism, growth, sleep, sexual functioning and reproduction, mood, and other functions. Diet is thought to be important not only because food sustains life but also because what you eat affects which genes are expressed or silenced. Thus, diet can contribute to the development of diseases such as cancer and cardiovascular disease or psychological issues such as depression.

Of particular importance to human behavior, however, is the effect of the social environment on epigenetic changes. Littrell (2015) discusses research that shows how important nurturing is to the production of proteins that determine whether a gene is expressed or not. She notes that, among rats, the genes responsible for the development of receptors for stress neurochemicals are silenced among babies that receive a lot of nurturing (in the form of their mothers licking them). These lucky rat babies are significantly less anxious than those that did not receive adequate nurturing. Importantly, Littrell mentions research showing that the same gene was silenced among humans who were abused as children and later committed suicide.

In the last chapter, I introduced you to the social engagement system, the neurobiological circuitry that develops in response to our need to live together as a social species. Fundamental to our inherent interconnectedness is the bond between a mother and her child that we call *attachment*. This earliest relationship affects all future relationships, and, even more fundamental to human behavior and social interaction, it literally builds the brain. In Chapter 6, I will provide an overview of attachment theory and discuss the neurobiological systems that drive the attachment system. In addition, I will explain how attachment is related to the regulation of emotion and mood. Then, in Chapter 7, I will introduce the four attachment styles that develop during childhood. Finally, in Chapter 8, I will suggest the clinical implications of this information. It is my hope that through these discussions practitioners will gain a clear understanding of how this earliest mother-child bond influences relationships and mental health in every stage of life. Please note that throughout this chapter (and indeed through the remainder of the book) when I say "mother," I do not necessarily mean the biological mother; it could be a father, a grandparent, a foster or adoptive parent, a nanny, an older sibling, or *anyone* who takes on that mothering role. What is important is not who does the nurturing but that nurturing is done.

Attachment Theory and Neurobiology

Introduction

Attachment has been characterized as an affective state that arises reciprocally between individuals, often described using the common term *love* (Condon, Corkindale & Boyce, 2008). Attachment is fundamental to the survival of the species because its primary function is to protect. Indeed, attachment is a life-and-death issue to human babies, who come into the world weak and utterly helpless; they will *surely* die if not cared for. They can do nothing for themselves; they are unable to feed themselves, they can't fight or run away from danger, nor can they keep themselves warm or clean. Therefore, Nature has hardwired them to attach to (to fall in love with) whomever takes care of them. This bond is extremely powerful and long lasting, relentlessly motivating them to seek out connection with a loved one not just in childhood but throughout the lifespan, especially in times of danger, distress, or illness (Bowlby, 1969/1982).

Brisch and Hollerback (2018) argue that, not just during childhood but in all developmental stages, the feelings of trust and safety associated with close contact with an attachment figure decrease aggression, fear, and sensitivity to both pain and stress. These researchers suggest further that "it is the special way that mothers communicate with their infants during the first year of life [*mind-mindedness*] that characterizes secure attachment relationships and that mediates the association between attachment and Theory of Mind" (p. 349–350) (see Chapter 4 concerning Theory of Mind, intersubjectivity and mentalizing). Mothers' "mentalizing language" (p. 350) gives their children words with which to talk about how their thoughts and behaviors are related to others' thoughts and behaviors. Thus, a mother's own mentalization builds her child's ability to mentalize and to make sense out of his or her own mind in relationship to others. Developing the ability to mentalize during infancy and early childhood can then help children to form and maintain well-differentiated, stable interpersonal relationships throughout both childhood and adulthood (Tremlow, Fonagy, Campbell, & Sacco, 2018). These authors argue that without the neuronal structure provided by the growing capacity to mentalize, children may be unable to fully recognize the pain and suffering that they can cause others, thus promoting bullying, violence, and other forms of victimization.

Attachment is a two-way street. That is, Nature has provided children with brain systems that spur the development of attachment, but it has also given adults the neurobiological impetus to attach to babies, especially their own. I will discuss how attachment affects the brains of both mothers and their children below. It should be noted, however, that as Mikulincer and Shaver (2016) have pointed out, the quality of the attachment bond is different for adult attachment figures since their role is that of caregiver. That is, they do not rely on the child to give them care and protection as the child relies on them. Indeed, if roles are reversed so that the child becomes a caregiver to the adult, psychological damage will occur because the child will not be sure that he or she has a safe haven and secure base. Mikulincer and Shaver acknowledge that if a parent loses a child, the reaction will almost always be extremely intense. However, they emphasize that the attached child "longs for the lost attachment figure's supportive presence and provision of comfort and security; the caregiver who loses a child tends to long for opportunities to care for the child and make restitution for failures of adequate care" (p. 17). Attachment is so important to the child that Nature has made it so that babies will attach even to adults who abuse them, often resulting in nonconscious seeking out of abusive relationships time and again well into adulthood (Chambers, 2017).

Although attachment centers on whomever assumes the primary care taking duties for the child during infancy, other loving attachments are made throughout life (Bowlby, 1969/1982; Mikulincer & Shaver, 2016). Relationships provide fundamental support for both mental and physical health from preconception through death (Doan & Zimmerman, 2003). It appears that Darwin was only partially correct with his survival of the fittest idea; it turns out that, at least for humans, it is survival of the loved and nurtured.

I will start this chapter with a brief history of the development of attachment theory. I will then discuss how the attachment behavioral system works both to ensure that the child is able to be close to caring adults who will see to his or her needs and to determine his or her sense of self in relation to others. Next, I will discuss who normally serves as attachment figures as individuals transition through developmental stages. Then, I will identify the parts of the brain and the neurochemicals associated with attachment. Last, I will explain how attachment influences the regulation of emotions and behavior throughout the life span.

A Short History of Attachment Theory

John Bowlby (1969/1982) introduced attachment theory to the world back in the late 1950s, arguing that through evolutionary processes babies developed instinctive (automatic) behaviors that he called the *attachment behavioral system*. These behaviors help them to gain and maintain proximity to caring adults, thus increasing the chances that they will be protected from danger, survive into adulthood, and have children of their own, thus perpetuating the species. In addition, he noted that the attachment behavioral system is interconnected with other behavioral systems, in particular the *exploratory behavioral system* and the *HPA* (fear) system.

Bowlby (1969/1982) understood that for children to grow up to thrive in the world they need, first, to be safe and then to be able to explore and master the world. He argued that when children have access to an available and responsive caring adult, they have a secure base from which to explore the world and a safe haven to return to in times of danger or distress. Bowlby recognized further that the felt safety provided by the secure base/safe haven system that available and responsive mothers offer them helps to manage their fear system (i.e., the HPA fight/flight and vegetative vagal freeze systems). Lastly, Bowlby (1973) noted that stored memories of how caregivers respond to their children's repeated attempts to feel safe gradually develop into mental representations concerning both what to expect (or not) in the way of care and safety in the world and how deserving (or not) they are of loving relationships. These representations of self and other become the foundation of the individual's personality.

Bowlby's colleague Mary Ainsworth expanded on his ideas concerning the attachment behavioral system (i.e., innate, biologically driven attachment processes through which babies seek and maintain proximity to their caretakers). In her research, Ainsworth focused on the bond that develops between a baby and his or her mother, discovering that some children are very secure in that relationship while others are less secure (Ainsworth, 1963; Ainsworth, Blehar, Waters, & Wall, 1978). In her Strange Situation research, Ainsworth tested children's behavioral reactions in a lab setting to being left by their mothers for a few minutes with a stranger and then calmed by them upon return. Based on their reactions, she was able to categorize most of the children she observed into one of three classifications—*secure* (visibly distressed by being left but easily calmed upon return), *anxious/avoidant* (not visibly distressed by being left and not seeking comfort upon return), or *anxious/ambivalent* (visibly extremely distressed by being left and difficult to calm upon return). Later, one of Ainsworth's students, Mary Main, and her associates (Main, Kaplan, & Cassidy, 1985; Main & Solomon, 1990) went on to define a fourth classification—*disorganized/disoriented* (odd or awkward behaviors, such as lying face down on the floor or freezing when mother entered the room). In addition to recognizing the extremity of these children's distress, Ainsworth came to realize that the mothers of disorganized/disoriented children were highly likely to have suffered trauma as children and to have developed a disorganized/disorganized attachment style themselves. Thus, she recognized the transmission of attachment style down the generations.

More recent theorizing on attachment suggests that it is a complex and multidimensional construct (Vivanti & Nuske, 2017). These researchers note that Ainsworth's (1963; 1978) Strange-Situation experiments tapped into only one dimension of attachment, the proximity-seeking behaviors associated with a fear response to stress/threat. They call this dimension an "externally driven response" (p. 252). This dimension is in contrast to what they call an "internally driven response" (p. 252) in which proximity to the attachment figure is not sought out because of an external threat but occurs instead in response to a drive for affiliation, a drive that is common to social animals. Citing Insel et al., they argue that "Affiliation is engagement in positive social interaction with other individuals [whereas] attachment is selective affiliation as a consequence of the development of a social bond" (p. 252). That is, they are suggesting that humans can seek proximity with an attachment figure for two quite different reasons: (1) it makes them feel safe, and (2) they like to be with them. They emphasize that both of these drives (attachment and affiliation) are extremely ancient and provide relevant adaptive responses that promote survival of our highly social species. Thus, we have one neural system that promotes survival through accessing a safe haven in times of distress (externally driven) and another neural system that promotes survival through social interaction (internally driven). As will be discussed in later chapters, things can go wrong in these systems due to abuse, neglect, or neurodevelopmental disorders like autism. However, in normal development, both attachment systems promote well-being.

From this brief discussion of the developmental history of attachment theory, it is clear that how a mother treats her baby has a lasting influence on his or her emotional and behavioral functioning. However, connectedness is so important to survival that Nature has given us the ability to attach to different people in what Bowlby (1969/1982) calls an attachment hierarchy.

The Attachment Hierarchy

As Maslow (1943) made clear, human beings have a natural drive to *affiliate* with others— to hang out together, to chat, play golf or watch movies with, etc. However, that kind of relationship is not what Bowlby (1969/1982) meant by *attachment*. As Mikulincer and Shaver (2016) explain

> An attachment interaction is one in which one person is threatened or distressed and seeks comfort and support from the other. An affiliation interaction is one in which both people are in a good mood, do not feel threatened, and have the goal of enjoying their time together or advancing common interests" (p. 17).

Thus, an attachment figure, to Bowlby (1969/1982), meant someone who is bigger, stronger and wiser who you run to when times get bad (safe haven/secure base), someone who if you are separated from or lose him or her, causes you intense and long-lasting sadness, perhaps even for the rest of your life. Thus, to be an attachment figure, an individual must meet three criteria: (1) be someone who the child will seek out when in trouble; (2) act as a safe haven for the child, reliably providing safety, support, relief and protection; (3) act as a secure base from which the child can explore the world safely. The same criteria apply to attachment relationships later in life also (Mikulincer & Shaver, 2016).

From an attachment perspective, the environment "is often referred to as the stage or setting in which care-giver-child interactions occur" (Donelan-McCall & Olds, 2018, p. 82). During infancy, the mother is, to a considerable extent, the child's environment (Schore, 2001). However, please remember that when I say "mother" I do not necessarily mean the biological mother. By "mother," I mean whoever takes on the role of safe haven and secure base and regularly takes care of the baby's needs. This person is considered the primary attachment figure. Moreover, this mother is not just the first attachment figure; she is usually also the deepest attachment figure.

Remember that attachment is a biological drive that occurs in all human babies because of its survival value. That is, babies will not survive if someone isn't there to take care of their needs, so having a relationship with a primary attachment figure is a matter of life and death. Therefore, separation from mother, or rejection by her, is perceived by the child as catastrophic. Look at it from the child's perspective: my mother feeds me every couple of hours during my first weeks and months of life, makes me comfortable by getting rid of my wet diaper, wraps me up to keep me warm, sings me gently to sleep when I am tired, upset, and crying. If she leaves me, I search for her, I long for her comfort and presence. I protest long and loud because **I will die without her.** Moreover, these are my earliest experiences of the world, experiences that are being encoded into right-brain memory, implicit and not available for conscious recall. Because my life depends on her, and because she is there again and again and again, hour after hour, day after day during a time when I don't even know what time is, her presence is my world. Thus, she has a profoundly privileged place both in my present and in my memory.

Some researchers believe, however, that the optimal situation for children is to have dual primary attachment figures (Newland & Coyle, 2010). This thinking is based on the understanding that both safety (safe haven) and exploration (secure base) are essential during childhood. Mothers have been found to be more engaged in caregiving activities, socializing, and teaching their children, while fathers are more engaged in rough-and-tumble physical play with them (Schoppe-Sullivan, Kotila, Jia, Lang & Bower, 2013). The mother, whose primary responsibility generally is to keep her children safe and to soothe them when the world knocks them on their head, may be unwilling to let them take chances that would help them understand the world better and take considered risks needed for growth. Having a second highly involved caregiver, often (but not necessarily) the father, can allow children, through excitement, play and joy, to safely stretch beyond their comfort zone and encourage them to try beyond what they think they can do, life skills that can be very useful in all developmental stages (Newland & Coyle, 2010). This does not mean, however, that families that do not have two parents involved in caring for their children and providing them with opportunities to stretch themselves cannot raise healthy and happy children. They absolutely can! It just means that having other attachment figures available who can help the mother out is a good idea.

The good news is that people other than the mother can also become attachment figures and can be an important source of social support when mom and/or dad are not available. Indeed, Siegel (2012a) has suggested that for human beings to thrive, they need a community of caregivers who collaborate to provide the nurturance in all stages of life. Although these secondary attachment figures may not offer felt security at quite the same level and may not hold quite the same privileged place in the heart as the one who takes hourly, daily care of the infant, they are still important. Thus, Bowlby (1969/1982) recognized that there is a hierarchy of attachment figures with the mother (and perhaps fathers) coming first, but with grandparents, older siblings and day care workers offering a sense of felt security, too.

Mikulincer and Shaver (2016) emphasize that attachment figures can include extended family during the early years. Then as the child matures and spends more time out in the community, teachers, coaches, and other mentors can become attachment figures. Even certain coworkers may take on this role when the individual enters the work world. Of course, romantic partners can become powerful attachment figures, especially when they have children together and need each other's support during stressful times. Indeed, even groups and institutions (e.g., religious organization) can serve as attachment figures, as can symbolic figures such as God, angels and saints, providing for some people real comfort and relief during the hardest of times. The good news for mental health practitioners is that we, too, can act as attachment figures to our clients whether they are children, adolescents, or adults. Indeed, some researchers argue that in effective therapy, the bond between clinician and client offers a corrective attachment experience in which the client "comes to know him- or herself in the process of being known by another" (Wallin, 2007, p. 57).

Attachment-Related Brain System

As explained in Chapter 1, the human brain evolved through three levels, the hind (lizard brain), the limbic system, and the neocortex. Each of these levels affects and is affected by attachment. Nature (genes) determines the basic structure of the brain as well as the neurochemicals that it produces, while Nurture (the environment) shapes the neural networks in those structures. A baby comes into the world with a brain equipped with experience-expectant plasticity. The part of the brain responsible for vision, for example, is present at birth, waiting on (expecting) light to activate it. When nerves are stimulated by light, the stimulus is carried to the visual cortex and that part of the brain begins to develop. Likewise, experience-expectant parts of the brain responsible for the attachment bond will be stimulated to grow in response to a baby's interaction with a bigger, stronger and wiser person who will become his or her primary attachment figure.

Exactly how those neural networks grow is dependent upon the kinds of interactions the baby has with his or her attachment figure(s)—experience-dependent plasticity. As Schore (2002a) has stated, "The baby's brain is not only affected by these interactions; its growth literally requires brain/brain interactions and occurs in the context of a positive relationship between mother and infant" (p. 62). That is, a mother's brain literally builds her child's brain. I will start this section with a discussion of the brain structures associated with attachment starting from the bottom (hindbrain) and going up (limbic and neocortex). Then I will discuss the attachment-related neurochemicals.

Hindbrain

The hindbrain is the most primitive part of the brain and is responsible for our most primitive bodily functions, such as heart and respiration rates as well as digestion and elimination. As you may recall, these functions are regulated by the ANS, which consists of the sympathetic and parasympathetic systems. The hindbrain is where the cranial nerves originate, the ancient vegetative vagus and the more modern smart vagus. In addition, the hindbrain is where our reflex actions originate. Each of these functions is important to attachment.

Attachment and the Smart Vagus

As discussed in Chapter 4, the smart vagus is largely responsible for our ability to communicate socially. Indeed, Schore (2001) argues that communication may be the most important process to take place over the first year of post-natal development. The smart vagus controls the muscles of the face, eyes, mouth, tongue, throat, ears and head, and controls heart rate and breathing in the absence of threat.

The smart vagus starts developing at around the 26th week of gestation and is mature enough at birth so that babies can give rudimentary signals to mom concerning their physical/psychological state (e.g., crying, grimacing, smiling, gazing). In addition, they are able to suck and swallow so that mom can meet their nutritional needs, and they can pick out their mom's voice from all the surrounding sounds, having heard it often in utero. These automatic activities and responses are essential for babies' immediate survival since they trigger mom's innate maternal behaviors. In addition, as mom responds to her baby's signals, she actively builds her child's smart vagus, thus influencing the development of his or her nascent social engagement system.

The social signals being sent and received by the smart vagus of a mother and her baby (vocalizations, eye gaze, smiling, etc.) are perceived during the primary analysis of stimuli (neuroception) as signs of safety, and this information is sent to the amygdala. The amygdala then produces both oxytocin and endorphins, resulting in a shared sense of well-being and happiness, followed by the production of dopamine and a resulting desire to be in each other's company. Thus, healthy functioning of the smart vagus is fundamental to the establishment of the attachment bond.

Reflex Actions

Cozolino (2014) notes that babies come into the world with innate behaviors that serve to "jump-start" (p. 94) attachment. Their reflex actions, such as crying, grasping, grimacing, yawning, etc., elicit responses from their caregivers. This two-way interaction is what is called *contingent communication* in which "mother and infant continually adjust to each other's sounds, gestures, movements and emotions in a lyrical duet" (p. 94).

All five senses involved in exteroception are available to babies at birth. Their olfactory lobe is sensitive to the smell of their mother's body and breast milk, and babies will actively seek their mother's nipple so that they can nurse. If you have ever placed your little finger against a baby's palm, you have probably noticed that their fingers reflexively close over and grip it in a most endearing fashion. Mothers are also very aware of this grasping capability since their children often grab onto their hair. Ouch!

Babies are born recognizing and orienting to their mother's voice, having heard her voice when they were still inside the womb. As babies turns their heads to find mom's voice, they also try to find her face. Babies are particularly interested in all human faces and begin to imitate facial expressions shortly after birth. Moreover, mothers mirror their babies' facial expressions, a practice that stimulates the development of babies' social engagement and mirror resonance systems. An especially important and expressive part of the face is the eyes. A baby's eyes reflexively lock onto his or her mother's gaze. Indeed, mothers and babies tend to spend a great deal of time gazing into each other's eyes, a practice that links their brains and their minds. Schore (2001) recognized the importance of mutual gaze, saying that when a baby is about two months old,

> the visual stimuli emanating from the mother's emotionally expressive [face] becomes the most potent stimulus in the infant's social environment, and the intense interest in her face, especially in her eyes, leads him to track it in space, and to engage in periods of intense mutual gaze. The infant's gaze, in turn, evokes the mother's gaze, thereby acting as a potent interpersonal channel for the transmission of "reciprocal mutual influences." (p. 18)

Another particularly important sense associated with attachment is touch. Cozolino (2014) notes that touch is the first sense to develop during gestation and that it remains important throughout the lifespan. Touch is important to intimacy, and having our bodies gently caressed, scratched, tickled, massaged or otherwise touched in a positive way is pleasurable at all ages. Indeed, immediately after her baby is born, a mother instinctively wants skin-to-skin contact, spending about 80% of the first nine minutes touching, rubbing, and stroking her newborn. This instinctive action helps the baby's hypothalamus to establish and maintain his or her body temperature. Furthermore, Schore (2005) suggests that the reason most women naturally hold babies in their left arm is that this allows the baby to see mother's face and hear her voice with his or her left eye and ear. Because of the brain's contralateralized structure, this information is then carried to the baby's right brain, the part of the brain that is developing during infancy. The baby's responses are then fed back into the mother's right eye and ear and carried to her right brain. It is thought that this right brain-to-right brain connection is essential to the attachment bond.

Limbic System

The limbic system is where we process emotions. Schore (2001) suggests that the visual, auditory (prosodic) and gestural signals constantly being sent between mother and child as they interact is a form of "emotional communication" (p. 22) that in essence "constitutes a conversation between limbic systems" (p. 22). Schore points out, however, that the limbic system is not limited to emotional processing; it is also responsible for learning. That is, it is where memories are encoded. For infants and young children, it is this area that produces the internal working model of self and others based on our memories of how we have been treated. It is on these memories that we will base our expectations concerning how we should treat ourselves and others, and how others should treat us. It is in this part of the brain that we store our earliest assumptions about whether others are trustworthy and whether the world is safe to live in.

The part of the limbic system most important to attachment is the amygdala. As discussed in Chapter 3, the amygdala is responsible for primary appraisal (neuroception) of a stimulus to determine its potential for either threat or safety. If it perceives danger, it triggers the sympathetic system's fight/flight responses. If it perceives safety, it remains calm and allows approach/engagement. Schore (2001) states that "the amygdala ... [is] in a critical period of maturation that onsets in the last trimester of pregnancy and continues through the first two months of human life, the earliest period of bonding" (p. 32). Since the amygdala is an integral part of the HPA stress regulation system that matures during this early attachment period, less-than-optimal attachment experiences may result in permanent problems with stress regulation.

The amygdala is also responsible for encoding emotional memories (implicit, nonconscious) into the right side of the brain. In infancy, these are the only kind of memories being encoded because the left side of the brain is not yet functioning. The amygdala starts laying down memories in the right side of the brain even before birth, and a baby who is only six days old can discriminate between the smell of his or her mother and that of another woman (i.e., remember what mom smells like). Thus, the very powerful early memories of how I have to be so that I can be with my mom are laid down by the amygdala and are not available for conscious recall. These nonconscious memories become what Wallin (2007) (citing Bollas, 1987) calls "the unthought known" (p. 3). These memories make up the schema contained in our internal working model and unconsciously influence our relationships and behaviors in all future developmental stages. The unthought known generally causes a hair-trigger, uncontrolled reaction, a response based not on rational reflection but on instantaneous, unexamined, generalized assumptions about our safety and/or acceptability.

In the triune brain, the limbic system developed on top of and encompassed the hindbrain, the amygdala being one of the first structures to evolve in the limbic system. Evolution, however, demanded more of the brain, resulting in the development of the cerebral cortex, starting with the cingulate and insula cortices and then, later, the orbitomedial prefrontal cortex. These cortical structures are highly connected with both the amygdala and the hindbrain, and together make up the attachment-related brain system. These later-developing cortical areas will be discussed next.

Cerebral Cortex

The areas of the brain that are most influential in attachment processes are the anterior cingulate, the anterior insula and the orbitomedial prefrontal (OMPFC) cortices. Siegel (2012a) notes that some researchers actually consider these regions to be part of the limbic system. However, others note their ability to act as an interface between the lower limbic system and higher cortical structures and refer to them as the *paralimbic cortex*.

Cozolino (2014) explains that, because of their location, these regions are in a prime position to "process internal and external information, combine it with past experience, and feed it forward to the prefrontal and parietal lobes for analysis, decision making and goal directed action" (p.43). The healthy functioning of these important areas is highly influenced by attachment experiences in the first year of life. Although the human cerebral cortex doesn't mature completely until early adulthood, the anterior cingulate and anterior insula are mature by the ripe old age of 15 months while the OMPFC continues to mature for another three months (Schore, 2001). As is clear, then, these structures are maturing in response to environmental stimuli occurring during the time of life when interactions with the mother constitute, to a great extent, the child's environment. Therefore, attachment-related experiences are highly influential in their development.

Anterior Cingulate and Anterior Insula

According to Schore (2001), the development of the anterior cingulate is experience-dependent and begins to mature when the baby is between two and four months old. The anterior cingulate of both mother and child are involved in a number of behaviors important to the attachment bond. For example, the anterior cingulate is involved in remembering faces, in particular, the baby being able to distinguish his or her mother's face from others. In addition, the mother's anterior cingulate prompts her response to the pain and separation cries of her baby. Then, at the age of around nine months, the baby's anterior cingulate starts to prompt expressions of separation anxiety such as stopping activities and seeking out mom in response to novel or threatening situations or strangers.

In addition, the anterior cingulate is involved in the production of emotional vocalizations like laughing and crying as well as in play behaviors. A mother whose anterior cingulate and smart vagus are well developed will understand her baby's emotional vocalizations (his or her particular cries that mean hunger, fear, or fatigue, etc.) and respond appropriately. Her emotional vocalizations (e.g., singing a lullaby, excitement when baby smiles) will be perceived by her baby's anterior cingulate and smart vagus, strengthening their ability to recognize social information. Play between a mother and her baby is particularly important because it results in positive emotional resonance and the beginning of intersubjectivity at around the age of nine months. As discussed in Chapter 4, intersubjectivity is the ability to *mentalize* (i.e., be aware of others' intentions, predict their behaviors and empathize with their pain), the very foundation of sociality.

Intersubjectivity also involves the anterior insula, a part of the cortex that is closely connected to the anterior cingulate (and in constant interaction with it) and allows us to feel a representation of someone else's pain in our own bodies. According to Schore (2001), the maturation of the anterior cingulate and anterior insula during infancy allows the development of *joint attention*. That is, a young boy is able to be aware of, say, a ball rolling on the floor and at the same time aware that his mother also sees the ball rolling. This teaches the child that other people have interests and awareness just like himself, and that it is possible for people to share experiences. It is thought that the development of joint attention as the anterior cingulate and anterior insula mature may also be related to the maturation of the prefrontal cortex, which I will discuss next.

OMPFC

The OMPFC, according to Cozolino (2014), "sits at the apex of the neural networks of the social brain ... [and] is as much an extension of the limbic system as it is a full citizen of the cerebral cortex" (p. 44). Its healthy functioning is, according to Schore (2001), essential to human functions critically responsible for the definition of an individual's personality, including social adjustment, emotion, mood and behavioral regulation, motivation, and responsibility. Connected with the anterior cingulate and anterior insula as well as with the amygdala and hypothalamus, the reward system, and the vagal system, it is important to the functioning of the social engagement, motivational, and HPA systems (see Chapter 3). According to Schore (2001), the OMPFC is a "control system [that] integrates the psychological and biological spheres of mind and body" (p. 36). It is a regulatory system that

> monitors, adjusts, and corrects emotional responses and regulates motivational control of goal-directed behavior. It thus functions as a recovery mechanism that efficiently monitors and regulates the duration, frequency, and intensity of positive and negative affect states, from high intensity joy and excitement to the affective-motivational aspects of pain. (p. 39)

All this, and it matures at the age of 18 months! The OMPFC, like the other parts of the social engagement system, acts on the basis of learned experiences, including those earliest attachment experiences that occur in infancy. For the OMPFC to develop and integrate well with the rest of the system, infants need their mothers to regulate their stress and affect until their brains mature sufficiently so that they can take over that chore. That is, they have to use their mother's OMPFC until they have one of their own.

Attachment-Related Neurochemicals

Interactions between a mother and her baby "result in a cascade of biochemical processes that stimulate and enhance the growth and connectivity of neural networks throughout the brain" (Cozolino, 2014, p. 117). The neurochemicals most closely associated with these processes are oxytocin, endorphin, and dopamine.

Oxytocin

Oxytocin appears to be central to the formation of the attachment bond. It is a neurochemical that is associated with social support and affiliation in all stages of life (Walker & McGlone, 2013). Oxytocin provides the sense of safety, security, and trust found in secure attachment. Oxytocin is involved in all mothering behaviors, including the making of babies, the birthing of babies, the care and feeding of babies, and attachment to babies. It is present during vaginal stimulation, copulation, and orgasm; it causes contractions of the uterus during labor; when a baby nurses, stimulation of the nipple releases oxytocin into the blood stream causing milk to be expressed. In addition, it also causes the mother to relax and enjoy the experience of nursing her baby (Cozolino, 2014), thus reducing the risk of maternal neglect (Strathearn, 2011). Oxytocin has receptors in numerous locations in the brain and actively influences the functioning of the HPA, reward/motivation, and social engagement systems.

Oxytocin and the HPA System

In the HPA system, oxytocin moderates sympathetic and vegetative vagal defense responses to stress and promotes feelings of safety and wellbeing (Walker & McGlone, 2013), feelings that are critical to secure attachment. Recall that human babies come into the world unable to do anything for themselves. This includes regulating their levels of stress. In essence, they must use the adults around them to manage their emotions. In the attachment bond, the sense of safety that oxytocin produces allows the vegetative vagus to function optimally in both mother and child, promoting healthy immune responses, sleep, digestion, and growth (Carter & Porges, 2011). Thus, oxytocin and secure attachment apparently work together to regulate the stress-response system (Chambers, 2017).

Oxytocin and the Social Motivation System

At normal levels, oxytocin is thought to promote mothers' nurturing behaviors and to facilitate proximity seeking in both mother and child. Nurturing behaviors include activities such as touching, stroking, hugging, singing, talking in "motherese" (prosody), mutual eye gazing, and other playful and affectionate behaviors. These behaviors stimulate the reward system in both mother and baby, triggering a positive feedback loop in which the mother's nurturing behaviors cause the release of oxytocin in both mother and child, which then goes on to influence their social behaviors and cognitions (Chen, Heinrichs, & Johnson, 2017).

Touch and eye gaze are especially critical to children's development. Indeed, lack of touch has long been known to be associated with infant mortality even in the presence of sufficient food, warmth, and hygiene (Walker & McGlone, 2013). Touch in infancy reduces HPA activity in stressed infants and is influential in the development of self-regulation and reduced aggression in children (Walker & McGlone, 2013). Concerning infant-mother eye gaze, Schore (2001) emphasizes, "The future capacity to receive and express essential visual-facial social information is expressed in face-to-face communications, a central aspect of all later intimate relationships, and is dependent upon care-giver-infant eye contact and visual gazing during early critical periods" (p. 34).

Oxytocin and the Social Engagement System

Oxytocin has also been found to affect parents' imitation of their babies' facial expressions (Korb, Malsert, Strathearn, Vuilleumier, & Niedenthal, 2016), an important factor in the development of the baby's sense of self and his or her mirror-resonance system. In addition, oxytocin is related to awareness of social cues, a factor in a mother's ability to attune and respond appropriately to her baby's needs (MacKinnon et al., 2018).

Lastly, adequate mothering behaviors promote the development of the oxytocin system in their daughters, thus affecting the quality of nurturing in the next generation (Strathearn, 2017). Women who were abused as children have lower levels of oxytocin in general and specifically during pregnancy and after their babies are born (Chambers, 2017). New mothers with low oxytocin levels are at high risk of developing post-partum depression and thus of placing their children at risk of developing mental health problems of their own (Tse, Siu, & Wong, 2017).

Endorphins

Endogenous opioids help humans to manage pain, and they also reward social interaction, providing a sense of pleasure and well-being. Since endorphins are released during contact between a mother and her child, both take pleasure in being together. Similarly, when they are not together, they feel anxious and are driven to seek each other out again to relieve separation-distress. They are released during the birthing process itself and appear to facilitate maternal nurturing behaviors immediately after birth (Walker & McGlone, 2013).

Moreover, endorphins are produced during social play. While attachment provides a sense of felt security (safety), it also provides a secure base from which to explore the world. Although oxytocin is also produced in both mother and child during interactive play, endorphin is particularly important to exploratory and rough-and-tumble play. Children use play as a way of exploring the world that they need to master as they grow, and the endorphins produced during play make it a very pleasurable experience. At around the age of eight weeks, infants tend to begin to engage in playful activities with their mother, which the mother, in turn, finds pleasurable.

Although endorphins are involved in the rewards associated with attachment, they also have a dark side. Recall that the activity social engagement system is dependent on there being no environmental threat. However, when there is a threat that doesn't yield to social cues, the older sympathetic HPA system will be activated, causing fight/flight or freeze responses. In times of unavoidable life threat, the vegetative vagus is flooded with endorphins, which inhibits both the sympathetic system (and its active defensive behaviors) and also the oxytocin system (and its relational behaviors). Thus, although endorphins can provide a sense of well-being and safety, the large amounts released during traumatic stress can cause dissociation and the loss of the relational (Lanius, 2014). Endorphins help us manage both fear and pain, not just physical pain, but also the pain of social rejection. The effects of this endorphin-mediated dissociative response on attachment cannot be overstated. Lanius explains that

> If, for example, a baby reaches for her mom but her mom is preoccupied with war or is drunk or otherwise unavailable, the baby would turn away, flinch, but be unable to leave, protest, and then would surrender and shut down. The next day, again the baby is hungry, wants physical reassurance and loving touch, engagement with mother, and again mother can't be there, physically or emotionally, and the baby doesn't protest very long. The third day, the baby doesn't try; the spike of distress is quickly transformed by endogenous opioid release." (p. 115)

Dopamine

When oxytocin and/or endorphins are released into the reward center in response to something pleasurable, they stimulate the release of dopamine, which is then projected up into the OMPFC where it regulates motivation. Dopamine stimulates motivated behavior in both mother and child and is responsible for behavioral reinforcement (Strathearn, 2011). That is, dopamine motivates mother and baby to seek each other out. In addition, when mother and baby interact in ways that produce the rewarding effects of oxytocin, dopamine acts to make them want to engage in those behaviors again. Dopamine is also associated with preference formation (Walker & McGlone, 2013), which is probably why a baby prefers mom's face to other faces, mom's voice to other voices, and why mom thinks her baby is the prettiest, smartest and most wonderful baby in the whole world even when he or she clearly isn't to other people!

Having provided a brief explanation of which neurochemicals are associated with initiating and maintaining the attachment bond, I will now discuss the parts of the brain involved in attachment.

Attachment and Affect Regulation

Schore (2000, 2001) has argued that attachment theory is, at its heart, a regulatory theory. That is, he holds that a secure mother, through two-way contingent communication, will unconsciously regulate her baby's levels of arousal moment by moment. It is the mother's capacity to regulate both her own and her baby's arousal that allows her baby to develop those same capacities. Moreover, the mother is not building her baby's ability to self-regulate his or her responses to just painful or distressing events but also to novel events. Human beings seek not only the (soothing) familiar but also the (exciting) new. Secure attachment supports both. That is, when there is sufficient safety, a child can freely explore the environment. In addition, the child will be able to mentalize (i.e., recognize/understand other people's social signals and have compassion), reflect on his or her own emotions and behaviors, and change them as needed (Gilbert, 2014). If the mother's ability to attune adequately to her baby's signals is impaired, and therefore she is ineffective at regulating the baby's levels of arousal, there will be permanent impairment in the child's production and utilization of the neurochemicals associated with emotional regulation—oxytocin, endorphin, and dopamine. Schore (2001) emphasizes that these deficits result in

> not just an unstable self-system but one with a poor capacity to change, a limited ability to continue to develop at later points in the life cycle. … This relationship between events in early development and a later capacity to change is due to the fact that the early social environment directly impacts the experience-dependent maturation of the limbic system, the brain areas specialized for the organization of new learning and the capacity to adapt to a rapidly changing environment. Because limbic areas in the cortex and subcortex are in a critical period of growth in the first two years and these same neurobiological structures mediate stress-coping capacities for the rest of the lifespan, early interpersonal stress-inducing and stress-regulating events have long-enduring effects. (p. 16–17)

For children to build the capacity to regulate their affect on their own, they need, first, to be protected from prolonged high intensity or overwhelming affective states during early infancy. That is, they need to live in a safe and calm environment that offers moderate levels of stimulation. Too little stimulation (as in neglect) will not prompt the brain to grow. However, they shouldn't be overly stimulated or placed in emotionally stimulating situations for too long (as in abuse or domestic violence). Too much emotional stimulation for too long can actually result in neuron death in the vagal nerve, the hypothalamus and the brain stem, areas of the brain associated with autonomic regulation (Schore, 2001).

In addition to protection from prolonged or overwhelming amounts of emotional stimulation, babies need to have the opportunity to move from regulation to dysregulation and back to regulation over and over again. This process tends to happen naturally with a "good enough" (i.e., adequately attuned) mother who responds consistently and sensitively to her baby's communications. According to Schore (2001), at around the age of two months, babies begin to engage in highly arousing face-to-face playful interactions with the mother. As a result of these interactions, the two begin to develop affect synchrony in a "highly organized dialogue of visual and auditory signals [that] is transacted in milliseconds, and is composed of cyclic oscillations between states of attention and inattention in each partner's play" (p.18). Remember that babies come into the world incapable of doing anything for themselves, including managing their level of excitement. They can sustain attention for only a short time before they need a break.

For example, babies will lock gazes with mom, and they will laugh and make faces at each other for a little while. When this becomes overly stimulating, babies look away. Sensitive mothers will recognize (at an unconscious level) that when their babies look away, it is time for a break in engagement. They will allow them to take a little respite and will wait for them to signal that they are ready before re-engaging in their play. Three important things happen during this cycle. First, babies get to experience high levels of positive affect in reaction to their mothers' empathic attunement with them. These are pleasurable feelings for both and are strongly supportive of the development of the attachment bond. Second, when the excitement gets to be too much and mothers allow their babies to calm themselves by withdrawing, babies learn that mom reacts to certain social cues and that they can count on them to respond in certain ways. This is the beginning of the internal working model of self and others. In optimal circumstances, this understanding can be generalized later into the assumption that they can count on other people to help them regulate themselves. Lastly, the movement from positive affect to negative affect and then back again can teach children that being uncomfortable can be endured and overcome, thus encouraging the development of resiliency in the face of stress.

Summary

Attachment is governed by both genetic and epigenetic influences. During gestation, genes construct brain structures and regions and provide babies with an automatic attachment behavioral system that prompts behaviors meant to attract the attention and care of the adults around them. Because human babies come into the world completely unable to do anything for themselves, attachment to someone bigger, stronger, and wiser is essential to survival.

As will be explained in Chapter 9, both before and after birth, epigenetic factors influence brain development. That is, the brain structures and regions built during gestation grow in response to the experiences provided in babies' specific environment by their primary attachment figure(s). These attachment figures generally include one or possibly two primary attachment figures but can also include other individuals such as siblings and grandparents. The neurochemicals produced during healthy attachment-related interactions between an attachment figure and a child are highly rewarding for both, thus building the social motivation and engagement systems. Then, as children begin to spend more time out in the community and in the company of peers, they may form attachments with friends and adults other than those in their family circle.

As will be discussed in Chapter 17, when they enter adolescence and young adulthood, individuals begin to form attachments in intimate relationships, including with romantic partners and their own children. However, the earliest attachment relationship with the primary attachment figure(s) provides the foundations for all future relationships, and many of the psychological issues mental health practitioners treat arise directly from disturbances in those earliest attachment experiences. Moreover, the level of safety provided children in the first one to two years of life affects the development of their HPA (stress regulation) and social engagement systems and influences their ability to self-regulate in all later developmental stages. In the next chapter, I will explain how an individual's early attachment experiences form an unconscious sense of his or her lovability and acceptability. In addition, I will identify two proximity-seeking strategies that insecure children use in their efforts to be close to their mothers that over time solidify into attachment styles that may persist through childhood and even into adulthood.

CHAPTER 7

Attachment Processes and Styles

LEARNING OBJECTIVES

After completing this chapter, readers should
- Understand how attachment experiences result in internal working models of both self and others.
- Be able to identify the secondary attachment strategies used by insecurely attached children in their efforts to be close to their attachment figures.
- Understand how the nonconscious memories created through preverbal attachment experiences affect later relationships.
- Be able to identify the four childhood attachment styles.

KEY IDEAS

1. Children's internal working model of self and of others is a mental representation of their relationship with their primary attachment figure(s) that informs their expectations for how worthy they are of love and attention and what they can expect from relationships.
2. Children whose attachment figures are not consistently available physically and emotionally tend to use hyperactivation strategies to ensure proximity to them.
3. Children whose attachment figures reward independence or punish the expression of dependency needs tend to use deactivation strategies to ensure proximity to them.
4. There are three insecure attachment styles and one secure attachment style.
5. Attachment is such a primal drive that even children who are abused are still biologically prompted to attach to their caregivers.

Introduction

Children who receive consistently loving and sensitive care develop a sense of felt security and a willingness to use the attachment figure as a secure base from which to explore the environment. Children who receive inconsistent care, or who are cared for by an insensitive, cold or frightened/frightening caregiver do not develop a sense of felt security and are not able to use the attachment figure as a secure base from which to explore the environment. These insecurely attached children are more likely than securely attached children to develop mental health issues in all developmental stages.

These earliest attachment experiences lay down implicit, nonconscious memories in the right brain that answer the survival-related question, *How do I have to be so that I can be with you (my all-important attachment figure)?* They also determine the assumptions that the child then makes about his or her safety and acceptability/lovability *(I am as I am treated)* in all future relationships.

Our job as mental health practitioners is, largely, to help our clients become consciously aware of their behavior patterns that are being caused by pernicious nonconscious memories. Wallin (2007) emphasizes that the individual who "cannot (or will not) articulate his own dissociated or disavowed experience will *evoke* it in others, *enact* it with others, or *embody* it" (p. 4). That is, as clinicians, we must understand that early attachment-related memories and assumptions are often the underlying foundation of the mental health issues we see in our clients. When a client evokes a feeling in us, we must be sensitive enough (and secure enough) to recognize it for what it is—their feeling, not ours—and use it in the therapeutic process for the client's benefit. When our client treats us with disrespect, manipulation, rage, or dependency, we must not take it personally but realize that these behaviors are transference, that is, concrete examples of what the client has experienced in life. Lastly, we must pay attention to the nonverbal signals that a client is sending to us in the form of posture, gestures, vocal intonation, breathing, eye movements, etc. since their bodies tell a story that their words may deny.

As Wallin (2007) cautions, "What begins … as biologically driven interactions may register psychologically as mental representations that continue lifelong to shape behavior and subjective experience whether or not the original attachment figures are physically present" (p. 24). This is good news and bad news. The bad news is that people may suffer for their entire lives because of less-than-optimal (or terrible) attachment experiences in infancy. The good news is that we can often help them, either by offering prevention programming that addresses inadequate or harmful parenting practice and parent mental health issues or by providing corrective attachment experiences as we engage them in therapy.

I begin this chapter with an explanation of how children internalize the interactions they have with their primary attachment figure(s) (usually the mom but optimally the mom and the dad) into what Bowlby (1969/1982) called an Internal Working Model. Please remember that when I use the terms "mom/mother" and "dad/father," I do so only because it is easier to use those words than it is to use the dry and clunky term "attachment figure," As stated in earlier chapters, "mom" and "dad" refer to anyone who takes on the role of primary caregiver or dual primary caregiver. Next, I identify two basic strategies used by children who develop insecure attachment due to less-than-optimal parenting and explain how these strategies tend to manifest in future relationships. Last, I provide a detailed description of each of the childhood attachment styles and point out the limitations to attachment theory and the opportunities for research that still exist.

Internal Working Models

Cassidy, Erlich & Sherman (2014) note that "although virtually all children become attached to their primary caregivers, the quality of the attachment varies as a function of the nature of the specific infant-caregiver relationship" (p. 129). Children learn during repeated interactions with their moms that their caregivers tends to react to proximity-seeking efforts in relatively predictable patterns in what Bowlby (1973) called representational models or internal working models. These are small scale models of reality that an individual carries in his or her head that can be used to imagine alternatives and make decisions concerning which is best to use in a given circumstance to get his or her need for proximity met (Wallin, 2007). These models provide information, based on thousands of bits of nonconscious memory, on what to expect of both other people and of self.

The foundation for the internal working model is laid down in the first two years of life. However, because the encoding and consolidation of these models is an ongoing process, changing circumstances can result in changes in the model, for good or for ill. That is, a secure child can become insecure if his or her caregiver becomes unavailable, inconsistent, or inadequate, while an insecure child may become secure if the caregiver makes the environment consistently and reliably safe. However, as Bowlby (1988) points out, the longer a working model is in place, the more resistant to change it becomes. That is, very young infants can change from insecure to secure fairly rapidly when placed into a secure environment, while older children, adolescents and adults have increasing difficulty in changing their assumptions about self and others once they are set.

Internal Working Model of Others

One internal working model that is formed during infancy is the *working model of others*, an assumption concerning how an infant can expect his or her caregiver to behave. This mental representation is likely to be generalized to others as he or she transitions through the developmental stages. Cassidy et al. (2014) explain how important it is to have a model of others being safe, stable, and predictable. As they put it, "... it is because securely attached infants are more likely than insecurely attached infants to predict caregiver availability and responsiveness that they are able to interpret a threat as manageable and respond to it with less fear and anxiety" (p. 130). That is, security builds the capacity for regulation of mood and behavior. As we have learned in previous chapters, less fear and anxiety means less activation of the sympathetic nervous system. Less sympathetic activity means that the vegetative vagus can do its job of resting, digesting, and fighting off disease, thus allowing the child to grow. In addition, the smart vagus can develop a strong social engagement system. Thus, the child can grow strong and healthy physically, psychologically, and socially.

Mikulincer and Shaver (2016) explain that children in secure attachment relationships go through a cycle hour after hour, day after day in which they will experience some kind of distress; they then seek protection and comfort from mom; they get relief from the distress and feel secure again; they return to exploration and fun. For them, it goes like this: it's bad; help me, mom; mom helps; I feel better; let's play. This cycle, which I discuss in greater detail below, becomes a prototype for managing both personal physical/emotional distress and interpersonal closeness. It teaches them that it is possible for an individual to have distance and autonomy as well as closeness and reliance on others, something that is essential for genuinely intimate relationships throughout. The cycle becomes a "script" (p. 13) that can be used to regulate negative emotions and maintain emotional balance and to support important relationships.

Experienced again and again over the first couple of years of life, memories of these experiences turn into what is called a schema. A schema is a nonconscious expectation that allows individuals to "efficiently predict, interpret, and guide their interactions with others" (Cassidy et al., 2014, p. 129). Although a schema influences an individual's behavior at a nonconscious level, it is (lucky for both them and us) open to change based on new experience. Thus, corrective experiences can be offered in a relationship with a caring other (e.g., therapist), though clients with insecure attachment may have more difficulty changing than those with a more secure attachment history (Wallin, 2007).

For the cycle mentioned above to work well, it is crucial that a mother be sensitive to her child's behaviors, emotional signals, and needs and be consistently and appropriately responsive to them in what is called contingent communication. As Wallin (2007) puts it, in contingent communication, "One party signals while the other answers with behavior that says, in effect, I can sense what you are feeling and respond to what you need" (p. 21). If a mother cannot read her child's signals adequately, contingent communication is impaired, resulting in the formation of an insecure attachment bond. Indeed, the mother's sensitivity to her child's cues is absolutely essential to the development of secure attachment (Juffer, Bakermans-Kranenburg, & van IJzendoorn, 2018). Furthermore, contingent communication affects the growth of integrative fibers in the brain that promote the development of self-regulation (Siegel, 2012a).

Schema develop regardless of how secure or insecure the attachment relationship is or how faulty or true the memories on which they are based are. Working models of others grow from whatever interactions happen repeatedly. For example, one child may learn that when I cry my mom comes and soothes me, while another child may learn that when I cry my mom comes and hurts me. One child may find that mom sometimes responds to her discomfort or fear with concern and compassion but other times laughs and belittles her. Still another child may learn that since my mom punishes me when I cry, I will cut off my feelings. In summary, given the importance of attachment to a child's survival, a schema answers the all-important question: *How do I have to be so that I can be with you?*

Internal Working Model of Self

At the same time that children are developing working models of others, they are learning fundamental lessons about themselves. Based on their caregiver's responses to their attempts to seek closeness in times of distress, they are learning about their ability to affect their world and about their value as individuals. Gilbert (2014) emphasizes that being valued is very different from being cared for, and not being valued can result in the development of shame and of psychopathology later in life. The child mentioned above who cries and whose mother consistently comes to soothe her learns that she is capable of making something happen in her world (I cried, she came, I feel better). At the same time, she learns that her mother values her enough to respond to her when she is uncomfortable or afraid. The child, however, who learns that his discomfort or fear will be met only with pain if he expresses those feelings (I cried, she came, I made it worse) will figure out how to escape those feelings. In addition, he learns that he is not valued if he expresses discomfort or fear even to someone who he is biologically driven to seek in times of stress. These earliest experiences with mother form nonconscious assumptions concerning the child's lovability and acceptability: *I am as I am treated.*

Attachment and Memory

The schema contained in internal working models of self and others are based on memory, and as was discussed in Chapter 3, memory is not necessarily reliable. Bowlby (1980) recognized this problem, pointing out that children (and adults) who grow up with insecure attachment may have a distorted schema for several reasons. First, these working models of self and others are internalized in the first months and years of life (from birth to about the age of 3), before the left brain has developed and can lay down conscious memories and before a child can put words to their experiences. Second, because being close to a caregiver is literally a matter of life and death for a child, and because these earliest experiences of self and others are developed through frequent repetition in the context of essential caretaking relationships, these assumptions of self and others are deeply etched into nonconscious memory. Third, because of the implicit nature of these early memories, they are difficult both to access consciously and to change. In addition, they become part of top-down information processing, inevitably coloring information that is coming from the bottom up (see Chapter 2). Therefore, later situations and relationships will inevitably be tinged with those early experiences. In times of need, old attachment schema will be automatically activated. That's not a bad deal for the child who acted to get her mother's attention and was soothed, but it may cause a less secure child, one who was not so lucky with his mother, to show up in your office later in life with emotional and behavioral problems.

Memories that are encoded after the left brain has begun to function can also be unreliable. For example, it is not uncommon for families to try to bury a traumatic or embarrassing event (e.g., suicide), never talking about it, shielding children from the memory of it, even if they actually witnessed it. It is also possible that children may be witness to things that are just too hard for them to bear (e.g., parental violence) and which they refuse to think about (consciously or unconsciously). Lastly, children sometimes do things or think about doing things that they are ashamed of, such as engaging in sexual acts or wishing a parent dead in a moment of anger. Thus, getting reliable information from a client who has developed insecure attachment can be challenging.

The good news for therapists is that, although internal working models are resistant to change and become harder to change over time, if the caregiving experience changes, the internal working model can also change (Weinfield, Sroufe, & Egeland, 2000). This means that early intervention in the infant-mother attachment relationship has the best chance of changing the outcome for an insecurely attached child. Indeed, insecure infants have been shown to develop secure behaviors in as quickly as one week when placed with sensitive foster parents (Dozier, Bernard, & Roben, 2018). In other cases, it is possible for an individual to find himself or herself in more secure environments as he or she gets older due to changes in circumstances and thus is able to develop a more secure attachment style (Sibcy & Knight, 2017). In some cases, the changed circumstances may include going into therapy many years later. In that case, the therapist can act as a new attachment figure, providing the client a corrective attachment experience and the opportunity to develop what is called earned security (Sroufe, Carlson, Levy, & Egeland, 1999).

Secondary Attachment Strategies

Attachment bonds take some time to develop, though they are generally firmly in place by the age of two. Bowlby (1969/1982) proposed four stages of attachment development that occur over time: (1) *preattachment*, from birth to about two months, during which time children are interested in and responsive to almost anyone; (2) *attachment-in-the-making*, from about two months to six months, during which time preferences for one person over another begin to appear; (3) *clear-cut attachment*, from about six months to about two years, during which time the primary caregiver(s) is (are) the clear focus of proximity-seeking behaviors and extreme separation reactions; and (4) *goal-corrected partnership*, two years and on, during which time children can handle longer separations and can coordinate their proximity-seeking with their caregiver's needs and wants. Over those two years, then, attachment security/insecurity will be influenced through repeated interactions with primary caregivers. Over thousands of interactions, babies try all sorts of things to develop a repertoire of behaviors that they can count on to gain and maintain proximity.

When a child's attachment figure is consistently available both physically and emotionally and responds appropriately to his or her bids for help in times of distress, a sense of security and trust develops. However, not all children have an attachment figure they can count on to be available or to respond appropriately. In these cases, the original distress caused by a threat that activates their attachment behavioral system is aggravated even further by their sense of helplessness and vulnerability (Mikulincer & Shaver, 2016). It's a double whammy: not only am I in trouble, but I also can't count on mom.

As their internal working models of self and others develop, the strategies to get the attention they want/need tend to settle into relatively predictable patterns. According to Mikulincer and Shaver (2016), when primary attachment strategies don't work to elicit mom's help when distressed, children are forced to use the secondary attachment strategies of hyperactivation, deactivation, or both. Which one is used will be determined by expectations for how successful the behavior will be in gaining proximity. The decision is not a conscious one. Babies are not stupid; they are just small! Their behaviors are based on past experiences of what has worked to achieve closeness, love, protection, or connection or of what has resulted in inattention, rejection, anger, or pain.

Hyperactivation

Hyperactivation strategies include exaggeration or amplification of primary attachment strategies. Hyperactivation is a ramping up of the attachment behavioral system in response to an attachment figure's unreliable or unpredictable care. Mikulincer and Shaver (2016) explain that these strategies tend to be employed under four conditions: (1) the mother is inconsistently available emotionally or physically; (2) she is intrusive, interfering with the child's development of self-regulation and autonomy; (3) she tells the child (implicitly or explicitly) that he or she is too stupid, weak, incompetent or helpless to make it in the world, or; (4) when trauma/abuse has occurred when mom wasn't there. In these situations, the child "thinks," I am ambivalent about my mom; I may not be afraid that she is going to hurt me, but I am also anxious that she will not be there for me when I need her.

The answer to the question, *How do I have to be so that I can be with you?* for children who hyperactivate their attachment behavioral system is: I have try very hard and persevere relentlessly until mom finally comes to help me. I am preoccupied with where mom is. If crying doesn't work to get the cooperation or protection that I need, I will cry louder, or I'll scream. I'll whine and make a nuisance of myself. If mom has left me alone and I don't know where she is, I will keep on crying even when she returns; it will be hard to soothe me because what if she leaves me again. I can't play anymore because I have to keep her in sight. I am anxious all the time because I am not sure that I am loved and safe. Moreover, because infants and young children are, according to Piaget's (1936/1952) theory of development, highly egocentric, the child will "think," if *I am as I am treated*, then I am not sure that I am worthy of love and safety.

Deactivation

Mikulincer and Shaver (2016) explain that deactivation strategies include minimizing or eliminating proximity-seeking behaviors and shutting down the attachment behavioral system. Deactivation occurs under four conditions: (1) mom is consistently rejecting, hostile, inattentive or emotionally cold; (2) she looks or moves away if her child appears sad, uncomfortable with and avoiding physical contact; (3) she is violent or abusive to the child, or; (4) she tells the child (implicitly or explicitly) that he or she needs to be self-reliant and not show neediness or vulnerability. Wallin (2007) emphasizes that "The attachment relationship to the caregiver(s) is critical to the infant's physical and emotional survival and development. Given the requirement to attach, the infant must adapt to the caregiver, defensively excluding whatever behavior threatens the attachment bond" (p. 2). In the situations mentioned above, children recognize implicitly that, although their natural instinct is to seek mom out for comfort and care, their efforts will be, at best, futile, and at worst, life-threatening. Thus, they do their best to exclude behaviors that either won't work or that could cause them harm.

In answer to the question, *How do I have to be so that I can be with you?* my vegetative vagus may shut me down because protesting (crying, screaming, etc.) may do more harm than good, or my attachment behavioral and HPA systems may be activated, but I dare not show it. Thus, as an infant, I may simply give up and lie helplessly in my cradle, going limp when held rather than cuddling or clinging. Or when I can get around on my own, I may act indifferent to mom or find ways of being close to her without actually asking directly. Perhaps I slowly edge closer to her so that she won't notice, or I may just stuff my feelings so that she won't move further away from me. In more dangerous situations, I may find ways of distracting myself, or I may even dissociate so that I don't feel what I am feeling. As with hyperactivation behaviors, I am anxious all the time because I am not sure that I am loved and safe. However, I don't show that anxiety. I learn to take care of myself because my experiences have shown me that no one else is going to help me. If *I am as I am treated*, then I am either not worthy of love and safety, or I am worthy only when I manage myself and don't bother my mother.

Combined Hyperactivation and Deactivation

Many insecure children are able to rely on the effectiveness of hyperactivation or deactivation and employ them as their go-to strategy in times of need; that is, they have an organized way of managing distress. However, other children are unable to find a coherent strategy that they can count on. Mikulincer and Shaver (2016) suggest that these individuals are extremely insecure in their attachment relationships. They describe these children as being characterized by "simultaneous or rapidly vacillating displays of approach and avoidance behavior toward an attachment figure and by aimless, disoriented, or confused actions in response to attachment figure unavailability" (p. 40). This disorganization occurs when mom is either frightening to or frightened by her child.

In answer to the question, *How do I have to be so that I can be with you?* I may have no viable option. If my mother is physically abusing me, for example, what am I supposed to do? My attachment behavioral system is activated, and my instinct is to run to her for comfort, but she is the *source* of my discomfort, so I have to run away from her! This results in a *biological paradox* in which there is no solution to my distress! Or imagine that my mother looks at me with an expression of terror on her face or with no expression on her face at all. Remember that in infancy, I learn about myself by my mother mirroring my facial expressions; when she smiles, I smile back, and when I smile, she smiles back; we have contingent mirroring. Fonagy et al. (2002), however, suggest that when a mother's face doesn't mirror her child's (non-contingent mirroring), a profoundly disturbed image of self results. If, for example, I see terror on my mom's face, I have no choice but to assume (at a nonconscious level, since only my right brain is functioning) that there is something terribly, irremediably wrong with me. If my own mom, this person who is bigger, stronger and wiser than me, is afraid of me, I should be *terrified*! Of myself! Perhaps even worse, if my mom has no expression on her face at all, do I even exist?!

You may well wonder why an adult would become terrified when looking at her baby. This can happen if the mother was herself traumatized/abused as an infant. The signs of her baby's distress can then trigger terrifying implicit memories that obliterate reality. Similarly, a blank face could be the result of dissociation, or it could be the result of depression (post-partum or major depressive disorder). In any case, the child cannot possibly know what is going on with mom. Thus, in contrast to the children above who are *unsure* that they are deserving of love and safety, with these children, if *I am as I am treated*, I am *sure* that I am neither loved nor safe, and I am *sure* that I am not worthy of love or safety.

Primary and secondary attachment strategies are intimately related to the patterns of behavior that develop over the first one to two years of life. These attachment styles will be introduced next.

Childhood Attachment Styles

Shaver and Mikulincer (2002) have defined attachment styles as being "systematic patterns of expectations, needs, emotions, emotion-regulation strategies, and social behavior that result from the interaction of an innate attachment behavioral system and a particular history of attachment experiences, usually beginning in relationships with parents" (p. 134). As explained earlier in the chapter, Ainsworth (Ainsworth et al., 1978) identified three possible attachment styles: secure, anxious/ambivalent, and avoidant. Main and Solomon (1990) later discovered a fourth style: disorganized/disoriented. These classifications were derived from Ainsworth's (1978) Strange Situation research. They reflect behaviors of children during separation from and reunification with their mother, interactions with a stranger both while the mother is still present and when she is gone, and mother-child interactions in a later home visit.

Although research shows that there is considerable variation in the distribution of these styles between cultures internationally (van IJzendoorn & Kroonenburg, 1988), it appears that among children in low-risk situations, 55% to 65% can be classified as secure, 5% to 15% as anxious/ambivalent, 15% as avoidant, and 15% as disorganized/disoriented (van IJzendoorn, Schuengel, & Bakermans-Kranenburg, 1999). However, these researchers noted that among children who live in high-risk situations (e.g., maltreatment, parental substance abuse or mental issues, poverty), approximately 80% could be classified as disorganized/disoriented (van IJzendoorn & Bakermans-Kranenburg, 2006).

These attachment styles, their causes and their characteristics are shown in Table 7.1. In the sections below, I will describe in detail the maternal behaviors that result in each style and which primary or secondary attachment infants use to seek proximity in times of distress.

TABLE 7.1   Attachment Styles and Characteristics

Secure
- Caregiver: available physically and emotionally, appropriately responsive (good enough)
- Results: easy expression of self (both positives and negatives)
- I am worthy of love, I can safely show all my emotions
- Develops into
  - Secure adult style; calm, confident
  - Deep sense of personal value
  - Willing to establish intimate and caring relationships
  - Willing to take considered risks
  - Relaxed exploration of self and the world

Anxious/Ambivalent
- Caregiver: inconsistent (self-absorbed); inconsistently appropriate/attuned in responses
- Results: hyperactivation strategies, anger on return
- I'm not sure I'm worthy of love; I must get your attention and help
- Develops into:
  - Preoccupied adult style; clingy, demanding, attention-seeking
  - Depression, anxiety, eating disorders, substance abuse, personality disorders

Avoidant
- Caregivers: distancing, neglectful, punishing dependency, rewarding independence
- Results: deactivation strategies; little visible distress on separation, turning away on return
- I'm not sure I'm worthy of love; I can show only certain emotions; I don't ask for help
- Develops into
  - Dismissing adult style; distancing, little intimacy, denial of negative emotions
  - Outwardly secure, inwardly stressed
  - Personality disorders, substance abuse

Disorganized/Disoriented
- Caregiver: frightened or frightening (origin of terror AND source of safety), intrusive, affective communication errors
- Results: biological paradox; collapse of proximity-seeking strategies; freezing, dissociation, rocking, head banging; serious self-regulation problems
- I'm not worthy of love; I must have your attention, but I am afraid you will hurt me
- Develops into
  - Fearful adult style, approach-avoidance behaviors, personality disorder, substance abuse, compulsive caregiving

Secure

Mothers of children classified as secure tend to be appropriately responsive to their children's proximity-seeking behaviors and to be consistently physically and emotionally available to them. Children with secure attachment can express negative emotions freely, and they feel comfortable seeking proximity to their mothers when distressed (safe haven). They also feel comfortable to explore the environment, expecting that they will be supported rather than interfered with and therefore able to turn all of their attention to play (secure base). Benoit (2004) explains that this style is considered to be *organized* because these children know "exactly what to do with a sensitively responsive caregiver, i.e., approach the caregiver when distressed" (p. 542). It would appear, then, that by the end of the first year of life, these children are able to use a *primary* attachment strategy to seek proximity, and they are able to use their mothers as a secure base for exploration. Because their mothers consistently meet their needs for closeness and security, they are likely to develop an internal working model of others that assumes that people will be available and helpful when needed, and they will be willing to ask for that help (Sroufe et al., 1999). These children will likely develop self-confidence and a sense of competence, mastery, autonomy and self-determination, and they will likely be resilient in the face of adversity (Siegel, 2012a).

Anxious/Ambivalent

Mothers of children in the anxious/ambivalent classification tend to respond to their children in unpredictable ways and are not consistent in their emotional or physical availability, or they may be intrusive and controlling. These children's behavior is considered to be *organized* because they know "exactly what to do with an inconsistently responsive caregiver, i.e., exaggerate displays of distress and angry, resistant responses, hoping that the marked distress response cannot possibly be missed by the inconsistently responsive caregiver" (Benoit, 2004, p. 542). Their demanding, strident bids for attention indicate that they are employing a secondary *hyperactivation* attachment strategy. They may eschew exploration and play, instead keeping their attention on attachment-related information, alternately whining, clinging to, and expressing anger at their mother. Granqvist et al. (2017) explain that "to the extent that the caregiver does respond by giving attention, the child's heightening of attachment behaviors can result in an organized, workable attachment strategy" (p. 538). They will be unsure of the safety and reliability their mother is providing, and they will not be able to count on her to provide a secure base for exploration. Their internal working model of others may, over time, assume that people cannot be trusted to be there when needed, and so they must be constantly hypervigilant for signs of abandonment. Their relationships are likely to be fraught with negative, disruptive emotions and behaviors (Sroufe et al., 1999). Their internal working model of self may assume that they are vulnerable and must constantly seek reassurance. Therefore, they likely will not be sure that they are accepted/loved as a person or worthy of acceptance/love.

Avoidant

Mothers of children in the avoidant classification are not appropriately responsive to their needs, and their children's attempts to communicate may be ignored or met with annoyance, anger, or rejection. They tend to be relatively cold, withdrawn, and punishing of neediness. Like the secure and anxious/ambivalent children discussed above, avoidant children are considered to have an *organized* attachment style because they know "exactly what to do with a rejecting caregiver, i.e., to avoid the caregiver in times of need" (Benoit, 2004, p. 154). Therefore, they may try to distract themselves from attending to anything in the environment that would trigger the desire to seek proximity. This secondary *deactivation* attachment strategy might then avoid making their mother uncomfortable and thus retain her availability. Granqvist et al. (2017) suggest that "As long as the caregiver continues to provide reasonable protection and monitoring in the context of more emotional distance, this adjustment allows the infant to achieve an organized, workable attachment strategy" (p. 538). However, although these children often remain outwardly calm, they are not calm on the inside; their HPA systems are activated as indicated by increased heart rates (Zelenko et al., 2005). These children will often develop an internal working model of others that assumes that no one is going to help them and that they are on their own. Their internal working model of self will be based on the assumption that they should never show vulnerability if they feel it, and that if at all possible, they should shut down any and all distressing feelings.

Disorganized/Disoriented

The mothers of children with disorganized/disoriented attachment tend to be a regular source of alarm to their children, either frightening to them or frightened by them. They may frighten their children through emotional, physical or sexual abuse, often having been abused themselves in childhood. Abusive behavior places children into the paradoxical situation of being driven by their own neurologically based attachment behavioral system to seek proximity to the very source of their fear. Thus, they may move toward and then away from mom or perhaps freeze in place. They may appear confused, conflicted, or apprehensive in regard to accessing their mother when distressed. However, Granqvist et al. (2017) point out that "at an evolutionary level, proximity to an alarming caregiver would likely have helped a human infant survive, given that infants are unable to fend for or regulate themselves" (p. 541). Thus, abused children are still biologically prompted to attach to their caregiver.

Some mothers' alarming behaviors may be much more subtle than those seen in cases of outright abuse. Indeed, disorganization can arise in situations where there is no abuse at all. Granqvist et al. (2017) point out that extended or repeated separation from an attachment figure (e.g., hospitalization, death, multiple out-of-home placements) can result in disorganized attachment. Mothers who have experienced trauma themselves may be triggered by their own infant (as in PTSD, for example), and if she shows fear or threat on her face (even unconsciously), the infant may experience terror. Even living in a family in which five or more socioeconomic risk factors are present can result in disorganized attachment if the caregiver who otherwise would be able to provide loving care is overtly frightened and distressed (Granqvist et al., 2017). In other cases, mothers who have post-partum depression, other mental illness, or substance abuse issues may be highly unpredictable and inappropriate, showing aberrant behavior around their children even when the children are not seeking them out. Infants in these situations may be unable to develop any organized strategy that reduces their distress.

While the anxious/ambivalent and avoidant children can rely on their secondary attachment strategies (hyperactivation and deactivation, respectively) to help them cope with their worlds, disorganized/disoriented children are unable to develop an organized and coherent strategy, cannot trust their mothers to provide safety or to be a secure base from which to explore the environment. They are likely to develop an internal working model of others as being, at best, unreliable and at worst, dangerous. At the same time, they may develop an internal working model of self as vulnerable and ineffective. Because individuals who develop a disorganized/disoriented attachment style often have serious psychological issues later in life, I discuss how this style develops in greater detail in Chapter 12.

Limitations of Attachment Style Identification

Granqvist et al. (2017) have cautioned that care must be taken when assessing and utilizing attachment categories in clinical work. For example, although the insecure attachment styles are associated with various psychopathologies, poor outcomes are not inevitable; if life circumstances change, attachment-related behaviors (and internal working models) can also change. In addition, even secure children exhibit behaviors associated with insecure attachment styles from time to time; care must be taken not to jump to conclusions based on incomplete/inadequate observations. Furthermore, attachment styles are relationship specific; that is, a child can be disorganized/disoriented with one person and secure with another. In my discussion above, I have centered on the maternal relationship because that is usually the primary attachment relationship. It is, however, possible to have other protective relationships that can buffer the child against insecurity. In addition, as children get older and develop more coping skills, they often find workable ways to manage their affect. Concerning disorganized/disoriented attachment specifically, although the vast majority of maltreated infants exhibit disorganized behaviors, not all disorganized infants have been maltreated. That is, disorganization may be a red flag, but care must be taken not to *blame* a mother for something that is not her fault. Lastly, factors other than the mother-infant relationship (e.g., genetics and temperament) influence behavior, so we should remain open to multiple avenues of intervention.

Regardless of the limitations associated with the attachment styles, an attachment perspective is still valid in clinical work. Helping clients to understand that their earliest relationship experiences are affecting their current behavior can provide needed insight and open the door to self-compassion and forgiveness. Although the best measurement tools for a thorough assessment of attachment (and the training to use them) may be out of the price range of most clinicians, understanding which behaviors observed in our clients (whether they be infants, children, adolescents, or adults) are indicative of early relational dysfunction can point the way to effective prevention and intervention efforts. To clarify why attachment is so powerful, let's take a look at the brain systems that are affected by it.

Summary

In this chapter I have introduced you to the concept of the internal working models of self and of others that children develop over the first two years of life. These models are based on thousands of moment-to-moment interactions with the primary attachment figure. Children who develop a secure attachment style are able to do so because their mother consistently and reliably acts as a safe haven in times of distress and as a secure base from which the world can safely be explored. Children whose mothers are inconsistently available as a safe haven and secure base discover through trial and error that hyperactivation strategies work to obtain assurance that their mother is available to keep them safe. Children whose mothers either reward their child's efforts to manage their own needs for safety or punish their attempts to seek proximity when distressed tend to find ways to deactivate their attachment behavioral system. Children whose mothers are actually frightening to them, or who are frightened by their child due to their own psychological issues, are unable to organize a set of behaviors that they can rely on to get the attention they need. These children develop a disorganized/disoriented attachment style.

An important point for mental health practitioners to remember from this chapter is that internal working models and the experiences that produced them reside in implicit memory. When triggered, these memories do not cause a feeling that they are from the past. Rather, they arise as assumptions about how lovable and deserving of love the individual is and about what he or she can expect from and within a relationship. They arise out of procedural memory, the same memory we use when we walk or ride a bicycle. Therefore, when an early attachment memory is triggered, clients in mental health treatment will often base their reactions to people and events on an "unthought known" (Wallin, 2007, p. 3, citing Bollas, 1987) rather than on rational, reflective consideration. Therefore, in the next chapter, I will discuss the clinical implications of attachment strategies and styles in both clients and practitioners.

CHAPTER 8

Implications of Attachment Theory in Clinical Work

LEARNING OBJECTIVES

After completing this chapter, readers should

- Understand how a client's attachment style may affect his or her relationship with his or her therapist.
- Understand how a therapist's attachment style may affect his or her relationship with his or her client.
- Be able to identify the five attachment-related tasks that influence the effectiveness of therapeutic interventions.
- Understand how attachment affects therapeutic processes.

KEY IDEAS

1. Both the client and the practitioner enter into the working relationship with personal attachment histories and orientations, which interact in ways that can lead either to a corrective attachment experience for the client or to an impaired therapeutic relationship.
2. Transference is a phenomenon in which clients with insecure attachment tend to transfer their negative models of self and others onto the practitioner, expecting the same level of rejection and abandonment they experienced as children.
3. Countertransference is a phenomenon in which a practitioner may misinterpret what the client's needs or may react to the client in nonconscious ways (emotions or behaviors) that reflect their own early insecure attachment.
4. It is important that practitioners identify their own tendencies toward attachment anxiety and/or avoidance and work to minimize or eliminate their effects on the therapeutic relationship.

Introduction

Everyone has an attachment style. This means that both mental health practitioners and their clients will come into the therapeutic relationship with an attachment heritage. It is important, therefore, for practitioners to have an understanding of how attachment influences human development because it affects all relationships, including the client-practitioner relationship. When clients enter a mental health practitioner's offices, they bring their mothers and fathers with them (whether their mothers and fathers are physically present or not). Moreover, practitioners' mothers and fathers (almost surely not physically present) are also in the office, making for a very crowded room indeed. These earliest relationships directly affect the neurobiological development of both our clients and practitioners, even before they/we are born, and continue until they/we draw our last breaths. Understanding that neurobiology and attachment are often the underpinnings of our clients' problematic behavior can help us to have deep compassion for them and can also guide our interventions. When we uncover what a client's life was like during gestation, infancy, and early childhood, how they are feeling and behaving may begin to make sense both to us and to them.

As mental health professionals, we must be aware that our clients' reactions to us and to the ways we try to help them may have little to do with us personally. The good news is that their nonconscious assumptions, expectations and behaviors provide us with a window into the origins of their pain. This understanding may then help us to have compassion for our difficult clients and suggest to us how we might be able to offer them a corrective attachment experience that can make them more secure. The bad news is our own attachment-related insecurities may manifest in response to our clients' (and even our colleagues') emotions and behaviors. It is important to understand that the interaction between a client's attachment style and a practitioner's attachment style can lead either to a corrective attachment experience for the client or to an impaired therapeutic relationship. In this chapter, I will discuss first how attachment-related anxiety and avoidance are related to many of the mental health issues we address. Then I will explain how practitioners' own attachment style can affect the therapeutic process.

Attachment and the Client

Insecure attachment has been shown to be associated with a broad array of mental health disorders (Mikulincer & Shaver, 2016). Moreover, existing attachment insecurity can be aggravated by "exposure to natural or man-made traumatic event, life transitions, or actual or anticipated loss of important material or psychological assets [that can] amplify the effects of other pathogenic factors such as poverty and learning disabilities" (p. 397). At the same time, early insecure attachment can aggravate an individual's response to a later traumatic event, resulting in the development of possibly severe PTSD. Becoming aware of how clients relate and react to the practitioners who are trying to help them is an indication of their attachment style (Main, 2000; Wallin, 2007). Thus, it is important for practitioners to gain an understanding of how the attachment dimensions are related to the problems that our clients bring into our offices. I will discuss how insecure attachment affects the development of specific mental disorders and problem behaviors in later chapters devoted to specific age groups.

Attachment and Therapeutic Processes

First of all, attachment style affects an individual's willingness to enter therapy in the first place. Clients with a more avoidant style (i.e., those who were rewarded for handling their own distress) are less likely to seek help than those with more secure attachment (Mikulincer and Shaver, 2016). However, individuals with a more anxious attachment may also be less likely to attend therapy than more secure individuals are because of their fear of being rejected or stigmatized (Nam & Lee, 2015). In addition, research has clearly shown that clients with more secure states of mind regarding close relationships have more positive attitudes about therapy

(Hill et al., 2012; Marmarosh et al., 2009; Shechtman & Dvir, 2006) and are more likely to engage in therapeutic tasks and activities (Saypol & Farber, 2010; Shechtman & Rybko, 2004). To complicate matters further, the therapeutic process can be affected not only by the client's attachment style, but also by the practitioner's.

Attachment and the Practitioner

From an attachment perspective, the practitioner's job is to help a client to "understand his or her accumulated, and often forgotten or misunderstood, attachment experiences, identify and reverse insecure working models by transforming them into more secure models, and learn about ways to achieve both comfortable intimacy and flexible autonomy" (Mikulincer & Shaver, 2016, p. 443–444). In order to achieve this goal, certain things must happen in the encounter between the practitioner and his or her client. The practitioner's attachment style can and does affect the relationship with the client. In this section I will first discuss five therapeutic tasks that Bowlby (1988) suggested need to be undertaken in order for therapy to be successful. Then I will discuss how the practitioner's attachment style may affect the therapeutic process.

The Five Therapeutic Tasks

Bowlby (1988) identified five tasks that must be undertaken by a practitioner for intervention to have a chance of being effective. First, the practitioner must act as a safe haven and a secure base from which the client can explore his or her emotions and behaviors. Yes, you need to be the good mother that client never had. Without this safety, the client is unlikely to divulge troubling and possibly embarrassing thoughts and feelings. The practitioner can act as a "stronger and wiser" person that the client can rely on to be there when the exploration of self and relationships gets scary.

Second, the practitioner must come to understand how the client is currently relating to others, what his or her behavioral patterns are and the consequences of those patterns, and the client's nonconscious cognitive biases that result in maladaptive interpretations of events and circumstances. To gain this understanding the practitioner must be sensitive and responsive to the client, forming a relationship that is similar to that of a mother to her child. At the same time, the relationship cannot be the same as a mother-child relationship. The therapeutic relationship is normally less intensely emotional and more objective than a parent-child relationship. In addition, it is normally a shorter relationship, generally involves financial remuneration, usually is not conducted in the practitioner's home, and is governed by professional ethical considerations. However, even though there are distinct differences between the therapeutic relationship and the relationship between a mother and her child, sensitive and responsive intervention will improve the chances that the practitioner can begin to understand the dynamics of the client's relational interactions.

Third, the practitioner must remain open to the client's development of transference. Transference is a phenomenon that can be recognized when the practitioner observes "a misfit between a practitioner's interventions and a client's response (e.g., the strength of the reaction may seem inappropriate, capricious, or unusually tenacious)" (Mikulincer and Shaver, 2016, p. 461). The client's reaction tells the practitioner that something is happening at a nonconscious level that has prompted the client to act defensively due to outdated internal working models of self and other. Clients with insecure attachment tend to transfer their negative models of self and others onto the practitioner, expecting the same level of rejection and abandonment they experienced as children.

It is essential that a practitioner recognize transference for what it is: a real-time example of what life was like for this client in childhood. This understanding will help the practitioner to avoid personalizing the client's rage, blame, threats, and/or resistance and provide insight into the early (nonconscious) factors underpinning his or her mental health issues. Thus, attachment-anxious clients' strident demands for love and attention (and their rage if they perceive that love and attention is not forthcoming) can be met with compassion and curiosity; attachment-avoidant clients' refusal to engage in treatment activities or their outright devaluation of the practitioner's person or qualifications can be met with understanding rather than with defensive fear and anger.

Just as important as recognizing the client's transference is recognizing your own countertransference. It is very possible that our clients' behavior will kick up our own (nonconscious) attachment issues, especially in practitioners new to the field when they are still unsure that school actually taught them what they need to know. Mikulincer and Shaver (2016) explain that in countertransference, a practitioner may misinterpret what the client needs or may react to the client in nonconscious ways (emotions or behaviors) that reflect their own early insecure attachment. To make matters even more complicated, a practitioner's countertransference may be initiated by the client's transference. Thus, being able to discern which emotions belong to you and which belong to your clients is essential to effective therapeutic intervention.

Siegel (2010) suggests that from an interpersonal neurobiology perspective, practitioners need to be able to track both their client's and their own emotional and physiological responses on an ongoing basis, moment to moment, during a session. As discussed in Chapter 4, because of our smart vagus, we are able to read other people's emotions (via their facial expressions, posture, gestures, vocal intonations, etc.) and to respond to them even without conscious knowledge of what we are seeing. Thus, it is possible to experience sadness in our own bodies in response to the sadness that our client is experiencing, even though the client may be saying that he is happy! Siegel suggests that a sensitive and well-integrated practitioner has the capacity for "nonconceptual knowing" (p. 139), in which we sense what is going on in another person even though the other person may not even be aware of it himself. Therefore, it is useful for practitioners to develop the ability to attune to their clients so that they can recognize when clients are transferring their nonconscious patterns onto them; when they themselves are transferring their own nonconscious patterns onto their clients; and when they are picking up on a client's unverbalized (and perhaps unverbalizable) emotional energies that may be the key to therapeutic success.

The fourth task that Bowlby (1988) enumerated is for clients to begin to reflect on how the internal working models of self and others that they developed during childhood are affecting their close relationship in the present (including, perhaps, their relationship with their practitioner). The understanding that they gain through this reflection may then help them in the fifth and final task of revising and updating their internal working models and moving toward a more secure state of mind concerning their close relationships. Mikulincer and

Shaver (2016) suggest that this exploration needs to take two forms. First is an exploration of past attachment experiences that can shed light on how the client engages in and reacts to current relationships. Second is exploration of current relationships and how they reflect the pain of early rejection and abandonment. They suggest that "Both kinds of therapeutic exploration encourage constructive overhaul of working models, and initiate and sustain a broaden-and-build cycle of attachment security, which facilitates therapeutic change and continued personal growth" (p. 445).

Effects of Practitioner Attachment Orientations

According to Mikulincer and Shaver (2016), the practitioner's attachment style can interact with their clients' attachment styles, particularly in the area of the working alliance. The working alliance "reflects an emotional alignment of client and practitioner based on trust and mutual regard as well as agreement about tasks and goals of therapy" (p. 454). In other words, practitioners become attachment figures to their clients. Many studies have shown that the formation of a good working alliance during the early stages of therapy is predictive of positive therapeutic outcomes (Horvath, Del Re, Flukiger, & Symonds, 2011). However, practitioners may have difficulty initiating and maintaining the emotional alliance if they have their own insecure attachment orientations. Miscommunications and misinterpretations can trigger habitual attachment-anxious hyperactivation or attachment-avoidant deactivation strategies in either the client or the practitioner or both.

A practitioner with a secure state of mind regarding attachment is likely to display the core traits of warmth, acceptance, open communication, and trustworthiness in their relationships with their clients, thus opening the door for clients to perceive them as a safe haven and secure base. In contrast, clients of practitioners with a more anxious attachment style report that they are more anxiously attached to them (i.e., they use hyperactivation strategies with their therapist) while clients of practitioners with a more avoidant style report that they are more avoidantly attached to them (i.e., they use deactivation strategies with their therapist) (Petrowski, Pokorny, Nowacki, & Buckheim, 2013). Interestingly, however, Mikulincer and Shaver (2016) suggest that a practitioner's use of "countercomplementary attachment proximity strategies" (p. 460) may provide his or her clients with a helpful corrective attachment experience. They explain:

> For avoidant clients, who prefer interpersonal distance and tend to elicit emotional detachment from others, corrective emotional experiences can be provided mainly when practitioners rely on hyperactivating strategies, tend to increase proximity, and insist on deepening clients' disclosures. For anxiously attached clients, who prefer to remain in an infantile, dependent position, compulsively seek a "savior" who will love and care for them, and tend to elicit compassion and rescue fantasies from others, corrective emotional experiences can be provided mainly when practitioners adopt deactivating strategies, maintain optimal distance from clients, and encourage clients to take an autonomous role in dealing with their problems. (p. 460)

They caution, however, that if these strategies are not intentional (i.e., if they are employed nonconsciously in response to the practitioner's attachment insecurity), they are less likely to be effective. Our clients' hyperactivation and deactivation strategies, mastered and honed over long years of practice, make it possible for them to elicit emotions in us that we may have to *consciously* ignore in order to provide that corrective attachment experience. It apparently takes a secure state of mind that promotes attuned and flexible sensitivity and responsiveness for countercomplementary strategies to be reliably effective.

This information concerning the effects of the practitioner's attachment state of mind should make it clear, first, that practitioners would be wise to recognize their own tendencies toward attachment anxiety and/or avoidance. Finding out your own attachment style is easy, and I highly recommend that you go to http://web-research-design.net/cgi-bin/crq/crq.pl and take the survey offered there. Using the Experiences with Close Relationships attachment measure (ECR-R; Fraley, Waller & Brennen, 2000), the survey will place you somewhere within one of the attachment quadrants, allowing you to see clearly your levels of attachment anxiety and avoidance and track changes in your attachment orientation over time.

> Please take the time to identify your own attachment style by visiting the following website and completing the questionnaire: http://web-research-design.net/cgi-bin/crq/crq.pl. Then take a moment to imagine how your attachment style may interact with your clients' styles and how that might affect treatment outcomes.

Second, armed with the information that the Fraley et al. (2000) survey provides, you can make a decision about whether you need to do your own work to move yourself into a more secure state of mind in regards to close relationships. Many of us have entered the mental health field after having been in therapy ourselves, and we oftentimes need to reenter treatment for a time in order to overcome persistent countertransference issues. Others of us have never been in therapy even though we may have benefited from addressing our own early attachment experiences. This would be true especially for those of us with avoidant/dismissing attachment since we tend to believe either that we can handle everything ourselves or that admitting that we have a problem would make us less than perfect. Beware! In my experience, practitioners genuinely want to be the best practitioner they can be; it may happen that admitting that we are not perfect ends up making us the best that we can be. If we don't do our own work, if we don't become as secure as we can, not only may we not be as effective as we could be, but we could actually harm our clients. I know, I know. You're busy, and therapy costs money. Just do it if and when you need to!

Summary

In this chapter, I have pointed out how important attachment is to the client-practitioner relationship. Realizing that the client sitting in front of you was a baby at one time and was biologically driven to attach to his or her mother in particular ways as a matter of survival may help the practitioner empathize with and have compassion for even the most difficult client.

In addition, acknowledging that you, the practitioner, had your own early attachment experiences that are still active in your relationship with clients may help you to have compassion for yourself as you do the hard work of sitting with someone who clearly needs your help.

In the coming chapters in Section III, I will discuss how the brain and early attachment experiences affect functioning in each of the foundational developmental stages, that is, the stages during which the vast majority of changes in brain structure occur. This information may offer you ideas concerning possible routes for entry into individual, family, and community systems that can influence mental health outcomes.

Neurobiology and Attachment in the Developmental Stages

Introduction

Researchers and practitioners in the field of prenatal and perinatal psychology (also called *primary psychology*) have developed a set of twelve core principles that act as guidelines for professionals, families, and communities who want to optimize early development and social functioning (McCarty & Glenn, 2008). These guidelines are shown in Table III.1.

TABLE III.1   Twelve Guiding Principles

1. **The Primary Period:** The primary period for human development occurs from preconception through the first year of postnatal life. This is the time in which vital foundations are established at every level of being: physical, emotional, mental, spiritual and relational.

2. **Forming the Core Blueprint:** Experiences during this primary period form the blueprint of our core perceptions, belief structures, and ways of being in the world with others and ourselves. These foundational elements are implicit, observable in newborns, and initiate lifelong ways of being. These core implicit patterns profoundly shape our being in life-enhancing or life-diminishing directions.

3. **Capacities and Capabilities:** Human being are conscious, sentient, aware, and possess a sense of self even during this very early primary period. We seek ever-increasing states of wholeness and growth through the expression of human life. This innate drive guides and infuses our human development. From the beginning of life, babies perceive, communicate, and learn in ways that include an integration of mind-to-mind, energetic, and physical-sensorial capacities and ways of being.

4. **Continuum of Development:** Human development is continuous from prenatal to postnatal life. Postnatal patterns build on earlier prenatal and birth experiences. Optimal foundations for growth and resiliency, including brain development, emotional intelligence, and self-regulation are predicted upon optimal conditions during the preconception period, during pregnancy, the birth experience and the first year of life.

5. **Relationship:** Human development occurs within relationships from the beginning. Human connections and the surrounding environment profoundly influence the quality and structure of every aspect of a baby's development. From the beginning of life, a baby experiences and internalizes what its mother experiences and feels. Father's and/or partner's relationships with mother and baby are integral to optimizing primary foundations for the baby. All relationships and encounters with mother, baby, and father during this primary period affect the quality of life and the baby's foundation. Supportive, loving and healthy relationships are integral to optimizing primary foundations for the baby.

6. **Innate Needs:** The innate need for security, belonging, love and nurturing, feeling wanted, feeling valued, and being seen as the self we are is present from the beginning of life. Meeting these needs and providing the right environment supports optimal development.

7. **Communication:** Babies are continually communicating and seeking connection. Relating and responding to babies in ways that honor their multifaceted capacities for communication supports optimal development and wholeness.

8. **Mother-baby Interconnectedness:** Respecting and optimizing the bond between mother and baby and the mother-baby interconnectedness during pregnancy, birth, and infancy is of highest priority.

9. **Bonding:** Birth and bonding is a critical development process for mother, baby, and father that forms core patterns with lifelong implications. The best baby and mother outcomes occur when the mother feels empowered and supported, and the natural process of birth is allowed to unfurl with minimal intervention and no interruption in mother-baby connection and physical contact. If any separation of baby and mother occurs, continuity of father's contact and connection with the baby should be supported. The baby responds and thrives best when the relationship with the mother is undisturbed, when the baby is communicated with directly, and when the process of birth supports the baby's ability to orient and integrate the series of events.

10. **Resolving and Healing:** Resolving and healing past and current conflicts, stress, and issues that affect the quality of life of all family members is of highest priority. Doing so before pregnancy is best. When needed, therapeutic support for mother, baby, and father provided as early as possible during this vital primary period is recommended for optimal outcomes.

11. **Underlying Patterns:** When unresolved issues remain or less-than-optimal conditions and experiences occur during conception, pregnancy, birth and the first postnatal year, life-diminishing patterns often underlay health issues, stress behaviors, difficulty in self-regulation, attachment, learning, and other disorders over the lifespan.

12. **Professional Support:** These early diminishing patterns embed below the level of the conscious mind in the implicit memory system, subconscious, and somatic patterns. Professionals trained in primary psychology (prenatal and perinatal psychology) can identify these patterns and support babies, children, parents, and adults to heal and shift these primary patterns to more life-enhancing ones at any age. When parents resolve and heal their own unresolved issues from their child's pregnancy and birth, their children benefit at any age.

The first of these principles refers to the *primary period* of human development as spanning from before a baby is conceived to the second year after birth. Practitioners and researchers who take this perspective argue that these earliest experiences affect how we perceive the world, what we believe, and how we relate to others for the rest of our lives. What happens during this time determines the structure of brain itself, thus impacting our ability to recognize and control our emotions and behaviors. Moreover, they hold that brain development and attachment are inextricably bound together.

The vast majority of brain development occurs during gestation and the first three postnatal years, and much of the postnatal development is strongly influenced by the attachment bond. However, the brain doesn't mature completely until early adulthood when the prefrontal cortex is fully connected with subcortical regions so that the individual is better able to manage emotions and responses than he or she was earlier in life. Therefore, Section III presents the changes in the brain and social connectedness that normally can be expected to occur among infants and toddlers and among children as they move through early and middle childhood and into adolescence and young adulthood. For each of the developmental stages, I present what can be expected in normal development first and then particular challenges faced by each age group.

The first four chapters of this section focus on brain and attachment development from before a baby is conceived to toddlerhood. During gestation, the basic structure of the brain is put into place in preparation for life outside the womb. After birth, the brain organizes itself in response to the environment it encounters, and that environment is, to a great extent, the social environment provided by the mother. Mosier (2013) puts it this way: "Genes are the brain's blueprint, and stimulus from the environment guides the brain's construction" (p. 81). He further points out that that 90% of an individual's brain is in place, and 50% of everything he or she is going to learn throughout life has been learned by age three. Thus, since the less complex circuitry present at this life stage serves as the platform on which more complex circuitry will be built as the individual matures, this stage of life is clearly of great importance to everything that comes afterwards. Therefore, I begin this section with chapters that focus on the very earliest brain and attachment formations beginning before conception and following them through to toddlerhood.

Because the formation of an attachment bond is biologically driven by neural circuitry determined both by the individual's genes and by epigenetic factors that may be present even before the baby is conceived, the first chapter in the section (Chapter 9) starts with a discussion of preconception influences on brain development. It then goes on to include information about how the brain grows from conception through toddlerhood with special emphasis placed on the development of the smart vagal system and other parts of the social engagement system. Chapter 10 then focuses on the neurobiology that is specific to attachment and goes on to discuss the attachment process itself from preconception to toddlerhood. In Chapter 11, challenges to conception itself are briefly discussed before going on to examine the effects of maternal mental health issues on a child's brain and attachment formation. Chapter 12 then goes on to look specifically at factors associated with the development of disorganized/disoriented attachment.

The next three chapters focus on the early and middle childhood developmental stages. I start in Chapter 13 with the major changes in the brain associated with the normal process of pruning that starts at the beginning of early childhood. I then go on to discuss the slow maturation of the prefrontal cortex that allows the development of executive functions and self-reflection and evaluation in the context of peer and community relationships. Next, I discuss the development of episodic memory, which is essential to the construction of a child's personal narrative and to his or her ability to engage in what Suddendorf and Corballis (2007) call "mental time travel" (p. 299). Chapter 14 is devoted to social development and the effects of insecure attachment on several important functions that develop in this age group: play, emotional intelligence, and morality. Chapter 15 focuses on the personal challenges facing children with a history of childhood trauma or who have mental health issues associated with attention deficits and/or autism. Chapter 16 focuses on interpersonal challenges associated with bullying and the increasing use of digital technology among this age group.

The last three chapters in this section are devoted to adolescence and young adulthood during which time significant changes in neurological structure and functioning result in a significant increase in risk-taking that doesn't abate until the prefrontal cortex finally matures around age 25 as discussed in Chapter 17. Chapter 18 focuses on the effects of early childhood attachment experiences on the attachments that adolescents and young adults make as they enter adulthood. Chapter 18 then focuses on the challenges associated with sexual maturation and the formation of intimate relationships and the special challenges of parenting during the teen years. Then the final chapter is devoted to three particularly difficult challenges for individuals in this age group—identity formation, addiction, and violence.

In addition to the information on brain development and attachment influences in these various developmental stages, I introduce four case studies that are interwoven into each of the chapters in this section. These case studies are meant to help the reader place this information into a practice context. The individuals presented are entirely fictional, though based on real-life situations that have occurred during my own clinical sessions and that other clinicians have related to me in supervision. They illustrate the four attachment styles as well as the challenges that children face as they transition through the stages.

CHAPTER 9

Brain Development from Preconception Through Toddlerhood

LEARNING OBJECTIVES

After completing this chapter, readers should understand:

- How genetic and epigenetic factors influence brain development before and during pregnancy and the first two years of life.
- The development of the brain through the three trimesters of pregnancy.
- How the social engagement system develops during infancy and toddlerhood.
- How mother-child interaction during infancy and toddler affect the development of the right hemisphere.

KEY IDEAS

1. The brain is influenced by epigenetic factors even before conception.
2. The brain starts to develop before the mother may even be aware that she is pregnant, making the brain extremely vulnerable to early insult that can affect the foundations of personality and behavior.
3. The intrauterine environment influences the molecular structure of the limbic, autonomic, and central nervous systems, thus laying the foundations for an individual's personality and behavioral functioning starting at conception.
4. Babies are born with brains that are extremely primitive, and it is the mother's face, voice, touch, and vocalizations that lay the foundations of her baby's social engagement system.
5. Implicit memories of the mother's face, voice, touch, and vocalizations are encoded into her baby's right brain and become the foundation for his or her ability to regulate his or her affect.

Introduction

Over 40 years of research in the field of prenatal and perinatal psychology have determined that "The core foundations of physical and mental health, emotional intelligence, and the ability to develop one's capacities and talents are established between preconception and the first postnatal year" (Glenn, 2015, p. 332). McCarty and Glenn (2008) have stressed that although the years between zero (meaning the moment of birth) and three have been identified as being critical to the development of good mental and physical health, it may be wise to consider the health and well-being of the mother even before a baby is conceived. They argue that raising public awareness about the effects of environmental toxins, prescription medications, and alcohol and drug use would be a valuable investment of public funds. In addition, education concerning the effects of preconception anxiety, depression, and stress as well as providing easily accessible mental health services for vulnerable women could go a long way toward preventing negative outcomes.

In the sections below, I will discuss genetic and epigenetic factors that influence brain development during this primary developmental period and then provide a synopsis of normal brain development from conception through toddlerhood. I will discuss how attachment affects pre- and postnatal development in the next chapter.

Preconception

Can a baby's brain actually be affected by what has been going on with the mother and the father before he or she was even conceived? Research shows that there are indeed factors that have been passed down from even earlier generations that can affect fetal brain development (Yehuda et al., 2005; 2009; 2016). In the introduction to Section I discussed how genes and the environment interact to build the human body and brain and to influence emotions and behavior. Epigenetic factors such as alcohol and drug use or smoking can affect fertility in both males and females, as can dieting/poor nutrition and high levels of stress (Babenko et al., 2015; Fifer, Monk, & Grose-Fifer, 2001; Monk et al., 2012). Moreover, they can result in serious mental health issues, such as schizophrenia, ADHD, autism, and anxiety and depressive disorders, which can then be transmitted to the next generation (Babenko et al., 2015).

Weinstein (2016) cautions that when a woman/girl gets pregnant, her life experiences and her beliefs, as well as her current perceptions and experiences, all influence her physiology and therefore affect the uterine environment in which her baby will grow. However, it is much more complex than that. Indeed, epigenetic influences start even before a baby's mother and father are born! Yes, you are reading this correctly. Environmental factors present while your mother was in your grandmother's belly may set your own baby up for problems later in life, or more positively, set him or her up for resiliency and healthy functioning. Early research shows that the precursor cells that will become eggs in an ovary are present in a female fetus at five months in the pregnancy (Finch & Loehlin, 1998). This means that, as Wolynn (2016) puts it, "before your mother was even born, your grandmother, your mother, and the earliest traces of you were all in the same body—three generations sharing the same biological environment" (p. 25). Weinstein (2016) explains

> We are only beginning to understand the myriad aspects of this relationship [between a mother and her unborn child], which begins when a human female's eggs develop during her own gestation in her mother's womb. Her eggs carry the potential for the next generation, which includes the genetic and epigenetic information from previous generations that will be selectively expressed as a result of her experiences when she conceives her own child. The sperm of the male with whom she conceives also carries the genetic and epigenetic information from previous generations. This information will also be selectively expressed in their child as a result of the mother's experiences after conception. (p. 55)

Conception

Among humans, the menstrual cycle is normally 28 days, starting on the first day of a woman's period. Fourteen days later, in response to hormonal promptings she releases an egg from one of her ovaries into a fallopian tube that begins to carry it slowly and gently down toward her uterus. This is the point during the cycle (days 14–16) that she is most likely to get pregnant, and if sperm are released into her vagina during this time, one lucky one may find that egg, punch through its cell wall and, BAM!, the miracle of reproduction begins.

The united sperm and egg form a single cell (carrying the genetic and epigenetic information of both the mother and the father) that floats down the fallopian tube, dividing again and again to form a round ball of cells called a *blastocyst*. When it reaches the uterus, it buries itself into the uterine wall. The outermost layer of cells then begin to multiply rapidly and differentiate to form supportive systems (amniotic sac, placenta, etc.) for the inner cells, which will become the *embryo*.

It is important to understand that even when a fertilized egg is nothing but a single cell, the environment in which it finds itself provides a "biochemical experience" that shapes how that cell functions (Verny & Weintraub, 2002, p. 155). Since that single cell divides into many exact replicas of itself as it makes its way down into the uterus, the mother's internal environment will necessarily influence the functioning of the cells even before they implant in the uterine wall. The implanted cells in turn will be influenced by the intrauterine environment as it changes in response to whatever the mother is experiencing as the embryo and fetus develop. This process is called programming and is considered to be "an epigenetic response that interacts with the external world of the mother, the mother's responses to this world, and the prenate's genetic inheritance; it prepares the prenate for the psychophysiological survival during postnatal development" (Thomson, 2012, 13). Verny and Weintraub (2002) explain that cells are structured at a molecular level to process and store information that they receive from the mother's hormonal system (e.g., cortisol when she is stressed or endorphin when she is happy). They argue that

> Before our children have even rudimentary brains, they are gathering, within the cells of their bodies, their first memories. Our earliest memories are not conscious, nor even unconscious in the standard sense. ... [W]e record experience and history of our lives in our cells. (p. 160)

Nature apparently assumes that the environment a woman lives in during her pregnancy is the environment into which her the baby will be born. Therefore, these cellular "experiences" or "memories" structure the developing brain in ways that may affect the individual for his or her entire life (e.g., by building a hyper-reactive HPA system or by building a well-developed smart vagus) (Weinstein, 2016). While problems associated with prenatal stress will be discussed in detail in the next chapter, in the next section, I will explain how the brain develops during the three trimesters of a normal pregnancy.

Fetal Brain Development

After the blastocyst implants in the uterine wall and the embryo begins to develop, one of the very first changes to occur is that the brain starts to develop. This starts about a week after the woman has missed her period, and if her periods are somewhat irregular, as is the case for many women, she may not even suspect that she's pregnant. Thus, she could continue to use alcohol or other drugs, smoke cigarettes, or engage in other risky behaviors that have been part of her life up to that point, inadvertently placing the developing embryo at risk. The first eight weeks of embryological development is the time in which most congenital anomalies occur in response to genetic or epigenetic influences (O'Rahilly & Muller, 2006). If she wasn't expecting to get pregnant and so wasn't alert to the possibility, her personal choices and circumstances could negatively affect the very foundation of her child's physical and mental functioning before she can make a conscious decision about what to do.

Verny and Weintraub (2002) argue that experiences in the womb form the molecular structure of the primary limbic, autonomic and central nervous systems. Therefore, whatever happens in the intrauterine environment affects the very foundation of an individual's personality and behavioral functioning. As Thomson (2012) has stated, "During prenatal development you live in two worlds: the world of your mother and the world into which you will be born" (p. 12). That is, a fetus' environment includes not just the mother's uterus but also her physical environment and psychological condition. The air she breathes, what she eats and drinks, drugs (prescribed or recreational) that she uses, the amount of physical and psychological stress she is under, environmental toxins she encounters, her emotions associated with her pregnancy, and numerous other factors can affect the intrauterine environment in which the fetus is floating. This is important to understand because, as Schore (2002b) notes, "maternal hormones regulate the expression of genes in the fetal brain, and … acute changes in maternal hormones induce changes in gene expression … that are retained when it reaches adulthood" (p. 250). In the sections below, I will give a summary of the changes that occur in the developing brain during the three trimesters of gestation when the uterine and maternal environments are conducive to development.

First Trimester

About three weeks after conception (and only about a week after the woman has missed her period), the mass of inner cells that form the embryo begins to form a groove that deepens over the next several days, eventually forming a hollow tube which when it closes will become the central nervous system, i.e., the brain and the spinal cord. The cells forming the brain itself begin to differentiate into what will eventually become the hind, mid-, and fore brains. By about the fourth week post-conception, the head begins to form with areas differentiated for the sense organs (eyes, mouth, nose, and ears). In addition, the body and internal organs are developing.

Up until six weeks after conception, the brain cells that have been growing have been structural only; neurons, the specialized cells that carry energy and information through the nervous systems, begin to be produced deep inside the center of the brain on day 42. Some of these cells migrate outward to the various areas of the neocortex (forming into the six layers discussed in Chapter 2). Others migrate to form the peripheral nervous system, the vegetative vagus migrating downward to the visceral organs and the body, forming dense clumps of nerves in the heart and gut and connecting all parts of the body with the brain. At the same time, the nerves of the smart vagus migrate upward to the head and throat and downward to the heart and bronchi. Once the neurons have reached their target destinations, they develop axons and dendrites that allow them to send and receive energy and information. By week eight post-conception, the basic structure and foundational innervation of the brain and the body are in place, and for the remainder of gestation, changes that occur in the brain are elaborations of these original structures. At this point, the embryo becomes what is called a *fetus*.

Second Trimester

All of the senses are important to the development and maintenance of both early attachment and later relationships, so it is important to understand that development of the senses starts very early and sets the stage for giving and receiving nurturance. During the fourth month of gestation, the eyes, though not yet fully formed, are able to move, and the thalamus has begun to develop the capacity to deal with visual input. In addition, the fetus may at this point be able to taste and smell through what Fifer et al. (2001) call "chemosensation" (p. 512) as it inhales amniotic fluid through its nose and mouth. Thus, the mother's preferences for specific foods and beverages may be passed along to the fetus and manifested in her child's food preferences later in life.

The vestibular system is the next to develop. This system resides in the fetus' inner ear and controls the sense of balance and of spatial orientation. Then, by the beginning of the sixth month, the fetus shows a primitive response to sound, indicating that the auditory system is developing. It is also in the sixth month of gestation that myelination begins. That is, during this time certain neural circuits begin to develop the fatty sheath around the axons that will triple the speed of transmission between and among neurons (LeDoux, 2002).

By week 26 post conception, all of the sensory systems are able to function at least to some extent, with sensory information following a feedback loop between the thalamus and the cortex (LeDoux, 2002; Stiles & Jernigan, 2010). It is important to understand that for the sensory system to develop normally, it needs to be stimulated. As Hart (2018) has pointed out, while food provides the energy and raw materials for the body to grow, stimulation provides the perceptual, cognitive, and sensorimotor systems what they need to become functional. However, too much of a good thing can be bad. For example, when a pregnant woman experiences mild stress in the third trimester, it actually strengthens the fetus' respiratory development and enhances its ability to learn and to self-regulate emotions after birth (Diego et al., 2002). However, other research shows that exposure to elevated levels of stress, especially anxiety associated with the pregnancy itself (Glynn & Sandman, 2011), results in numerous negative physiological, cognitive, and behavioral outcomes not just during pregnancy and birth but throughout childhood, adolescence, and adulthood (Entringer, Buss, & Wadhwa, 2010; Glynn & Sandman, 2011; Lupien, McEwen, Gunnar, & Heim, 2009).

Third Trimester

LeDoux (2002) points out that although the production of neurons has been ongoing since day 42 after conception, the vast majority of these cells are produced in the third trimester, with around 250,000 neurons being produced every minute. At this point in the pregnancy, the fetus experiences the world through its sensory system. In addition, its vagal system is rapidly developing so that it is prepared for social connection when it is born.

Sensory Development

During the seventh month of pregnancy, the developing fetus has some limited capacity for vision. It can see light and dark and can see relatively large patterns if they are close. The visual cortex has matured and is ready to process information once it is stimulated by the postnatal environment. Babies arrive in the world somewhat nearsighted, which actually works to their advantage since their eyes are perfectly structured to see their mother's face. Their visual systems will continue to develop, though, so that they can see objects across the room within a couple of months and then see as well as an adult by age eight months (LeDoux, 2002).

The fetus' auditory system is also maturing, and by the ninth month of gestation, it can hear well. The sounds most available to a fetus are the mother's heartbeat, digestive gurgles, and voice. Having become familiar with the mother's voice in utero, the baby will show a clear preference for her voice in early infancy (LeDoux, 2002).

That babies show a preference for their mother's voice after they are born shows that during the last trimester, their brains have developed sufficiently to provide some very basic memory functions. Indeed, a fetus can become *habituated* to loud sounds that occur near mom's belly. That is, the fetus will be startled by the sound at first, but if the sound is repeated regularly, it becomes used to it, suggesting that it has learned (remembers) that no harm is associated with the sound. Lastly, a baby recognizes the smell of his or her mother's breast milk, a phenomenon suggesting that he or she remembers tastes and smells associated with mom's diets while in utero (LeDoux, 2002).

The above description of the development of the sensory systems shows that when babies come into the world, they are able to see their mother's face, smell her body, and hear her voice; they can feel her loving touch and taste the sweetness of her life-giving breast milk. All of their senses, then, let their mom bring them pleasure and make them feel secure, thus laying the foundation for the development of secure attachment.

Vagal Development

Although the vegetative vagus is working at birth, the smart vagus needs to continue to mature for several months postpartum. As discussed in Chapter 4, the smart vagus innervates our social engagement system, making it possible for us to send and receive social signals that will help us to get our needs met and to recognize and understand the social signals others are sending us. In addition, the smart vagus controls the vagal brake, suppressing the sympathetic system so that adrenalin and cortisol don't have to be secreted to support basic mobilization (e.g., crying and sucking) and overriding the shutdown response of the vegetative vagus during feeding that could cause the baby to stop breathing (Porges & Furman, 2011).

While the vegetative vagus and the sympathetic nervous system are not myelinated, the smart vagus is, allowing it to respond virtually instantaneously to external and internal signals and to calm the body during times of perceived safety. However, the smart vagus doesn't start to myelinate until week 24 of gestation, with significant myelination not in place until around week 30–32 of gestation. Therefore, preterm babies are at risk of entering the world with a smart vagus that isn't yet supporting their survival. In addition, a poorly regulated heart rate at birth (mediated by the smart vagus) is associated with poor development of self-soothing, attention, and social engagement during infancy and toddlerhood. Porges and Furman (2011) caution that

Without a functioning myelinated vagus, social behavior would be compromised, and more primitive defense strategies, such as fight-flight mobilization and tantrums (mediated by the sympathetic nervous) and shut down behaviours (mediated by the unmyelinated vagal system) would be more frequently expressed. Clinically, the status of myelination becomes critical for the newborn and the young infant as they attempt to engage and disengage the caregiver and to explore social reciprocity as a mechanism to regulate physiology and behavior. (p. 113)

Infant/Toddler Brain Development

All of a baby's major neural pathways, shaped by input from the environment, will have formed by age three. Although the number of neurons actually declines during infancy and toddlerhood, the brain's volume increases dramatically as well as the number of connections between neurons. According to Knickmeyer et al. (2008), the total brain volume of a two- to four-week old baby more than doubles in the first year (going from 36% to 72% of the volume of an adult) and increases by another 15% in the second year (to 83% of an adult volume). Hart (2018) points out that even though the newborn's brain is so much smaller than an adult's brain, it actually has between 15% and 85% more neurons than the same sections of an adult brain. The increase in the brain's volume over those first couple of years is primarily due to the production of *glial* (support) cells since the number of *neurons* will actually decline through a natural die-off process so that by the age of three, the child has the about same number of neurons he or she will have as an adult. After this natural die-off, the number of neurons should then remain fairly stable for the rest of the individual's life.

As you may recall from Chapter 1, the number of connections between neurons will rise rapidly during infancy in a process called *blooming* so that about eight months after birth, an infant will have eight times as many connections as she or he had when first born. This overabundance of connections is apparently nature's way of making sure that there are plenty of available pathways to accommodate the experiences that the baby will have after birth. That is, the infant's brain is *experience-expectant*.

For example, the cerebellum triples in size during the first year of life to accommodate the development of the essential motor skills that it "knows" is coming. The brain "expects" that it will see faces, and when the visual cortex receives stimuli from mom's face, this part of the brain begins to develop normally. A newborn can see immediately after birth and can distinguish between happy and sad faces, though his or her area of focus is limited to that distance between his or her eyes and mom's face (Dirix, Nijhuis, Jongsma, & Hornstra, 2009). However, by the age of three months, he or she will be able to see as well as an adult. Mosier (2013) explains that the brain "expects" to hear words. Similarly, when mom talks to her baby, her baby's language centers in the frontal and temporal lobes begin to develop so that he or she will naturally begin to learn the language being spoken as these centers mature. In addition, the more mom talks to her baby, the more neurons are devoted to language in her baby's brain. The hippocampus also matures over the first year just in time for the toddler to remember and repeat words and phrases he or she has been hearing and quadrupling his or her vocabulary during the second year of life. Moreover, during the third year of life the prefrontal cortex produces twice as many connections as it will need, providing essential networks for the regulation of thoughts, emotions, and behavior.

In addition to synaptic blooming and establishment of major neural pathways, as babies interact with their world, more and more areas will be myelinated, speeding up transmission of energy and information and making the brain more and more efficient through childhood and adolescence and even on into adulthood. However, the importance of this developmental stage cannot be overstated, with Perry (2002) cautioning, "While experience may alter the behavior of an adult, experience literally provides the organizing framework for an infant and child" (p. 87).

Siegel (2001), however, cautions that many parents today, having heard that babies need stimulation for their brains to develop, may actually overstimulate them. He cautions that

> This is an unfortunate misinterpretation of the neurobiological literature—that somehow "more is better." It is just not so. Parents and other caregivers can "relax" and stop worrying about providing huge amounts of sensory bombardment for their children. ... Attachment research suggests that collaborative interpersonal interaction, not excessive sensory stimulation, can be seen as the key to healthy development. (p. 72)

Although there will be a pruning of unused connections starting around age four, new connections and interconnections will continue to be made, probably up until the very moment of death (LeDoux, 2002).

Development of the Social Engagement System

During the last trimester of gestation, the ANS develops rapidly so that when babies are born, they are able to breathe, ingest and digest food, and maintain their body temperature. Porges and Furman (2011) suggest that this prenatal development of the ANS constitutes a "neural platform" (p. 107) that will underpin babies' abilities to interact successfully with their caregivers and others in their physical and social environment. Although newborns are unable to care for themselves in any way, they are able to elicit help from their caregivers so that their basic needs for food, warmth, and protection will be met. As their bodies and brains develop over infancy and childhood and provide them with more and more independence, they become able to function on their own, though their need for social contact never goes away. Although they may become less dependent on their moms and dads as they transition into adolescence and young adulthood, they will continue to search for supportive friends, partners, and mates throughout their lives, not just to help them handle the hassles of the world (homework, moving, etc.) but also to help them regulate their moods and behaviors.

Four parts of the brain—the smart vagus, the closely related anterior cingulate and insula, and the OMPFC—are particularly involved in babies' developing social engagement system. I will discuss the vagal system first followed by the anterior cingulate and insula and then the OMPFC.

The Vagal System

In addition to innervating the face and throat, the smart vagus also acts to regulate heart and respiration rates in the absence of life-threatening danger. As mentioned above, the smart vagus controls the muscles of the mouth and throat so that a newborn can suck, swallow, and breathe without choking. However, beyond addressing the physiological need for food to nourish the body, the heart-face connection provided by the smart vagus is of profound importance to a baby's ability to manage his or her emotions and to form mutually satisfying relationships as he or she matures.

For example, when a mother feeds her baby, she is not just providing him or her with food; she is strengthening the connection between the face and the heart and laying the foundation for her child's social engagement system. During feeding, the smart vagus releases the vagal brake (allowing the heart to speed up) to provide energy for sucking and swallowing and then applies it again to conserve energy and allow the vegetative vagus to promote rest and digestion. This releasing and applying of the vagal brake regulates the infant's physiological and emotional state, moving him or her from a state of discomfort (hunger) to a state of comfort and positive affect. At the same time, a loving, sensitive and responsive mother will naturally smile, coo, and speak in "motherese" as she is feeding her baby, providing social cues of safety. As the baby's smart vagus matures over the first six months of life, it gradually allows the baby to move from sucking as a way to regulate his or her state to using the social engagement system to engage with and be soothed by others. (Panksepp & Watt, 2011).

When a well-developed smart vagus releases the vagal brake on the heart in response to something in the environment, it promotes a state of vigilance. Remember that this is a process of neuroception, not of thinking. The baby's senses take in the environment and send that information to the hindbrain and the amygdala. If risk is perceived, the baby will first try social communication mediated by the smart vagus (e.g., whimpering or screwing up its face and starting to cry). If that doesn't work, he or she may go into fight/flight mediated by the sympathetic system (protest, full-throated screaming, waving of fists and kicking). The baby will subside into still silence if no one comes to help (despair), most likely a response by the vegetative vagus in the hope that if the predator doesn't hear the baby, it will pass on by. However, if neuroception determines that the environment is not dangerous after all, the smart vagus will engage the vagal brake again, the heartbeat will return to normal, resulting in a calm and happy baby (Panksepp & Watt, 2011).

The Anterior Cingulate and Insula

Schore (2001) explains that at the same time the smart vagus is beginning to mature at around two to four months of age, the anterior cingulate is also beginning to mature. The two are very closely connected. The anterior cingulate is associated with both play and separation behaviors (in both mothers and their babies) and with the sounds produced during those kinds of activities (e.g., laughing or crying). In addition, it is associated with face recognition. Thus, the anterior cingulate mediates the expression of separation anxiety in early infancy and stranger anxiety in later infancy.

Before a baby is two or three months old, he or she doesn't worry much about mom not being there as long as somebody is there to relieve uncomfortable physical sensations. However, as the anterior cingulate matures, the baby comes to recognize mom's face and protests when mom is out of sight. When a baby's brain has developed sufficiently to realize that mom is gone, her absence activates the GRIEF/separation (attachment behavioral system) and consequent proximity seeking behaviors and social signals of distress (mediated by the smart vagus). Knowing that mom is close by, however, prevents activation of the fight/flight/freeze responses and allows heart rate and breathing to remain calm. Then, by eight to ten months of age, the infant's anterior cingulate has matured to the point that his or her FEAR system will be activated when exposed to novel or threatening situations or to people whose faces are not recognized (stranger anxiety), again utilizing social signals of distress meant to activate mom's CARE system and avoid danger.

Importantly, the anterior cingulate has a primary role in consciousness. Consciousness is hard to explain, and neuroscientists are still struggling with how to define it and to explain the processes associated with its origin. However, there is some agreement that consciousness has to do with awareness and attention, and the three terms are often used almost interchangeably. If you are *unconscious* during surgery, for example, you are *not aware* that the doctor is cutting you with his scalpel, something that you would surely be *aware* of if you were *conscious*. When you are paying close *attention* to your professor as she explains how the brain works, you may be *unaware* that there is a storm coming until you become *conscious* of it when lightning strikes a tree outside the window and instantly captures your *attention*. But then, you refocus your *attention* on the professor's lecture when the lights come back on and the nervous laughter of all your classmates subsides. Your conscious awareness and conscious transfer of attention from one focus to another occurs in the anterior cingulate.

Schore (2001) suggests that the healthy maturation of the anterior cingulate develops in response to social-emotional communications (mediated by the smart vagus) occurring between mother and baby in the first year of life. That is, a baby is indeed conscious (when he or she is awake) of the light shining on the bouncing mobile over her crib, of the sounds of mom's footfalls as she approaches the nursery, of the discomfort of hunger or a wet diaper, etc. However, that primary consciousness will expand into more complex states of consciousness that are informed by memory in the context of relationship across time (right brain, implicit during infancy but expanding to left brain, explicit during toddlerhood). Thus according to Schore, consciousness "is a product of that part of the brain that handles human relations [i.e., the anterior cingulate and the smart vagus], and is a property of the brain that is and has been in communication with other brains" (p. 34).

As discussed in Chapter 2, the anterior cingulate and the insula are very closely connected. The anterior cingulate is involved in the conscious awareness of stimuli coming in from the outside. It is also involved in conscious awareness of internal bodily sensations that are sent to it via the insula. As the insula processes internal sensations, it generates an image of the individual's physical state and emotional reaction to that state that is laid down in memory (implicit memory in infancy since explicit is not yet active). In addition, the insula is involved in the processing of others' facial expressions, setting off an alarm if whatever is processed suggests that something bad is about to happen.

During infancy, these two functions of the insula (processing internal sensations and reacting to facial expressions) lay the foundations for the development of a sense of self. I feel things in "my" body, and I see "myself" reflected back to me in your facial expressions. Then, in concert with the anterior cingulate, an awareness and recognition of self will develop and provide a platform on which autobiographical memory will be based in toddlerhood (Schore, 2005). In addition, since the insula processes internal sensations associated with the social signals sent by others, it lays the foundation for the development of mentalization (the image of other peoples' thoughts, attitudes, and intentions), both of which are essential to the development of his or her internal working models (see Chapter 7) and the development of an attachment style.

The Orbitomedial Prefrontal Cortex

The OMPFC in conjunction with the anterior cingulate and the amygdala form what Schore (2001, p. 35) calls a "social editor" that processes social signals of all kinds including the social intentions of others. Its successful development results in individuals being able to regulate their moods as well as their reactions and interactions with others, to control and direct their impulses, and to assume responsibility for their actions. In addition, the OMPFC has a reciprocal relationship with the vagal system and thus is able to modulate approach/avoidance behaviors and levels of arousal in interpersonal behaviors. Schore stresses the importance of the healthy development of this part of the brain by saying that

> this regulatory system monitors, adjusts, and corrects emotional responses and regulates the motivational control of goal-directed behavior. It thus functions as a recovery mechanism that efficiently monitors and regulates the duration, frequency, and intensity of positive and negative affective states, from high intensity joy and excitement to the affective motivational aspects of pain. (p. 39)

He then goes on to emphasize that the healthy development of these capacities is dependent upon the development of a secure attachment and the mother's acting as a secure base for her child's exploration of the world. Although the OMPFC doesn't mature completely until young adulthood, it starts in infancy and toddlerhood. In his early authoritative book on emotional development and affect regulation, Schore (1994) argues forcibly that "the interval between 10–12 to 16–18 months is a critical period for the final maturation of a system in the prefrontal cortex that is essential for the regulation of affect over the rest of the lifespan" (p. 24). This is so because the infant brain begins a natural pruning process around the age of 24 months, and thus the neural pathways devoted to attachment, though not impervious to change, are well defined (Chambers, 2017).

Development of the Right Hemisphere

Although all areas of the brain are developing during infancy and toddlerhood, the right hemisphere is by far the most active. It is important to remember that the right brain lays down only implicit memories, memories that manifest not through words but through emotions, assumptions, and images. The words that mom is using when she talks or sings to her baby mean precisely nothing to the baby; all baby understands is mom's tone of voice and level of intensity, facial expressions, posture and movement, gestures, and even subtle physiological changes (her social signals mediated by her smart vagus). In loving interactions, baby and mom share a "conversation between limbic systems" (Schore, 2002b, p. 257) in which they open "a two-way channel of emotional communication" (p. 261) that they create together.

Siegel (2001) stresses that this kind of contingent communication in which mom and baby respond to each other's social signals is the foundation for building the baby's social brain.

Schore (2002b) goes so far as to say that when they are in spontaneous, resonant communication, mother and baby literally become a single biological unit in which

> the mother is downloading emotional programs into her infant's right brain. The child is using the mother's right hemisphere as a template for the imprinting, the hard wiring of circuits in his own right hemisphere that will come to mediate his expanding affective capacities, an essential element of his emerging personality. (p. 258)

Mom's and baby's emotions become synchronized in such a way that she actually regulates her baby's emotions. She is able to help her baby experience higher levels of positive emotions and to minimize his or her experience of negative emotions.

As his brain develops through these interactions, the baby will eventually begin to be able to regulate his own affect. In addition, he will internalize at a nonconscious level that he can use other people to help him regulate his emotions when the going gets really rough. The baby is on his way to recognizing his own emotions and the emotions of others. Schore (2002b) argues that this early development of the structures that support intersubjectivity and empathy (see Chapter 4) is crucial to moral development. Therefore, early attachment experiences are the substrate for all subsequent social engagement and socially responsible behavior, making what happens during this early stage of life of critical importance to the very survival of our essentially social species.

Summary

This chapter has offered an overview of brain development from before a child is conceived through about age three. As you learned in Section I of this book, brain growth and functioning is influenced by both genetic and epigenetic factors. From a mental health practitioner's perspective, then, gathering information about a client's past may mean not just asking about his or her own childhood but perhaps about his or her mother's or even grandmother's past as well. How much stress a pregnant woman experiences affects the intrauterine environment, programming the fetal brain for the environment that it is likely to encounter, thus likely affecting how that baby reacts to stress for the remainder of his or her life. It is important to remember that different parts of the brain develop at different times during a pregnancy, so there are windows of vulnerability that occur throughout fetal development. However, since later brain growth is based on earlier brain growth, damage from toxins, stress, and trauma early in a pregnancy can have pervasive negative effects on the outcome.

As discussed in Chapter 4, healthy functioning of the social engagement system promotes connectedness and good affect regulation throughout the lifespan. This system has its origins in the very earliest weeks of prenatal growth, and its functioning is optimized by good parenting and secure attachment. In the next chapter, I will explain how the attachment system active in a baby and the CARE/nurturing system active in a mother work together to promote secure attachment. Then I will go into the specifics of the pre- and postnatal attachment processes.

CHAPTER **10**

Attachment from Preconception to Toddlerhood

LEARNING OBJECTIVES

After completing this chapter, readers should understand that:

- The care-seeking and nurturing systems work together to establish and maintain the parent-child attachment bond.
- The attachment bond can begin to form well before a baby is born in both the mother and the father, and its presence before birth is predictive of the development of secure attachment postnatally.
- While mothers form a strong attachment within hours of their baby's birth, babies go through three stages of attachment over about two years before the bond is firmly in place.
- There are five major elements needed to foster secure attachment during infancy and toddlerhood.

KEY IDEAS

1. Attachment between mother and infant is supported by two distinct but interconnected brain circuits—the nurturing system and the attachment behavioral system.
2. Postnatal maternal attachment is correlated with prenatal maternal attachment.
3. The fostering of secure attachment depends of five factors: collaboration, reflective dialogue, repair of ruptures in communication, mother's coherent narrative, and adequate emotional communication.

Introduction

Schore (2001), one of the world's most influential researchers on attachment and the brain, suggests that "attachment theory is, in essence, a regulatory theory" (p. 14), meaning that the attachment bond builds the systems that allow babies to appraise the environment and cope with stress. Secure attachment results in a balance between bottom-up and top-down processing of information received from the environment (see Chapter 2) and optimizes the ability to learn new things and adapt to a changing environment. Schore emphasizes that the earliest experiences a baby has (whether positive or negative) happen in the context of the attachment relationship with his or her mom. Whether mom is available, sensitive, and attuned or hopelessly inept and abusive, attachment happens. However, whether a child develops secure or insecure attachment during infancy is crucially important since these earliest experiences are carried forward into all later developmental stages and influence how an individual later seeks out, interprets, and reacts to the experiences she or he encounters (Sroufe, Egeland, Carlson, & Collins, 2005). As Benoit (2004) puts it, "... the question is never 'is there an attachment between this parent and this child?' Instead, the question is 'what is the quality of the attachment between this parent and this child?'" (p. 543). Moreover, Panksepp (2012b) suggests that this earliest relationship is of primary importance to mental health, stating, "It is becoming increasingly clear that mothers and loving others are the ones who can offer us the gift of a happy life" (p. 313).

The purpose of this chapter, then, is to explain the neurological underpinnings of the infant-mother attachment bond and discuss pre- and perinatal attachment through the first two years after birth. In an effort to make these concepts as real as possible for my readers, I will introduce a case study, little Sophia Ramirez and her family, and show how secure attachment develops in infancy and toddlerhood.

Neurological Underpinnings of Caregiving and Care Seeking

Attachment is a neurobiological phenomenon that, as discussed in the previous chapter, is supported by genetically programmed circuitry and is influenced by epigenetic factors that may be present even before the baby is a gleam in his or her parents' eye. Bowlby (1969/1982) proposed that two parallel systems evolved to support the survival of infants—the attachment behavioral system (proximity seeking) and the caregiving system (detection of and response to cues associated with a child's stress). The attachment behavioral system becomes active soon after birth, while the caregiving system doesn't mature until late adolescence when puberty produces hormonal and neurobiological changes associated with reproduction (Lenzi, Trentini, Tambelli, & Pantano, 2015). Thus, moms' and babies' brains are structured to support the behaviors that make it most likely that those babies will grow up to have babies of their own. The mother's care *giving* circuit (nurturing system) and the baby's care *seeking* circuit (attachment behavioral system) provide the neurobiological underpinnings of attachment. Below, I will discuss the nurturing system first followed by the attachment behavioral system.

The Nurturing System

Women (and to a somewhat lesser extent, men) have developed, through evolutionary pressures across the millennia, a limbic brain system that maximizes the probability that their babies will be able to survive, what Panksepp (2009) calls the CARE/nurturing system. (Please see Chapter 3 for a discussion of Panksepp's understanding of emotions and the use of all caps to label them). In Chapter 6, I suggested that it is the CARE/nurturing system rather than just physical strength that makes a person most fit to survive in the world—survival of the nurtured.

The impulse to nurture is embedded in the CARE system. Because we are a social species, this system urges us to care not only for our own children but to take an interest in and nurture other people's children, too. Think about how you feel when you see a tiny baby in the grocery store being pushed through the aisles by her mother. This wrinkled, blotchy, often hairless little being with a face that only her mother can love just makes you go "Awwww," doesn't it? If you see a toddler wandering around the mall unaccompanied, you may well rush over and protect him or her until the authorities can take over the process of finding the mother. People are perfectly happy to adopt a complete stranger's baby and love it just as much as they love their own biological children. Indeed, Panksepp (2009) emphasizes that this CARE system is so powerful that it actually prompts the nurturing of not just human young but even of other species' young (think of how we watch all those YouTube videos of puppies and kittens, and how distressed we become when a baby bird falls out of the nest).

Panksepp (2012b) explains that a mother's desire to CARE for her baby arises because of her production of oxytocin and endorphins in response to the touch, sight, smell, and sound of her infant. She actually starts producing high levels of oxytocin toward the end of her pregnancy, probably in response to increased levels of estrogen (which is probably responsible for her urge to "feather her nest"). The oxytocin in her system initiates both milk production and the maternal urges to nurture and protect her baby when he or she is born. Interestingly, after maternal behaviors have been established during the first couple of postnatal weeks, oxytocin levels do not affect her nurturing activities. Instead, it appears that her loving interactions with her baby become something of a matter of habit, probably reinforced by the production of the feel-good endogenous opiates (endorphin). As you may remember from Chapter 3, oxytocin and endorphins activate the reward system, which in turn causes dopamine to be produced in the reward system and the OMPFC. When dopamine reaches the OMPFC, it activates a SEEKING response, in the case of a mother-child relationship, urging her to SEEK out and CARE for her baby.

Maternal behaviors are laid down permanently in the mother's right brain as she experiences providing maternal care to her first baby, and her caregiving competencies are available for access for the remainder of her life. It's kind of like once you learn to ride a bicycle, you never really forget. Panksepp (2012b) also notes that oxytocin (and vasopressin) is involved in the strengthening of social memories. Thus, the production of oxytocin may well be responsible for the mother being able to pick out her baby's face, smell, and cry from other babies' and to remember how good it feels to be with her baby.

Although childcare practices are clearly influenced by the culture into which a baby is born, the traditional role of men as breadwinners rather than caregivers may have its origins in men's lower levels of estrogen and consequent lower levels of oxytocin. Panksepp (2012b) suggests that

> most human fathers who participate in infant care probably nurture in more routine and less deeply emotional and empathetic ways than mothers. Mothers typically exhibit more natural warmth and desire to be with infants. It is also usually mothers who more persistently carry on sensitive affective communication with babies, especially with happy babies but also with those in distress. (p. 299)

Thus, although the nurturing impulse may be somewhat reduced among men, the CARE system is present in their brains and definitely can be activated. According to Hart (2009), while mothers tend to do things that calm their young children, fathers tend to do things that intensify their children's level of arousal and push them to see what is happening in the world around them. That is, while mothers tend to provide safety in an unsafe world (a *safe haven*), fathers tend to provide a *secure base* from which to explore the world. Please notice, however, the words *tend to*; fathers can, indeed, act as a safe haven and mothers as a secure base.

The Care Seeking System

In reciprocal interaction with the CARE/nurturing system is the GRIEF/separation system (Panksepp, 2012b). This GRIEF/separation system is the brain system that Bowlby (1969/1982) calls the attachment behavioral system. It is active not only in infancy and early childhood but throughout the lifespan. While nurturing produces delightful feelings of warmth, security, and wellbeing, separation from or loss of an attachment figure feels absolutely terrible. When the GRIEF/separation system is activated, the young of social species (including humans) will signal their need for CARE by sending out highly charged emotional sounds that grab the attention of their caregivers, activate their CARE systems, and urge them to SEEK and help their baby. The presence of the caregiver (sight, sound, and touch) then releases oxytocin and endorphins in the baby, resulting in her or him being soothed and calmed. Human babies can (and do) cry at birth. In addition, they develop a repertoire of behaviors in their attachment behavioral system that facilitate proximity seeking as discussed in Chapter 6.

When a baby is born, he or she can experience only a few emotions (fear, comfort, joy, and curiosity) and has very little ability to regulate those emotions (Mosier, 2013). In the first couple of months of life, babies cry and fuss in response to distress caused by hunger or other physical discomforts, and they are soothed when those discomforts are relieved. However, by about two months of age, they begin to feel distress in the form of separation anxiety when they realize that mom is not present. Their brains have developed to the point that they can notice when mom isn't there. Because being close to mom increases the chances that the baby will survive, nature has made being close to mom feel good and being separated from mom feel bad. When feel-good neurochemicals are high, babies are happy, but when they are low, babies cry.

Interestingly, infants cry in response to both separation and fear. However, according to Panksepp (2012b), the feeling that infants experience during separation is not FEAR. FEAR is a separate system activated by danger, not by separation (even though separation from mom may place the baby in danger). To understand the difference, imagine a time when you have been scared by something; then imagine a time when you have lost someone you love (a romantic breakup, perhaps, or when someone close to you died). Although both fear and separation/loss are painful, the feelings are quite different, aren't they? Panksepp (2012b) notes that babies will respond to either fear or separation (or both) by crying in an intense effort to be reunited with mom. However, the response to fear may be to freeze (nature's way of hopefully keeping a predator from noticing the baby) while the response to separation is to scream and cry inconsolably to gain attention and, among those who are mobile, to run around frantically in search of mom.

Crying is an action and is mediated by dopamine. (Remember that dopamine, although having some pleasurable effects, is more about action/movement than about pleasure.) Thus, the SEEKING system is activated both by fear and by separation. In cases in which there is chronic fear or separation (e.g., abuse or neglect), the pleasurable aspect of the dopamine in the SEEKING system may become depleted, resulting in decreased "joy-of-life resources" (Panksepp, 2012b, p. 317). Among infants, this situation may be lethal as in cases of "failure to thrive" in which babies simply die even though their physical needs are being met. In addition, this deficiency may lead to chronic mood disorders and personality disorders later in life, and because sadness is associated with decreased opioid activity in the brain, may lead to the use of opiates and other addictive substances in an attempt to self-medicate psychic pain that is rooted in early separation. In addition to dopamine, stress hormones are also produced when the GRIEF/separation system is activated. Therefore, in cases of long-term separation, babies' HPA systems may be chronically upregulated, resulting in anxiety disorders and panic attacks activated not by fear but by feelings of separation and loss.

The discussion above shows that mother-child attachment and their reciprocal interactions during infancy and toddlerhood are deeply rooted in brain functioning. In the next sections, I will discuss how important attachment is even before a baby is conceived. Then I will show how attachment changes and grows across infancy and into toddlerhood. Lastly, I will suggest how secure attachment can be fostered during this developmental stage. In addition, I will introduce you to little Sophia Ramirez and her family. We will be following Sophia's story and several other case studies that will be introduced in later chapters to see how the concepts being discussed relate to real life.

Pre- and Perinatal Attachment

As discussed in Chapter 1, neuroplasticity allows the brain to change in response to experience. However, neuroplasticity does have limits. There are critical periods during which some of these experience-*expectant* parts of the brain (structured by genes) are experience-*dependent* (structured by epigenetic influences). Attachment is experience-dependent. For example, research with monkeys shows that baby monkeys will not develop normally if they don't have certain attachment experiences within 90 days of birth. Beyond that, irrevocable psychological damage occurs so that they remain highly disturbed and reactive to stress for the remainder of their lives (Harlow, 1958, 1959). Humans are born with a brain that expects to have attachment experiences, too. If that expectation is met, the child will feel safe and will be able to explore the world with relative ease. If, however, that expectation is not met, serious and irrevocable damage can occur (Bowlby, 1973). This possibility is discussed in depth in the next chapter.

Sroufe (2005) is careful to point out that development across infancy, childhood, and adolescence is an extremely complex process that includes not only early attachment experiences but also non-attachment-related parenting experiences, sibling and peer relationships, and changes in contexts and conditions over time. While cautioning that parent-child attachment is related only probabilistically to outcomes and saying that parent-child attachment is not "inexorably related to any outcome whatsoever" (p. 365), he emphasizes that attachment

> is an organizing core in development that is always integrated with later experience and never lost. While it is not proper to think of attachment variations as directly causing certain outcomes, and while early attachment has no privileged causal status, it is nonetheless the case that nothing can be assessed in infancy that is more important. Infant attachment is critical, both because of its place in initiating pathways of development and because of its connection with so many critical developmental functions—social relatedness, arousal modulation, emotional regulation, and curiosity, to name just a few. Attachment experiences remain, even in this complex view, vital in the formation of the person. (p. 365)

Understanding the foundational influences of attachment is, then, important for mental health practitioners. In this section, I will discuss first discuss how prenatal maternal and paternal attachment is formed. Then I will discuss what is known about the formation of attachment bonds in infancy and toddlerhood.

Prenatal Attachment

Doan and Zimerman (2003) suggest that it is possible for attachment between a mother or a father and their baby to form well before the baby is born, and a considerable amount of research shows there is a correlation between levels of maternal prenatal attachment and levels of attachment after the baby is born (Alhusen, 2008; Rossen et al., 2016). There is less research on paternal prenatal attachment than there is on maternal. However, that research shows that the two most influential factors in a father's level of attachment to his baby are his level of prenatal attachment with the fetus and the quality of the relationship between him and the mother. In other words, though the strength of the attachment bond is open to change, generally the stronger the mother's and father's attachment bonds with their baby before birth, the stronger the bonds after the baby is born.

Doan and Zimerman (2003) argue that it is important to recognize that pregnancy is simply one part of a developmental sequence that starts well before conception and unfolds across the lifespan. Women enter pregnancy with abilities, skills, and experiences that influence their attitudes and behaviors not just while they are pregnant but also after their baby is born. Most women have sufficient cognitive ability to think abstractly and imagine fetal development. However, maternal attachment tends to increase after she feels her baby begin to move and after she sees an ultrasound of her fetus (Condon, Corkindale, Boyce, & Gamble, 2013). In addition, Doan and Zimerman (2003) point out that, although the research is somewhat inconsistent, the mother's own attachment status may significantly affect her ability to attach to her developing fetus. That is, women who have a secure attachment style are more likely to have a strong attachment to their fetus even early in their pregnancy than insecure women are. Environmental factors such as availability of and willingness to access marital or family social support are also important to the development of prenatal attachment.

Attachment in Infancy and Toddlerhood

Fortunately, nature has set it up so that a mother starts forming a strong attachment to her baby within hours of birth (especially, as discussed above, if she has already become attached before the baby is even born). The baby, on the other hand, takes much longer to form a solid bond with his or her primary attachment figure. Up until about the age of two months, babies are in a *preattachment* stage in which they respond to almost anyone who is taking care of their basic needs. Then in the *attachment-in-the-making* stage that goes from about two to six months of age, they begin to show a preference for one caregiver over another. *Clear-cut attachment*, in which the primary caregiver becomes the one that babies clearly prefer and seek out (and who they scream for when separated from them) starts developing at about six months and is fully formed by age two and a half. In this section, I will discuss how attachment forms during these three stages.

Preattachment: Birth to Two Months

As Schore (2002b) explains, early socioemotional experiences are laid down in the right brain during a growth spurt that starts in the last trimester of pregnancy and continues to about age one and a half to two (i.e., toddlerhood). During pregnancy, the mother's hormones induce genetic expression of structures in the fetus' brain, and her interactions with her baby during infancy induce epigenetic (environmental) influences on those structures. Thus, citing Cicchetti and Tucker (1994, p. 538), Schore emphasizes that since maturation of the brain is experience-dependent, "nature's potential can be realized only as it is enabled by nurture." Nurture in this age group is provided primarily by mom, and the sooner she starts nurturing, the better.

The literature indicates that, for optimal outcomes (both post-birth and later in life, and for both baby and mom), nurturing in the form of skin-to-skin contact needs to occur as soon after birth as possible. Sometimes called "the golden hour," the newborn should have skin-to-skin contact with his or her mother beginning immediately after birth and continuing until after the baby has nursed for the first time. This means that, after a vaginal birth the baby is laid directly on the mother's bare abdomen immediately after he or she has been dried off, even before the umbilical cord is clamped, and then be moved up to her chest after the cord is clamped. For C-sections, the recommendation is to place the baby on the mother's chest as soon as she is alert and responsive (which may be immediately, if she has had an epidural or spinal anesthetic and has been conscious throughout the process) (Crenshaw, 2007).

With this skin-to-skin contact, oxytocin begins to surge in the blood streams of both mother and baby, encouraging both to relax. In addition, the mother's brain releases endorphins, providing her with both pain relief and pleasurable reinforcement of contact with her baby. During post-birth skin-to-skin contact, babies instinctively search for the mother's breast so that they can suckle after which they then tend to fall into a relaxed sleep. During breastfeeding levels of endorphins increase in both mother and baby, thus reinforcing breastfeeding, an activity that is important both to short- and long-term physical health and to the attachment process (Crenshaw, 2007). Sometimes, mom is not able to start nurturing her baby immediately. In the worst case, she may have died during childbirth. Or perhaps she had a complex C-section and needs time to recover. Or perhaps the baby is removed by child services because the mother is not capable of caring for her baby. Whatever the situation between birth mother and baby, *someone* needs to start the nurturing process as soon as possible.

Interestingly, research has shown that although babies are born with a functioning amygdala, this part of the brain (which, if you remember, is associated with fear) is relatively weak during early infancy (Landers & Sullivan, 2012). Thus, babies are spared the fear that they might have experienced associated with the overwhelming novelty of their new environment since virtually everything is new to them, including everything that mom is doing to and with them. This attenuated amygdala, then, actually suppresses fear and the avoidance that comes with it and facilitates the formation of attachment (Tareen & Tareen, 2014). Moreover, according to Schore (2001), in the first couple of postnatal months, babies interact with their mom through their senses of *taste, touch, and smell*. Breast milk is sweet and therefore not only provides relief from the distress of hunger but also is pleasurable because of its taste. Gentle stroking, touching, and holding releases oxytocin and endorphins in both baby and mom (resulting in feelings of comfort, wellbeing, and happiness in both), and permanently downregulates the baby's production of stress hormones. Moms find the smell of their own baby pleasurable, and babies find their mom's smell soothing. Although baby is not yet solidly attached to mom, these pleasurable stimuli set the stage for attachment to occur.

Although the left side of the hippocampus, the side associated with the encoding of explicit, verbal memories, will not become active until later in infancy, the right is involved with spatial and emotional memory and matures at about age two to three months. This maturation is important to the development of attachment because it allows the baby to recognize his or her mother and remember that she provides good things, like food, dry diapers, gentle and soothing touch, etc. (Chambers, 2017).

Attachment-in-the-Making: Two to Six Months

At about the age of eight weeks, changes in the baby's maturing occipital lobe make mom's face and the emotions expressed there the most important positive stimuli in his or her social environment (Schore, 2001). *Vision* now becomes important to the developing attachment bond. At this age, babies start paying very close attention to mom's face, especially her eyes. Interestingly, Schore (1994) explains that the eye actually begins to develop during early gestation at the same time that the brain starts to develop and can actually be considered an extension of the brain itself. Thus, direct eye-to-eye contact between baby and mother in essence allows them direct access to each other's brain. Mom and baby tend to lock gazes, and if you have ever seen a mother and her baby while they are sharing this kind of intense mutual eye contact, you have surely recognized that they are head-over-heels in love with each other. There's all sorts of smiling and cooing going on as mom mirrors her baby's expressions and sounds, a process that is essential to her baby's development of a sense of self. This interaction between mom and baby is a form of play and can lead to high levels of positive affect in both of them that supports the development of attachment (Schore, 2001).

However, it is important that baby be in charge of this interaction. That is, because the intense level of emotional communication that is happening during mutual gazing is highly stimulating, a baby may break the gaze in an effort to reduce the level of stimulation. Therefore, mom needs to be sensitive to her baby's signal that that he needs a bit of rest (looking away or stopping smiling) and to his signal that it's time to play again (re-engaging eye contact). Schore (2001) suggests that

> The more the psychobiologically attuned mother tunes her activity level to the infant during periods of social engagement, the more she allows him to recover quietly in periods of disengagement, and the more she attend to the child's reinitiating cues for reengagement, the more synchronized their interactions … [a process that is] fundamental to the healthy affective development of the infant. (pp. 18–19)

In "an infant-leads-mother-follows sequence" (Schore, 2002b, p. 254), a sensitive mother can read her baby's signals within a split second, recognize that he is overstimulated, and act in ways that will allow him to calm down. When this is done well and consistently, it results in the baby experiencing the joy of being the gleam in the parent's eye, and of having the secure feeling that [he] is under the watchful eye of the mother, even when she's not physically present, [thus supporting and nurturing] the infant's burgeoning positive self-esteem. (p. 261)

This pattern of attunement, disengagement, and reengagement (attunement, rupture, and repair) generally takes place beneath the level of consciousness. However, it is necessary that the mother be able to discern (be conscious of) and regulate her own affect as she interacts with her baby, especially her negative emotions. It is not unusual for a mother to miss or misunderstand what her baby is trying to communicate, resulting in a rupture of the attachment bond. Indeed, Stern (as cited in Wallin, 2007) notes that even among highly sensitive mothers, ruptures occur at least once every 19 seconds! This is not necessarily a bad thing if the rupture is repaired relatively quickly. Indeed, a pattern of disruption and repair between a sensitive and attuned mother and her baby gives the baby a chance to move from a positive to a negative affect and back again, letting the baby learn that a negative affect can be both endured and overcome. In addition, if the mother repairs the rupture reasonably quickly and thus restores comfort and security, her baby learns that mom can be trusted to help her or him out when things go bad, a message that promotes the development of attachment during the attachment-in-the-making stage and leads to clear cut attachment toward the end of the first year.

Clear Cut Attachment: Six Months to Two and a Half Years

As mentioned in the section on the development of the social engagement system above, a mother's consistent, appropriate, attuned, and sensitive interactions with her baby (all associated with the formation of a secure attachment style) stimulate her baby's experience-dependent anterior cingulate and insula. By about the age of nine months, these brain regions will have matured in such a way that the understanding that other people have thoughts and feelings just like she or he does can develop. Moreover, she or he will come to understand that it is possible for both to actually recognize and share their thoughts and feelings. In addition, by the last quarter of the first year, a baby's anterior cingulate will have developed to the point that he or she can pay attention not only to his or her mother but can shift his or her attention to whatever his or her mother is paying attention to (joint attention). That is, if mom points, baby looks. This indicates the development of intersubjectivity (see Chapter 4) and the earliest forms of social engagement (Schore, 2001).

Schore (2001) emphasizes that during the baby's first year, a mother is responsible not just for minimizing her infant's negative emotions through soothing and comforting but also for amplifying and intensifying his or her positive emotions through play. As discussed in Chapter 6, attachment has two purposes: (1) provision of a sense of safety in times of perceived danger and (2) provision of a safe haven from which a child can explore the world. Mom's early regulation of her baby's affect does both of those things. It allows him or her to feel safe and to express curiosity about both self and the environment, particularly after the baby starts to walk.

In his seminal book on attachment and affect regulation, Schore (1994) notes that profound changes occur in the mother-child relationship over the course of infancy and toddlerhood. During this time, the mother's role shifts from being the one who *cares for* her baby to the one who *socializes* her baby. From the time of conception to about one year post birth, babies are carried around (in the belly, in the arms, in a papoose, in a stroller, etc.). However, things change once a child begins to walk and talk. Toward the end of the first year, children tend to experience heightened levels of positive affect associated with their ability to explore and play in their expanding world. They love that their bodies can do things, build things, tear things down, open things, close things, stick things into other things and then pull them out, make noise, and go where they want to go when they want go. Wow! What a world this world is to a two-year-old!

However, as you know if you have ever dealt with a two-year old, he wants what he wants when he wants it. Schore (1994) points out that during toddlerhood, children have higher levels of narcissism than at any other time of life. What are a toddler's favorite words? "No" and "mine." Up until this point, mothers have spent the vast majority of their time (about 90%) in positive interaction with the baby, and the oxytocin and endorphins have been flowing. Seldom (only about 5% of the time) has she had to redirect or correct her infant. In toddlerhood, however, she constantly has to redirect and correct her child so that he or she doesn't get hurt while exploring the environment, but also so that he or she can begin to delay gratification and get along with others. Instead of the goo-goo, ga-ga, look-at-the-pretty-little-baby language he or she has been hearing up to this point, it becomes No! Stop! get-over-here-this-very-instant language. Baby is now running up against all kinds of limitations just when he or she is experiencing in his or her body what feels like unlimited possibility.

This can be a very hard time for toddlers because the smart vagus is not yet fully developed and has only tenuous control over the sympathetic nervous system. The sympathetic nervous system is associated with not only fight/flight responses to fear but also with excitement and joy. Therefore, during early toddlerhood, children are excited a lot of the time and seem to have boundless energy that requires constant monitoring. How mom responds to her toddler's desire to explore and to become an autonomous individual will affect his or her brain development at a critical stage. As discussed above, during the last quarter of the first postnatal year and then extending well into the second year, the OMPFC goes through a growth spurt in which it connects with the amygdala. Strong connection between the OMPFC and the limbic system at this stage of life will allow the child to begin to regulate his or her emotions and responses in later stages. Importantly, development of those connections is highly dependent upon attachment security.

Although toddlers are extremely active and curious about everything in the world, they also are not ready to let mom go completely; they still need to know that the safe haven is still there. During infancy, there was a lot of long, drawn-out eye-gazing going on between mom and baby. However, as Schore (1994) explains, although eye contact between a mother and her toddler is much briefer (averaging about 1.33 seconds), it is still important. The toddler who is exploring his environment will frequently check to see if mom is still there. If she is not there, he will immediately stop exploring and go in search of her. If she is there, though, he will scrutinize her face and eyes for information about her emotions. The toddler is interested not only in what mom thinks about the environment (e.g., does she see danger that he doesn't see?) but also in how mom feels about his exploration. If mom is happy, excited, and supportive, he gains in confidence; he is mastering his world and is proud of himself.

This constant demand for attention places a pretty heavy burden on mom, as you may imagine; how much emotional energy she has or is willing to invest in her interactions with her toddler will affect the security of their attachment bond at this developmental stage. Moreover, how she responds to her toddler influences his understanding of how he or she should react to people, things, and events. As Schore (1994) puts it, her response tells her child "how to feel, how much to feel, and whether to feel" (p. 108), establishing the parameters for how much he or she can enjoy life and how intensely feelings should be expressed. Remember, the memories that a child lays down during this time will probably go into the implicit memory system and become the foundation for his or her developing internal working model of self and other. Remember also from Chapter 7 that these early interactions with mom answer the survival question, *How do I have to be so that I can be with you?* The answer to this question then determines the child's attachment style, solidly set into place by about age two. In addition, these interactions lay down fundamental assumptions about the self, with the child forming the assumption that *I am as I am treated.* These assumptions are, however, completely nonconscious.

By the middle of the infant's second year, though, the hippocampus starts to lay down explicit memories in the left side of the brain that are accompanied by the sensation that the memory is being recalled from the past. When the OMPFC begins to connect to the hippocampus over the next couple of years, the child will begin to develop what is called *autobiographical memory,* that is, a story about who he or she is, where he or she comes from, and what has happened over the course of his or her life. There are two important factors to consider, though. First, language develops rather slowly, so memories between the ages of about two and four may have few words attached to them. An average twelve-month-old has a vocabulary of only about three words, and a fifteen-month-old has only about nineteen words. Thus, when people look back on their toddlerhood, they may not have any explicit (verbal) memories of that time. Secondly, explicit memories will be filtered through those earliest implicit memories, those memories that are laid down during early the attachment relationship with mom.

Fostering Secure Attachment

What has to happen between mothers and their babies so that they can establish secure attachment and consequent positive internal working models of self and other? Siegel (2001) suggests that there are five basic elements of mother-infant relationship (shown in Table 10.1) that need to be in place for this to happen. Let me provide an example of how security can be developed during infancy and toddlerhood. Please read Case Study 10.1 in which I introduce you to little Sophia Ramirez and her parents and provide a little background for Sophia's infancy and toddlerhood. Below, I go on to explore Sophia's and her mother's interactions in the context of Siegel's ideas. I will be introducing you to several other families as we go through the remaining chapters of this book, but let's first take a look at what a securely attached family looks like.

- **Collaboration:** During infancy, mother and baby share contingent communication in which both respond directly to each other's *nonverbal* signals to form a resonant connection in which each "feels felt" by the other. They co-create their experience.

- **Reflective Dialogue:** As the infant begins to understand language, the mother shares *verbally* her own mental states and also verbalizes to her child what she thinks is her child's mental state, thus creating meaning for her child and showing him or her that the emotions, perceptions, ideas, beliefs, and attitudes held in one person's mind can be recognized in, and shared with, another.

- **Repair:** The mother repairs inevitable ruptures in her and her child's contingent communication as quickly and appropriately as she can.

- **Coherent Narratives:** The mother must have a coherent autobiographical narrative of her own life that connects her own past to the present so that she can help her child construct stories about his or her own life experiences that include both activities and the mental life of the people in it.

- **Emotional Communication:** The mother (and other attachment figures) both amplify and personally share in the joyful experiences in her child's life while also remaining connected with her child when he or she is experiencing and acting out negative emotions, helping him or her to reduce his or her distress.

Source: Siegel, D. (2001). Toward an interpersonal neurobiology of the developing mind: Attachment relationships, "mindsight" and neural integration. *Infant Mental Health Journal*, 22(1–2), 67–94.

CASE STUDY 10.1 SOPHIA: BORN INTO LOVE

Nilda Ramirez was considered by some of her friends to be something of a "health nut" who intentionally prepared for her pregnancy for six months before going off the pill. She joined a gym, stopped drinking alcohol entirely, ate well, and took folic acid tablets along with a multiple vitamin every day. Her husband Nelson was thrilled when he found out that they were going to have a baby girl and, though working as a traveling sales representative and frequently away from home, he pitched in to prepare the nursery on weekends.

Nelson and Nilda were overwhelmed with love both for each other and for their baby after they saw the results of their first sonogram. They settled on the name Sophia Maia and planned to call her Sophia. Nelson frequently placed his face close to Nilda's growing belly and hummed songs to Sophia, much to Nilda's delight. A month before her due date, Nilda quit work as a bookkeeper at a small pest control company, planning to spend a minimum of six months as a stay-at-home mom before going back to work. Nelson planned to take family leave for eight weeks and wanted to be an active participant in Sophia's care.

Life was busy around the Ramirez house as the months passed, but Nilda's mother, who lived only two miles away from them, saw her several times a week, even going grocery shopping and doing laundry for Nilda when she began to be tired and uncomfortable toward the end. She moved into the guest bedroom and stayed for a month after Sophia was born so she could be there to provide whatever support Nilda needed.

Nilda's labor was difficult, but after 14 hours, Sophia came wailing into the world and was placed immediately on Nilda's chest. Nilda said later that she thought she was going to simply die from the love she experienced as she felt her daughter wiggle and squirm and heard her little voice for the first time. Nelson, who was holding Nilda's hand and encouraging her throughout the entire process, burst into tears when he saw his daughter and vowed to himself that no harm would ever come to the prettiest little girl who had ever been born.

Nilda had decided to breastfeed Sophia until she returned to work. It was hard at first, feeding her every two hours round the clock, but holding her brought her such a sense of peace and well-being, and because Nilda's mother was there to help, she was able to get adequate sleep and healthy food to eat. The new parents were somewhat anxious at first since they had never taken care of a newborn, but with Nilda's mom's advice, they settled into routines so that within just a couple of months Sophia was sleeping through the night.

Soon they noticed that when Sophia saw her mom's face, she would light up with a smile that just melted their hearts. Nilda's mother returned to her own home a month after Sophia came home but came to visit often, giving Nilda an opportunity to rest. Nelson returned to work after two months. Nilda loved being at home with her baby. She and Sophia played well together, enjoying each other's company. Going back to work after six months was really hard for Nilda; she cried and cried when she left Sophia at day care. But Sophia seemed to thrive in the lively and welcoming day care environment, so Nilda eventually was able to leave her comfortably. Life was good for the Ramirez family.

Siegel's (2001) first element in the mother-child relationship, collaboration, involves "eye contact, facial expressions, tone of voice, bodily gestures and timing and intensity of response [that work together to] create a joining of two minds at a basic level of 'primary emotions'" (p. 78). Chambers (2017) suggests that the interaction between a mother and her baby is akin to a "sensitive and nuanced dance" (p. 545) with both partners contributing through non-verbal communication in a way that allows the baby "to feel understood in a unique way" (p. 545). Similarly, Siegel (2001) emphasizes that this kind of communication is about "feeling felt," not simply about delivering information. He states, "Collaborative communication is far more than sharing linguistic packets of verbally understood words" (p. 84), a very important point since infants don't understand words, and toddlers have limited vocabulary and verbal understanding. For example, imagine that Sophia in Case Study 10.1 is three months old, and her mother Nilda is changing her diaper. Sophia kicks her little feet and smiles. Nilda smiles back and tickles Sophia's feet, making her giggle and kick harder. Then Sophia glances away, feeling overstimulated by the tickling, and Nilda stops amplifying her mood. Thus, Nilda and Sophia work together to find the right amount of stimulation. What Sophia learns from such an attuned interaction is, first, that it is fun to connect with someone else and that social engagement is a good thing. Second, she learns that mom can be trusted to let her be who she is without negative consequences.

In reflective dialogue, the second element, the mother recognizes what kinds of internal experiences her child is trying to communicate and reflects them back to her child. This creates "a sense that subjective experience is both important and can be communicated and shared" (Siegel, 2001, p. 79). For example, imagine that Sophia is 18 months old and is toddling over to her mom in the kitchen. She says, "Cookie" and points at the box of cookies on the counter. Nilda says, "Not now, sweetie, it's time for your lunch." Sophia then frowns and imperiously demands, "COOKIE," to which Nilda says firmly, "Not now." Sophia goes into meltdown (because she is no good at delayed gratification since his OMPFC is not yet well connected with her limbic system and doesn't provide much impulse control) and throws a tantrum. Nilda then stops making lunch, gets down on the floor and says, with her face mirroring Sophia's distress, "I know you really, really want a cookie right now and not getting it makes you really angry. But I'm your mommy, and it is my job to keep you healthy, so I can't give you a cookie right now. We can have one together right after lunch." In this scenario, Nilda mirrors her child's emotions, letting her know that she has been seen and understood. In addition, she has labeled Sophia's feelings as "angry" and shown her what anger looks like on a face. She has also collaborated with her by giving her what she wanted, albeit later than she wanted it, and shown her that this will make her happy, too. According to Siegel, when reflective dialogue is combined with collaboration, the two processes result in reciprocal communication of mental states and support the child's development of mentalization, or as Siegel terms it, "mindsight" (p.79) (i.e., my mind can see your mind, and your mind can see mine).

The third element of the mother-child relationship, repair, is critically important to secure attachment. The rupture of attuned communication is inevitable, and as mentioned above, not necessarily a bad thing since it can "teach the child that life is filled with inevitable moments of misunderstandings and missed connections that can be identified and connection created again" (Siegel, 2001, p. 79). For example, picture Sophia as a six-month-old infant who is hungry. However, Nilda has been on the phone for the last half hour with her mother-in-law who just won't stop talking. Therefore, Sophia has been experiencing intense negative emotion for what to her seems like forever—I'M HUNGRY, AND I'M GOING TO DIE IF I DON'T GET FED THIS VERY INSTANT. When Nilda finally gets to hang up (Whew!), she repairs this rupture by recognizing that Sophia is miserable. She engages in reflective dialogue by picking Sophia up and saying in soothing baby talk and with a look of misery on her face that mirrors Sophia's look of misery, "Aw, poor little baby is so hungry and upset, poor little thing. Let's get that sweet thing fed." Because she has been seen and her misery recognized, and because Nilda responds to her distress and takes her discomfort away, Sophia replies to her by stopping crying and putting an expression on her face that tells Nilda, "I'm feeling better now, let's eat."

The fourth element that fosters attachment, coherent narrative, refers to the mental health of the mother. In Chapter 5, I discussed Siegel's (2003) ideas concerning the need for various forms of neural integration (e.g., cortical-subcortical, left brain-right brain, etc.). One of those forms of integration is called *narrative integration* in which we develop a coherent story (mediated by our autobiographical memory) concerning who we are and what we have done that lets us make sense of our lives and the world we live in. This story is constructed from both right-brain-implicit, often preverbal, memories as well as left-brain-explicit memories that are often experienced with words. When a mother is able to make sense of, and verbalize, her past and can let those memories inform her present situation and circumstances, she is able to reflectively and collaboratively co-construct her child's perception of the world.

In Sophia's case, imagine that Nilda was loved and cared for by her own mother and father (and probably members of her extended family, too). She developed a secure attachment style, and her brain developed well during her childhood so that her OMPFC connected with her limbic system in such a way that she was able to develop both emotional regulation and autobiographical memory. Therefore, she can make sense out of her own life by reflecting on the events that happened to her and her family as well as on the mental lives of both herself and other important people in her life. This allows her to remain present with Sophia rather than becoming stuck in past pain or a terrifying future.

The last element for the fostering of attachment suggested by Siegel (2001) is emotional communication. This element derives from the other four. That is, when a mentally healthy mother engages with her child during the first three years of life with collaborative, contingent communication and reflective dialogue, her child will "feel felt" and have a sense of connection to others. When that mother responds to ruptures in attuned communication in a consistently and predictably loving way, her child will feel safe and will look forward to exploring the world around her.

In Sophia's case, when Sophia (at three months of age) stops playing with her mom and looks away, Nilda doesn't jump to the conclusion that Sophia doesn't love her and react with fear or anger; she realizes that Sophia just needs a little rest. When Sophia goes into meltdown over a cookie as a toddler, Nilda doesn't take it as a personal attack on her authority; she sets limits in a loving way without shaming Sophia or losing her temper. Because Nilda's family provided her with experiences that allowed her to develop empathy, she can meet Sophia's negative affects with compassion, thus building and strengthening their attachment bond. The message Sophia gets repeatedly is that sometimes bad things happen in life, but mom can be trusted to take care of her. She learns that even though life may be painful sometimes, pain isn't permanent. Sophia's repeated experiences of her mother's joyful interactions with her, as well as her mother's repeated acceptance of her negative affects, provide Sophia an answer to the all-important question *How do I have to be so that I can be with you?* The answer for her is: I can be however I am, and my mom will still love me and be there for me. At the same time, since Sophia knows at an instinctual level that *I am as I am treated*, she will form the implicit and nonconscious assumption that she is, at her core, both loved and lovable. This is the essence of security.

It is important to note that in each of these scenarios, security was provided not through toys, beautiful clothing, or high-tech strollers and digital gadgets. Security was provided through intensive, consistent, timely and attuned face-to-face mother-child interaction and through repair of inevitable (and useful) rupture. As Siegel makes clear:

> The heart of the emotional transactions with the growing child can be described as being the sharing and amplification of positive emotional states, and the sharing and reduction of negative states. These repeated and reliable emotional transactions allow a child to feel connected to the world. It is also these communications that allow a child to initially rely on the caregiver for help in regulating her own emotions, and then later to develop a more autonomous form of flexible self-regulation. In this manner attuned emotional communication with secure attachments leads to a healthy and flexible capacity of self-regulation. (p. 85)

Summary

In this chapter, we have learned how the human brain is structured to support the giving and receiving of care. The CARE/nurturing and SEEKING systems in adults' brains urge them to provide the experiences that their young children need to survive and thrive in the world, while the GRIEF/separation and SEEKING systems in the brains of infants and children urge them to attach to their caregivers and maintain proximity to them through their attachment behavioral systems. We also learned how the brain develops during pregnancy and after the baby is born, stressing the importance of both genetic and environmental influences on healthy development of the social engagement system and the right hemisphere. Lastly, we learned how attachment can begin even before a baby is born and how secure attachment can be optimized through collaborative, contingent communication and reflective dialogue between mother and baby, and timely repair of ruptures in their attuned communication. In the next chapter, I will discuss some of the things that can go wrong before a baby is born, resulting in the increased probability of a child developing insecure attachment and impaired mental and emotional functioning. Then in Chapter 12, I will identify how things can go wrong for infants and toddlers.

CHAPTER 11

Prenatal Challenges to Brain Development

LEARNING OBJECTIVES

After completing this chapter, readers should understand that:

- Chronic stress can interfere both with a woman's ability to conceive and with her baby's brain development.
- Prenatal stress can result in poor postnatal neurodevelopment and cognitive development, difficult temperament, and mental and physical health problems.
- A woman's history of interpersonal trauma can affect her levels of stress hormones and thereby place the fetus' developing HPA system at risk.
- That the use of psychoactive substances during pregnancy can place a baby at increased risk of growth deficits, attention problems or ADHD, problems with executive functioning, depression, anxiety, future substance use and abuse, and intellectual disability associated with Fetal Alcohol Syndrome.

KEY IDEAS

1. Infertility issues may arise among women who have experienced chronic stress since the body perceives the environment as being less than optimal for reproduction.
2. Fetal brain cells are structured at the molecular level by the intrauterine environment, and stress, anxiety, or depression during pregnancy can program the baby's central nervous system and HPA stress response systems (fight/flight/freeze) for hyper-reactivity to stress.
3. A maternal history of interpersonal trauma is associated with prenatal PTSD, and women with prenatal PTSD are at increased risk of substance abuse, eating disorders, and suicidality.
4. Alcohol, illicit drugs, and some prescribed medications can pass the fetal blood-brain barrier and negatively affect fetal brain development.
5. Alcohol or drug use in the first trimester of pregnancy may interrupt the manufacture, migration, and organization of fetal brain cells on which the remainder of the brain will be built, possibly resulting in permanent and catastrophic structural and functional deficits.

Introduction

As McCarty and Glenn (2009) have pointed out, many women of childbearing age in the world are very vulnerable, including

- adolescent girls whose bodies and brains are not yet fully developed;
- those who have suffered trauma or loss during or even before their childbearing years;
- those who have developed PTSD or dissociative disorders because of that trauma;
- those who have experienced or are currently suffering from the chronic stress of racism and discrimination, incarceration, or homelessness;
- those who are malnourished due to poverty or eating disorders;
- those with addiction or other mental or physical illnesses.

The children of these women are at heightened risk of a wide variety of negative outcomes, including many of the psychopathologies that mental health practitioners address. In the previous chapter, I discussed general factors that influence pre- and postnatal brain development and the development of secure attachment. In this chapter, I will discuss how things can go wrong during this life stage.

Before beginning, however, I think it is important to remember what should be happening during infancy and toddlerhood for optimal development. According to Erikson (1963), infancy is the *Basic Trust vs. Basic Mistrust* stage in which the main developmental task is for the infant to gain a sense that the world is a reasonably safe place and that his or her needs are going to be taken care of. This sense of safety is provided by a caregiver who meets the baby's physical, emotional and social needs reasonably well (a good-enough parent). If those needs are not well met, the infant will develop an assumption (completely nonconscious and completely unavailable for rational analysis) that he or she is not safe. Moreover, the sympathetic and vegetative vagal systems will predominate over the smart vagal system, resulting in amplified fight/flight and freeze responses to stress.

During toddlerhood, Erikson's (1963) *Autonomy vs. Shame and Doubt* stage, the main developmental task for children is to gain self-confidence and a sense of mastery over their bodies and environment by using their newly developed motor skills. If you have ever spent any time around a toddler, you may have noticed that it appears that their two favorite words are "No!" and "Mine!" (although my nephew Matthew's favorite word was "bacon!"). This behavior is completely normal; they are simply trying to exert agency over their world, looking for where the limits are, finding out how things work and how much they can do (and if they can get mom to fry up some bacon). Toddlers are biologically driven to explore their environments, and they need to be allowed to do so within the bounds of safety. According to Erikson, if they are not allowed a certain amount of autonomy in this exploration of self and surroundings, they will develop a deep sense of shame and begin to doubt their ability to manage themselves and their world. Remember that the assumptions they make about themselves at this stage are stored mostly in the right brain and thus are not available for conscious analysis.

In the previous chapter, I introduced you to the Ramirez family and their daughter Sophia (Case Study 10.1), a close-knit and loving family who appear to be securely attached. In this chapter, I would like to introduce you to Sally Weisman and her sons Jet and Luke in Case

Studies 11.1 and 11.2 and consider the unfortunate events that lead to the boys' adoption by Helen and Hank Wolverton discussed in the next chapter. Keep these case studies in mind as well as the developmental tasks mentioned above as you read the sections below. I begin with a section on the challenges associated with getting pregnant. Next, I discuss how maternal stress, anxiety and depression, unresolved trauma or loss, and substance abuse can negatively affect the fetal brain, followed by a discussion of how these same factors can negatively affect brain development after the baby is born.

CASE STUDY 11.1 JET: A ROUGH BEGINNING

Sally Weisman was 16 years old when she got pregnant. She had no idea who the father was because she had been trading sex for drugs (methamphetamine and crack co-caine) for the past year and had had sex with maybe 50 boys and men. She had been living with her mom and dad and going to school sporadically, but they never really paid attention to where she was or what she was doing. They had never wanted her and were quick to tell her so. She had few memories of her childhood, but what she did remember were the angry faces and voices directed at her. In addition, her father had sexually abused her starting at age seven. She didn't dare tell her mother for fear of getting a beating from her. It was even possible that the baby was his. When they found out she was pregnant, her parents threw her out of the house.

Homeless and unable to get a job, she began prostituting herself to survive. She was given a place to live by a man she met on the street in return for turning over whatever she earned to him. He also kept her supplied with drugs in return for sexual favors. Although he was kind to her in the beginning, when her pregnancy couldn't be hidden any longer, he started beating her and telling her how fat and ugly she was. Finally, he turned her out onto the streets again. Stunned and desperate, Sally wandered the streets for two days before running into another prostitute who she knew and had been friendly with. She told her what had happened, and this girl let her sleep on her couch and shared her food with her when she could.

Sally drank alcohol and used drugs throughout her pregnancy, adding heroin to the mix after she moved in with her friend. She wasn't exactly sure how far along she was in her pregnancy since she had never seen a doctor, but when she realized she was in labor, she was pretty sure it was early. She gave birth to a four-pound, eight ounce baby boy in the emergency room. He was taken away immediately and placed on a respirator because of breathing irregularities; she didn't even get a chance to look at him. Lying exhausted and alone in her hospital bed after the delivery, Sally decided to name him Jet, after a dog the family had had, the only one she could count on for comfort. When they let her see Jet six hours later, she was overwhelmed with anxiety; he was so very small! He had tubes in his nose and a needle taped to his arm. She couldn't imagine how she was going to take care of him, but she knew she wanted to give him a better life than she had had.

Jet went into withdrawal when he was born since he was no longer getting any heroin through his mother's bloodstream, and the hospital called child protective services (CPS) because of their concerns for his welfare. Sally begged her mom and dad to let her return home with the baby, just until she could get on her feet, and they reluctantly agreed. Sally stopped using drugs and attended parenting groups in compliance with CPS requirements, and she did everything she could not to antagonize her parents; she was terrified that CPS would take her baby from her and that she would never see him again. He was, she said, the best thing that had ever happened to her. But when she came home one afternoon after leaving Jet in the care of her mother, Sally found cigarette burns on his chest. She immediately packed the baby up and disappeared onto the streets again.

Sally continued to prostitute herself to put food on the table and to pay for the small room she rented, and, of course, she started to use alcohol and drugs again. She allowed many men into her home, and there were frequent loud parties, violence, and chaos. She fed Jet at odd times, left him in soggy diapers, and often simply did not respond when he cried. Sometimes she would bare her teeth and growl at him when a client was disturbed by his crying. When she did this, Jet would get very quiet and not move for several minutes.

Things got a bit better for Jet when Sally got pregnant again. She cut way back on her drug use and was more aware of his needs. However, shortly before Jet's brother was born, Sally started using meth again. The doctors discovered her drug use and called CPS. Because Sally had left Jet at home unattended when she went into labor, CPS removed both him and his newborn brother, who Sally named Luke after her favorite *Star Wars* character, and placed them in foster care. She could get them back if she complied with their requirements—substance abuse treatment, parenting classes, and full-time employment. CPS helped Sally find a job and a safer place to live, and this time she made a real effort to change her life. After six months, CPS allowed her to take her children back. Unfortunately, six weeks later, Sally was found dead from a heroin overdose. Jet and Luke had lived for two days with no care at all. When the police and CPS arrived, Luke was listless, and Jet was terrified. They were again placed into foster care and put up for adoption.

When the boys arrived at their foster home, Jet was a year and a half old, and Luke was seven months old. Jet was underweight and dehydrated, and his body showed evidence of both physical and sexual abuse. He did not like to be touched. For six months after his arrival, he woke frequently during the night, screaming and inconsolable. His foster mother eventually gave up trying to calm him and left him to cry himself back to sleep. "The truth is," she said to Jet's case manager, "I just don't like the child; he's too much trouble, more than anyone can handle."

Luke, on the other hand, was different from his brother. He seldom cried and would lie in his crib in the morning, sucking his fingers, making silly noises, or simply staring at the mobile dancing in the sunlight overhead. He would eat hungrily whenever fed but would not look his foster mother in the eye while she was feeding him. She was, however, completely charmed by Luke when he would smile at her. She would pick him up and carry him around with her, chatting to him about whatever she was doing. If he got fussy, she would put him back in his crib and leave the room.

The foster mother found it hard to believe that the boys were so different. When Luke started walking and talking, rather than being noisy and active, he was mostly quiet and passive. Jet, however, continued to act out in many ways as he got older. He would explode in rage for no apparent reason, resisted redirection, threw horrific tantrums, and even physically attacked his foster mother. When his brother acted out like this, Luke would put his thumb in his mouth and get a distant look in his eye, as if he couldn't hear or see anything his brother was doing. Sometimes the foster mother would hear Luke whimpering in his room, but when she would come to see what he was doing, he would grow quiet and look away from her. Truthfully, she was glad that Luke was so quiet and required so little care since Jet demanded so much attention. She could leave Luke quietly entertaining himself for hours at a time while she chased Jet around and cleaned up whatever mess he was making. She was relieved when Jet and Luke were adopted together three years later by a family who lived several states away.

CLASS DISCUSSION

Which childhood attachment style do you think Jet is developing? Which do you think Luke is likely to develop?

Challenges to Conception

Infertility is a relatively common issue that affects about 10% to 20% of couples of childbearing age (Center for Disease Control and Prevention, 2018c; Jacobs, Boynton-Jarrett, & Harville, 2015; Suna et al., 2016). Aside from the obvious problems of low sperm counts and poor sperm motility, ovarian dysfunction, tubal issues, and timing of sexual intercourse, a number of other issues can affect a woman's ability to get pregnant. Stress is one of the factors that may contribute to these problems. Sometimes the stress is related to the attempt to conceive itself. As Noorhasen (2014) has pointed out, there are many anecdotes about couples waiting months or years to have a baby and then getting pregnant shortly after adopting a child. However, other research has shown that chronic stress occurring in the woman's early life, especially the stress of abuse, neglect, parental substance abuse, and family violence, may result in fertility issues later in life (Jacobs et al., 2015). These problems probably are due to alterations in the functioning of the HPA (stress) system that suppresses fertility because the body perceives the environment as being less than optimal for reproduction.

As Carter and Porges (2011) have made clear, feeling safe allows social animals to relax and enjoy each other's company, while feeling unsafe triggers fight/flight/freeze responses. Although women obviously can get pregnant whether they enjoy sexual intercourse or not (e.g., in the case of rape), a lack of safety results in a lack of oxytocin in the bloodstream. That lack of oxytocin and the consequent lack of feelings of well-being and emotional warmth may result in attenuated sexual desire and inhibited sexual intercourse. Moreover, since oxytocin is involved in the birthing process itself as well as in bonding and breastfeeding, having a safe environment for loving sexual activity and support from a loving partner or other caring individual(s) throughout pregnancy and during the perinatal period is of primary importance.

Challenges to Prenatal Brain Development

Maternal stress can also be problematic after a woman gets pregnant. Stressors may come in many forms, ranging from the extremes of natural disasters or the death of a loved one to domestic violence and family chaos to relationship problems, stressful work environments, and illnesses to daily hassles and annoyances (Glover, 2014; Kinney, Munir, Crowley, & Miller, 2008). Moreover, the intrauterine environment is affected not only by the mother's physical state but also by her psychological state.

It is not uncommon for women to have mental health issues during pregnancy, with research showing that between 8% and 12% of pregnant women meet DSM criteria for a mental disorder (Fisher et al., 2012; Howard et al., 2015). Unfortunately, this may be an underestimation of the problem since other research shows that about 30% of pregnant women report some kind of daily stress, such as job strain or symptoms of anxiety or depression for which they may not seek professional help where a diagnosis would be recorded (Van den Bergh et al., 2017). The stress of depression, anxiety (especially anxiety concerning pregnancy), bereavement, or emotions associated with a poor relationship with a partner can all affect the baby's developing brain (Glover, 2014). Moreover, if a woman has trouble finding a balance between personal, family, and work issues, the pregnancy itself may become the source of additional stress (Van den Bergh et al., 2017).

Another major challenge to fetal brain development is maternal prenatal substance use and abuse. Substance use may be associated with the woman's attempt to manage her stress, anxiety and/or depression, or it may be an ongoing lifestyle choice or addiction. In any case, alcohol and drug use (whether recreational or prescribed) during pregnancy can result in catastrophic impacts on fetal brain development. In this section, I will first discuss the effects of maternal prenatal stress, anxiety, and depression and then the effects of substance use during pregnancy. To help place these issues in context, please make sure you have read Case Studies 11.1 and 11.2 concerning Sally Weisman and her sons Jet and Luke, and keep them in mind as you read the sections below on challenges to prenatal brain development.

Stress, Anxiety, and Depression During Pregnancy

In the previous chapter, I explained the process of *programming* in which fetal brain cells are structured at the molecular level by the intrauterine environment. Glynn and Sandman (2011) argue that

> The human fetus has evolved mechanisms to acquire information about the environment and guide its development. ... the fetal-placental unit's detection of stress signals from the maternal environment (e.g., cortisol) "informs" the fetus that there may be a threat to survival. This information primes or advances

the placental clock, resulting in earlier delivery. Concurrently, the fetus adjusts its developmental trajectory, modifying its nervous system to ensure survival. (p. 384)

In other words, maternal stress can result in both premature birth (with consequent immaturity of the brain and other internal organs) and programming of the baby's central nervous system and HPA stress response systems (fight/flight/freeze) for hyper-reactivity to stress. Kinney et al. (2008) summarize the effects of prenatal stress on postnatal functioning, saying

many different studies—involving different species, research designs, types of prenatal stressors, and measures of postnatal sensitivity to stress—have found that prenatal stress tends to produce a number of behavioral abnormalities, such as making individuals hyperaroused when faced with novel or challenging postnatal stimuli. (p. 1525)

These researchers suggest that when the maternal prenatal environment presents stressful challenges, the mother's stress hormones (some of which are passed on to her fetus through the placenta) increase. Moderate levels of maternal stress hormones are important to the normal development of the fetal brain during the third trimester, encouraging neuronal maturation and myelination (Glynn & Sandman, 2011; Lupien et al., 2009). However, too much results in an HPA system that does not develop normally over the long term. Effects can include cognitive abnormalities such as impaired attention and increased distractibility, neurological abnormalities such as seizure disorders and neuroinflammation, and immune system impairment. These researchers also note that, at least in animals, adverse effects do not occur just in response to severe or chronic prenatal stress but also in response even to relatively moderate or brief stressors (Kinney et al., 2008).

Numerous studies have found correlations between maternal prenatal stress and later offspring psychopathology, including anxiety, depression, ADHD, and even autism and schizophrenia (Babenko et al., 2015; Brannigan et al., 2019; Kinney et al., 2008). In addition, prenatal stress has been implicated in infant/toddler sleep problems, impaired cognitive performance, increased fearfulness, and difficult temperament as well as emotional and behavioral problems (anxiety, depression, ADHD and conduct disorder) in later childhood (Glover, 2014; Van den Bergh et al., 2017). Van den Bergh et al. (2017) conducted a very thorough systematic review of articles concerning prenatal stress and offspring outcomes from infancy through late adolescence in the areas of neural and cognitive development, temperament, and mental health (please see Table 11.1). The list of mental health disorders associated with prenatal stress should be of real interest to mental health practitioners since so many of the disorders we treat may have their origins in utero. Indeed, a review of the literature on fetal programming and postnatal mental health found research showing that fully 87% of male ADHD cases were predicted by perceived level of stress during pregnancy (Babenko et al., 2015). This is not to suggest that the postnatal environment is not influential, of course. Nor is it to suggest that all prenatal stress inevitably results in serious mental illness or cognitive impairment. However, research makes clear that stress during pregnancy has the clear potential to affect human development negatively to some significant degree across the entire life span.

TABLE 11.1 Effects of Prenatal Stress on Postnatal Development

Neurodevelopment:
- Poor state regulation
- Sleep problems
- Neurobehavioral maturity
- Decreased gross and fine motor skill development (especially boys)
- HPA system development (both higher and lower cortisol reactivity)
- ANS development
  - Higher baseline fetal heart rate and lower vagal tone
  - Impaired immune functioning

Cognitive Development:
- Decreased word comprehension and vocabulary development
- Decreased non-verbal communication
- Lower IQ
- Decreased problem-solving ability

Temperament:
- Negative affectivity and difficult temperament
- Arrhythmic temperament
- Irritable temperament
- Active-reactive temperament

Mental Health:
- Externalizing problems (aggressiveness and conduct disorders)
- Internalizing problems (anxiety and depression)
- Attention disorders
- Bipolar disorder
- PTSD
- Borderline personality disorder
- Eating disorders
- Schizophrenia
- Psychosis
- Suicide attempts and completions
- Autistic traits
- Impulsivity
- Impaired social behavior
- Other psychiatric problems

Physical Health:
- Altered gut microbiome
  - Weak immune system (more illness)
  - Metabolic problems (development of diabetes and metabolic syndrome)
  - Accelerated aging

Source: Van den Bergh et al. (2017). Prenatal developmental origins of behavior and mental health: Influence of maternal stress in pregnancy. *Neuroscience and Biobehavioral Reviews*, no pagination. Doi: https://doi.org/10.1016/j.neubiorev.2017.07.003

Kinney et al. (2008) suggest that maternal stress may affect fetal brain development through one or a combination of several mechanisms. For example, it can result in reduced blood flow to the placenta, with a consequent reduction in fetal oxygen availability. In addition, it can cause obstetric complications such as extended labor that can also cause low fetal oxygen levels as well as cerebral hemorrhage. The fetus may produce high levels of testosterone in response to its mother's stress, a factor associated specifically with the development of autism, poor social functioning, and lack of empathy. Moreover, maternal stress may produce epigenetic changes in the fetus's HPA system that can produce lifelong over-reactivity to stress that can be passed down to the next generation. The mechanisms that drive the negative effects of a mother's mood disorder on her developing fetus are not yet well understood. However, it appears that her mood affects the delicate balance between the hormones and neurotransmitters that structure the developing fetus' arousal and emotional regulation systems (Gao et al., 2019).

One important factor influencing outcomes associated with prenatal stress and mental health is the *timing* of it (Glynn & Sandman, 2011). There are sensitive periods throughout gestation in which a disturbance in the uterine environment can influence whatever happens to be developing within the body and brain of the fetus at that time. As van den Bergh et al., (2017) puts it, "the entire length of gestation represents a series of critical periods that are each vulnerable for one or more offspring outcomes, since different functions and structures of the brain are developing in each period" (p. 21). As mentioned in the previous chapter, the fetus is particularly vulnerable during early gestation because it is during this time that the foundations are laid for the brain and other important organs. During early gestation, the placenta offers some protection against maternal stress hormones. However, about halfway through the pregnancy (between weeks 19 and 26), the barrier becomes less active, leaving the fetus's brain vulnerable to the mother's stress (Glover, 2014). Other research has found that children whose mothers had experienced a major hurricane during the fifth or sixth month of their pregnancy were almost four times more likely to develop autism than women who didn't experience that trauma (Kinney et al., 2008). Unfortunately, there is not much research on windows of prenatal vulnerability yet, so we are unable to predict when a fetus is at heightened risk for specific developmental problems.

Maternal History of Trauma

One very important stressor that can affect both fetal development and later child outcomes is a maternal history of interpersonal trauma. Research shows that women who have experienced childhood abuse are 12 times more likely than those without an abuse history to have prenatal PTSD (Seng, Low, Sperlich, Ronis, & Liberzon, 2011). In addition, they are at increased risk of having clinical levels of depression, generalized anxiety, somatization, dissociation, or emotional dysregulation during their pregnancies (Seng, D'Andrea, & Ford, 2014). In turn, women with PTSD during pregnancy are at increased risk of substance abuse, eating disorders, and suicidality (Schwerdtfeger & Goff, 2007). All of these mental health issues can affect the mother's levels of stress hormones and place the fetus's developing HPA system at risk.

Substance Use During Pregnancy

Recent research shows that the brains of between 11 and 50 children per 1,000 have been affected by their mother's use of alcohol during pregnancy (May et al., 2018). Illicit drug use, such as methamphetamines, cocaine, heroin, fentanyl, marijuana, etc., can also pass the blood-brain barrier and affect fetal brain development directly. However, drugs that do not have direct effects on the fetus may still mimic the physiological effects of stress, with similar negative outcomes. Moreover, symptoms similar to those found among children whose mothers used alcohol during pregnancy can be found among the children of mothers who used prescribed drugs (e.g., drugs used for general anesthesia or anti-seizure medication) during their pregnancies (Creeley & Olney, 2013). Thus, it is clear that use of psychoactive substances during pregnancy should be avoided unless not using them would result in even worse effects.

According to Ross, Graham, Money, and Stanwood (2015), use of psychoactive drugs is associated with a host of neurodevelopmental, physical, behavioral, and mental health problems. Maternal use of almost all drugs of abuse place the developing fetus at increased risk of growth

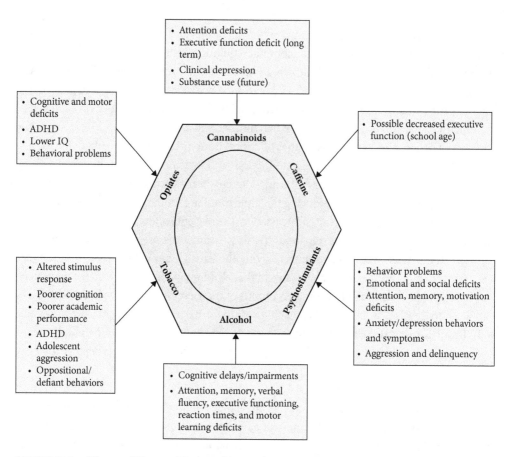

FIGURE 11.1   Effects of Maternal Prenatal Drug Abuse

Adapted from Emily J Ross, et al., Schematic Summary of Effects of Distinct Drug Classes on Offspring Development from "Developmental Consequences of Fetal Exposure to Drugs: What We Know and What We Still Must Learn," Neuropsychppharmacology, vol. 40, no. 1, pp. 77. Copyright © 2015 by Springer Nature.

deficits both in the womb and after birth, including infancy through adolescence. These deficits are not limited just to birth weight and physical size but are also apparent in head circumference, brain volume, and brain anomalies. Moreover, heart/cardiovascular formation and functioning as well as respiratory functioning may be compromised among children born to mothers who abuse drugs during their pregnancies.

Of particular interest to mental health practitioners are the effects of maternal prenatal drug use shown in Figure 11.1 since many of the disorders we treat may originate there.

For example, attention problems or ADHD are related to maternal use of cannabis (e.g., marijuana, hashish, etc.), psychostimulants (e.g., methamphetamine, amphetamine, MDMA (Ecstasy), cocaine), alcohol, tobacco, and opiates (e.g., heroin, fentanyl, morphine, etc.). Problems with executive functioning (decision making, problems solving, emotional control, impulsivity, etc.) are associated with maternal prenatal use of cannabis, caffeine, psychostimulants, alcohol, tobacco, and opiates. In addition, depression, anxiety and future substance use are all related to mother's use of cannabis while pregnant (Ross et al., 2015).

Although alcohol is a psychoactive substance that is widely used in western society (and legal over the age of 21), it is related to a number of detrimental neurobehavioral effects, even when used in moderation (Ross et al., 2015). The term **fetal alcohol spectrum disorders (FASD)** is used to characterize a range of deficits associated with maternal prenatal use of this substance. FASD is considered one of the leading causes of intellectual disabilities in the Western world and is entirely preventable. That is, if a woman does not drink alcohol during her pregnancy, her baby is 100% sure not to be born with an FASD.

Disorders included under the umbrella of FASD are fetal alcohol syndrome (FAS), alcohol-related neurodevelopmental disorder (ARND), alcohol-related birth defects (ARBD), and neuro-behavioral disorder associated with prenatal alcohol exposure (ND-PAE) (see Table 11.2 for a list of symptoms commonly found among children on the FASD spectrum). It should be noted that symptoms of FASD disorders can present as a mixture of problems and can range from mild to severe. Some children may present with facial or cranial abnormalities, although the majority of affected children do not. How severe the effects are depends on how often the mother drank, how much she drank, and at what point in the pregnancy she drank. For example, when a woman drinks during the first trimester of her pregnancy, she may interrupt the manufacture, migration, and organization of her baby's brain cells on which the remainder of the brain will be built (CDC, 2018b), while drinking during the third trimester has been linked to malformations in the cerebellum, hippocampus, and prefrontal cortex (Davis, Desrocher, & Moore, 2011). These structural and functional deficits can have permanent and catastrophic effects.

TABLE 11.2   Symptoms Associated with Fetal Alcohol Spectrum Disorders

- Abnormal facial features, such as a smooth ridge between the nose and upper lip (this ridge is called the philtrum), wide-set eyes
- Sleep and sucking problems as a baby
- Small head size
- Growth problems: Shorter-than-average height, low body weight
- Poor overall intellectual functioning; low IQ
- Poor memory and learning disabilities; poor academic performance (esp. math)
- Speech and language delays; problems with writing
- Slow reaction times
- Delayed motor development; poor coordination; problems with procedural learning
- Hyperactive behavior
- Difficulty with attention, perseveration, attention shifts
- Deficits in executive: self-regulation, working memory, cognitive flexibility, inhibition/impulsivity, planning, organization, judgement, cause-effect
- Mental health problems: depression, anxiety, withdrawal, oppositional-defiant, hyperactivity, psychosis
- Behavioral functioning: delinquency, lying/cheating/stealing, lack of guilt, cruelty, social skills deficits
- Physical abnormalities: vision, hearing, heart, kidneys, bones

According to Davis et al. (2011), researchers believe that the wide range of symptoms associated with FASD is a result of one or a combination of factors, including reductions in brain size, asymmetrical growth of the hippocampus (memory, learning, visuospatial functioning), damage to the cerebellum (procedural learning, coordination, and balance), and/or atypical patterns of pruning and myelination (slow reactions). In addition, many of the problems seen in individuals with FASD appear to be related to atypical development of the corpus callosum. If you remember from Chapter 2, the corpus callosum is the structure that separates the left and right hemispheres of the brain and allows the two sides to communicate effectively with each other. In individuals with FASD, this structure may be only partially developed or, in severe cases, completely absent. Without a well-formed corpus callosum, the individual will have difficulty performing tasks that require coordination of the hemispheres, such as learning, reading, verbal memory, and executive or social functioning. In addition, the facial abnormalities that are found in some individuals with FASD appear to be related to an absence of growth in the middle areas of the head, the same area in which the corpus callosum is located.

There are two things that I would like to stress to mental health practitioners concerning prenatal alcohol use. First, FASDs are often accompanied by co-morbid mental health issues. According to Davis et al. (2011), six secondary disabilities are very likely be found in individuals with FASD (percentages are shown in parentheses): mental health problems (90%), school problems (60%), problems with law enforcement (60%), mandated residential treatment or incarceration (50%), sexual acting out (50%), and/or substance use problems (30%). It is important, then, to assess individuals who come into our offices for possible prenatal exposure to alcohol so that we can make sense of, and have compassion for, their maladaptive behaviors. FASD is, after all, brain damage that occurred before the individual was even born.

CLASS DISCUSSION

How many mental health issues can you identify in Case Studies 11.1 and 11.2, and how may they affect the outcome of those pregnancies?

Secondly, I am constantly amazed when I teach about FASD in my classes that my students will tell me that their doctor told them that it was okay to drink a glass of wine during their pregnancy. There is no doubt that many women who have consumed alcohol while they were pregnant went on to give birth to healthy children who had no observable ill effects and who matured into happy and productive citizens. However, the risk is there, be it ever so small. FASDs are 100% preventable; if a pregnant woman doesn't pick up an alcoholic drink, she cannot drink to excess or drink during a sensitive developmental period. Therefore, if a woman is trying to get pregnant, or if she thinks there may be a chance that she is pregnant, it is my opinion that she should stop drinking. Remember that some of the worst neurodevelopmental effects can happen even before she realizes that there is a baby growing in there.

Summary

In this chapter, I have emphasized the negative effects that maternal stress can have on conception and pregnancy outcomes. Stress can make it difficult to get pregnant to begin with, either by making sexual activity less attractive or by prompting the body to delay reproduction or miscarry. After conception occurs, stress can affect fetal brain growth, organization, and functioning, programming the developing brain at a molecular level to be hyper-reactive to subsequent stress. Thus, stress reduction before and during pregnancy is strongly advised.

A history of interpersonal trauma is a significant risk factor for maternal stress, anxiety, and depression, and in an attempt to self-medicate these issues, a woman may resort to substance use and abuse, placing her unborn baby at increased risk of multiple, and sometimes catastrophic, physical and mental health problems. It is important, then, that mental health practitioners assess carefully for mental health and substance use problems among clients who are or want to become pregnant so that their babies have the best chance to have a healthy beginning. In the next chapter, I will discuss some of the issues that infants and toddlers face, focusing primarily on the factors that promote disorganized attachment.

CHAPTER 12

Infant and Toddler Attachment Challenges

LEARNING OBJECTIVES

After completing this chapter, readers should be able to identify:
- How disorganized/disoriented children tend to present for clinical observation.
- Primary and secondary frightening/frightened behaviors associated with disturbed attachment.
- The effects of child neglect on attachment representations and childhood behaviors.
- The effects of maternal psychological problems on childhood attachment processes.

KEY IDEAS

1. Frightening maternal behaviors such as those that occur in maltreatment can cause high levels of fear in a child and consequent alterations in brain structure and functioning as well as disorganized attachment.
2. Primary frightening/frightened maternal behaviors include dissociative behaviors as well as hostility, intrusiveness, aversive rejection, environmental chaos/violence, and frightened facial expressions.
3. Secondary frightening maternal behaviors associated with the development of disorganized attachment include timid or deferential behaviors, sexualized behaviors, or behaviors associated with the mother's own disorganized/disoriented attachment style.
4. Extreme childhood neglect can result in a diagnosis of reactive attachment disorder or disinhibited social engagement disorder.
5. The risk of disorganized attachment is increased among children whose mothers are diagnosed with substance abuse, postpartum anxiety and depression, or other mental health disorders.

Introduction

As was made clear in Chapter 7, mothers who respond to their infant's dependency needs inconsistently tend to produce an anxious/ambivalent attachment style in their children while those who reward independence or punish age-appropriate dependent behaviors tend to produce children with an avoidant style. Benoit (2004) explains that both of these attachment styles are considered to be insecure but *organized* styles. That is, these mothers have not been physically or emotionally available, or they have not been optimally responsive, sensitive, or attuned to their children's needs. Therefore, they have not promoted the developments of secure attachment. However, their children have managed somehow to organize their proximity-seeking behaviors in ways that have succeeded in getting the attention they require (through hyperactivation or deactivation strategies). However according to Lyons-Ruth and Jacobvitz (2017), approximately 15% of infants from middle-class families and 34% of infants from low-income families are unable to organize a set of behaviors that work reliably to relieve their attachment needs. These infants tend to form what is called a disorganized/disoriented attachment style characterized by a collapse of attentional and behavioral strategies when they are under stress (Hesse & Main, 2006) and result in the observable behaviors shown in Table 12.1.

TABLE 12.1   Disorganized/Disoriented Behaviors Observed During the Strange Situation

- Sequential display of contradictory behavior patterns: For example, the crying infant dashes to the parent, then immediately falls silent and turns away to the wall.
- Simultaneous displays of contradictory behavior patterns: For example, the infant approaches the parent with head averted or leans sharply away while clinging. Then, while smiling, the infant suddenly strikes or claws at the parent's face.
- Undirected, misdirected, incomplete, and interrupted movements and expressions: For example, the infant wanders about the room with no reference to toys or persons or moves sobbing to the wall, not the parent, when distressed.
- Stereotypies, asymmetrical, and mistimed movements and anomalous postures: For example, the infant rocks hard on hands and knees immediately on reunion, greets the parent with a one-sided smile with the opposite side expressing fear or distress, or repeatedly raises arms straight forward at shoulder height with eyes closed.
- Freezing, stilling, and slowed movements and expressions: For example, the infant moves very slowly toward the parent, as though moving under water or against physical resistance, or the infant freezes all movement for 20 seconds with hands in the air.
- Direct indices of apprehension regarding the parent: For example, the infant places hands to mouth at parent entrance with a frightened expression or, again at parent entrance, backs against a wall with a fearful smile.
- Direct indices of disorganization and disorientation: For example, the infant wanders about the room in a disorganized fashion or, immediately upon parent entrance, the infant brightly greets the stranger and raises arms.

Source: Hesse, E. & Main, M. (1999). Second-generation effects of unresolved trauma in nonmaltreating parents: Dissociated, frightened, and threatening parental behavior. *Psychoanalytic Inquiry*, 19(4), 481-540.

As you look at Table 12.1, though, please take into consideration that it is fairly common for children to display these kinds of behaviors at times. For example, many children engage in repetitive often seemingly purposeless habitual behaviors in an effort to self-regulate. They may suck their thumb, twirl their hair, bite their nails, lips, or arms, or even bang their heads. These kinds of behaviors are most likely to occur during illness, exhaustion, unrelenting pain, neurological disturbances, or extreme situational stress such as brief separation from mother when lost at the grocery store. However, in normal circumstances, they tend to simply disappear over time as the child gets older. In other cases, some of the behaviors may persist, but rather than being indicative of disordered attachment, they may be evidence of other serious disorders such as autism or neurological dysfunction.

Granqvist et al. (2017) strongly caution practitioners not to jump to conclusions about the parent-child attachment relationship when they see a child exhibiting any of the behaviors in Table 12.1 for three reasons. First, the list of behaviors was derived from observations during the Strange Situation experiments, not during mother-child interactions at home where a broad range of transient behaviors can be expected. Second, for them to be of clinical significance, the behaviors would need to be relatively severe. Last, these researchers caution that the list of behaviors is valid only for children under the age of 20 months since over that age, children may have developed other more sophisticated strategies to cope with distress. These behaviors may certainly serve as "red flags" for practitioners to follow up on. However, social services should probably not be involved without first having the child assessed by a clinician trained and accredited in the Strange Situation protocol.

Recent research suggests that disorganized *behavior* does not necessarily indicate disorganized *attachment*. That is, the presence of disorganized behavior could be the result of trauma not associated with adverse caregiving (Duschinsky, 2018) or even of temperamental factors present at birth (Padron, Carlson, & Sroufe, 2014) and not due to serious disturbances in the mother-infant relationship. Thus, jumping to conclusions that the mother (or other caregiver) is responsible and calling child protective services would be both insulting and counterproductive.

Moreover, the good news is that a disorganized attachment style is not a fixed trait but is specific to a particular relationship (Granqvist et al., 2017). For example, a child may have disorganized attachment with mom but secure attachment with dad, grandma, or someone else. Thus, he or she still may be able to form secure relationships later in life. What is important for mental health practitioners who work with these families, however, is to identify disturbed attachment as early as possible and offer attachment-based treatment not just for the child but also for the parent.

Although some caveats are associated with the identification of disorganized/disoriented attachment, it is important to identify it when it exists because it is a sign of serious mother-child problems. The behaviors associated with disorganized attachment in infancy are caused by repeated experiences of the caregiver being a source of *alarm* (Duschinsky, 2018; Lyons-Ruth & Jacobvitz, 2017; Main & Solomon, 1990). Alarm may arise for a number of different reasons, such as the mother is frightening *to* her child, the mother is frightened *by* her child, the mother rejects her child, or the child is confused by the mother's behavior.

It is important to remember that, as discussed in Chapter 3, human beings are constantly scanning the environment for cues that indicate that something may benefit them or place them in danger (primary appraisal). If something is deemed dangerous, the individual is prompted to react. This is true for babies as well as for everybody else. However, when a baby's primary appraisal of his or her mother's behavior suggests danger, there is a real problem. Remember that babies instinctively know that they are completely helpless and completely dependent on mom to keep them safe and take care of their survival needs. Take Jet in Case Study 11.1 in the previous chapter, for example. When Sally engages in frightening behaviors such as screaming at Jet or baring her teeth and growling at him, Jet is going to feel helpless and out of control, his attachment behavioral system is going to be activated, and he will be prompted to approach his mom for safety. However, since Sally is the source of his terror, what is he to do? This kind of behavior from his mom places Jet into what is known as "fright without solution" (Hesse & Main, 1999, p. 484) or a "biological paradox" (Siegel, 2004, p. 278). What results is a "feedforward 'looping' of attention [that can be expressed] as a self-perpetuating series of *if-then* (italics in the original) propositions, namely, 'IF toward, then away, IF away, then toward, IF toward, then away, and so forth'" (Hesse & Main, 2006, p. 310). When Jet finds himself chronically in a state of "fright without solution," he may be unable to organize his behaviors effectively to get the attention that he needs, and he will be likely to develop a disorganized/disoriented attachment style.

Why, you might well ask, would a mother frighten her child or be frightened by her child? After all, mothers are biologically driven to bond with their babies so that there is the best chance that the baby will survive to adulthood, and babies come equipped at birth to elicit those very survival-enhancing behaviors from their mothers. If only it were that simple! Take Sally's case for instance. Obviously, Sally was once a baby herself, and she developed an attachment style of her own in response to the parenting she received. As will be discussed in much greater detail in Chapter 17, the internal working models of self and other that are formed in infancy and early childhood tend to influence later attachment relationships. These relationships include romantic partners and one's own children, in particular. Sally's mother wasn't sensitive and attuned to her needs, and her father was even worse. Thus, Sally developed an insecure attachment style, most likely disorganized/disoriented, that she is likely to pass on to her son.

Mikulincer and Shaver (2016) explain that although there is only low to moderate correlation between child and adult attachment styles (since so many things can change between infancy and adulthood), there is some evidence that individuals who had secure attachment in childhood often go on to have *secure* (also called autonomous) adult relationships. Those who were anxious/ambivalent tend to develop a *preoccupied* adult attachment style in which they engage in attention-seeking behaviors due to (often nonconscious) fears of abandonment. Those who were avoidant tend to develop a *dismissing* attachment style, preferring to be independent and having more distance in their relationships. Those who developed a disorganized/disoriented attachment during infancy may go on to develop a *fearful* adult attachment style that may include both fear of abandonment and deep distrust of close relationship (with consequent approach-avoidant behaviors).

Many women in this latter category (e.g., Sally Weisman in Case Study 11.1, Jet has a rough beginning) have survived one or more traumatic events in their lives, including physical and/or sexual abuse by an attachment figure or loss of an important attachment figure through death. Hesse and Main (2006) suggest that women in this situation may still be psychologically overwhelmed by their maltreatment or loss, having been unable to resolve it and integrate it into their life narrative (please see Chapter 5 for the discussion of narrative integration as presented by Siegel [2012a]). Because fear can shut down the connection between the prefrontal cortex and the hippocampus and thus affect the formation of explicit memories (see Chapter 3), women with unresolved trauma or loss may have distorted or partial memories of events that occurred when they lapsed into primitive fight/flight or freeze responses during the trauma. Remember that when trauma occurs in infancy or toddlerhood before the left brain has matured sufficiently to allow the encoding of explicit memory, the individual stores memories in the right brain (implicit memory). When these memories are triggered later in life, they do not feel like memories at all. They are experienced as feelings, images, emotions, assumptions, and expectations. Thus, a mother who experienced trauma (e.g., physical or sexual abuse) or loss of an important attachment figure as an infant can be triggered by many things within her environment, including her own baby, and act in ways that cause her baby to become alarmed.

Hesse and Main (2006) have identified a number of alarming behaviors that a mother may exhibit (see Table 12.2). These behaviors may occur only very briefly and may be quite subtle.

However, babies are amazingly quick to notice atypical or disruptive behaviors in their mothers. These researchers place maternal frightening/frightened behavior into either primary or secondary categories. Primary behaviors include dissociative behaviors, anomalous forms of parental threat, and anomalous forms of parental fright. Secondary behaviors include timid/deferential behavior or role inversion, sexualized behaviors, and parental behaviors compatible with infant disorganized behaviors. I will explain these behaviors below.

TABLE 12.2   Frightening Parental Behaviors Associated with Disorganized Attachment

Major or Primary Aspects of Frightening Parental Behavior Expected to Directly Evoke Infant Alarm

1. Direct indices of entrance into a dissociative state: for example, parent suddenly completely "freezes" with eyes unmoving, half-lidded, despite nearby movement, or parent addresses infant in an "altered" tone with simultaneous voicing or devoicing ("haunted" sound, as can be produced by elongating the sounds of "Hi," "huh," or "ah" while pulling in on the diaphragm)
2. Threatening behavior inexplicable in origin and/or anomalous in form: for example, in nonplay contexts and in the absence of metasignals of play, stiff-legged, stalking of infant on all fours, exposure of canine tooth, hissing or deep growls directed at the infant
3. Frightened behavior patterns inexplicable in origin and/or anomalous in form: for example, sudden frightened look (fear mouth, exposure of whites of eyes) in absence of environmental change; also frightened retreat from the infant or approaching the infant apprehensively as though a dangerous object

Minor or Secondary Frightening Parental Behaviors not Expected to Directly Evoke Infant Alarm

1. Timid/deferential (role-inverting) behavior: for example, parent submissive to infant aggression, hands folded, head bowed while infant engages in obviously painful slapping, hitting, or hair pulling; also turning to the offspring as a haven of safety when alarmed
2. Sexualized behavior toward infant: for example, deep kissing, sexualized caressing
3. Disorganized/disoriented behaviors compatible with childhood disorganized/disoriented attachment behaviors: for example, mistimed movements, anomalous postures, approaching infant with head averted, or any observable "collapse of behavioral (caregiving) strategy," such as becoming motionless while infant is crying

Source: Hesse, E. & Main, M. (2006). Frightened, threatening, and dissociative parental behavior in low-risk samples: Description, discussion, and interpretations. *Development and Psychopathology*, 18(2), 309–343.

Primary Parental Frightening/Frightened Behaviors

Maltreatment can, of course, cause a child to experience high levels of fear and consequent alterations in brain structure and functioning as discussed above. Moreover, research shows that between 80% and 90% of maltreated children form disorganized attachment (Cyr, Euser, Bakersman-Kranenburg, & van IJzendoorn, 2010). However, it is important to understand that not all children who develop a disorganized attachment style have been abused or neglected in any way. In this section, I will discuss maternal behaviors that Hesse and Main's primary parental frighten or frightened behaviors: dissociative behaviors and anomalous frightening and frightened maternal.

Dissociative Behaviors

Dissociation is a very common human behavior; we all do it from time to time. Have you ever been driving down the interstate and missed your exit because you were absorbed in thinking about a problem? That's a mild form of dissociation. Hesse and Main (2006) explain that clinical levels of dissociation, however, are the result of activation of the mammalian fright responses—fight (attack), flight (withdrawal), or freeze (dissociation) responses. If you recall from Chapter 4, when the smart vagus is unable to solve problems through activation of the social engagement system, the sympathetic nervous system will be activated to allow fight or flight responses. If those don't/can't work, the vegetative vagal system will take over and cause a freeze or collapse response. Dissociative disorders (such as trance states, ideas of possession, depersonalization, derealization, fugues, and/or dissociative identity disorder) can develop in response to overwhelming trauma or loss. These disorders constitute "a disturbance or alteration in the normally integrative functions of identity, memory, or consciousness" (p. 331).

There are real differences between low levels of dissociation, such as becoming absorbed in a daydream or trying to remember what you had on your grocery list that you left at home, and clinical levels of dissociation in which you become completely still with a trance-like stare and glazed eyes, and babies instinctively know this difference. Hesse and Main (2006) explain that "dissociative behavior can itself be sufficiently alarming to leave the infant without a strategy for maintaining behavioral, emotional, and attentional organization" (p. 321). They note that research has shown a high incidence of disorganized/disoriented attachment among children of mothers with anxiety disorder (65%) and suggest that these mothers may be in a disconnected state of consciousness similar to dissociation and thus may cause their baby to be chronically alarmed. They note further that because manifestations of clinical dissociation are clearly abnormal alterations in consciousness, they become a source of alarm for the infant.

Likewise, strangely altered facial and vocal expressions such as grimacing or cackling like the Wicked Witch of the West with no indication that this is done in play will cause a baby to become alarmed (Hesse & Main, 2006). A baby has the capacity to make sense out of his or her mother's silence and facial expressions during brief daydreams or times of thoughtfulness. However, he or she can't make sense out of a mother who sits in a trance or makes weird noises, and thus his or her primary appraisal system will activate the attachment behavioral systems and send him or her into "fright without solution."

Anomalous Frightening Behaviors

Hesse and Main (2006) note that some mothers may engage in behaviors that would easily be expected to cause their baby alarm. These would include things like making strange or unusual movements similar to those made by predatory animals (stalking, growling, baring teeth, mauling), apparently while in a dissociative state. Absent any signal from her that she is playing, the child is likely to become alarmed. If she were doing it in play, the baby could make sense of it and deal with the excitement. However, since the person he or she would be approaching for safety is the growling animal that appears intent on eating him or her for lunch, he or she is again placed in the position of "fright without solution."

It is easy to imagine how dissociation or the odd behaviors mentioned above could be highly alarming to a baby. In addition, as discussed in the next sections, maternal hostility, intrusiveness or aversive rejection can also result in alarm.

Hostile Maternal Behaviors

Lyons-Ruth and Jacobvitz (2016) have suggested that in addition to the kinds of frightening behavior mentioned above, babies can also be alarmed by a mother's overt or covert hostility. Hostility can include maliciously mocking or teasing him or her. Alternatively, it could include abruptly invading his or her personal space, touching his or her body in uncomfortable ways, impatiently forcing him or her to go somewhere he or she doesn't want to go. Hostility could also include silently looming in her baby's face or glaring in anger.

Intrusive Maternal Behaviors

Intrusive maternal behaviors include controlling, interfering, overly directive, overwhelming or overprotective behaviors (Swanson, Beckwith, & Howard, 2000) or as Sroufe (2005) puts it, "doing things to the baby for which the baby [is] not prepared" (p. 356). Examples of intrusiveness can include, for example, a mother's insistence on touching her child even when the child does not need and is not asking for emotional comfort (Tse, Siu, & Wong, 2012). Other examples include overpowering or overstimulating the child; not allowing the child to lead when mother and child play together; frequently interfering with the child's choice of toys, games and movement; stressing the educational aspects of play rather than the fun aspects; stressing the importance of performance over enjoyment; frequent limit setting and rigidity; physically looming over the child; or doing too much for the child (Swanson et al., 2000).

This last example, doing too much for the child, is often seen today in what has become known as overparenting or "helicopter parenting." Overparenting includes such behaviors as "developmentally inappropriate levels of parental directiveness, tangible assistance, problem-solving, monitoring, and involvement in the lives of children" (Segrin et al., 2013). Being overly protective or micromanaging a child's behavior can interfere with a child's ability to experience autonomy (Munich & Munich, 2009). As mentioned in the introduction to this chapter, Erikson (1963) suggests that during toddlerhood, children need to experience considerable autonomy as they begin to explore the environment. In addition, they need use their newly developed motor skills to manipulate things (e.g., stacking things up and them knocking them down, pulling, pushing and banging on things, etc.). If they are not allowed some autonomy in deciding what to do, how to play, and what to play with (i.e., free play), they will develop shame and doubt. For cases in which a mother intrudes again and again on a toddler's play when it is not necessary, in my imagination I hear the child say (even though he or she may have very little language yet), "There must be something wrong with me. Every time I start to do something, mommy stops me and tells me I am wrong. I need to know how the world works, but since mommy is taking over, I guess I'm just not smart enough to manage anything on my own." Without the opportunity to try, fail, try again, and finally succeed (that is, if mom jumps in and does it herself or tries to fix every mistake), a child may later have difficulty taking personal responsibility not only for his or her mistakes but also for his or her successes.

According to Munich and Munich (2009), parents who overparent generally do so because of an exaggerated desire to ensure that their vulnerable little child makes it in a world that they perceive as being highly competitive and fraught with dangers and pitfalls. Failure, to them, is not an option. These parents may be basing their own self-esteem on their child's success, perhaps stemming from their own early attachment issues. Instead of focusing on their child's mental state and growing ability to master the world, they focus on their own fears, leaving little space for their child to develop a healthy sense of self and competency. Thus, often starting in infancy or toddlerhood (if not before the baby is even born), they start pushing their child to do things perfectly. Of course, the child can't do things perfectly (since human beings generally don't do things perfectly), so they jump in and try to make it right. However, what may start out as simply frustration to a two-year-old can turn into low self-esteem, lack of initiative, and a sense of entitlement with a concomitant sense of emptiness and confusion in an adolescent or young adult. Instead of being helpful, these parents promote traits that can actually stand in the way of the child's success—anxiety, withdrawal, depression and insecurity—by not allowing the child to develop effective problem-solving and coping skills (Segrin et al., 2013).

Aversive Rejection

Duschinsky (2018) points out another frightening maternal behavior that can result in disorganized attachment—severe aversive rejection. For example, she may stiffen or pull away from her baby or actually push her baby away when he or she is seeking comfort. She may hold the baby away from her body with stiff arms rather than touching and soothing. Duschinsky notes that although these kinds of behaviors could be due to the mother's fear or hostility, they could also be due to her own aversion to touch. However, the baby is not going to understand that his or her mother is acting this way because of sensitivity to being touched. He or she is simply going to experience rejection. A baby knows instinctively that a rejected baby is likely to be a dead baby and may slip into "fright without solution."

Environmental Factors

The alarm associated with an infant's development of disorganized attachment isn't restricted just to interactions between the mother and child. Duschinsky (2018) suggests that if there is interparental domestic violence or other kinds of chaos in the home that cause "a cacophony of daily forms of alarm" (p. 25), the mother simply may not be available physically or emotionally to assuage her child's fear. Moreover, the probability of disorganization is increased since she is not only unavailable to soothe her baby and repair the rupture to their communication, but she is an integral part of the frightening chaos. Thus, she may become frightening herself. Children in this situation may perceive that "their safe haven is itself under attack…. [and] associate alarm with the very individual that the attachment system is prompting them to approach with the expectation of safety" (p. 25).

Disorganized vs. Avoidant Attachment

Hostility, intrusiveness, rejection and environmental chaos all suggest a mother who is unavailable for sensitive response to her child's normal needs and healthy curiosity, energy, and autonomy. Lack of sensitivity, or poor attunement to a baby's needs, is strongly associated with the development of insecure attachment as discussed at length in Chapter 6. Both Lyons-Ruth and Jacobvitz (2016) and Duschinsky (2018) point out that these behaviors are hallmarks for the development of *avoidant* rather than *disorganized* attachment. However, Duschinsky argues that the difference between avoidant and disorganized attachment is to a great extent a matter of degree. Avoidant children have been able manage their distress by finding ways to shift their attention away from the mother and toward their toys or something else that can reduce their stress. It is important to understand, though, that these children are not avoiding their mother (or other caregiver); indeed, they want to be as close to their mother as they can get. Instead, they are avoiding the negative dependency-related emotions that, if exhibited, only make things worse. In contrast, children who are unable to reduce their stress because of the severity or manner of their mother's behavior are likely to develop a disorganized/disoriented attachment style and accompanying problematic emotions and behaviors.

Anomalous Frightened Behaviors

Hesse and Main (2006) suggest that most of the frightened behaviors that some mothers manifest are presumed to be caused by the triggering of implicit memories of trauma or loss. When these nonconscious memories cause fear to show on the mother's face, her baby will try to figure out what is making mom afraid. However, since the fear is being generated internally, there are no external threats that he or she can identify. Thus, the baby can't make sense of what his or her mother is expressing and will experience alarm as a result. To make matters worse, in this kind of situation not only is the mom the source of the alarm, but she is also unavailable as a safe haven.

In other cases, the mother may act as if her baby is the *cause* of her fright. It is presumed that her fear is the result of a dissociative experience in which she identifies her baby with her own traumatic experience. She may back away from her infant with fear on her face and in her voice, or she may cautiously step around her baby as if trying to escape danger. Her baby perceives danger in his or her mother's expressions and actions, which causes alarm and activates his or her attachment behavioral system. However, the baby perceives that he or she is the very source of his safe haven's fear. How can he or she possibly make sense of this and organize a response that will provide safety? Hesse and Main (2006) suggest that in order to escape from this intolerable situation, a child may actually split into two or more "selves" (resulting in the development of dissociative disorders). Alternatively, noting that some animals chase other animals who flee from them, they suggest that a child may actually become aggressive and attack his or her frightened parent, which would result in escalating fear on the part of the frightened mother!

Secondary Parental Frightening Behavior

According to Hesse and Main (2006), secondary behaviors—timid/deferential attitudes or reversed roles, sexualized behaviors, or behaviors similar to infant disorganized behaviors— are unlikely in themselves to cause alarm in the infant. However, because they imply that the mother is an altered state of consciousness, they may still result in disorganized infant attachment responses.

Timid/Deferential Behaviors or Role Inversion

Hesse and Main (2006) explain that mothers who think of their babies as being somehow superior to them or as having more power than they do tend to be very timid with their children, afraid that they are going to offend them in some way or acting humble and deferential with them. They may simply allow the child to slap or hit them or pull their hair without defending themselves or disciplining the child. They may even have distorted thoughts in which they believe their child to have supernatural powers. These researchers believe that these parents may be confusing their and their baby's relationship roles. That is, if her baby is distressed and seeks her out for comfort or safety, this may trigger alarm in her based on early memories of trauma or loss, which makes her want to seek out a safe haven, too. She may then reach out to her baby for that safety, prioritizing her needs over her baby's, which of course doesn't help the baby deal with his or her own distress and may cause disorganization.

Lyons-Ruth and Jacobvitz (2016) suggest that some women with unresolved trauma or loss may have feelings of helplessness as a parent, either afraid of their child or afraid that they will not be able to control themselves in relation to their child. These mothers may commit "affective communication errors" (p. 678) such as telling her baby to come to her while she continues to move away from him or her. She may engage in withdrawal behaviors such as simply leaving her baby crying on the floor or freezing when her baby cries, not responding at all. Interestingly, these children tend to show disorganized/disoriented behaviors during infancy and toddlerhood but then develop controlling behaviors by about age six in which they either become controlling and punishing of their mother or take on the role of parent and take care of their mother. This latter response tends to result in later maternal role confusion and caregiving helplessness with their own children.

Sexualized Behavior

Although Hesse and Main (2006) suggest that it is rare for a mother to show overly sexualized behavior with her infant, researchers have witnessed relatively mild sexual behaviors, such as provocative looks and intimate kissing in certain mothers. These authors state that

> It is hard to imagine that these parents in the westernized nations where these studies were undertaken could (a) lack the capacity to monitor their actions sufficiently to permit observation of sexualized behavior toward their infants without (b) having had experiences rendering them vulnerable to exhibiting overtly dissociative and/or [frightening/frightened] behavior in other contexts. (p. 325)

Both Hesse and Main and Lyons-Ruth and Jacobvitz (2016) believed that these women may have been unconsciously reenacting actions that they had witnessed or experienced long ago. This kind of sexual attention would be incomprehensible to the woman's baby. This strange behavior could be perceived by the child as alarming and, if it happened often, could result in disorganized responses.

Disorganized/Disoriented Behaviors

Because mothers who have experienced unresolved trauma or loss are likely to have adopted a disorganized/disoriented attachment style in their own infancies, they are likely, according to Hesse & Main (2006) and Lyons-Ruth and Jacobvitz (2016), to display many of the odd, out-of-context or disoriented behaviors that their disorganized/disoriented baby would display (see Table 12.1). Thus, a mother might approach her baby in the same way a baby who is afraid of his or her mother would approach her, perhaps with head averted. She may move in slow motion or with awkward, clumsy or stiff actions. The baby will have trouble making sense of these actions and perhaps respond with disorganized behaviors of his or her own.

Child Neglect

Lyons-Ruth and Jacobvitz (2016) note that while child abuse is clearly associated with disorganized/disoriented attachment, children with five or more socioeconomic risk factors are also at significantly elevated risk for this attachment style. Parents who have multiple socioeconomic stressors may have little or no energy or attention to spare on their children even if they love them very much, and their neglect can have devastating effects on the formation of the attachment bond. Moreover, children who are institutionalized (e.g., orphans) tend to develop serious attachment problems even when housed in high-quality institutions that provide good physical and medical care and plenty of educational and recreational resources, most likely due to lack of sensitive and attuned caregiving (Oliveira, Fearon, Belsky, Fachada, & Soares, 2015).

There are two forms of disordered attachment that can arise from grossly inadequate (negligent) parenting in infancy and toddlerhood that should be discussed—disinhibited social engagement disorder (DSED) and reactive attachment disorder (RAD). The DSM5 (APA, 2013) provides a diagnosis of DSED for children who seek close physical contact with or who go off readily with a stranger. Normally, infants over the age of about seven months are naturally afraid of strangers. Moreover, mothers generally emphasize to their children that they should never talk to or go anywhere with a stranger. However, research on children (ages 12–31 months) raised in orphanages in eastern Europe in which extreme neglect and poor socialization occurred shows that they were highly likely to show indiscriminate attachment to strangers (Zeanah, Smykes, Koga, Carlson, & the Bucharest Early Intervention Project Core Group, 2005). Children who have been severely neglected like those orphans may actively pursue and happily talk with strangers, sit on their laps, hug them, tell them how much they love them, or willingly and without question leave with them. This, of course, places these children at high risk for victimization. They are often described as being overly bright in affect and friendly to the point of causing discomfort to whomever they are focused on. Often highly attention-seeking, these children may become aggressive in their efforts to get the attention they desire.

Because children who have been socially deprived often have attention problems and are overly active, children with DSED may also have a co-morbid diagnosis of ADHD. In addition, those who have experienced maltreatment in addition to neglect may also meet criteria for PTSD (Zeanah, Cheser, Boris, and the American Academy of Child and Adolescent Psychiatry [AACAP] Committee on Quality Issues [CQI], 2016). The good news is that, when children with DSED are placed as early as possible into a good foster care or adoptive home where secure attachment can be established, some if not all of the early damage can be repaired. However, the indiscriminate behaviors may continue in some of these children even after they have established secure attachment with foster or adoptive parents.

In contrast to children with DSED, children diagnosed with RAD are not interested in interacting socially with others whether they are caregivers or strangers. They do not engage in proximity- or comfort-seeking behaviors with caregivers in times of emotional need even when their caregivers have had significant and regular interaction with them. They show little social reciprocity or empathy, and their affect is generally not positive, sometimes showing inexplicable sadness, fearfulness, or irritability around their caregivers. In addition to severe neglect, many of these children have also suffered significant trauma and thus may have co-morbid diagnoses of PTSD or depression, may engage in stereotypies, and show evidence of cognitive delays and learning disorders (Zeanah et al., 2016).

Zeanah et al. (2016) emphasize that both DSED and RAD are rare disorders and should not be given unless there is clear evidence of extreme deprivation during infancy and early childhood. This extreme neglect is most likely to occur in an institution (e.g., an orphanage) in which there was a high ratio of children to staff and consequent inadequate physical contact and socialization, or in which there were large numbers of caregivers working irregular shifts.

In addition, it is important to rule out differential diagnoses. For example, children with suspected DSED must be distinguished from those who are simply high in sociability, the degree to which the child deviates from accepted social norms concerning social boundaries as well as the level of functional impairment being the defining characteristics. In addition, they must be differentiated from children with ADHD. Impulsivity in DSED children is purely social in nature, while that seen in ADHD children is usually behavioral or cognitive. Children with suspected RAD should be distinguished from those with autism (ASD) (suggested by their social withdrawal and reduced social reciprocity) or global developmental delay (GDD) (suggested by their cognitive delays).

CLASS DISCUSSION

Which attachment style would you say that Jet is manifesting in his foster home? Which is Luke manifesting? Is there any evidence for a diagnosis of DSED or RAD for either Jet or Luke?

In both DSED and RAD, attachment problems arise because of a lack of attention to basic psychosocial-emotional needs, often in the context of institutional care. In the next section, I will discuss how maternal mental illness can result in disorganization.

Maternal Psychological Issues

Lyons-Ruth and Jacobvitz (2016) have noted that the probability of developing disorganized attachment is elevated in children whose mothers have mental health diagnoses. Both substance abuse and postpartum anxiety and depression are relatively common disorders among women with infants and toddlers and are discussed in the sections below.

Substance Use and Abuse

While a mother's use of substances can affect fetal brain development, it can also have a devastating effect on her baby's postnatal growth and development. Research has shown than approximately 19% of women who abuse alcohol before becoming pregnant continue to abuse it during pregnancy (Kelly, Zatzick, & Anders, 2001). This is unfortunate since recent research indicates that only 7% of babies whose mothers had been using substances recently or at the time of birth scored in the optimal range on a neurological exam immediately after birth (Tuhkana, Pajulo, Jussila, & Ekholms, 2019). In contrast, 95% of babies born to women who did not use alcohol or drugs during their pregnancy reached optimal scores. Moreover, 63% of those babies needed follow-up services, and 12% continued to show suboptimal neurological functioning at twelve months.

As for relationships between substance use and attachment, Swanson, Beckwith, and Howard (2000) note that about 46% of children whose mothers abuse alcohol while pregnant form an insecure attachment by toddlerhood. Moreover, they also report that 68% of the children of mothers who abuse drugs during their pregnancy are insecure, with 45% of these drug-exposed children characterized as having a disorganized/disoriented attachment style. Reasons for the development of insecure attachment among alcohol- and drug-exposed children can be found in research that shows that mothers who use substances may have diminished intensity of feelings toward their child both before and after birth (Rossen et al., 2016). In other research, mothers who used substances during their pregnancy were at greatly enhanced risk of interfering with the child's autonomy during toddlerhood, a risk factor for the development of disorganized attachment as discussed above (Swanson et al., 2000).

Children of substance-abusing mothers are at significant risk of developing disorganized attachment because their mothers are likely to be intrusive and/or to have unresolved trauma or loss. For example, Swanson et al. (2000) noted that within their sample of 51 mothers who had used drugs during their pregnancies discussed above, all of the women had a history of physical or sexual abuse, exposure to extreme family violence, or death of an important attachment figure. Moreover, most of them continued to use substances after their babies were born. Thus, their babies were likely to have experienced times when their mothers were unavailable either because they were high or because they were in an altered state of consciousness due to dissociation. Moreover, their mothers may have been frightening to them because of their erratic drug-related behaviors. Thus, these children are at greatly increased risk of developing disorganized attachment and subsequent emotional and behavioral disorders.

Postpartum Depression and Anxiety

Maternal postpartum depression and anxiety have clear negative effects on babies' development, with research showing that postpartum depression is associated with infant behavioral and emotional regulation problems as well as poorer cognitive performance (Reck, Tietz, Muller, Seibold, & Tronick, 2018). Postpartum anxiety, on the other hand, is associated with increased infant stress reactivity and reduced social engagement. Approximately 13% of postpartum women experience depression, and 12% experience anxiety, usually appearing two to three months after giving birth (Reck et al., 2018). Symptoms can range from mild (e.g., sadness, "baby blues") to clinical levels of depression that may include psychosis. Although research has shown only a modest correlation between maternal depression and development of disorganized attachment in infancy, the more severe and chronic the depression is, the more likely it will affect the bond (Lyons-Ruth & Jacobvitz, 2016).

It should be noted that postpartum depression and anxiety are found not only in mothers but also in fathers. One study that explored this issue among men whose spouse gave birth through C-section found that more than one third of the fathers became depressed. Risk factors for fathers include financial problems, relationship problems with the mother, having a female newborn, and having a spouse with postpartum depression. The effects on the baby and on the couple's relationship is similar to the effects of maternal depression (Stanescu, Balalau, Ples, Paunica, & Balalau, 2018).

Although the mechanisms associated with the development of these disorders are not yet completely identified, Brummelta and Galea (2016) point out that disturbances in the production of estrogen, progesterone, and oxytocin, as well as abnormal functioning of the HPA system occurring after a baby is born are most likely involved. Postpartum depressed women tend to have significantly higher levels of cortisol in their blood and significantly lower levels of oxytocin than non-depressed women do. Moreover, Pawluski, Lonstein, and

Flemming (2017) emphasize that numerous studies show that post-partum depression or anxiety affects maternal sleep patterns and affective states, but also affects mothers' 'hedonic' responses to stimuli, executive function, and cognition. Moreover, we know that executive function deficits have a clear impact on the quality of mothering behavior exhibited during the first postpartum year.

These problems may affect the mother's ability to connect with her infant. If you remember, oxytocin is associated not only with labor and lactation but also with mother-baby interaction. Thus, an oxytocin deficit in mothers with postpartum depression may be responsible for the fact that they are more likely to terminate breastfeeding earlier than nondepressed mothers, that they don't touch their babies as much as unaffected mothers, and that their touch is not as loving and affectionate (Brummelte & Galea, 2016). These mothers do not smile at or talk to their babies as much and tend to show more negative or disengaged behaviors with their babies. In addition, the research shows that anxious mothers tend to be colder, more negative, and more criticizing and catastrophizing than mothers without anxiety (Reck et al., 2018). In addition, they tend to be "more intrusive with, and irritated by, their infant (although many depressed mothers are detached and withdrawn), and respond less sensitively, less contingently, and more negatively to their infants compared with nondepressed mothers (Pawluski et al., 2017, p. 113).

Existing psychological disturbances may also predispose women to development of these disorders. Research by Meuti et al. (2015) has shown that significant risk factors for post-natal depression include a personal history of previous psychiatric disorders (especially depression, anxiety, and bipolar disorder) (53% vs. 16% among controls); psychiatric disorders among family members (especially depression among their mothers) (50% compared to 30% among controls); and relationship problems with current partner (33% compared to 5% among controls).

Moreover, other research notes associations between maternal attachment styles and post-natal depression. For example, Meuti et al. (2015) explored attachment among a sample of postpartum women and found that depressed women had significantly higher mean scores for both attachment anxiety and attachment avoidance than women without depression. In addition, while only 41% of women with depression had secure attachment, 90% of women without depression had this attachment style. Moreover, 30% of women with depression had fearful attachment compared to only 1% of women without depression. This last finding is of particular importance because women with fearful attachment are likely to have had a disorganized/disoriented attachment style due to attachment-related trauma during their own infancy (Mikulincer & Shaver, 2016). As discussed above, when attachment-related trauma is unresolved, mothers tend to act in ways that promote disorganized attachment in their children, thereby passing their own trauma on to the next generation. As Schwerdtfeger and Goff (2007) point out, women who have a history of interpersonal trauma may

> "pass on" their trauma symptoms or reactions to their children, either through the children's direct exposure to the parents' symptoms or through the parents' potentially traumatizing (e.g., abusive) behavior. Additionally, depression, anxiety, psychosomatic problems, aggression, guilt, and related issues may be common in the children of trauma survivors. (p. 40)

Prematurity, Maternal Psychology, and Attachment

According to the CDC (2019), almost 10% of births in 2016 were premature (< 37 weeks gestation). However, clear differences in preterm birth rates were associated with race: Whites, 9%, Hispanics, 9.5%, and Blacks, 13.6%. Research indicates that in about two-thirds of cases there is no clear explanation for the preterm birth, though clear risks are associated with previous preterm delivery, preeclampsia, multiple gestations, age (older), and poor maternal mental health (Martin & Osterman, 2018). Prematurity is associated with a host of mental (e.g., motor and cognitive delays and impairments, and later behavioral, conduct, and relationship difficulties) and physical problems (e.g., mortality, feeding and breathing problems, cerebral palsy, etc.) for the baby with, of course, effects being more severe according to how premature the baby is (Anderson & Cacola, 2017).

Hallin, Bengtsson, and Stjernqvist (2011) note that many children who are born prematurely go on to adjust well as they transition into adulthood. However, they point out that when multiple risk factors are present, preterm infants may face some real challenges to optimal development. While postpartum anxiety and depression are not uncommon problems as discussed above, the probability for their development is greatly increased among women who give birth early (>40%) (Jubinville, Newburn-Cook, Hegadoren, & Lacaze-Masmonteil, 2012). As discussed above, severe maternal postpartum anxiety and depressive disorders are associated with the infant developing disorganized attachment. Although there have been mixed results among studies exploring attachment disorganization and preterm birth, there is some clear indication of a relationship between the two (Pennestri et al., 2015; Wolke, Eryigit-Madzwamuse, & Gutbrod, 2014). Research suggests that prematurity is associated with higher levels of maternal insensitivity, hostility, intrusiveness, and controlling behaviors as well as reduced synchronous and cooperative mother-baby interactions (Hallin et al., 2011; Nuccini, Paterlini, Gargano, & Landini, 2015). Moreover, since depressed mothers are less likely to engage actively in either verbal or play physical with their child, preterm infants are likely to show deficits in their motor development, which in turn may affect their cognitive development (Anderson & Cacola, 2017).

Premature births are frequently traumatic for the mother, leaving her vulnerable to acute stress reactions, including the development of PTSD (Jubinville et al., 2012; Nuccini et al., 2015). Cantle (2013) explains that instead of allowing a "golden hour" of skin-to-skin contact between a mother and her premature infant, doctors and nurses often whisk the child away to the hospital neonate intensive care unit (NICU). There, they place him or her in a room full of high-tech equipment where he or she may be placed into an incubator, with tubes in the nose for feeding and monitors incessantly beeping. For these mothers there may be no rush of oxytocin prompted by the sights and sounds of their babies. When they visit the NICU, they may be overwhelmed by the medical environment and overwhelmed by their baby's tiny size and obvious vulnerability. They may be afraid to touch the baby and indeed may not even recognize the infant as being theirs. Indeed, they may feel "as if their baby belongs to the hospital, as the staff have taken over responsibility for his care and feel that they have barely any useful role" (p. 263). This is not to condemn neonatal nurses and doctors; they are doing their best to keep the preemie alive, and they generally have systems in place to promote attachment (Anderson & Cacola, 2017). However, what they have to do to keep the baby alive is clearly not optimal for the development of a secure attachment bond.

Summary

In this chapter, we have identified many challenges that can result in the development of inse-cure attachment, especially disorganized attachment. When the mother's mental health is significantly affected by unresolved trauma or loss, she is at increased risk of engaging in behav-iors with her infant that are frightening to the child, placing him or her into a state of "fright without solution" that can result in disorganized attachment. Although disorganization may result from directly frightening maternal behaviors, a baby can also become disorganized if his or her mother appears to be frightened by him or her or if she engages in odd dissociative behaviors that a child simply can't make sense of.

Extreme neglect, such as that found among children who have been hospitalized or other-wise institutionalized or who are born to parents who ignore their most basic needs may be deprived of essential social interactions with a primary attachment figure. Therefore, their attachment behavioral systems do not develop normally, and they are at increased risk of developing serious attachment disorders. They may seek close physical contact with almost any adult they encounter. Alternatively, they may have no interest in interacting socially with others and do not seek comfort from anyone and have extreme deficits in social rec-iprocity and empathy. A mother's psychopathology, such as substance abuse, post-partum depression and anxiety can also interfere with the development of a secure bond and result in disorganized attachment.

Children with disorganized or distorted attachment behaviors can be very difficult to treat and their families can be desperate for help. However, a number of attachment-focused ther-apies are being developed that can help the practitioner when faced with this challenge. In addition to the well-known attachment-based therapy models such as Attachment-based Family Therapy (ABFT) (see, for example, Diamond, Russon, & Levy, 2016) and Theraplay (see, for example, Booth, Lender, & Lindaman, 2018), new therapies are currently being devel-oped. For example, attachment issues are being addressed from a neurobiological perspective and based on polyvagal theory in a modality that uses sound (Richards, 2016). In addition, Steele and Steele (2018) have compiled a collection of studies on 21 empirically validated attachment-based interventions that include a wide range of modalities from home-visits to parent-child dyadic work, to multifamily groups, to video-feedback targeting at-risk chil-dren ranging in age from infancy through adolescence. Other modalities are being devised to prevent or minimize attachment problems from developing to begin with, such as the FirstPlay Infant Massage and Storytelling (see https://firstplaytherapy.com/ and Courtney & Nowalski, 2019).

Moving on to the next life stages, early and middle childhood, I will discuss normal changes in neurobiological and social functioning that occur during early and middle childhood in the next three chapters. In addition, you will get to know Jet's brother Luke better and meet Macy Oster as they enter the school system and navigate the stresses of mastering academic and social skills.

CHAPTER **13**

Brain Development in Early and Middle Childhood

LEARNING OBJECTIVES

After completing this chapter, readers should understand:
- What pruning is and how it affects the brain's efficiency.
- What executive functions are and why they are important to social functioning.
- How the slow maturation of the prefrontal cortex affects executive functioning during childhood.
- How self-evaluation is related to a growing sense of self in this age group.
- What episodic memory is and why "mental time travel" is important.

KEY IDEAS

1. During early childhood, although the brain becomes more efficient through the process of pruning, essential functions that are not in place by then may never develop or may develop poorly.
2. During early and middle childhood, the prefrontal cortex develops reciprocal connections with the subcortical brain that promote the development of executive functions and self-evaluation.
3. Development of good executive functioning allows an individual to set and work toward goals, to take another's perspective and interpret his or her emotions and motives, and to interact with others in socially acceptable ways.
4. The growing capacity for self-reflection afforded by the maturing prefrontal cortex allows individuals to begin to compare themselves and their academic and social performance with that of other individuals.
5. The maturing brain increases an individual's ability to engage in "mental time travel," i.e., to imagine what is going to happen in the future based on things that have happened in the past, providing motivation and planning for the future and adaptive behavior in the present.

Introduction

As children leave infancy and toddlerhood and enter school environments normally encountered in early and middle childhood, their neural circuitry becomes more complex. It is to be expected that over time the various regions of the brain will become more and more integrated, forming connections between cortical and subcortical structures and between the right and left hemispheres. Children will become less dependent on the adults around them to regulate their emotions as they build conscious awareness of their own and others' feelings and intentions. Because language and explicit memory are now available to them, they will begin to form an autobiographical narrative of their lives and a sense of self that includes both events that have occurred to and around them and their emotional reactions to those events. Thus, given adequate parenting and the compassionate attention of adults within the community, children in these age groups can be expected to develop their mentalization capabilities so that they become better and better able to discern and verbalize their own feelings and take others' perspectives and feelings into consideration as they navigate their social environment.

Experience-dependent changes occur in the brain that support the acquisition of language, the ability to focus (and move) attention at will, to utilize both working and long-term memory, and to self-regulate emotions and behaviors (Guyer, Perez-Edgar, & Crone, 2018). The current literature on neurobiology during early and middle childhood tends to focus on three areas: the natural elimination of unused or weak synaptic connections, the slow maturation of the connections between the prefrontal cortex and subcortical regions of the brain, and the development of episodic hippocampal memory. I first discuss how the brain changes during early and middle childhood as children face the transition into school and the broader social world. Then, I examine how increasing connection between the prefrontal cortex and multiple subcortical regions results in gains in executive function and in self-reflection capacities that impact both academic performance and social functioning. Last, I discuss the development of episodic memory, which allows children to learn from their mistakes and successes so that they can plan and adapt to their more complex social environment.

First, however, I invite you to read Case Study 13.1, Jet and Luke Find a Home. As you read the sections below, be thinking about how their experiences in infancy and toddlerhood may affect their brain development. A little later in the chapter, I will introduce you to Macy Oster and her mother Tara in Case Study 13.2. Notice the similarities and differences between these families, and see if you can imagine how these children will handle the pressures associated with the increased academic and social pressures associated with entering the school system.

CASE STUDY 13.1 JET AND LUKE FIND A HOME

Unable to have children of their own, Helen and Hank Wolverton had been talking about adopting for a while. When Helen saw the pictures of Jet and Luke on an adoption web site, she felt that her dreams might come true. At four and a half years old, Jet looked solemn and grown up with his arm protectively holding his younger brother; Luke's smile was adorable. Helen had grown up as the only child of two professional parents who were preoccupied with their careers and social lives, and she was often extremely lonely. She had always wanted to have children so that she could shower them with the love and attention. Hank was skeptical, but agreed to go meet them, and when he saw Helen's face light up when she saw them, he agreed to the adoption.

Within three months of bringing the boys home, Helen's dream began to crumble. Luke wasn't a problem. At three years of age, he was remarkably well behaved. He played quietly by himself and did what he was told without complaint. He didn't seek her out or ask for attention, but he responded to her hugs and appeared to enjoy it when she read him a story at bedtime.

Jet, however, was a different story. Although he was polite when he first arrived, he soon started testing her every minute of every day. He refused to follow direction, threw food, and just smiled at her when she spanked him. He woke up screaming in the middle of the night. Sometimes he just sat in the middle of the kitchen floor and rocked forward and backward, not responding to any of her attempts to get his attention. Helen took this as a direct insult to her mothering abilities. She began to wish that they had taken just the younger brother, though she felt guilty for thinking it. This was not at all what Helen had expected. She had thought the boys would be grateful for a stable home and was angry and hurt that Jet didn't show any gratitude.

Hank escaped the chaos at home by going to work early in the morning and not coming home until well after dark. He still expected that the house would be orderly and that Helen should have dinner ready, but he offered her no help. After all, she wasn't working, and it was she who wanted these children. Depressed, overwhelmed and exhausted, Helen called the adoption agency to ask what she should do with Jet, secretly hoping that they would offer to take him back. They suggested therapy and gave her a list of referrals. However, she didn't trust having a stranger know all her business, so she never called.

Over the past two years, the family has slowly adjusted. They have recently begun to notice that Jet's bad behavior seems to come in waves. For weeks, he will be calm and cooperative. He will play with Luke and is willing to help Helen. Then he becomes sullen and mean. Helen suspects that he is stealing money from her purse but can never catch him at it, and he lies to her for no apparent reason. In first grade now, he has already been suspended twice because of his aggression, and they have finally agreed to try therapy. She has little hope, though; nobody can fix this child.

Helen often tells Luke that she is glad that he isn't like his brother and compliments him on how he can play so well by himself. Luke does his best to live up to her expectations. In kindergarten now, he is the delight of his teachers, never causing trouble, always compliant and quiet. However, they note that he seldom plays with the other children and seems to be in his own world.

Pruning

As discussed in Chapter 1, after a period of exuberant growth in synaptic connections (blooming) during infancy and toddlerhood, all of the major neural pathways are in place by the end of the third year of life. At that point, synaptic connections that are weak or unused are eliminated through a process called **pruning**. The strong synapses that survive pruning then form into networks, or "neuro-clusters" (Mosier, 2013, p. 84) that are unique to the individual. Because the functioning of the brain requires a considerable expenditure of energy even in a resting state, this reduction in synaptic connections allows for essential energy conservation. Thus, the good news about pruning is that it both increases brain efficiency and decreases energy consumption. However, the bad news is that some brain functions develop primarily during specific sensitive periods, and if development doesn't occur during that time, that function may never develop or may develop poorly.

For example, Knudsen (2004) explains that among ducks and chickens, hatchlings have a period of only a few days in which they can imprint on their mother. If they don't imprint during that time, they will never recognize their mother as their mother and utilize her for care and protection. Similarly, some baby songbirds learn their species' characteristic songs by memorizing it as sung by their father. If the father is absent, they may memorize some other dialect of the song or even the song of another bird species altogether to which they have been exposed. In cases of absolute song deprivation during the critical period, these unfortunate birds will grow up to sing, but their songs will be highly abnormal.

Knudsen (2004) goes on to point out that among humans, there are sensitive periods for the development of a number of functions, such as stereoscopic vision and language proficiency. In addition, he suggests that there are sensitive periods for the capacity to form attachment relationships and proximity-seeking behaviors. Thompson (2001), however, argues that humans do not have the same kind of sensitive periods that are critical to duck, chicken, and songbird attachment imprinting. Instead, he points out that (as already discussed in Chapter 7) virtually all children attach during the first two years of life to whomever is taking care of them, even if that care is grossly inadequate. The *quality* of the attachment in children who are severely deprived in those first two years of life, though, may suffer seriously and persist into adulthood.

CLASS DISCUSSION

How do you think Jet's early experiences will have affected the pruning process as he enters early and middle childhood? Will Luke's experience be any different? Why or why not?

Although the damage done by inadequate attachment experiences may not permanently affect the architecture of the brain, after pruning begins in early childhood, those networks that were so carefully crafted by our brains during repeated experiences of insensitive parenting, neglect or abuse will become ever more difficult to replace. After all, Thompson (2001) cautions that the research on Romanian orphans shows that about one third of those who were adopted into loving families after one year of age showed atypical, bizarre or disorganized attachment years later. Sometimes, apparently, we just can't overcome our early programming. Knudsen (2004) points out that the neural circuitry devoted to early attachment is complex and extensive. However, he offers some hope to practitioners and their clients, saying that some molecular and cellular changes that occur during early childhood can be reversed. Moreover, several interventions have been developed that increase plasticity significantly in the neural circuitry of adult brains that have been shaped by their early attachment experiences. However, more research needs to be conducted to determine which interventions can effectively build that new circuitry.

Maturation of the Prefrontal Cortex

During early and middle childhood, the prefrontal cortex develops reciprocal connections with the subcortical regions of the brain responsible for attention, emotions, and social connection (e.g., the anterior cingulate, anterior insula, limbic area, amygdala and hippocampus) (Barrasso-Catanzaro & Eslinger, 2016). Thus, it is involved in two important developmental features—executive functions and self-evaluation—that are essential to successful transition through these stages.

I invite you to read Case Study 13.2, Macy Oster's First Years. Keep it in mind as you read the sections below and consider the questions in the sidebars.

CASE STUDY 13.2: MACY OSTER'S FIRST YEARS

Tara Oster was surprised when she got pregnant at age 42 after having tried unsuccessfully to get pregnant for ten years with her husband. She had been having an affair for seven months, and when her husband found out about it and realized that he wasn't the father of the baby, he filed for divorce. When she told her lover that she was pregnant, he demanded that she have an abortion. She was not willing to terminate her pregnancy, and he simply disappeared.

Macy was born a month and a half early. At five pounds, two ounces, she was too small to take home from the hospital immediately, but a week later Tara brought her home to stay. It was extremely hard for Tara during the first six months because it took Macy a long time before she was able to sleep through the night, and this left Tara exhausted. She had to return to work just weeks after she brought Macy home, so she called on her mother, Hazel, for help. Unfortunately, at age 63, Hazel had some health issues that drained her of energy on many days, and Macy was a real handful. She was a difficult baby with frequent digestive problems, and she was often restless and hard to soothe. Over time she grew into a difficult toddler, extremely active, into everything. She had a powerful temper, too.

As Macy got older, Tara would put her to bed as soon as she got home from Hazel's, sometimes singing her a lullaby or reading from one or another of her favorite books until Macy fell asleep. Many times, though, she was simply too tired to spend time with her daughter and would put her down in front of the TV so that she could do chores and get ready for work the next day.

Macy was relentlessly energetic, and she became clingy, whiny, and attention-seeking. Tara would often lament to Hazel, "What are we going to do with this child?! She's just like her father! He couldn't sit still either." They both did the best they could, but there were times when one or the other would lose her temper and yell at Macy. Afterwards, they would try to make it up to her, playing with her or giving her special treats, showering her with attention.

When Macy entered kindergarten, her teachers found her difficult to deal with. She was inattentive and squirmy. She had a hair-trigger temper and often struck out at her classmates impulsively. By second grade, she was becoming isolated and was regularly getting failing grades. Her classmates were reluctant to play games with her because she had trouble learning and following the rules. She wanted so badly to win that she would either start a fight or storm off if she found that she was losing. She was held back a grade in the hopes that she would mature somewhat and learn how to get along with others better.

When Macy was in fourth grade, the school suggested to Tara that she have Macy tested for ADHD, and sure enough, she was diagnosed and placed on psychostimulant medication. The medication helped Macy to contain her impulsivity and to focus on her schoolwork, but it also upset her stomach, so she resisted taking it. Sometimes, Tara just didn't have the energy to argue with her and would send her to school without it. The prescribing psychiatrist suggested that Tara and Macy also see a family social worker. She instructed Tara in how to enact a behavior modification plan for Macy, but Hazel couldn't keep up with it, and Tara eventually stopped bringing Macy to treatment.

Executive Functions

As discussed in Chapter 1, the prefrontal cortex is in charge of what is known as executive functions. According to Blair (2002), good executive function is the product of a brain that is able to integrate working memory, flexible attention, and effortful control in the service of goal-directed planning and activity. Successful development of executive functions over time allows the brain

> to organize cognitive and emotional resources effectively toward achieving goals and, ultimately, rewards … [to develop] sociomoral abilities such as perspective-taking, empathy, moral dilemmas, interpretation of the emotions and motives of others, and social emotions such as gratitude, embarrassment, and fear. (Barrasso-Catanzaro & Eslinger, 2016, p. 108–109)

Barrasso-Catanzaro and Eslinger (2016) group executive functions into three distinct categories—representational knowledge, operational processes, and self-regulation. In its earliest manifestation, representational knowledge allows a child to recognize that words stand for things. When Macy's grandmother says the word "bottle," obviously the word is not the bottle itself but *represents* a bottle. When she says the word and hands the bottle to Macy, Macy eventually gains the representational knowledge needed to understand that the word stands for the object. As her brain matures over childhood and adolescence, these kinds of representations become much more sophisticated and may include family or cultural rules, conventions, and norms, as well as abstract thought and the reading of other's intentions (mentalization).

The second executive function, operational processes, includes the ability to shift one's attention flexibly and efficiently; to use ones working memory to temporarily hold onto and manipulate information; and to utilize long-term memory in the service of organizing and planning so that one can set and reach one's goals (Barrasso-Catanzaro & Eslinger, 2016). Both attention and memory are important to learning. Imagine, for example, that Macy is in class on a day when her mom let her go to school without her medication, and the teacher is trying to teach her students how to add and subtract, but Macy is fascinated by a bird's nest in the tree outside the classroom window. What the teacher is putting on the blackboard isn't getting into Macy's working memory because her attention is elsewhere. Is it likely that she is going to remember how to add two and two? Will she be able to use that information to pass a test or to understand other arithmetic concepts? Probably not. Because Macy spends a large part of her time in school at this age, operational processes are essential to her successful transition through early and middle childhood. As she proceeds through these stages, not only does she need to be able to concentrate for longer periods of time, but she must be able to shift her attention in response to changes in context as well as to the requirements of various goals (Diaz, Blankenship, & Bell, 2018). Given her difficulty in shifting and maintaining attention, Macy may not be able to pay close attention her teachers' instructions or prioritize the information being presented in her classes. It is no wonder that her grades are suffering.

The third executive function, self-regulation, includes the capacity to inhibit negative emotions and manage behavioral responses to them (Barrasso-Catanzaro & Eslinger, 2016). If you remember, in Chapter 3 we learned about bottom-up ("low road") and top-down ("high road") processing. When a stimulus from the environment is perceived, it is sent simultaneously to the amygdala (bottom-up, "low road") and to the prefrontal cortex (top-down, "high road"). The amygdala makes decisions about approach and avoidance, almost instantaneously producing emotional responses that may result in automatic behaviors. The prefrontal cortex acts considerably more slowly but allows an individual to respond to stimuli in more reasoned ways. When the prefrontal cortex is adequately connected with the amygdala and the hippocampus, it can modulate the amygdala's response and avoid sending the individual into fight/flight/freeze responses. Thus, self-regulation is highly dependent on adequate functioning of the prefrontal cortex.

CLASS DISCUSSION

Think for a moment about how Jet's history of trauma and neglect may have affected his bottom-up and top-down processing capabilities. If his reactions to his peers are "low-road" responses, could that explain his aggression?

In addition to the inhibition of the fear responses, the prefrontal cortex also allows what is known as effortful control. This is the ability to shift one's attention and integrate information from the environment so that one can decide what to do in a given circumstance. It has to do with inhibiting pulses delaying gratification in order to receive a greater benefit later. This last ability is essential to motivation, and it depends on an individual's ability to self-regulate his or her needs and desires. Blair (2002) notes that self-regulation emerges during early childhood as the prefrontal cortex begins to mature at just about the time that children start school and under normal circumstances should increase and stabilize with age. However, a poorly functioning prefrontal cortex impairs an individual's ability to self-monitor, to plan, to shift and sustain attention, and to respond to impending reward or punishment. Therefore, he argues that a child's readiness for school is dependent upon his or her self-regulatory skills.

CLASS DISCUSSION

Do you think that Macy's premature birth has anything to do with her problems in school? What do you think Macy's attachment style is? Could that have anything to do with her grades or her social problems?

Children learn self-regulation skills from their early caregivers. Just as parents label their children's body parts when they say things like, "Just look at your chubby little cheeks!" or "Isn't that the cutest little button nose?" (examples of representational knowledge, by the way), they also label their children's emotions for them so that they come to know the words associated with their feelings. In addition, parents model responses to their own emotions (for good or for ill) and thus teach their children which emotions are appropriate to display, which should remain hidden, and at what level given emotions can be expressed.

When this is done well, children are prepared to think about, experience, and respond to their own and others' emotions. When it is not done well, they struggle to get their own needs met and to relate constructively to peers, teachers and other adults. In addition, if they are unable to manage their emotions adequately, their ability to think clearly may be impaired, diminishing their ability to plan, make good decisions, resolve conflicts and find good solutions to problems (Mosier, 2013). Take Luke, for example. Helen is giving him clear feedback about which emotions she approves of and which she doesn't approve of. She is encouraging Luke to manage his negative emotions on his own, praising him for not acting like his big brother, telling him that she loves him for being quiet and calm. He is learning his lessons well and generalizing them to the school setting. However, he pays a dear price, doesn't he? He has learned that he is loved and approved of because of what he does, not because of who he is.

Szalavitz and Perry (2011) suggest that it is through ongoing positive adult relationships both within and outside the family that children develop the ability to identify, understand, and constructively express their emotions. With help from responsible adults, they can gradually increase their ability to read, understand, and express empathy for others' emotions and regulate their behavioral responses to them. Importantly, with this ongoing care and attention, children gradually develop a sense of personal agency and self-efficacy as they navigate their physical and social environments. Thus, when the prefrontal cortex is given the opportunity to connect well with lower portions of the brain, the stage is set for positive outcomes across all of the later life stages.

CLASS DISCUSSION

What would you say to Helen about how she can help Luke to express his emotions?

Self-Evaluation

Individuals begin to develop a sense of self starting at about seven months of age (Marchetti, Massaro & Di Dio, 2017; Stern, 1985) when they begin to realize every time they move that they have bodies made up of muscles, bones, and joints, and that this body is separate and distinct from their mother's body. When the left brain begins to function during toddlerhood, they are able to form explicit memories about their experiences and to interpret events that have occurred. Over time, this capacity provides them with an autobiographical narrative of who they are, where they come from, what they can and can't do, what they like and don't like, and what they can expect for themselves and others. In contrast to early, implicit memories, this narrative is available for conscious analysis and interpretation and can be put into words.

Related to this growing sense of self is a global sense of self-worth based on the individual's evaluation of self in relation to others, a process that requires self-reflection. Self-reflection is a conscious process through which an individual first determines whether environmental cues apply to him- or herself and then makes decisions about what should be done if they do apply (van der Meer, Costafreda, Aleman, & David, 2010; Pfeifer, Dapretto, & Lieberman, 2010). The ability to self-reflect becomes particularly important at this time of life when children begin to move out into various community contexts (day care, kindergarten, and school, sports, etc.) where they begin to compare themselves to a broad number of other individuals. Thus, "having an accurate representation of one's traits, abilities and attitudes is important in evaluating one's own behavior and comparing it with the behavior of other human beings" (van der Meer, Costafreda, Aleman, & David, 2010, p. 936). It is the maturing prefrontal cortex that mediates their ability to reflect on their qualities and behaviors.

According to Pfeifer, Dapretto, and Lieberman (2010), self-evaluation during early childhood is considerably less sophisticated than it is during middle childhood, which is in turn less sophisticated than it is in adolescence. Moreover, evaluations of self are based not just on what individuals think of themselves, but also on what they think other people think of them. As children enter early childhood, they tend to base their descriptions of themselves on single instances of behavior. The prefrontal cortex is not yet well connected to their hippocampus, so, as will be discussed in the section below, explicit memory retrieval of multiple instances of evaluation may not be available yet. In addition, they tend to base their opinions of themselves on valence (i.e., their intrinsic goodness or badness). For example, at age four or five, Macy might evaluate herself by saying, "I am a good girl because I helped my mommy fold the laundry."

In contrast, by about the age of eight, the prefrontal cortex is normally developing reciprocal connections with the hippocampus, amygdala, anterior and posterior cingulate and anterior insula that allows them to base their understanding of self on generalizations about their behaviors, abilities, and attitudes that recur over time. At this age, Macy might describe herself by saying, "I am a good person because I am friendly and smart." However, in late middle childhood, the prefrontal cortex is even better connected, and the social engagement system has developed to the point that she can take other people's perspectives into consideration. At that point, Macy's self-evaluation may extend these same kinds of assessments to include how other people see her. She might say something like, "Other kids in my class think I am friendly and smart." In addition, as Macy approaches adolescence, she will be able to differentiate between the various domains of her life (e.g., academic performance, athletic performance, conduct, physical attributes, and sociability). For example, in late middle childhood she may describe herself by saying, "I'm really good at science but terrible at sports."

CLASS DISCUSSION

What are Jet's and Luke's self-evaluations based on? How do you think they see themselves?

Development of Episodic Memory

It is important to remember that during infancy, right brain functions are dominant. Memories are encoded during this time by the amygdala and thus are not available for conscious recall. At about the time a child starts to talk, however, his or her hippocampus comes on line and starts encoding memories on the left side of the brain, memories that are recognized as coming from the past and which are generally expressed in words. As the years pass during early childhood, children become increasingly able to remember and recount the details of events and interpret them in light of their own and others' emotional reactions to them.

In addition to the development of explicit memory capabilities, children begin to develop a capacity called *prospection*, which is "the ability to mentally project forward in time in order to pre-experience future events" (Coughlin, Lyons, & Ghetti, 2014, p. 97). Suddendorf and Corballis (2007) call this capacity "mental time travel" (p. 299). That is, between the ages of three and five, children begin to gain the ability to remember something that has happened to them and to use this memory to imagine what is going to happen in the future. This capability is essential to motivation and planning for the future and also to adaptive behavior in the present. Unfortunately, it also means that children who are exposed to chronic family violence or other stressors may develop maladaptive behaviors based on past experiences and expectations for the future that can interfere with their ability to manage their recollections and/or moderate their fear responses in the present (Cross, Fani, Powers, & Bradley, 2017). That is, when a fearful memory is triggered by something in the environment, the expectation that something terrible is going to happen may pop up automatically, as frequently happens in children with PTSD.

CLASS DISCUSSION

How do you think Jet's memories of his experiences in foster care are affecting his relationship with his adoptive parents? His teachers? How is this different from how Luke's experiences in foster care may affect his relationship with his adoptive parents? His teachers? How are both of these different from how Macy or Sophia's experiences in infancy and toddlerhood might affect their expectations for their relationship with their families? Their teachers?

Growing Importance of Peers

It is important to understand that the neurological changes discussed above occur to a great extent in the context of peer relationships established in school and in the community. During early and middle childhood, children tend to become more active in the broader community, attending school and extracurricular activities and playing out in their neighborhoods. They begin spending more time with their peers and less time with their families, and peer relationships become increasingly important. Sroufe et al. (2005, p. 56) provide an excellent summary of the issues that children face as they begin to negotiate their relationships with peers during these stages (see Table 13.1). I have included the information on adolescents in that table to show clearly how relationships get more complex as children approach adulthood. Successful development of peer relationships is supported by the neurological growth discussed above.

In addition, relationship skills in one stage provide the foundations for the skills in the next stage. Thus, peer relations in early childhood are actually built on the attachment relationships established in infancy and toddlerhood.

TABLE 13.1   Issues Associated with Peer Relationships During Early and Middle Childhood and Adolescence

Preschool: "Positive Engagement of Peers"

1. Selecting specific partners
2. Sustaining interactive bouts
   a. Negotiating conflicts in interaction
   b. Maintaining organization in the face of arousal
   c. Finding pleasure in the interactive process
3. Participation in groups

Middle Childhood: "Investment in the Peer World"

1. Forming loyal friendships
2. Sustaining relationships
   a. Negotiating relationship conflicts
   b. Tolerating a range of emotional experiences
   c. Enhancement of self in relationships
3. Functioning in stable, organized groups
   a. Adhering to group norms
   b. Maintaining gender boundaries
4. Coordinating friendships and group functioning

Adolescence: "Integrating Self and Peer Relationships"

1. Forming intimate relationships
   a. Self-disclosing same-gender relationships
   b. Cross-gender relationships
   c. Sexual relationships
2. Commitment in relationships
   a. Negotiating self-relevant conflicts
   b. Emotional vulnerability
   c. Self-disclosure and self-identity
3. Functioning in a relationship network
   a. Mastering multiple rule systems
   b. Establishing flexible boundaries
4. Coordinating multiple relationships
   a. Same-gender and cross-gender
   b. Intimate relationships and group functioning

Source: Sroufe, L. A., Egeland, B., Carlson, E., & Collins, W. A. (2005). Placing early attachment experiences in developmental context: The Minnesota Longitudinal Study. In K. E. Grossman, K. Grossman and E. Waters (Eds.), Attachment from infancy to adulthood: The major longitudinal studies *(pp. 48–70). New York, NY: Guilford Press.*

Sroufe and his associates (2005) emphasize that secure attachment during infancy and toddlerhood allows a child "to acquire the attitudes that support engagement with peers, personal capacities to stay engaged and to be attractive to peer partners, and a fundamental understanding of what relationships require" (p. 57). Therefore, parents who provide a secure base and safe haven, who regulate their child's levels of stimulation and arousal until their child can do this on his or her own, and who act as positive roles models for conflict resolution and problem-solving are setting the stage for relationships for the rest of the child's life. Parents who provide sensitive limit-setting and adequate socialization early in life and then honor their child's growing need for relative independence as he or she matures are setting their child up to establish the social support he or she will need to thrive in the world. Then, "As development continues, early attachment, later family experiences, and peer experiences together provide the foundation for the intimate relationships of maturity. These adult partner relationships, in turn, of course, are additional foundations for parenting and other tasks of later adulthood" (Sroufe et al., 2005, p. 67). Thus, secure attachment is passed onto the next generation.

Summary

The neurobiological changes discussed above impact children's ability to establish and maintain relationships as they begin to leave their families to go out into the wider world of school, neighborhood, and community. Children in this age group have active imaginations and want to explore and engage with their worlds. Erikson (1963) assumes that children need to begin to plan and initiate action on their own during early childhood and to experience remorse for actions that hurt others. As they move into middle childhood, children need to master both academic and social skills. These tasks, essential to successful transition into adolescence, require that children be able to recognize, understand, and manage their own emotions so that they can get along with other children and adults and get their wants and needs met in socially acceptable ways. In addition, they need to learn how to become acceptable members of society so that they can make their way in the world without undue restraint and can strengthen the social structure so that it can, in turn, support its members (morality). Thus, they need to develop both morality and emotional intelligence during these childhood development stages. Much of this learning is done during early childhood in the context of play with friends and peers. Therefore, in the next chapter, I will discuss how play aids development during this life stage and how emotional intelligence and moral behavior arise in the context of family and community.

CHAPTER 14

Social and Intellectual Development in Early and Middle Childhood

LEARNING OBJECTIVES

After completing this chapter, readers should understand:

- Why play is important to successful transition through the early and middle childhood developmental stages.
- What emotional intelligence is and how it develops during early and middle childhood.
- What the neurobiological foundations of emotional intelligence and morality are.
- How emotional intelligence and morality affect social relationships.

KEY IDEAS

1. Although family remains important throughout early and middle childhood, relationships with peers become of increasing importance.
2. Play is critical to the development of emotional and behavioral regulation that allows positive social connectedness and mental health.
3. Emotional intelligence entails the ability to manage one's own and others' emotions and behaviors and is built on a foundation of secure attachment.
4. Neurological changes during early and middle childhood affect the individual's ability to establish a sense of self and manage peer relationships.
5. Closely associated with emotional intelligence, morality is an innate human ability that manifests among individuals with well-functioning social engagement systems.

Introduction

According to Erikson (1963) children between the ages of three and five are in the *Initiative vs. Guilt* developmental stage. During this stage, they need to begin to initiate purposeful actions and manage the frustrations they experience associated with parental and environmental restrictions of those actions. Then in middle childhood (Erikson's *Industry vs. Inferiority stage*), they need to be industrious and to persevere in the face of frustration as they develop and master academic and social competencies that will eventually support their adult relationships and activities (e.g., marriage, children, work, etc.). Thus, during these stages, children must begin to do things and make decisions on their own, accept correction, and feel remorse when their mistakes hurt others. In addition, they must figure out how to get along with both peers and adults as they progress through school and enter the wider community.

Panksepp (2012b) suggests that much of the maturation of the brain and consequent emotional regulation needed for success in these stages occurs in the context of play. Play allows children to gain some emotional independence from their parents and to learn to enjoy and maintain friendly relationships outside of the family, setting the stage for normal individuation during adolescence and young adulthood. According to Marks-Tarlow et al. (2018), when children play, they learn the various social roles and rules of their culture. In addition, they "push the very edges of what is tolerable and understandable as they wrestle, spin, twirl, hurl, and leap into novel states of mind" (p. 1). In this way, they come to better understand and regulate their own and others' emotions and behaviors, thus developing what is known as *emotional intelligence.*

Emotional intelligence arises out of a well-functioning social engagement system that allows accurate perception of others' social signals and one's own response to them. Because humans are social animals, they have developed neural circuits that promote concern not just for the well-being of one's own self but also for that of others, something that is essential to the social skills that children need to master. In addition, these kinds of concerns are the foundations of *morality*. It is thought that children have an innate ability to care for others and to learn the moral messages embedded in their families and their cultures, much like their inborn ability to learn any language that is spoken to them (Gazzillo et al., 2019).

In this chapter, I begin with a discussion of the importance of play to the maturation of neural networks and social connectedness and then delve into the literature on emotional intelligence as it influences the mastery of social skills that allow successful transition through these stages. Last, I consider how attachment and parenting practices influence the development of morality. To help you connect this information to your work as mental health practitioners, I will explore how Sophia Ramirez and her parents (from Chapter 10) handle some of the changes associated with this developmental stage.

Play

Play is a powerful context for children to learn how to successfully establish and maintain peer relationships. In the next section, I will discuss how the brain and attachment support this essential activity. Please read Case Study 14.1 concerning Luke's early experiences and think about how they are affecting his ability to engage with his peers as he enters middle childhood.

CASE STUDY 14.1: LUKE GOES TO SCHOOL

When Luke entered the school system, he continued to be quiet and to cause little trouble. Indeed, his second grade teacher commented to a co-worker that she sometimes forgot that he was even in the classroom. After he moved on to the third grade, the teacher remembered his name but couldn't remember what he looked like. His grades were adequate, but he seemed strangely lacking in curiosity and never showed any particular interest in any subject. He never asked for help from his teachers and refused his mother's offers for help on homework.

In eighth grade now, Luke maintains his solitude. He seldom plays with other children unless he is assigned an activity with someone. During recess, he tends to play by himself and avoids competitive games. He is almost always the last one to be chosen as a teammate; he is overweight and slow, and he shows little enthusiasm for sports.

For the past several years, Luke has spent most of his time either in his room watching TV and playing video games on a tablet, or wandering alone through the woods behind his house. He loves his older brother but is also afraid of him. Jet will sometimes play mean pranks on him and then tell Luke that if he tells on Jet, Jet will beat him up. It only took once for Jet to follow through on that threat before Luke learned to simply get out of the way when his brother is around.

Recently, Luke discovered online gaming, and since then, he has spent every minute he could following the pros and playing with friends he meets online. He admires those kids who win the tournaments and earn the big prizes. For the first time in his life, he has a group of friends he can hang out with. They know him as "SkyWalkinGamer" but don't know who he is or what he looks like, and they don't care about what grades he gets or what kind of clothes he wears. They are just interested in the same things he is interested in. If things get too personal, he just signs off, and if Jet and his mom and dad are fighting, he can escape to a much better place.

Papousek (2016) points out that, like attachment, play is a basic psychobiological need among young children, and they engage in play in one form or another most of their waking hours from infancy to adolescence. Moreover, research has shown that when children are not allowed to play, they are at increased risk of developing cognitive, emotional, social, and physical problems over the long term (Brown & Eberle, 2018).

Because of the proven value of play to optimal child development, the United Nations has declared play to be the right of every child (Ginsburg et al., 2007). Play is not just "a simple joy that is a cherished part of childhood" (p. 183). Instead,

> Play allows children to use their creativity while developing their imagination, dexterity, and physical, cognitive, and emotional strength. Play is important to healthy brain development. It is through play that children at a very early age engage and interact in the world around them. Play allows children to create and explore a world they can master, conquering their fears while practicing adult roles, sometimes in conjunction with other children or adult caregivers. As they master their world, play helps children develop new competencies that lead to enhanced confidence and the resiliency they need to face future challenges. Undirected play allows children to learn how to work in groups, to share, to negotiate, to resolve conflicts, and to learn self-advocacy skills. When play is allowed to be child driven, children practice decision-making skills, move at their own pace, discover their own areas of interest, and ultimately engage fully in the passions they wish to pursue. (p. 183)

To see how important to physical and social development play is, take a moment to look at the numerous benefits that play provides shown in Table 14.1.

TABLE 14.1   Benefits of Play

Opportunities to Develop:

Physical:
- Adaptive responses to the unexpected
- Dexterity
- Agility

Interpersonal:
- Realistic interpretation of social signals
- Communication skills
- The ability to communicate coherent narratives
- Metacommunication skills (communicating about communication)
- Social competence
- An understanding of culturally acceptable roles, rules, and relationships
- Empathy through perspective-taking
- Problem-solving skills

Intrapersonal:
- Meaning making
- Regulation of affect (emotional stability)
- Identity (who one is and who one wants to become)
- Symbolic representation
- Imagination
- Creativity/invention
- Intelligence
- Problem-solving
- Divergent thinking
- Novel forms of speech, thought, behavior and social interaction
- Pride
- Satisfaction
- Sense of accomplishment
- Self-efficacy

Source: Siegel, D. & Hartzell, M. (2003). *Parenting from the inside out: How a deeper self-understanding can help you raise children who thrive.* New York, NY: Penguin. Doi: https://doi.org/10.1007/s10615-009-0226-0

Characteristics of Play

Hughes (2010) holds that an activity must have five essential characteristics for it to be considered play. First, it must be *intrinsically motivated.* That is, it is done simply for the satisfaction it provides; it is engaged in as an end in itself, simply for the fun of it. Second, the player must *freely* choose it. That is, if the activity is assigned (educators, listen up!) or if the individual is coerced into it (overzealous parents, listen up!), he or she may regard it as work (or perhaps as punishment) rather than as play. A third requirement of play is that the activity must be *pleasurable*; if it isn't fun, it isn't play; it's something else. A fourth requirement for an activity to be considered play is that it must be *non-literal.* All young mammals play in ways that let them *simulate* behaviors that are important to survival. Even rough-and-tumble activities and organized sports can be considered simulations of real-life activities. However, players must use facial expressions, vocalizations, and actions during these simulations that indicate that the activity is meant to be play. A last requirement for a playful activity is that the player must be *actively engaged* in it. That is, for it to be considered play, the player must be physically and/or psychologically engaged, not simply passively present with no real interest in the activity.

As you might suspect, because play is such an ancient and survival-oriented activity, it is embedded in our neural circuitry. In the next section, I will discuss how our brains are involved in play.

Neurobiology of Play

Stagnitti (2017) notes that "true play is good brain chemistry, as there is a release of a symphony of 'feel good' hormones such as opioids, oxytocin, and dopamine when we are engaged in physically interactive play" (p. 186). If you remember from Chapter 2, one of Panksepp's (2009) seven affective/emotional neural circuits is PLAY. He argues that the PLAY system is a genetically programmed drive present in all social animals and is just as important as other drives such as hunger, thirst, and sex. Brown & Eberle (2018) emphasize the importance of play to human survival and development by stating that "we are built to play, and built through PLAY" (p. 38), pointing out that play-deprived individuals exhibit cortical imbalances similar to those found among sleep-deprived individuals, though the effects may take longer to manifest. Some of you may know from experience what sleep deprivation feels like. However, this research suggests that a lack of play may, over time, affect you just as negatively as lack of sleep. Any of you mental health practitioners or student interns, take heed! To tweak an old adage slightly, all work and no play makes Jack a less effective therapist!

> **CLASS DISCUSSION**
>
> How do you incorporate play into your own self-care? How might you incorporate play into your treatment with clients?

Repeated experiences of play that is both safe and exciting, that brings the child joy while teaching him or her the boundaries and limitations of engagement with others, builds resilience and widens what Siegel (2006) calls their window of tolerance. The size of the window of tolerance depends on how well the limbic system and the prefrontal cortex are integrated (Badenoch & Kestly, 2015). In Figure 14.1, the social engagement system (which determines the size of the window of tolerance) is characterized as *a zone of optimal arousal* in which an individual is on a continuum of arousal from low to high. When an individual feels safe in a zone of optimal arousal, he or she can have fun, smiling and laughing, relaxed and flexible. Thus, children can have fun while happily playing together in rough-and-tumble or silly activities (mobilization without fear). However, if the face-to-face interaction with another becomes too stimulating, rambunctious or aggressive (physically or relationally), it's not fun anymore, stops being play, and turns into fight or flight (mobilization with fear).

On the other side of the window of tolerance, children may play together gently, enjoying each other's company quietly, hiding or pretending to be asleep (immobilization without fear). However, if the play turns hurtful, a child may first try smart vagal responses like talking, smiling, etc. but then resort to sympathetic fight or vegetative vagal responses—leaving physically in shame or perhaps leaving psychologically through dissociation.

Reasonably safe play can widen a child's window of tolerance. It allows him or her to practice a wide range of social behaviors and to manage both positive high-arousal emotions

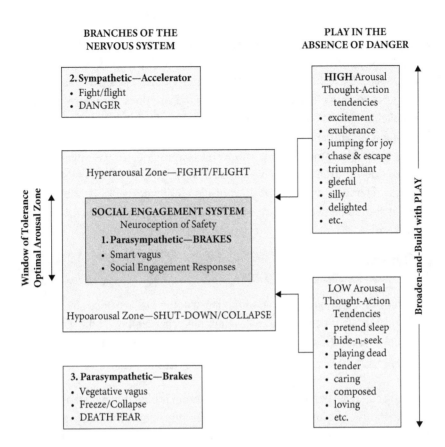

BRANCHES OF THE NERVOUS SYSTEM

2. Sympathetic—Accelerator
- Fight/flight
- DANGER

Hyperarousal Zone—FIGHT/FLIGHT

SOCIAL ENGAGEMENT SYSTEM
Neuroception of Safety
1. Parasympathetic—BRAKES
- Smart vagus
- Social Engagement Responses

Hypoarousal Zone—SHUT-DOWN/COLLAPSE

3. Parasympathetic—Brakes
- Vegetative vagus
- Freeze/Collapse
- DEATH FEAR

Window of Tolerance Optimal Arousal Zone

PLAY IN THE ABSENCE OF DANGER

HIGH Arousal Thought-Action tendencies
- excitement
- exuberance
- jumping for joy
- chase & escape
- triumphant
- gleeful
- silly
- delighted
- etc.

LOW Arousal Thought-Action Tendencies
- pretend sleep
- hide-n-seek
- playing dead
- tender
- caring
- composed
- loving
- etc.

Broaden-and-Build with PLAY

FIGURE 14.1   **Play in the Nervous System: Hierarchy of Arousal Zones**

Theresa Kestley, Play from "Presence and Play: Why Mindfulness Matters," *International Journal of Play Therapy*, vol. 25, no. 1, pp. 19. Copyright © 2016 by American Psychological Association.

(excitement, delight) and positive low-arousal emotions (tenderness, caring) (Kestly, 2018). Children have to *learn* how to manage themselves with others, and they must be "taught the requirements of intimacy and playfulness on an individual basis" through well-supervised but free and open play (Panksepp, 2018, p. 266).

Panksepp (2018) is very outspoken about how important play is to the developing child. He argues that, "In the long term, lots of joyous physical PLAY probably helps build and strengthen the reflective, inhibitory resources that facilitate adult prosocial planning" (p. 252). He argues further that

> PLAYfulness reflects that emotional system's urge to positively engage with others, routinely as well as creatively, allowing youngsters to learn about diverse social dynamics in pleasurable ways. This can lead children to CARE about others more while they SEEK to understand and become affectively positive productive actors in their social worlds. (p. 254)

However, he also emphasizes how necessary adult attention is, saying, "Woe to the child who does not have emotionally responsive and resilient CARE providers. Woe to the child who has too much FEAR, RAGE, and PANIC, which can lead positive creativity to shrivel" (p. 247). He goes so far as to suggest that western culture does not appreciate the value of play to the development of cognitive and social resources, stressing instead the importance of academic achievement and behavioral compliance and the use of pharmacological interventions among overly-rambunctious children to support them. He suggests instead that we should provide children with "play sanctuaries" (p. 264) in which children are allowed to play freely, preferably in nature, with minimal adult intervention. When intervention is necessary, it should be used as an opportunity to teach social skills and empathy, not to punish or control.

CLASS DISCUSSION

Do you think that providing children with "play sanctuaries" is a good idea? If so, what would it take for your community to develop "play sanctuaries" in the schools within your school district? What would be one step that you could take to make that happen?

As already discussed in earlier chapters, a child's brain is built during infancy in response to interactions with his or her mother. Many of the activities that a mother engages in with her baby are infused with playfulness. Therefore, play and attachment are closely related. In the next section, I will discuss how play is related to attachment style.

Attachment and Play

How a mother responds to her child's play becomes part of his or her internal working models of self and others. That is, play and attachment are intimately bound together, and the attachment style that develops during infancy influences how a child (and later an adult) plays. Secure attachment is fundamental to the development of healthy and happy play (Papousek, 2016). Indeed, as Schore and Marks-Tarlow (2018) explain, "Love is capable of energetically jump starting all of the positive emotions and behavior, including interest, excitement, joy, curiosity, exploration and play …, [resulting in] passionate engagement throughout life, including a love of life itself" (p. 65).

Gordon (2014) uses some metaphors (shown in Table 14.2) that suggest ways that secure and insecure attachment styles affect playfulness. Because having a secure base to access when something goes wrong while exploring the world, a child with secure attachment can simply play. Even in circumstances in which there are ambiguous social signals or it is not clear that the situation is appropriate for play, he or she is open to the possibility of looking, examining, manipulating, pushing, pulling, running, tumbling, laughing, approaching, or whatever, knowing that mom is both available and aware. Gordon emphasizes that when such children make the assumption that the world is a playground, it doesn't mean that they are *too* trusting or *too* optimistic. Instead, she argues that their attachment security allows them to read others' social cues accurately and either to recognize and avoid danger or to recover from dangerous situations relatively easily.

Play among insecure children is very different. An anxious/ambivalent child can't be sure that mom will be available, aware, or responsive if trouble arises, so the focus may be more on staying close to mom and getting her attention than it is on play. When encountering a stranger, whether it is another child or an adult, children with anxious attachment may either actively seek out the stranger's approval or defend themselves against the need for their approval (or perhaps both). These tendencies are likely to remain as the child begins to interact with peers and adults in school and out in the community. Remember that anxious attachment has to do with the fear of abandonment and with an uncertainty about one's acceptability. Thus, these children may focus on pleasing others, and they may become extremely upset if they lose a friend.

TABLE 14.2   Playground Metaphors

METAPHOR AND ATTACHMENT STYLE	CHILD EXPECTATIONS
World as Playground: secure	• World is friendly and adventures will be enriching • Ambiguity and uncertainty are exciting • Strangers are potential playmates • New environments are potential playgrounds
World as Proving Ground: Anxious/ambivalent	• World may not provide support • Little trust in self; must test others and the world constantly to determine who/what is trustworthy • Ambiguity and uncertainty are threatening and must be controlled • Strangers approval must be won • Societal/cultural expectations must be met even if it doesn't provide happiness
World as Battleground: Avoidant	• World is hostile or indifferent, unwelcoming or unsafe • Little trust in others; do not ask for support • Ambiguity and uncertainty cause phobic or counterphobic responses and stress • Prefer relatively small environment that they can control
World as Prison: Disorganized/disoriented	• World is a perpetual threat • Little trust in self or others • Ambiguity and uncertainty cause disorganized fight/flight/freeze responses (dissociation or eruptions of violence) • Avoidance of others

Source: Gordon, G. (2014). Well played: The origins and future of playfulness. *American Journal of Play*, 6(2), 234-266.

Children with avoidant attachment, on the other hand, assume that they are on their own in a world that is scary and dangerous. Given what you know about Luke's early attachment experiences from the case studies you have read so far, it shouldn't come as a surprise that he avoids social interaction. In addition, since children like Luke may actively avoid novelty and excitement in an effort to control their anxiety (even if there is no clear danger), you can see how this can contribute to their isolation. Interestingly, avoidant children may have become experts at denying negative emotions such as anxiety and may actively seek out novelty and excitement even when it is actually dangerous. Either response, however, is accompanied by a ramped up HPA system and reactivity to stress.

Disorganized/disoriented children have the most trouble playing because playing requires feelings of safety (Porges, 2011). These children seldom feel safe enough to have fun because to them the world is always dangerous and they have found no reliable way to defend themselves (Gordon, 2014). If they do play with others, they may have difficulty with the excitement of the game, lose control of their emotions and reactions, and ruin the fun for everyone. They may be desperately lonely but terrified of being abandoned if they make friends.

Children start playing very early in life, and how they play, and who/what they play with necessarily change as their bodies and brains grow. What does play look like in children at different stages of development? In the next section, I will describe play among infants and toddlers and how that changes in early and middle childhood.

Types of Play

There are two basic forms of play during childhood—physical play and social play. Physical play has been described as being "so central to child development that it should be included in the very definition of childhood" (Milteer, Ginsburg, the Council on Communications and Media, & Committee on Psychosocial Aspects of Child and Family Health, 2012, p. e204). It builds dexterity, agility, and endurance, allows children to explore how the physical world works, and promotes the development of motor and cognitive skills. It is important throughout childhood, not just to physical development but also to the development of creativity, an attribute that is of profound importance to a successful and happy life (Blair, 2002; Ogden, 2018).

In contrast, lack of physical activity has been linked to childhood obesity (Singh, Siahpush, & Kogan, 2010). Childhood obesity is related in turn to numerous physical health issues as well as to mental health problems (e.g., depression, eating disorders, and low self-esteem) not just in childhood but also in adulthood (Basset, John, Conger, Fitzhugh, & Coe, 2015; Ma, Frick, Crawford, & Guyer, 2015). It is important to address obesity early in life since research shows that overweight preschoolers are five times more likely to be overweight at age twelve than are their normal weight peers, and obese adolescents are as much as 20 times more likely to become obese adults than are their normal-weight peers (Ma et al., 2015). Thus, physical activity during childhood may help to reduce the very high personal and societal costs of obesity.

Social play is normal among all mammals. Among humans, it provides opportunities for social connectedness both within and beyond the family unit, and the development of social skills, emotional regulation, cooperation and healthy competition that are essential to the well-being of the individual in society (Hughes, 2010). Moreover, if a child doesn't have the opportunity for social play, there is a high likelihood that he or she will develop mental health problems. Indeed, Vanderschuren, Achterberg and Trezza (2016) state that "the importance [of social play] should not be underestimated because of the fact that social impairments, including aberrant social play, are core symptoms of pediatric mental disorders, such as autism, disruptive behavior disorders, attention-deficit/hyperactivity disorder and early-onset schizophrenia" (p. 87).

In the sections below, I will discuss the two types of play as they manifest among humans in infancy and toddlerhood and then in early and middle childhood.

Infant and Toddler Physical Play

Babies come into the world ready to connect with their environments. Over the first two months, that connection happens, according to Gordon (2014), through normal sensorimotor stimulation as a child smells, tastes, touches, and moves. Play at this stage doesn't look like what we generally think of as play—foot kicking, rocking, for example (Pelligrini & Smith, 1998). This is a kind of primitive object play in which the child explores his or her own body as an object, noticing the physical sensations that it provides, engaging in motor activity simply for the pleasure of moving. However, play at this age does not include the intellectual awareness and intentionality required to be considered real play (Hughes, 2010). Instead, it seems to be primarily for the purpose of developing the motor systems within in the brain.

Hughes (2010) notes that by around the age of five months, infants begin to engage in genuine object play, and by the age of nine months tend to seek out new objects in preference to more familiar objects. At around the age of one, children begin to engage in exercise play (i.e., vigorous, playful gross locomotor movements), which evolves into rough-and-tumble play (Pellegrini & Smith, 1998). By toddlerhood, children tend to become incredibly and relentlessly active, curious, and imaginative. They are interested in almost anything that is new to them, whether it be toys, bugs, flowers, activities, or people, and they engage with them in what is known as exploratory play. Gordon (2014) suggests that this kind of play during this early stage of life should be called *protoexploration* since it "leads to increasing complexity in physical expression (sports, dance, and similar activities), the arts and sciences, adventure, performance, experimentation, hobbies, risky or deep play, vertiginous play, games of chance, and personal growth as a whole. ..." (p. 244).

Infant and Toddler Social Play

Hughes (2010) points out that, although they are not yet actively playing with other children, even during the first few weeks and months of life babies take an active interest in their peers, gazing at them with intense curiosity and even leaning towards them as if to take a closer look, waving their arms in excitement. However, the mother is the first real playmate.

At eight weeks of age, an infant's visual cortex matures sufficiently to make eye contact possible, which in turn makes it possible for the baby to recognize and respond to his or her mother's facial expressions. This milestone opens the door to the first form of social play—infant-mother attuned play (Gordon, 2014). This interaction results in synchronized waves of alternating stimulation and soothing through which the baby learns how to manage emotions associated with the normal novelty and stress of being alive. Dissanayake (2017) explains that in

> ordinary face-to-face play, both mother and baby are doing something quite specialized, based on inborn competencies and sensitivities. Using rhythmic head and body movements, gestures, and facial expressions as well as vocal sounds, the pair create and maintain communicative sequences that are exquisitely patterned over time. Even newborns show sensitivity to temporal sequence and pattern and engage in behavioral turn-taking as early as eight weeks of age. ... It heralds our later social lives, whether in conversation, social play, lovemaking, and ... music, dance and other performance arts" (p. 147).

Infant-mother playfulness could be called *protosocial* play because it is followed by "myriad forms of more complex social play including rough-and-tumble play, joking, mimetic play, agonistic play, social games, team sports, contests, festivals, celebrations, and rituals" (p. 244). It provides a foundation of joy and curiosity on which the child can build interest, passion, and vitality for the remainder of his or her life (Schore, 1994).

The secure attachment that comes from maternal attunement and sensitivity promotes a willingness in the child to begin to explore the environment even more once he or she reaches toddlerhood. Their joint play "assumes a central role in the development of intersubjective emotional relatedness, shared intentionality, social cognition, and empathy" (Papousek, 2016, p. 165). Two-year-olds tend to engage in either solitary play or onlooker play rather than engaging in cooperative play (Hughes, 2010). They may also engage in parallel play at this stage in which they engage in the same activities and at the same time as other children around them but remain separate from them. This may be a transitional kind of play between immature solitary and more cooperative forms of play that require a higher level of sophistication that appear around the age of three or four.

CLASS DISCUSSION

How do you think Jet's experiences during infancy affect his ability to play as a toddler? When he enters the school system? How may his play affect his ability to master social skills?

Early and Middle Childhood Physical Play

Children have enormous amounts of energy during early and middle childhood. In preschool, children enjoy playing outdoors, where they can play noisily, make messes, explore, and experiment without as much adult supervision and control as tends to happen indoors. They particularly love natural settings with plenty of vegetation, and they make good use of any materials they find there to stimulate their imaginations—old tires, lumber, empty boxes, rocks, mud, etc. In large open spaces, whether indoors or outdoors, they can let off steam by running, jumping, and other rough-and-tumble activities. In smaller spaces, they can enjoy playing with clay and paint, and building things (Hughes, 2010).

In middle childhood, children's brains are becoming better integrated, and logical thinking begins to emerge, with a concomitant need for order. Children begin to enjoy collecting things (stickers, coins, stamps, Barbies, toys offered by fast food venders, etc.) and tend to add chants and rituals to their play (e.g., "step on a crack, break your mother's back," "eeny, meeny, miny, mo"). In addition, they are able to play games that have rules (e.g., hopscotch, tag, dodge ball). Eventually, rule-based games come to include organized sports (Hughes, 2010).

Unfortunately, there has been a steady decline in physical activity among children in the past 40 years related to changes in modes of transportation (i.e., less walking and more riding to school and other destinations), less physical education in school as well as less outdoor play in general (Basset et al., 2015). In addition, many schools have curtailed recess and free play in favor of more academic offerings (Brez & Sheets, 2017). At the same time, there have been increases in opportunities for passive entertainment provided by television (and DVD recordings), video and computer games, cell phones, and tablets (Basset et al., 2015). Communities have attempted to address these lower rates of physical activities among children by increasing structured, after-school activities. However, Panksepp (2018) argues that organized sports are "a pale imitation of real PLAY," and that unstructured free play (that is, play that the child chooses and that serves no function other than to simply have fun) is essential to "full social brain and mid maturation" (p. 264).

Although the research mentioned above stresses the importance of physical activity to child development, and even though the U. S. Department of Health and Human Services (2018) recommends a minimum of 60 minutes of physical activity per day for children, some researchers believe that sedentary play should not be completely demonized (Alexander, Fusco, & Frolich, 2015). These researchers argue that the current emphasis on physical play by governmental organizations and obesity-prevention programs may have unintended negative consequences. Their research shows that children are internalizing the pro-physical exercise messages to mean that any form of play other than physical activity is unhealthy. Thus, some valuable forms of play and relaxation (those activities associated with parasympathetic activation such as drawing, modeling with clay, daydreaming, and even reading) may be perceived as being somewhat shameful since *real play* has to be active.

Alexander et al. (2015) also note that parents may be confused by contradictory messages concerning physical play. On one hand, they are encouraged to send children outside to play, but on the other they are warned that physical play outside can be dangerous and then feel guilty if they allow their child to play quietly indoors in activities that he or she may enjoy and benefit from. At the same time, they may be overly protective of their children when they do go outside, possibly interfering with moderately risky activities that could actually help them learn how to handle the challenges that life will most surely send their way. Thus, it must be remembered that play is not just for health; it is also for fun.

Early and Middle Childhood Social Play

By age three, children are engaging in pretend play (role-play, dramatization, etc.), often acting out the adult roles that they see in their homes. They may use everyday objects as symbols (e.g., using a building block as a teakettle, an empty box as a spaceship, or leaping tall sofas with a single bound). They also begin to pretend play with other children in which they learn to abide by implicit rules provided by their cultures and come to understand and respond to social cues, reflecting the emergence of empathy and the social engagement system (Yuill, Henske, Williams, & Leith, 2014). Even when children engage in rough-and-tumble play like running, chasing, or wrestling, there is an element of pretend in the activity since their voices and facial expressions indicate that they are playing rather than attacking, and so these activities are important to socialization (Hughes, 2010).

By preschool, children are able to create shared meanings with other children, introduce new ideas and props, and communicate both verbally and nonverbally about whether they like a playmate's ideas and actions (Stagnitti, 2017). In addition, they are capable of producing things through arts and crafts, activities that help them to develop symbolic thinking, creativity, purposeful behaviors, and persistence (Sheina, Smirnova, & Ryabkova, 2017). At this age, children are better (though certainly not experts) at sharing, waiting their turn, and cooperating with both adults and peers. In addition, they move from solitary and parallel forms of play to associative play in which they continue to stay focused on their own play but begin to share and lend toys, take turns, pay attention to and communicate with their peers. Finally, they make the transition to cooperative play in which they have common goals that require that they work together in harmony to achieve them (Hughes, 2010). Each of these transitions (from solitary to parallel to associative to cooperative) is indicative of maturation of neural circuits in the contexts of motor and social development.

By about age five to seven, children are able to understand more clearly other playmates' perspectives and are able to negotiate, organize, and resolve conflicts, skills that should improve over middle childhood. They are better able to initiate and maintain joint attention and shared understanding and to cooperate in joint actions and ideas (Yuill et al., 2014). At this age, they can begin to play games that have specific rules that are not open to negotiation. Children in this age group need to learn norms and rules and be able to regulate their emotions and behavioral responses whether they win the game or lose it (Sheina et al., 2017). These capacities are essential to the development of social skills they need to successfully transition into adolescence and adulthood.

According to Hughes (2010), as children enter middle childhood and mature towards adolescence, there is an increased need for acceptance within a group (belonging). They begin to spend more time with peers and less time with their families, and they need to learn the skills that will make it possible for them to be desirable playmates. Thus, they need to learn the social rules of their peer group(s) such as how to behave in various situations, how to dress and talk, and how to play games and abide by the rules. It is through play with peers that children gain the physical and intellectual skills needed to gain acceptance to a group. Unusual dress, differences in spoken language or accents, dysregulated behavior, socioeconomic status and cultural traditions, and other differences can result in exclusion (sometimes delivered in harsh terms). Indeed, Hughes emphasizes that "It should not be surprising, considering the amount of free time children spend of playing, that the battleground is often the playground— figuratively and literally" (p. 134).

As they approach adolescence, children's prefrontal cortex will have matured considerably, allowing them to think logically and abstractly, to be able to imagine clearly what others may be thinking or feeling, and to construct complex narratives concerning themselves and their worlds. In addition, their pretend play tends to become less concrete as they grow older, changing from "playing on the floor with toys to age-appropriate activity forms, such as drama, school musicals, improvisation and the ability to follow complex emotional and social behaviours in interactions of others" (p. 189).

The importance of children in this age group mastering social skills cannot be overstated. Remember that middle childhood is Erikson's (1963) stage of *Industry vs. Inferiority*. The term *industry* refers to the ability to persevere in the face of frustration until competence is achieved. This perseverance must occur not only in academic endeavors (skills that are, of course, extremely important) but also in social endeavors, learning how to get along with others, how to play a game without it devolving into a fight, how to win and how to lose, how to make and maintain friendships. Thus, play in early and middle childhood serves an essential purpose that supports all future life activities and relationships. If a child in this age group is unable to master social skills during this time in which both academic and social competence become of central importance, he or she will transition into adolescence with a sense of inferiority that may become solidified as a part of his or her identity (Erikson, 1963).

As children make their way through middle childhood, they learn about how to get along with each other, what is right and what is wrong, what is fair and what is unjust. These are all concepts that children must learn how to manage if they are to become adults who can regulate their own emotions and relationships so that they can get their needs met. In addition, because children are social beings, they must begin to behave in ways that are acceptable to their communities and to society in general. Therefore, in the remainder of the chapter I will discuss how emotional intelligence and morality can be expected to develop in this life stage.

Emotional Intelligence

During infancy and toddlerhood, children lay down the foundations of emotional regulation that may affect their lives and relationships not just during childhood but also quite possibly for the remainder of their adult lives (Sroufe, 2005). These foundations are constructed through interactions with primary attachment figures, who influence the development of the child's brain and of his or her internal working models of self and expectations for relationships with others. Although problems in the management of emotions may be apparent during infancy and toddlerhood, those problems occur mostly within the confines of the family. As children enter the wider community through school and other activities, however, these problems may seriously affect the developmental tasks that children face. That is, in early childhood (Erikson's *Initiative vs. Guilt* stage) children need to begin to initiate purposeful actions and manage the frustrations they experience associated with parental and environmental restrictions of those actions. Then in middle childhood (Erikson's *Industry vs. Inferiority* stage), they need to be industrious and to persevere as they develop and master academic and social competencies that will eventually support their adult relationships and activities (e.g., marriage, children, work, etc.). Academic achievement is associated with better self-regulation and higher levels of motivation, even after IQ level is controlled (Blair, 2002). Thus, awareness and regulation of one's own emotions and awareness and regulation of others' emotions becomes increasingly important as children move through these stages.

Petrides and Furnham (2003) define emotional intelligence (EI) as the extent to which individuals "attend to, process, and utilize affect-laden information of an intrapersonal (e.g., managing one's own emotions) or interpersonal (e.g., managing others' emotions) nature" (p. 39). In other words, EI is a form of intelligence that involves both processing emotions and using emotions to help optimize one's life. Mayer, Salovey, and Caruso (2004) consider EI to be a set of four *abilities* that are hierarchical in nature (i.e., each builds on the one below) that allow the individual (1) to *perceive* emotions accurately, (2) to *use* emotions to help in thinking, (3) to *understand* emotions, and (4) to *manage* emotions. Table 14.3 shows what these abilities entail.

TABLE 14.3   Emotional Intelligence

ABILITY:	INDIVIDUAL CAN:
1. Accurate perception	• read others' social cues (facial expressions, gestures, vocal tone, etc.)
2. Retrieval and generation	• recognize the internal physiological signs associated with one's own emotional responses to those cues • use them in thinking, planning, decision-making, and problem-solving

3. Understanding	• label and analyze what one is feeling
	• place it into context, recognizing where the emotion came from and how it will likely play out over time
4. Regulation	• manage one's emotional and behavioral responses
	• manage the other's emotional and behavioral responses

Source: Mayer, J. D., Salovey, P., & Caruso, D. R. (2004). Emotional intelligence: Theory, findings and implications. Psychological Inquiry, 15(3), 197-215.

Emotions are, of course, a product of the limbic system but are influenced by multiple other brain regions. In the next section, I will discuss which brain regions support these abilities.

Neurobiology of Emotional Intelligence

There isn't a lot of research on the neural circuitry associated with EI yet. However, Raz and Zysberg (2015) emphasize that there is not a single place in the brain where it can be said that EI is located. Instead, EI appears to be the product of complex functional connectivity between a number of different brain regions. The parts of the brain associated with EI appear to include the amygdala, hippocampus, anterior insula, anterior cingulate, and parts of the prefrontal cortex (Raz & Zysberg, 2015; Tarasuik, Ciorciari, & Stough, 2009). In addition, it involves the smart vagus and both hemispheres. In the sections below, I will discuss these brain regions as they are associated with each of the four elements of EI mentioned above.

Accurate Perception of Emotions

The accurate perception of emotions requires that an individual be able to read accurately the social cues that another person is sending (Rash & Prkachin, 2013). Thus, EI is related to functioning of the smart vagus and the social engagement system. Remember that when social signals are perceived, they are instantly sent to the amygdala (just like all other stimuli coming in from the environment) to determine if they constitute a danger and to activate the fight/flight system if danger is detected. This system is, if you recall, the "low road" in the brain, which is fast but primitive and will cause a virtually instantaneous emotional response to social cues that have not yet been processed by the rational parts of the brain.

Use of Emotions to Assist Thinking

Whenever an individual receives social cues from another person, he or she will have an emotional response of some sort that is felt physically. This internal sensation is mediated by the anterior insula. If an individual can consciously access these physiological sensations, he or she can utilize them to aid in planning responses and solving problems (Mayer et al., 2004). The sensations that our insula provides us can inform our rational decisions. Thus, the insula is a link between emotions and thinking (Mayer et al., 2004). As discussed in Chapter 2, although we often think that decision-making and problem-solving are purely rational, left-brain activities, they are actually highly influenced by right-brain emotions. However, recall that emotions are located to a great extent in the right side of the brain, while rational thought and analysis are located in the left side. Adequate connection between the two hemispheres, then, is needed for an individual to be able to allow emotions to inform thinking.

Understanding Emotions

If you recall, the anterior insula is closely connected with the anterior cingulate, a part of the brain that is particularly important to the interpretation of social information and which is very closely connected with the OMPFC. At the same time that social cues are being routed to the amygdala (on the "low road"), they are also being sent to the OMPFC, which quickly scans the memories in the association cortex to determine whether the signals suggest danger. This is the "high road," which is slower than the "low road" but sees matters much more clearly. If the OMPFC is adequately connected to the anterior cingulate, the insula, and the amygdala, it can calm the amygdala's fear reactions, activate more nuanced emotions, and avoid irrational, fear-driven behavioral reactions. These are left-brain activities that allow labeling feelings, putting them into words, and discriminating between them (Mayer et al., 2004).

Managing Emotions

When individuals perceive others' social signals accurately, recognize their own emotional responses to those signals, and link them to rational thought processes, they are in a good position to regulate their emotions and respond reasonably to the other person. Moreover, because human beings have the ability to co-regulate each other, they are also in a good position to influence the other person's emotions and behaviors. This is the very essence of the social engagement system—awareness and management of the self, and awareness and management of the other. Of course, the more mature an individual is, the better connected these neural circuits should be. That is, a two-year-old's ability to understand and manage his or her emotions is generally less advanced than a 12-year-old's, which is generally less advanced than a 32-year-old's (Mayer et al., 2004).

Let me provide an example of how EI works. Take a moment to read Case Study 14.2 in which Sophia Ramirez (from Chapter 5), now four years old, and her mother Nilda have gone to the grocery store. Remember that Sophia developed a secure attachment style during infancy and toddlerhood because her mother was attuned, sensitive, and available as a safe haven and secure base. In this scenario, Nilda is able to read Sophia's emotions accurately, recognize her own responses to Sophia's emotions, and analyze the situation rationally. Therefore, she is able to manage her own emotions and behaviors so that she can down-regulate Sophia's emotions and behaviors. Thus, Nilda proves herself to be an emotionally intelligent person who is building EI in her child. One reason that things went well in this case study is that Sophia and Nilda have a secure attachment bond. In the next section, I will discuss how EI and attachment are related.

CASE STUDY 14.2: EMOTIONAL INTELLIGENCE IN SOPHIA AND NILDA

Sophia, who is sitting in a grocery cart, sees a box of Gooey Fruity Sugar Bomb cereal and reaches out to grab the box. Nilda quickly moves the cart so that Sophia can't reach the cereal, and Sophia instantly twists around in the cart, frowns and starts to cry and whine loudly. Nilda accurately perceives Sophia's facial expression, body language, and vocal tone as meaning that Sophia is outraged. In response to Sophia's signals of outrage, Nilda experiences annoyance (felt as a tightness in her throat and a frown on her face). However, she realizes as she places her and Sophia's emotions in context, that her reaction, though understandable in the moment, is inappropriate to the situation. That is, she realizes that Sophia is only four years old and doesn't have enough control over her impulses yet to resist reaching for the cleverly marketed box of cereal. She also realizes that giving in to her annoyance and getting angry at Sophia will probably only escalate the problem. So instead, Nilda speaks to Sophia in a reasonable tone of voice, telling her that she can't have that cereal but that when they get home she can have a popsicle. Sophia gradually stops crying and whining, and they continue with their shopping.

Emotional Intelligence and Attachment

Research has shown repeatedly that secure attachment is related to good emotional regulation, while insecure attachment is related to emotional regulation problems and psychopathology (Sroufe et al., 1999). The above scenario with Nilda and Sophia illustrates how EI can manifest in secure attachment. Both Sophia and her mother would appear to be psychologically healthy and able to handle emotional situations well. It is a different story for individuals with attachment insecurity. Research has shown, for example, that among adults there are inverse relationships between EI and both anxious and avoidant attachment (Marks, Horrocks, & Schutte, 2016). That is, the more anxiously or avoidantly attached an individual is, the lower their EI tends to be. Of particular importance to mental health providers, the lower an individual's EI, the more likely he or she is to have psychological problems (somatic complaints, anxiety and insomnia, social dysfunction, and severe depression).

In other research, EI and self-esteem have been found to moderate the relationship between insecure attachment (anxiety and avoidance) and the individual's sense of overall well-being (Li & Zheng, 2014). First, these researchers found the more attachment avoidance or anxiety an individual reported, the less well-being he or she reported (i.e., attachment insecurity *directly* affects well-being). However, attachment insecurity was also related to lower levels of both EI and self-esteem, both of which in turn affected the level of well-being (i.e., attachment insecurity affects well-being *indirectly* through EI and self-esteem). Thus, individuals with insecure attachment appear to be at risk of a double whammy in which insecure attachment has both direct and indirect effects on their sense of well-being.

As social animals, human beings need to be able to get along with each other well enough to ensure social cohesion. The development of EI therefore makes it possible for children to begin to empathize with and help others who are in need. In addition, they begin to make judgments concerning their own and others' behavior as being acceptable or not (based to some extent, but not entirely, on cultural expectations of behavior). Thus, EI and morality are closely interrelated. In the next section, I will discuss how early attachment and the maturing brain influence the development of morality in this life stage.

Moral Development

Hennig (2004) defines morality among humans as "doing the right thing, at the right time, toward the right people, for the right ends, in the right way, and with the right motives" (p. 62). I, personally, might expand that slightly to include doing the right thing at the right time to the right *beings, including the Earth,* but he certainly seems to have hit most of the idea. It includes concepts such as justice, fairness, respect, tolerance, altruism, commitment, duty, responsibility, and cooperation, the presence of which facilitate the functioning of society in general and shapes the behavior of the individual.

Morality apparently has deep evolutionary roots, arising in response to the development of the complex cooperative skills needed for social harmony (Price & Brosnan, 2012). That is, among social species, each member of the social group (herd, pack, tribe, etc.) depends on the survival of the group for its own survival. This "forced interdependence" (Gazzillo et al., 2019, p. 2) is thought to have arisen out of the care system that governs parental caregiving behaviors and over time generalized to the protection and care of other individuals in need (Churchland, 2014). Thus, moral thought and behavior is "driven by intuitive processes that form the understructure of a natural, untaught, and unlearned moral core, molded by natural selection in order to facilitate social cohesion and cooperation" (Chen, Martinez, & Cheng, 2018, p. 4).

One of the earliest researchers on morality, Kohlberg (1969, 1976) believed that morality is a cognitive process that involves conscious reasoning. His *cognitive development* approach to morality dominated the research and discourse on morality for decades, defining morality as the capacity to make, and act on, moral decisions and judgments that are based on moral principles. Kohlberg's model has been criticized for several reasons. First, Gilligan (1977) pointed out that his research had used primarily male subjects and that its focus on reasoning and logic could not be generalized to women. Therefore, she developed an alternative theory that was not so focused on judgment but was instead focused on the ethics of caregiving. Morality is now thought to include elements of both justice and care (Narvaez & Vaydich, 2008).

Kohlberg's model also has been criticized because of its assumption that morality is the product of purely rational, deliberative thought processes that inform intentional, rule-based choices. Likely assuming as most people did at that time that these processes are not available to young children, Kohlberg never explored morality among infants or toddlers. Therefore, he was unable to imagine, as is thought today, that morality might have much earlier roots (Narvaez & Lapsley, 2005). Indeed, it appears, as discussed below, that the capacity to develop morality is an inborn trait of human beings based in neural structure.

Neurobiology of Moral Development

Churchland (2014) explains that moral values arise out of ancient caregiving circuitry, saying,

> that anything has value *at all* and is motivating *at all* (italics in the original) ultimately depends on very ancient neural organization servicing survival and well-being. With the evolution of mammals, the rudimentary "self-care organization" is modified to extend basic values of being alive and well to selected others—to *Me and Mine* (italics in the original). Depending on the evolutionary

pressures to which a species is subject, caring may extend to mates, kin, and to friends. Social mammals do tend to show attachment and caring behavior to others besides their own offspring. (pp. 288–289)

She suggests that the systems involved in morality include the pain centers in the anterior cingulate as well as the emotional salience center in the amygdala and that the good feelings that we get when we do something good come from the production of oxytocin, vasopressin, endorphins, and endocannabinoids. She suggests, then, that we are moral because it feels good, the same way that caring for one's baby feels good.

Although moral reasoning and resultant behavior may be left-brain functions, they are profoundly influenced by the right brain, and although they may require a well-functioning prefrontal cortex, that prefrontal cortex must be well integrated with the limbic system. Indeed, Damasio (1999) argued that when reason is used without input from the emotions, it is not effective for good decision-making. Moreover, research showing that moral judgments are more likely to be informed by gut feelings and emotional reactions than by the conscious and deliberate weighing of law and human rights or other abstract moral values (Prehn & Heerkeren, 2014).

Recent research, however, shows that children are "hardwired for moral sensitivity" (Narvaez & Vaydich, 2008, p. 297). Gazzillo et al. (2019) point out that by age three months infants can tell the difference between pro- and antisocial behaviors (e.g., helping, comforting and fair distribution of goods vs. hurting, hindering and unfair distribution of goods) and show clear preference for pro-social behaviors. These researchers suggest, therefore, that moral sensitivity "reflects our fundamental social nature [and] is an expression of the care and play/cooperation motivational system. ..." (p. 4).

As children move into the second year of life, their brains are better organized, and they show evidence of mentalization. The ability to detect another person's distress is fundamental to empathy, and empathy is fundamental to morality (Chen et al., 2018). By toddlerhood, children begin to spontaneously offer help to others who are having difficulty (e.g., helping mom open the door when she has an armload of groceries) even though they don't expect to receive some kind of tangible reward. Then by the age of about three, children begin to understand that they are members of a group and begin to develop "collective morality" (p. 5) in which they recognize and share the social norms and behavioral standards expected within their particular culture. Although different cultures may have different ideas of what constitutes right and wrong, good and evil, "cultural norms do not create morality, they simply shape it" (Chen et al., 2018, p. 5). Although mentalization is rather primitive among children between the ages of four to six, by the time they are six to eight years old, children become focused on fairness. It becomes very important to them that they both *be* good and *do* good, attributes that can be encouraged by reminding them of times in the past when they were generous or did a good deed (Tasimi & Young, 2016).

The neural foundations of morality are laid down during infancy and toddlerhood when children's brains are being constructed through their interactions with their attachment figures. Therefore, in the next section, I will discuss how attachment and morality are related.

Morality and Attachment

Shaver and Mikulincer (2012) argue that

> An abiding inner sense of attachment security (based on experience) promotes a pervasive faith in other people's good will; a sense of being loved, esteemed, understood, and accepted by relationship partners; and optimistic beliefs about being able to handle frustration and distress" (p. 258).

That is, secure attachment provides the inborn capacity for empathy and the desire to help others. As Narveaz and Vaydich (2008) put it, "responsible parenting fosters securely attached children who in turn show earlier conscience development" (p. 297).

Govrin (2014) argues that it is the mother-infant relationship that triggers the acquisition of moral principles. She states, "It is somewhat like a car: when we turn the key, the car operates like a car—not a boat—simply because it is built like a car. However, if we don't turn the key, nothing happens" (p. 11). Thus, secure attachment is the key to later moral development. Children learn prosocial and moral behavior through direct experience of their parents' behaviors. That is,

> a secure person comes to show genuine interest in others' welfare and a desire to help them by knowledge of what it is like to be cared for by considerate others and by modeling one's behavior on the observed behavior of one's own parents (Shaver & Mikulincer, 2012, p. 260).

These authors go on to suggest that insecure attachment interferes with an individual's ability to notice and focus on others' needs. Those with anxious attachment are likely to be so focused on their own attachment-related distress that they can't attend accurately or consistently to anyone else's needs. Alternatively, because of their need for constant closeness, they may engage in *compulsive caregiving* in which they martyr themselves, caring for others to the detriment of their own health. They may help more out of a desire for approval than out of a genuine desire to relieve someone's distress.

Individuals with avoidant attachment, on the other hand, may be unwilling to help others who are in distress, detaching themselves in an effort to shut down the uncomfortable feelings that the other's distress provokes. If they do extend a helping hand, it may be more because they want to avoid the other's negative reaction to their lack of empathy or because they think they will get something in return for providing assistance (Shaver & Mikulincer, 2012).

It is through the child's relationship with a responsive and loving caregiver during the first two years of life that he or she internalizes parental expectations for behavior and develops "committed compliance" (Narvaez & Lapsley, 2004, p. 250): I do the right thing because I want to please my mommy. This commitment to doing the right thing becomes a part of the internal working model of self, laid down in the right brain as an implicit sense of "this is who I am, and this is what I do" which becomes as automatic and unconscious as riding a bicycle—a procedural memory that requires no analysis. It is no longer a matter of I do the right thing for my mommy because I want to please her but instead becomes a sense of moral obligation that "expands, moving from concern for self, to concern for known others, to concern for the welfare of strangers" (p. 257). That is, it tends to move from Kohlberg's preconventional stage in early childhood to his conventional stage in middle childhood and then to his postconventional stage in adolescence and adulthood.

CLASS DISCUSSION

How do you think Sophia's early life experiences will affect her moral development? How does this compare with Jet's and Luke's experiences? With Macy's?

It is clear that how parents parent their children has an enormous influence on the development of their child's moral judgments and behaviors. Kuntoro, Dwuputri, and Adams (2018) suggest that parents with a *conformity-oriented* parenting style (authoritarian, rules-focused, not interested in the child's opinion or perspective) tend to produce children who have difficulty understanding that others may have different perspectives from their own. In addition, they may have a restricted ability to use their own critical thinking skills to make decisions about moral matters, instead simply relying on their parents thoughts and opinions as to what should or shouldn't be done. In contrast, an *autonomy-oriented* parenting style (authoritative, taking into consideration the child's opinion and perspective) tends to produce children who can use their own thoughts and opinions in making moral decisions. Because these parents are likely to discuss with their children how their actions have affected others and how others may perceive their actions, their children are more likely to have developed accurate mentalization concerning why others are doing what they are doing and act with empathy.

Narvaez and Lapsley (2004) warn that, although a secure attachment bond is of primary importance to the development of morality, the child enters the attachment relationship with a given temperament. Children naturally want to please their parents and are anxious if their parents disapprove of them. Therefore, if parents are conscious of their child's temperament, they can tap into his or her natural anxiety to promote the behavior they want to see. That is, parenting style needs to vary to some extent according to the dictates of the child's temperament. For example, they point out that some children are naturally fearful (cautious, shy, timid) and others are naturally fearless (adventurous, outgoing). Parents of more fearful children will be able to elicit good behavior by using a "silken glove" approach that "capitalizes on the child's own discomfort to produce the optimal level of anxiety that facilitates the processing and retention of parents' socialization messages" (p. 251). However, the answer to the more fearless child's behavior is not to use an "iron-hand" approach, which will likely result in the child simply becoming angry and resistant to the socialization message, but rather to utilize his or her positive emotions. That is, for more fearless children, catch them being good and praise them extravagantly.

Summary

As discussed in the previous chapter, the prefrontal cortex should begin to form strong connections with subcortical regions during early and middle childhood. This maturation allows children to develop emotional intelligence, a capacity in which they gain the ability to manage their emotions and relationships as they progress through early and middle childhood and into adolescence and adulthood. At the same time, these changes in neural connection support the development of morality. Both emotional intelligence and morality develop largely in the context of play, through which children develop motor, cognitive, and social skills over the course of their childhood. The attachment style developed during infancy and toddlerhood influences the play experience during early and middle childhood as well as emotion regulation and morality. In the next chapter, I will discuss some of the important mental health issues that practitioners address when working with children.

CHAPTER 15

Challenges to Mental Health in Early and Middle Childhood

After completing this chapter, readers should understand:
- How trauma, abuse, and neglect affect mental health in early and middle childhood.
- How trauma, abuse, and neglect affect brain development in early and middle childhood.
- How does the use of electronic media affect brain development?
- What the similarities and differences between attention deficit/hyperactivity disorder and autism spectrum disorder are.
- How attachment affects outcomes of children with attention deficit/hyperactivity disorder and autism spectrum disorder.

KEY IDEAS

1. Adverse childhood experiences such as trauma, abuse, and neglect negatively affect brain development and frequently result in behavioral problems and psychopathology.
2. Attention deficit/hyperactivity disorder and autism spectrum disorder are two very common mental health disorders that can have serious effects on successful transition through early and middle childhood.
3. Recent research indicates that attention deficit/hyperactivity disorder and autism spectrum disorder may be a single spectrum disorder, with attention deficit at the milder end.
4. Secure attachment is related to better outcomes for both attention deficit/hyperactivity disorder and autism spectrum disorder.

Introduction

As children leave toddlerhood and enter early childhood, they enter Erikson's (1968) third developmental stage, *Initiative vs. Guilt* in which they begin to take purposeful action in the world, to plan and initiate ideas, to make decisions based on their own preferences, and to take more control over their environments. Moreover, their brains have developed sufficiently for them to experience remorse when they have done something that is against family values or have hurt someone. Unfortunately, some parents are too controlling, or they may consistently criticize or interfere with their children or hurt them physically or emotionally in response to their desire to do things on their own. Children who are treated this way may internalize their parents' actions as evidence that when they try to initiate something on their own or do things their own way, they think they are doing something wrong. They may come to depend on others to make decisions for them, or if they make a mistake (which, of course, they will since they are human), they may simply give up and stop trying. In addition, they may develop chronic feelings of shame and guilt that develop into either internalizing disorders such as depression, anxiety, and eating disorders, or externalizing disorders such as hostile aggression or self-destructive behaviors.

Then, as they enter middle childhood, children transition into Erikson's (1963) fourth developmental stage, *Industry vs. Inferiority*, in which they must master both academic and social skills. If they are not able to do this, they are likely to develop a sense of being inferior and incompetent compared to their peers. These skills are built on the foundation of trust, autonomy and initiative developed in the earlier stages. However, if things went wrong during infancy, toddlerhood, or early childhood, that foundation may be shaky, and unfortunately, as any mental health practitioners knows, an optimal developmental process from birth to middle childhood often doesn't happen.

In this chapter, we will look at several common mental health challenges in school-age children. I will start with a discussion of the negative effects of trauma, abuse, and neglect on the developing brains and attachment relationships of children in early and middle childhood. Then, I will discuss two common neurodevelopmental disorders that tend to manifest during childhood, attention deficit/hyperactivity disorder (ADHD) and autism spectrum disorder (ASD). Last, I will explain how attachment affects the outcomes of these disorders among children transitioning through these stages.

Trauma, Abuse, and Neglect

In the late 1990s, Felitti and his associates (1998) began exploring the effects of adverse childhood experiences (ACEs) (e.g., childhood abuse, community violence, parental psychopathology or death, etc.) on physical and mental health. Since that time, research has consistently shown that family environments characterized by hostility, chaos, abuse, neglect, and/or trauma are highly significant contributors to childhood mental health problems (Sheikh, Abelsen, & Olsen, 2016; Shonkoff, Garner, & the Committee on Psychosocial Aspects of Child and Family Health, 2012). Effects can range from minor to profound, depending on the age of the child, the frequency and severity of the trauma, how involved important caregivers were with the trauma, and individual vulnerability and resiliency factors (French, 2008). Moreover, the effects of trauma during early childhood can have lasting effects across the life span on mood, thought, attention, and behavior. Trauma disrupts the development of neurobiological systems associated with emotion regulation and information processing (van der Kolk, 2005), in particular the amygdala, hippocampus, prefrontal cortex, anterior cingulate, and the HPA system (Fonzo et al., 2016; French, 2008). I invite you to read Case Study 15.1, Jet's Downward Spiral, and think about it as you read the sections below concerning trauma, abuse, and neglect.

Just two weeks before he died, Hank Wolverton, Jet's father, complained to a friend, saying, "I just don't understand. Jet never looks on the bright side of things and constantly finds something negative to say. For example, last Sunday was his tenth birthday, and Helen baked him a chocolate cake. He sat there eating it with this awful frown on his face. I asked him, 'Jet, why the frown? This is your favorite thing in the world to eat,' and do you know what he said? He said, 'So what? I have to go back to school tomorrow,' threw his fork down and stormed off to his room. What am I supposed to do with that?"

Hank had tried to spend time with Jet over the years, but his work schedule kept him away from home a lot of the time. He traveled out of state about two weeks out of the month, so there wasn't much he could do. Besides, Jet was kind of uncoordinated, and it wasn't much fun to play ball with him. On top of that, when Jet messed up somehow, he would just lose it, crying and stomping around, kicking and breaking things, and Hank would have to send him to his room. Hank had tried taking Jet camping a couple of times, but Jet got lost once, and they had to call the police to find him. The other time, he came down with the flu and threw up all over the car. Neither one of them really wanted to try camping again. From Jet's perspective, it was a relief that his dad stopped asking him to do things with him. He never felt comfortable with his dad and could tell that his dad was bored playing with him.

Then Hank had a heart attack and died. Jet had many feelings about this loss but couldn't put a name on any of them. There was confusing mixture of rage, sadness, betrayal, and loneliness. Helen sank into depression for several months, and it often fell to Jet to make sure that they all got fed; it was that or go hungry. He had been doing well in school, but now his grades started falling. He started getting into fights in the hallways over minor and imagined slights. Jet was small for his age, and some of the bigger boys started picking on him and calling him names. One day, they stole his book bag that had his homework in it. His teacher didn't believe him when he said someone had taken it and gave him a failing grade. As soon as he got home that day, he went into his brother's room, tore up a set of drawings Luke was working on, and dared him to tell Helen.

The next day, Jet went online using the cell phone his parents had given him for his birthday and started leaving mean comments on photos that girls had posted on their social media sites. He had no fear that anyone would come after him about it; it was all anonymous and faceless, and it gave him a sense of power.

Prevalence of Trauma, Abuse, and Neglect in Early and Middle Childhood

Unfortunately, childhood interpersonal trauma is not an uncommon occurrence. Felitti et al. (1998) conducted a study exploring the prevalence of various types of ACEs. These experiences included physical, sexual or emotional abuse; physical or emotional neglect; exposure to domestic violence; substance abuse or mental illness in the home; or parental separation or divorce or incarceration of a family member. Results indicated that only one in three respondents reported no such experiences. Moreover, 87% of those with at least one adverse experience reported at least one additional experience. Later research on childhood adversity has found 20% of their sample reported five or more adverse experiences by age 12 (Flaherty et al., 2009), a particularly troublesome statistic since there is a positive relationship between the number of childhood adverse experiences reported and the number of childhood health complaints and behavioral problems, as well as adult health risks reported.

CLASS DISCUSSION

How many ACEs have Jet and Luke experienced? How may these experiences affect their mental and physical health now and in the future?

The Center for Disease Control and Prevention (2018d) provides the dismal current statistic that about one in seven children today is the victim of neglect or of physical, sexual, or emotional abuse. These children do not have the sensitive, attuned, and responsive attachment relationships needed to develop secure attachment. In addition, they are at increased risk of developing gross deficiencies in sensory, cognitive, and social stimulation needed for healthy brain development that support cognitive, associative, and implicit learning, executive functioning, and neural function and structure (Lupien et al., 2009; McLaughlin, Sheridan, & Nelson, 2017; Teicher & Samson, 2016; Tyrka, Burgers, Phillip, Price, & Carpenter, 2013). In the sections below, the mental health and neurobiological consequences of trauma, abuse, and neglect will be discussed in detail.

Consequences of Trauma, Abuse, and Neglect in Early and Middle Childhood

Research on the consequences of childhood trauma, abuse and neglect has targeted both the mental health and neurobiological outcomes. I will discuss consequences to mental health first and then the neurobiological effects.

Mental Health Consequences

Mental health problems are, regrettably, not uncommon among even young children. According to the CDC (2018a), over 7% of children age three through seventeeen have a diagnosed behavioral problem, while 7% and 3% have clinical levels of anxiety and depression, respectively. Moreover, mental health problems in early childhood can have multiple adverse effects on outcomes in adulthood such as substance abuse/dependence, depression, suicide, number of sexual partners and sexually transmitted diseases, obesity, heart disease, cancer, lung disease, bone fractures, and on and on (Ma et al., 2015; Sciaraffa, Zeneah, & Zeneah, 2018). Thus, early childhood mental health is an issue that affects not just the individual child and his or her family but entire communities and society in general.

Neurobiological processes associated with trauma and maltreatment are clearly associated with these mental health issues. It appears that the reward pathway that stretches between the ventral tegmentum and the OMPFC may be damaged by maltreatment, resulting in problems with both mood and motivation (see Chapter 2). For example, Hanson et al. (2015) found that cumulative exposure to stress, especially interpersonal adversity, among children in either kindergarten or grade three blunted children's engagement with positively valenced stimuli and increased their engagement with negatively valenced stimuli. In other words, these children are less likely to be able to sustain positive affect and optimism and more likely to experience negative mood and hopelessness than children who haven't experienced adversity. Thus, children with a history of chronic interpersonal problems (such as emotional neglect or physical or sexual abuse) are at higher risk of mental health issues associated with negative mood, apathy, and hopelessness and are less motivated to learn and persevere in the face of frustration. In addition, a lack of motivation and perseverance during middle childhood, a time when mastery of academic skills becomes so important (Erikson, 1963), can have devastating effects on an individual's preparation for adult life.

CLASS DISCUSSION

What mental health issues to you see developing in Jet? How do you think these issues will affect his ability to master social and academic skills?

Van der Kolk (2005) has suggested that chronic or multiple exposures to trauma during early childhood (including multiple medical/surgical procedures; physical, sexual or psychological/emotional abuse; witnessing or being the victim of domestic violence; traumatic loss; neglect) can result in what is now commonly called "complex trauma" (p. 402). He argues that although children who suffer abuse may exhibit symptoms of PTSD, they are likely to develop a host of other psychiatric problems in adolescence and adulthood instead of or in addition to PTSD (e.g., dissociative, eating, anxiety and mood, borderline and antisocial personality, substance use, and somatoform disorders). In addition, they may develop physical health issues such as cardiovascular, metabolic, immune and sexual disorders. Moreover, he argues that

> These experiences engender intense affects, such as rage, betrayal, fear, resignation, defeat, and shame, and efforts to ward off the recurrence of those emotions, including the avoidance of experiences that precipitate them or engaging in behaviors that convey a subjective sense of control in the face of potential threats. These children tend to reenact their traumas behaviorally, either as perpetrators (e.g., aggressive or sexual acting out or in frozen avoidance reactions). Their physiological dysregulation may lead to multiple somatic complaints, such as headaches and stomachaches, in response to fearful and helpless emotions. (p. 406)

Van der Kolk (2005) goes on to point out, however, that, even in the face of horrific abuse and neglect, these children are attached to their families; they are loyal and they learn to keep secrets exceedingly well. They do whatever they have to to deal with their feelings of helplessness. Over time, they tend both to expect and to prepare for their trauma to happen again and are triggered easily by even small reminders of the original event(s). This hypervigilence affects their ability to manage their emotions and responses and to establish trusting relationships, often for the remainder of their lives. In addition, they often have little insight into how they themselves may contribute to repeated traumatic relationships. It is a sad, sad story that mental health professionals see in their practices over and over again.

Neurobiological Consequences

Concerning the effects of trauma and maltreatment on the developing brain, the literature indicates widespread negative effects that can result in adverse outcomes in early and middle childhood (Lupien et al., 2009; Teicher & Samson, 2016; Tyrka et al., 2013). This research shows consistently that adverse childhood experiences are associated with upregulation of the HPA system and consequent damage to the PFC and hippocampus and increased sensitivity of the amygdala, providing a pathway to childhood psychopathology.

One group of researchers suggests that childhood adversity affects both educational attainment and social functioning by impacting neurodevelopment through two pathways—environmental deprivation (neglect, inadequate cognitive and social stimulation) and threat (abuse, violence, and trauma) (McLaughlin et al., 2017; Sheridan & McLaughlin, 2016). They constructed a model specifically to explain how poverty (one element of particular importance in childhood adversity) affects educational attainment, suggesting that there is heightened risk of deprivation and threat among children living in poverty. However, their model can be used to explain how children in other socioeconomic conditions who are abused or neglected could also be affected (see Figure 15.1). I will focus on neglect (environmental deprivation) first and then discuss trauma and abuse (threat).

Neurodevelopmental Effects of Neglect

McLaughlin et al. (2017) argue that environmental deprivation (i.e., neglectful parenting, institutionalization, poverty, etc.) can result in impairments in global cognitive ability, associative

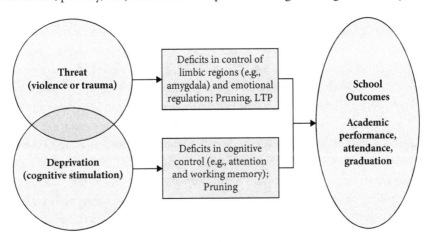

FIGURE 15.1 **Effects of Childhood Abuse, Trauma, and Neglect on Educational Outcomes**

Adapted from Margaret A. Sheridan and Katie A. McLaughlin, School Outcomes from "Neurobiological Models of the Impact of Adversity on Education," *Current Opinions in Behavioral Sciences*, vol. 10, pp. 110. Copyright © 2016 by Elsevier B.V.

and implicit learning, language, executive functioning, cortical structure and myelination. In normal families, caregivers naturally provide their infants with sensory, linguistic, cognitive, and social stimulation that provides neural pathways for the development of associative and implicit learning upon which all future functioning will be based. Children with serious deficits in these kinds of experiences have smaller brains, widespread thinning of the cortex, reduced myelination of the corpus callosum (important for horizontal integration) and the PFC (important for vertical integration and emotion regulation). They also have reduced volume of the cerebellum, the part of the brain in which procedural memory is processed and stored). Moreover, deprivation can lead to accelerated and extreme pruning of synapses that would have survived had they been adequately stimulated and would have provided a foundation for future, more complex learning and behavior.

Similar to children living in poverty, neglected children may have many deficits in experience, such as little verbal interaction with parents and few opportunities to spend time in the company of caring adults. Their parents may have little interest in providing enriched environments that promote brain development, such as afterschool activities and cultural and art events. Therefore, neglected children are at a distinct disadvantage when they enter the school system (Sheridan & McLaughlin, 2016).

Neurodevelopmental Effects of Trauma and Abuse

In contrast to deprivation, threat in early childhood (e.g., violence occurring in abuse) results in a brain that is poorly connected vertically as well as supersensitive to other threats (due to an overly reactive amygdala). That is, cortical structures (e.g., the prefrontal cortex) are not able to provide the input to subcortical regions needed to control negative emotions and activation of fight/flight/freeze responses. In addition, the neural pathways that encode the violence become strong through the process of long-term potentiation (as discussed in Chapter 2) and thus become part of associational memory. Abuse, then, can affect children who are entering and navigating their way through the school system in two ways. First, they may have reduced control over their negative emotions, and second, they may have difficulty learning and remembering (Sheridan & McLaughlin, 2016).

In addition to their negative effects on academic performance, trauma and maltreatment can also negatively affect social engagement. French (2008) has studied the effects of trauma and maltreatment on the developing brain with results that suggest that these kinds of adversity are associated with both aggressive behavior and victimization. Similar to Sheridan and McLaughlin's (2016) findings discussed above, French explains that maltreatment during infancy and early childhood results in disruptions to the development of the amygdala and its connectivity with the prefrontal cortex. French, however, focuses on how these deficits result in an individual becoming overly reactive to stress and acting out with what French calls "hot" aggression. In "hot" aggression, the individual lashes impulsively in response to perceived threat or frustration. He or she may end up in a mental health practitioner's office due to oppositional defiant behavior, attention problems, and/or mood and anxiety disorders, or in the most extreme cases, self-harm (e.g., cutting, suicide attempts).

Alternatively, French (2008) notes that in some individuals who have suffered trauma or maltreatment the amygdala may become *under* reactive so that they do not respond to social cues concerning other people's distress in the same way that individuals who were not maltreated do. He explains that

> During normal development, caregivers reinforce desired behaviors and punish undesired ones. During a transgression, a victim's distress, pain, or sadness (unconditioned stimuli) results in activation (unconditioned response) of an aggressor's threat response system, which leads to autonomic arousal (and usually) postural freezing. This association of unpleasant unconditioned cues in the victim with unpleasant, unconditioned responses in the aggressor leads a normally developing child to experience the pain of others as aversive (aversive conditioning). Caregivers then, by focusing the transgressor's attention on the victim and connecting the cause of his or her suffering (and that being experienced by the transgressor) to the act committed by the transgressor, are able (through instrumental conditioning) to promote moral socialization and the induction of empathy. ..." (p. 47)

In addition to problems with amygdala function, the anterior cingulate, insula, and OMPFC may also be affected by trauma and abuse. Fonzo et al. (2016) have shown that children who were maltreated in childhood tend to have difficulty recognizing others' facial expressions (mediated by the anterior cingulate), empathizing with their pain (mediated by the anterior insula) and controlling feelings of anxiety and anger (mediated by the OMPFC). Therefore, maltreatment may impair the individual's ability to recognize someone's distress or experience empathy for him or her, possibly resulting in extreme cases in psychopathy and/or self-serving antisocial behaviors (French, 2008). In the next section, I will discuss how this lack of empathy for others and dysregulation of emotion caused by maltreatment and trauma may negatively affect social relations through bullying and peer rejection.

ADHD and Autism

Although precursors to both ASD and ADHD can be identified in infancy and toddlerhood, children generally are not diagnosed with them until early childhood at the earliest (Perry & Flood, 2016). School can present serious challenges to children with either or both of these disorders because of increased expectations for self-regulation and sustained attention that they have difficulty meeting. Children who have trouble regulating their emotions and behaviors face difficulties in initiating and maintaining friendships and are at risk of peer rejection, and those who have trouble shifting and sustaining attention are at an academic disadvantage. Thus, these children are challenged to master the skills needed to transition successfully through Erikson's (1963) early and middle childhood stages. Deficits in cognitive and executive functions, attention and motivation may "cascade into more serious learning and interpersonal problems, possibly associated with school failure, poor-decision-making, and peer rejection" (Campbell, Halperin, & Sonuga-Barke, 2014, p. 438).

In the sections below, I will first introduce recent research that suggests that ADHD and ASD may be on a single continuum with common neurobiological underpinnings. That is, autism is already considered a spectrum disorder, but recent thinking suggests that ADHD may be on that spectrum. Then I will identify similarities and differences of the disorders in terms of neurobiology and social deficits. Lastly, I will discuss how attachment acts either as a risk or protective factor as it interacts with the symptomatology of the disorders.

The Possible ADHD/ASD Spectrum

It may seem odd to you at first glance that this section includes both ADHD and ASD rather than addressing these disorders separately. However, some researchers have begun to consider the possibility that these two disorders fall on a single continuum, though there remains controversy around this possibility (Mikami et al., 2019). For example, Kern et al. (2015) point out that both ADHD and ASD are neurodevelopmental disorders that manifest in early childhood and tend to persist for the remainder of life; both are common disorders and both have risen dramatically in prevalence over the past twenty years; both are more common among males than females; both present similar associated medical conditions; they have similar social and communicative profiles; and they are frequently co-morbid. These researchers point out that over 90% of autistic children show evidence of abnormal sensory processing (i.e., receiving, organizing and understanding sensory stimuli). Some children may be overly sensitive to tactile, oral, visual, auditory, and vestibular stimuli, while others may be relatively insensitive to them, and still others may have a combination of sensitivity and insensitivity. Moreover, they point to research that suggests that children with ADHD have very similar sensitivities.

Taddei and Contena (2017) note that each of these disorders is characterized by problems in both attention and planning, though the level of impairment tends to be significantly more severe for those with ASD. Furthermore, both ADHD and ASD are highly heritable (LaBianca et al., 2018). That is, about 76% of children with ADHD and 80% of children with ASD have a family member (or twin) with the same disorder. In addition, the high rates of co-morbidity of the disorders strongly suggests shared genetic and neurocognitive pathways (Lau-Zhu, Fritz, & McLoughlin, 2019). Therefore, some researchers speculate that ADHD and ASD may be "expressions of one overarching disorder, with ADHD being the milder expression" (Rommelse, van der Meer, Hartman, & Buitelaar, 2016, p. 957).

ADHD is the more common primary diagnosis, with a prevalence of between 5% and 8% compared to between 1% and 2% for ASD. However, there is considerable overlap between the disorders, with 31% to 95% of children with a primary diagnosis of ASD showing significant symptoms of ADHD and 15% to 25% of children with a primary diagnosis of ADHD presenting with symptoms of ASD (Mikami et al., 2019). Moreover, there is a significant genetic overlap between the two disorders evident even when children with both disorders are excluded from analysis (Thapar, 2018). Research on children with combined ADHD/ASD symptoms is only in its infancy because it was only with the publication of the latest (5th) edition of the DSM that diagnosis of ADHD/ASD as a co-morbid disorder was sanctioned.

DSM5 (American Psychiatric Association, 2013) criteria for a diagnosis of ASD include deficits in social communication and interaction and restricted, repetitive, and stereotyped patterns of behavior, interests, and activities. It may also include hyper- or hypoactivity to sensory input and and/or intellectual impairments. In addition, autistic children may have some level of language impairment, including delayed language development as well as difficulties using language for social purposes (e.g., taking turns, appreciating humor, appropriate greetings and leavings, processing metaphors).

The defining characteristics of ADHD, in contrast, are inattention, hyperactivity, impulsivity and/or a combination of these symptoms. Children with ADHD are likely to be extremely rambunctious as well as overly reactive and difficult to soothe. They tend to be noncompliant and to throw tantrums in response to parental prohibitions and other frustrations. However, social problems are not part of the DSM diagnosis for ADHD even though they constitute a major challenge to the large majority of children with the disorder (about 80%) and even though they are closely associated with its core symptoms (Mikami et al., 2019).

Given the current diagnostic criteria, the two disorders would appear to be quite different, but upon closer examination, there are some real similarities between them. For example, both disorders are associated with sleep disturbances and anxiety. Motor difficulties are also associated with both disorders, including problems with fine and gross motor skills, impaired movement, timing and balance, and muscle weakness. In addition, both disorders affect social functioning in numerous ways (Kern et al., 2015; Mikami, 2019). Table 15.1 provides a comparison of children with ADHD and those with ASD in terms of social behavior, social cognition, and peer regard. In the sections below, I will discuss these similarities and differences in terms of social deficits and in terms of neurobiological functioning.

TABLE 15.1 Comparison of Social Symptoms among Individuals with ADHD and ASD

ADHD SYMPTOMATOLOGY	ASD SYMPTOMATOLOGY
Social behavior: • Elevated negative social behaviors • Obtrusive and impulsive behaviors • Social behavior problems occur when losing a game • Know what to do socially but don't do it (impulse control problems = impaired performance) • May not respond to social skills training; may respond to behavior modification • Poor relationships with adults (due to conflict and resistance)	**Social behavior:** • Absence of positive behaviors • Social withdrawal, rigidity in routines, impaired language • Social behavioral problems occur when others break/change the rules of a game • Don't know what to do socially (impaired intersubjectivity=impaired knowledge) and don't care (reduced reward sensitivity) • May respond to social skills training; may respond to non-didactic (fun) social games • Poor relationships with adults (due to reduced cognitive skills and reward sensitivity)
Social cognition: • Poorer understanding of social emotional cues than typical children • Poorer executive functioning than typical children • Poorer effortful control than typical children • Lack of opportunities (e.g., playdates) to practice social cognitive skills due to negative behaviors and peer rejection • Emotion recognition and intersubjectivity impairments may improve/remit with age	**Social cognition:** • Poorer understanding of social emotional cues than typical children *and children with ADHD* • Poorer executive functioning than typical children *and children with ADHD* • Poorer effortful control than typical children • Lack of opportunities (e.g., play dates) to practice social cognitive skills due to peer rejection • Emotion recognition and intersubjectivity do not improve/remit and may worsen with age

Peer regard:
- Less accepted and more rejected than typical children *and children with ASD*
- More difficulty being accepted (and not rejected) by a larger peer group than children with ASD
- Stigmatization by peers
- More social distancing by adults than children with ASD
- ADHD often not considered to be a valid mental health disorder (blaming the child for his or her behavior)

Peer regard:
- Less accepted and more rejected than typical children
- Impaired ability to establish friendships compared to typical children
- Stigmatization by peers
- Less social distancing by adults than children with ADHD
- ASD regularly recognized as a valid mental health disorder

Source: Mikami, A. Y., Miller, M., & Lerner, M. D. (2019). Social functioning in youth with attention-deficit/hyperactivity disorder and autism spectrum disorder: Transdiagnostic commonalities and differences. *Clinical Psychology Review*, 68, 54–70. Doi: https://doi.org/10.1016/j.cpr.2018.12.005

Similarities and Differences in Social Deficits

Both ADHD and ASD include problems with intersubjectivity, executive function, and effortful control. If you remember, intersubjectivity includes a child's ability to feel empathy for others and to take another person's perspective. Executive function has to do with the ability to manage one's time, organize and plan, solve problems, and make decisions. Effortful control pertains to the ability to shift attention, inhibit impulses, detect errors, and integrate information relevant to the selection of behaviors. Impairment in any of these functions can clearly affect how well a child can interact with others (LaBianca et al., 2018).

However, while there are similarities between the two disorders, there are also differences, some of which are associated with degree of symptom severity and others that are associated with the ways the symptoms manifest. For example, Mikami et al. (2019) note that, although both disorders involve deficits in reading facial expressions and other social cues, these deficits tend to be more severe among children with ASD. Both disorders involve problems with attention and planning, but the impairment is also more severe for children with ASD (Taddei & Contena, 2017). In addition, other researchers point out that children with ASD also tend to have more severe problems with emotional responsiveness than children with ADHD have (McCrimmon, Climie, & Huynh, 2018). They also have more problems with eye contact and with language and communication than ADHD children have. In addition, they engage in stereotypies and odd and repetitive handling of objects, and they tend to lack the ability to engage in imaginative play (Mikami et al., 2019).

Some interesting differences between ADHD and ASD exist regarding impairments in social behaviors. In ADHD, the impairments tend to include the *presence of negative behaviors* while impairments associated with ASD tend to include the *absence of positive behaviors*. That is, children with ADHD, especially those with combined symptomatology, are often aggressive and noncompliant, butt into games without invitation, don't wait their turn, can't keep their hands off other people's things, and other obtrusive and annoying behaviors. Children with ASD, however, tend to be withdrawn, do not to seek out peers for play, and engage primarily in solitary activities. Moreover, children with ADHD tend to know how they should behave in social situations (e.g., wait their turn, not hit others), but act anyway because of poor impulse control. In contrast, children with ASD may either genuinely not know what is expected of them socially, or they may simply not care. Autistic children are known to have an aberrant social reward system (i.e., social interaction is just not pleasurable) and therefore lack motivation to enact socially appropriate behaviors (Mikami et al., 2019).

Interestingly, although peers tend to reject children with either ADHD or ASD, they are friendlier with autistic children than they are with those with ADHD. Similarly, adults tend to distance themselves more from children with ADHD than from those with ASD. It may be that peers avoid interaction with their ADHD classmates because of the negative behaviors they tend to exhibit but are not so put off by the withdrawn behavior of their autistic peers. Adults, on the other hand, may stigmatize children with ADHD more than children with ASD because of a perception that ADHD behaviors are more controllable than ASD behaviors. That is, they may tend to blame children with ADHD for their impulsivity and resistance but excuse the same behaviors when they are exhibited by an autistic child, perhaps feeling that ASD is a valid disorder while ADHD isn't (Mikama et al., 2019).

Similarities and Differences in Neurobiological Functioning

Kern et al. (2015) have provided a review of studies exploring the neurobiology of autism and ADHD. They identify a group of metabolic/endocrine conditions present in both disorders, including oxidative stress, decreased methylation, and hormonal and genetic abnormalities. Oxidative stress occurs when the body doesn't have enough antioxidants to neutralize the byproducts of energy production, which when it occurs in the brain can result in inflammation and even cell death. Methylation is a molecular process involved in energy production, the cleansing of toxic levels of hormones, chemicals, and heavy metals from the body, cell repair, immune responses, gene expression, and other essential metabolic processes. These researchers note that decreased methylation is thought to be associated with attention problems, an issue in both ADHD and ASD. Moreover, both ASD and ADHD appear to be associated with toxic metal exposure (especially mercury for ASD and lead for ADHD), increased susceptibility to exposure, or impaired detoxification and excretion. Lastly, they note that levels of cortisol (a neurohormone associated with HPA system functioning) in both ADHD and ASD are lower than among typically developing children and emphasize that the greater the HPA dysfunction, the more severe the symptoms in both disorders. However, Teague, Gray, Tonge, and Newman (2017) note that oxytocin levels also tend to be lower among children with ASD than among typical children. Oxytocin has not been the focus of any studies concerning ADHD.

Kern et al. (2015) also point out certain brain pathologies common to ADHD and ASD. For example, they note that in ASD there is decreased blood flow to the frontal and prefrontal cortices, the anterior cingulate, and the anterior insula and other brain regions associated with attention, anticipation of reward, decision making, social evaluation, and emotion regulation. Likewise, there is decreased blood flow to brain regions associated with attention, reward processing, decision-making and inhibitory control in ADHD. In addition, these researchers point to a large body of research showing deficits in the ability of the brain to synchronize neuronal firing across neural networks as well as abnormalities in brain connectivity that limit the ability of the brain to process and coordinate sensory, social, and emotional information in both ASD and ADHD.

Although there are clear indications that ADHD and ASD are associated with neural and metabolic deficits, as is true of a great deal of human behavior, the outcomes for these disorders are also influenced by the social environment. In the next section, I will discuss how attachment is related to ADHD and ASD.

Attachment in ADHD and ASD

Researchers have found that raising a child with ADHD or ASD can be fraught with difficulty (McRae, Stoppelbein, O'Kelley, Fite, & Greening, 2019). They point out that parents of a child with one or both of these disorders face serious challenges in multiple areas, including managing their child's behavior on a day to day basis; getting accommodations and support at school; both finding treatment and support and finding ways to pay for them; and managing marital discord associated with these stressors. The amount of time they must spend and the drain on their physical, emotional, and financial resources can result in adjustment difficulties in both the parents and their child. Importantly, how parents adjust to their child's diagnosis and react to his or her behavior influences how the child adjusts and behaves above and beyond the severity of his or her symptoms. Those parents who do not adjust well or who become depressed or anxious are more likely to engage in inconsistent or authoritarian disciplinary practices. As discussed in earlier chapters, these kinds of parenting behaviors are associated with increased internalizing and externalizing behaviors in their children, which may in turn exacerbate negative parent-child interactions and result in a pattern of negative interaction that perpetuates itself. They emphasize that when a child with these disorders acts out on top of the already stressful core symptoms of his or her disorder, the parent

> Might also experience guilt about the child's difficulties and parent stress, anxiety about the child's current and future functioning and well-being, and stress about choosing appropriate school systems, interventions, and accommodations to meet their child's needs ... which might further increase their risk of experiencing poorer parental adjustment. (p. 676)

What a mess! Thus, it is clear that mental health practitioners who work with ADHD and/or ASD must consider parental needs as well as the needs of the children and where possible provide supports to help them develop warm/supportive, consistent, sensitive parenting. Environmental factors such as good parenting may not be able to overcome the genetic underpinnings of these disorders completely, but they may be able to at least diminish symptoms rather than exacerbate them.

Affectionate, consistent, sensitive parenting, as we have learned, is associated with the development of secure attachment and positive internal working models of both self and others. This broad generalization remains true even for children with disorders like ASD and ADHD that include serious barriers to social interaction. Research exploring associations between attachment and ADHD/ASD outcomes on a possible single continuum is not yet available. Therefore, I will discuss the current literature concerning the disorders separately.

Attachment and ADHD

Although it is clear that there is a strong genetic component to ADHD, researchers generally agree that multiple psychosocial and family correlates influence individual outcomes. Attachment is clearly one of those factors, and unfortunately, research has shown that only about

7% of children who have been diagnosed with ADHD have secure attachment, compared to 62% of children in the general population (Storebo & Simonsen, 2014). Indeed, a review of 29 studies examining associations between attachment and ADHD show that insecure attachment and ADHD are inextricably intertwined. That is, a child with insecure attachment is at risk of developing ADHD, and a child with ADHD is likely to develop insecure attachment (Storebo, Rasmussen, & Simonsen, 2016). Consider Macy, for example. I invite you to read Case Study 15.2 and consider how Macy's diagnosis of ADHD is affecting her relationship with her mother and how her mother may be contributing to Macy's problematic behaviors. There are apparently multiple factors at play in the relationship between parenting and ADHD outcomes. For example, as mentioned above, parental adjustment is an important factor in ADHD outcomes. That is, parental mood and behavior affect child mood and behavior. Of course, parental adjustment can be influenced by the parent's own attachment and mental health histories. In Chapter 6, I discussed how maternal psychological issues such as unresolved trauma/loss and depression can create insecure attachment. In addition, a mother's parenting style tends to be based on her own experience of being parented. If her own parents rejected her, or if they were only inconsistently available, she is likely to treat her own children the same way and place them at risk, especially if they have genetic susceptibility, of developing ADHD.

CASE STUDY 15.2: MACY STRUGGLES

Macy has never had many friends. In the younger grades, she had had difficulty controlling herself. Physical activity with the other children during recess frequently devolved into fighting that required adult intervention. In pretend play, she was bossy, and if she didn't get her way, she would throw tantrums and blame the other girls for being unfair. She also blamed her teachers for her poor grades. However, her teachers told Macy's mother, Tara, that they felt that she was very smart but unmotivated. She wasn't failing, but she felt like her teachers, her mother and her grandmother were constantly nagging her to do better. Her mother often said, "How are you going to be a doctor if you can't get into med school, for goodness sakes?!" Macy hated that she was such a disappointment to her mother, but she just couldn't get interested in many of the subjects at school, and if she wasn't interested, she simply wouldn't work. Besides, it felt to her like nobody noticed when she did something well; people only paid attention when she did something wrong.

Now that Macy is entering sixth grade, she is starting at a new middle school. She tries hard to make friends, but it isn't easy for her. She tends to become friends with someone for a few days or weeks and then erupts into anger when the friend expresses an interest in having other friends join them. Then she moves on to form a friendship with someone else. Each time she loses another friend, she feels worse about herself. In an effort to get others to like her, she starts making up stories about herself, exaggerating her accomplishments. The others suspect that she is lying and shun her all the more.

Then, her grandmother is hospitalized because of a stroke. Hazel had been caring for Macy for her entire life, and the thought of possibly losing her is absolutely overwhelming. Hazel survives the stroke but can no longer talk; in addition, she has lost some functioning in her legs, making her susceptible to falls. She can take care of her basic needs herself, but Tara insists that she move in with her and Macy so that they can help her adjust to her disabilities. Macy doesn't know what to do or how to help.

Over the next two years, Tara is strained as she tries to care for both her mother and her daughter, and tempers flare. Macy is constantly anxious. She is afraid that her grandmother is going to die, and terrified that her mother could die, too. She knows this fear is irrational, but she just can't stop it. Sometimes she creeps into her mother's bedroom at night to make sure she is still breathing. Not wanting to add to her mother's stress, she says nothing about her fears and simply isolates in her room after coming home from school. Her mother got her an I pad for Christmas last year, and she spends more and more time on social media sites. She has some friends there, and she spends hours chatting with them. Because she is safe at home and not causing any trouble, Tara leaves her alone, somewhat relieved that Macy seems to have finally found some friends.

Moreover, how a parent relates to his or her child can be affected by the personal characteristics of the child. It is known, for example, that infants with relatively difficult temperaments (e.g., irritable, hard to soothe, highly reactive) and toddlers with dysregulated affect, attention, impulse control, and activity levels are at increased risk of receiving an ADHD diagnosis in early childhood (Campbell, et al., 2014). Thus, there is an intertwining of intergenerational factors that can affect both parent and child and the stresses implicit in their relationship.

The attachment relationship serves as the foundation for a child's self-regulation skills. Children with ADHD tend to have significant deficits in self-regulation, and research indicates that insecure attachment, especially the anxious/ambivalent and disorganized styles, are associated with ADHD symptomatology (Sempio, Fabio, Tiezzi, & Cedro, 2016). Anxious attachment tends to generate hyperactivation strategies (demanding, clinging, intrusive, attention-seeking behaviors) as a means of getting attention from an inconsistently available care giver, while disorganized attachment may also include hyperactive responses to stress and various acting out behaviors (Mikulincer & Shaver, 2016); both involve compromised self-regulation. In contrast, secure attachment is associated with toddlers' willingness to comply with parental and teacher directions, with adequate problem-solving, and with the ability to self-regulate and delay gratification when they enter the school system (Sempio et al., 2016). Thus, with children who have a genetic predisposition to attention and self-regulation issues, insecure attachment will most likely exacerbate their problems. When they enter the school system, their problems may be compounded by teacher expectations and impatience, often resulting in punishment of behaviors over which they have little control.

CLASS DISCUSSION

Given what you know of the importance of mastering both academic and social skills during the school-age years, what do you think of psychostimulant medication for children with ADHD?

It is important to note that there are much higher levels of ADHD found among foster children, children who have been institutionalized (Dahmen, Putz, Herpertz-Dahlman, & Konrad, 2012), and adopted children who have suffered neglect in the first month of life (Roskam et al., 2014). These researchers also note that ADHD is significantly more common among children whose families are faced with the stresses of poverty, marital discord, large family size, or the presence of parental criminality or mental illness. These findings suggest that early deprivation has a strong impact on ADHD development and symptomatology such that "the less the rearing environment corresponds to a normal family setting, the more ADHD symptoms can be observed" (Dahmen, et al., 2012, p. 1026). Thus, although not all children who suffer early pathogenic care go on to develop ADHD, deprivation and attachment deficits certainly increase the risk.

Attachment and Autism

Research suggests that there is considerable overlap between symptoms of autism and symptoms of attachment insecurity in the areas of rigidity, play, social interaction, intersubjectivity, communication, emotion regulation, sensory integration, and executive function (Moran, 2010). Therefore, according to McKenzie and Dallos (2017), children who have serious attachment problems may be misdiagnosed as being on the autism spectrum and may improve significantly when placed in a loving home where they can find secure relationships.

In a systematic review of the literature concerning attachment among children on the spectrum, Teague et al. (2017) found secure attachment in about half of the children sampled in the studies (compared to about 65% in typically developing children). Among those identified as insecure, approximately 22% appeared to have a disorganized style (compared to only 15% reported among typically developing children). Moreover, these researchers suggest that there are common features between autism and two serious attachment disorders (reactive attachment disorder and disinhibited social engagement disorder), both of which are associated with extreme neglect or abuse. However, McKenzie and Dallos (2017) argue that determining attachment insecurity among children on the spectrum has thus far proven to be quite difficult for two reasons. First, they suggest that tools used to measure attachment among autistic children appear to be somewhat inadequate. Secondly, they point out that

> Children with autism may develop a complex set of symptoms that may derive from the developmental implications of autistic traits, combined with insecure attachment, leading to a blurring and exacerbation of symptoms associated with the two conditions. Over time, the symptoms of one condition may mask the other or become so entangled that it is no longer possible for clinicians to distinguish which symptoms may be attributable to autism. (p. 641)

However, they go on to suggest that, although it is difficult to draw firm conclusions from the mixed results of the studies currently in the literature, it appears that autistic children can and do develop secure attachment. Interestingly, children with ASD tend to have lower baseline levels of oxytocin than normally developing children (Teague et al., 2017). However, research shows that those levels become equal to those of typically developing children when they are interacting with their parents but then fall again with 15 minutes of stopping that interaction.

As I am sure you recall from Chapter 4, oxytocin is associated with secure attachment, and these researchers suggest that there is a need for more research on the role that oxytocin (and other neurohormones) play in attachment in this population.

McKenzie and Dallos (2017) emphasize that, although children with ASD can develop secure attachment, they face multiple factors that place them at increased risk of developing insecure attachment. For example, autistic children who also have intellectual disability, and those who have more severe autistic symptoms, are at higher risk of insecure attachment (Grzadzinski, Luyster, Spencer, & Lord, 2014; Teague et al., 2017). Teague et al. (2017) point out that it may be difficult for autistic children to develop trust in their parents' availability and responsiveness because their disorder has compromised their ability to understand, predict, and/or control their parents' behaviors. As you may recall, trust is fundamental to healthy development during infancy (Erikson, 1963). Without trust, autistic children may have difficulty using their caregiver as a safe haven when distressed, and since they also have difficulty reading and understanding their parents' social signals, they may respond in maladaptive ways (Teague, Newman, Tonge, Gray, & the MHYPsDD team, 2018).

McKenzie and Dallos (2017) argue that, as is true with all children, parents' own experiences of parenting and attachment will inevitably influence their attachment with their children; that is, insecure parents tend to produce insecure children, and secure parents tend to produce secure children. However, the stresses associated with parenting an autistic child can exacerbate any attachment issues a parent brings into the parent-child relationship. Autistic children do not provide the same level of emotional feedback that typical children do, and they may avoid eye contact and be unresponsive to their caregiver's attempts to communicate, leaving the parent unable to read their needs effectively (McKenzie & Dallos, 2017; Teague et al., 2018). Moreover, given the high rates of heritability in autism, it is possible that the parent may also have autistic traits and be lacking to some degree in empathy or the ability to read their child's social signals.

Van IJzendoorn et al. (2007) notes that even the most sensitive and attuned parents have difficulty parenting an autistic child. Therefore, autistic children of parents with mental health issues of their own, whether they be autistic traits, substance abuse, depression, anxiety, or unresolved trauma, may have difficulty, too. Similarly, the risk of developing an insecure attachment style may be significantly increased among autistic children whose parents had negative parenting models or insecure attachment themselves (Teague et al., 2017).

Secure attachment, on the other hand, is a powerful protective factor among children with ASD. Autistic children with secure attachment are, for example, more engaged with others, and they initiate social interaction more often than children with insecure attachment do. They also show fewer behavioral problems and more prosocial behaviors such as turn-taking and reciprocal smiling. In addition, they tend to engage in more joint attention, have higher levels of intersubjectivity, and better language development (McKenzie & Dallos, 2017). Similarly, Teague et al. (2017) note that securely attached children on the spectrum show more complex play behaviors, have more friends and are less jealous, and tend to have better academic performance that those who are insecure. Moreover, parents whose autistic child has a secure attachment style have lower levels of depression anxiety and stress levels than those who have children with an insecure style, suggesting a bi-directional relationship between child attachment and parenting quality (Teague et al., 2018).

It is clear, then, that mental health practitioners who work with the families of children on the spectrum should consider assessing for parental sensitivity and attunement and providing supports that will help them with the parenting practices that promote secure attachment. In addition, since parents of autistic children are less likely to have an authoritative parenting style than parents of typical children (Teague et al., 2018), it may be wise to provide them with parenting skills trainings.

Unfortunately, autism cannot be cured by simply improving attachment and parenting. As Vivanti and Nuske (2017) point out, although a child on the spectrum may be securely attached, he or she may still have profound deficits in social motivation and social-emotional reciprocity due to faulty brain development and functioning. As mentioned in Chapter 4, these researchers hold that two distinct neural pathways are involved in attachment: the system that drives proximity-seeking during times of danger/distress (help me!), and the system that drives proximity-seeking to satisfy the desire for affiliation (let's be friends!). They argue that in children on the spectrum the safety-seeking system apparently remains relatively intact (i.e., they will seek proximity to their attachment figure when frightened or sick). However, the affiliation-seeking system is damaged in such a way that social interaction is not as rewarding as it is for more typically developing children. Because of their impaired ability to imitate, to share emotions, and to pay attention to what others find interesting, they lose out on the social learning opportunities provided by the moment-to-moment social interaction with their caregiver during infancy and therefore do not have the foundation for later social relationships. Thus, even though secure attachment is associated with better outcomes, improving parental sensitivity and attunement can only go so far.

Summary

In this chapter, I have identified several important and (unfortunately) common challenges to development in early and middle childhood. Trauma and maltreatment (neglect and abuse) have been shown to cause changes in neural structure and function that promote behavioral and mental health issues during childhood that may continue into and through adulthood. Insecure attachment and poor parenting practices are closely associated with neglect and abuse and are risk factors for poorer outcomes in children who have suffered adverse childhood experiences. Moreover, they are associated with the development of ADHD symptomatology and with poorer outcomes for children with ADHD, ASD, or both disorders. Although genetic factors may make some children more vulnerable to negative mental health outcomes, practitioners may want to consider using attachment-focused interventions targeting children and families who present with these problems.

In the next chapter, I will address several problems associated with the increase in social connectedness and activity among children in school-age children. Specifically, I will explore how neurobiology and attachment are affected by and affect bullying and the use of digital technology, including the use of social media.

CHAPTER 16

The Social Environment of Early and Middle Childhood

LEARNING OBJECTIVES

After completing this chapter, readers should be able to identify:

- Personal and neurological characteristics of bullies and victims of bullying.
- Short- and long-term social consequences of bullying.
- The effects of insecure attachment on increased aggressive behavior toward peers (bullies), increased victimization by peers (victims) or both (bully-victims).
- Relationship between early attachment experiences and problematic use of electronic media.
- Physical and mental health issues associated with technology use.

KEY IDEAS

1. Both bullying and victimization are correlated with poorer academic performance, suicidal thoughts and actions, and involvement in violence and crime later in life.
2. Dysregulation of the stress regulation system is associated with both bullying and victimization.
3. Children with secure attachment are significantly less likely than their insecurely attached peers to be involved with either bullying or victimization.
4. The use of electronic devices by children can have a positive impact on their learning but is also associated with both physical and mental health issues.
5. Social media use during childhood can increase connectedness but can also result in increased levels of anxiety and depression.

Introduction

In previous chapters we have learned that trauma, abuse, and neglect during the early years of life are associated with the development of maladaptive behaviors and emotional dysregulation that can interfere with the important tasks that school-age children need to master in order to transition successfully into adolescence and adulthood. These factors are also associated with two problems that are of particular interest in today's world: bullying and the use of digital technology.

Bullying is an on going problem among school-age children, with between 25% and 33% of students reporting that they have been bullied at least once in a given month (Plessis, Sneekens, Cillessen, Whittle, & Guroglu, 2019; stopbullying.gov, 2018). Bullying includes behaviors that are intentionally directed by one or more individuals (the *bully/bullies*) against another individual (the *victim*) for the express purpose of inflicting distress or harm (Olweus & Limber, 2010). It frequently involves a group of individuals who gang up on a victim in an effort to hurt, humiliate, harass, or intimidate him or her. It is not unusual, however, for a bully also to have been the victim of bullying, and thus is known as a *bully-victim*. Bully-victims may be impulsive children who act out aggressively in response to being bullied, or they may transition from victim to bully over some period of time (Shetgiri, 2015). Research has shown that in a sample of adolescents, bully-victims outnumbered both just-bullies (36.6% bully-victims to 11.7% just-bullies) and just-victims (36.6% bully-victims to 19.5% just-victims), and that only 31.1% of the sample had neither been bullied nor victimized (Young et al., 2015). Given the widespread presence of bullying in current society, it is likely that mental health practitioners will encounter this problem if their practice includes work with children.

Similarly, in today's world, digital technology is widely available and used by even very young children. The use of digital devices by children has grown by leaps and bounds in recent years. One report shows that in the United States, 98% of homes with children age eight or younger have at least one mobile device, 95% have a smart phone, and in 78% of the homes, children have access to a tablet of some sort (Rideout, 2017). Moreover, this report indicates that 42% of children have a tablet for their own personal use, up from 7% in 2013 and 1% in 2011. All told, children age eight and under spend a little over two and a quarter hours a day watching one screen or another (televisions, computers, tablets, cell phones, etc.), an amount of time almost unchanged since 2011. However, the amount of time children spend on their mobile devices has increased dramatically, increasing from only five minutes a day in 2011 to 15 minutes in 2013, and to 48 minutes in 2017. It is important, then for mental health practitioners to be aware of the possible advantages and disadvantages of technology use among school-age children. Therefore, in this chapter, I will discuss the personal characteristics of bullies and victims, neurological factors associated with bullying, and the effects of attachment experiences in its development. Then I will explore the literature on the use of technology among school-age children with a special focus on the rising use of social media.

Bullying and Victimization

Bullying can be physical, verbal, or relational in nature, usually includes a clear power differential (e.g., physically stronger or a member of a majority group) between the bully/bullies and the victim, and usually happens repeatedly (see Table 16.1 for the kinds of behaviors associated with different types of bullying). This last characteristic (repetition) is not considered by some researchers to be essential for an act of aggression to be considered bullying. Rather, they suggest that it may be considered bullying if a victim simply remains afraid that the aggression will be repeated (Monks, Ortega Ruiz, & Torrado, 2002).

TABLE 16.1 Behaviors Associated with Bullying

TYPE OF BULLYING	BEHAVIORS
Physical	Hitting, pushing, choking, kicking Forcefully taking something from the victim Forcing the victim to do something Defacing or destroying the victim's property Making faces or obscene gestures
Verbal	Name-calling, taunting, tattling, malicious teasing Verbal threats and psychological intimidation Racist and sexual comments and gestures
Relational	Gossip, slander, sabotage Convincing others to exclude the victim
Cyberbullying	Same as above, but utilizing electronic devices such as cell phones, emails, text messaging and instant messaging, and other social media platforms to embarrass and humiliate the victim

Source: Shetgiri, R. (2013). Bullying and victimization among children. *Advances in Pediatrics*, 60, 33–51.

Bullying can occur in many different locations and contexts: school, playground, neighborhood, home, and online (cyberbullying). Although cyberbullying happens less often than other forms of bullying (stopbullying.gov, 2018), it is thought to be particularly pernicious since social media and humiliating websites can reach such a broad audience (Charalampous et al., 2018). Since it can be anonymous, it is hard to trace, which may embolden the bully since it is unlikely that he or she will be identified and held accountable. In addition, cyberbullying can reach the victim even in his or her home every time he or she reads emails or checks social media accounts; there is no respite and no safe place. In this section, I will discuss the personal characteristics of bullies and their victims and the short- and long-term neurological and social consequences of bullying. Then I will discuss bullying from an attachment and parenting perspective.

Characteristics of Bullies

Although bullying tends to occur most frequently during late middle childhood and adolescence (Craig & Pepler, 2007; stopbullying.gov, 2018), research suggests that much younger children are able to recognize the effect that their aggression can have on someone else and act with the intention to cause physical or emotional pain (Williams, Smith, & Winters, 2016). Moreover, they point out that children as young as four can recognize power differentials and exploit them to get what they want.

In general, bullies tend to enjoy socially dominating others, have positive attitudes toward violence, have little empathy for others, and they tend to perceive hostility in ambiguous situations (Pontzer, 2010). Not all bullies are alike, however. For example, Young et al. (2015) describe bullies as having higher levels of anger, lower levels of happiness, more interpersonal problems and physical altercations, more substance use, and poorer academic performance than non-bullies have. However, they also emphasize that a substantial portion of bullies have normal levels of social intelligence and popularity. They argue that most research on bullying has not delved deeply enough into bullies' subjective sense of happiness and social connectedness. Indeed, their research shows that more bullies report being happy and socially connected than report being unhappy and disconnected. Happiness of bullies who are highly engaged with a social group might be attributed to a sense of satisfaction associated with gaining or maintaining dominance within the group (Shetgiri, 2013). Alternatively, it may be that a bully may be rewarded for bullying by his or her peer group, which would result in feelings of happiness derived from a sense of group acceptance and belonging (Young et al., 2015). This assumption makes sense in light of research by Kokkinos and Panayiotou (2004) who report that bullies tend to have high self-esteem, which could be related to happiness. Moreover, they point out numerous negative mental health characteristics of bully-victims compared to bullies, including low self-esteem, less effective problem-solving and social skills, less popularity, and higher levels of depression than bullies.

Characteristics of Victims

According to Shetgiri (2015), victims of bullying tend to be physically smaller and more emotionally sensitive than their bullies. In addition, they tend to be more socially anxious and lonely and to lack assertiveness (Navarro, Larranaga, & Yubero, 2018; Shetgiri, 2015). A child who has few friends or who has friends who are not supportive or protective is at increased risk of bullying. In addition, victims tend to have difficulty regulating their emotions and defusing negative interactions with peers and thus encourage victimization by bullies who enjoy seeing their victims' distress. Interestingly, researchers have found that although many children may go online in the hopes of making new friends, those who go online due to serious social anxiety and loneliness are at high risk of severe cyberbullying (Navarro et al., 2018).

Consequences of Bullying and Victimization

Shetgiri (2015) notes that bullying and victimization can have both short- and long-term consequences. Importantly, both bullies and their victims are at increased risk of poorer school performance, which can affect their productivity later in life. Moreover, both are at heightened risk for suicidal ideation, attempt and completion. Childhood bullies tend to continue to bully into adulthood, and childhood victims tend to continue to be victims (Beduna & Perrone-McGovern, 2019). In addition, bullies are likely to go on to develop serious externalizing and antisocial behaviors including intimate partner violence, fighting and weapon-carrying, delinquency in adolescence, and multiple criminal convictions in adulthood. Furthermore, they are more likely to have children who become bullies (Shetgiri, 2015).

In contrast, victims have increased levels of low self-esteem and internalizing problems such as depression and anxiety, and they are more likely to develop PTSD than children who are not bullied. Their academic performance tends to be affected, perhaps due to increased absenteeism associated with social phobia or fear of going to school or riding the school bus where the bullying is happening. They report higher levels of insomnia and nightmares as well as somatic complaints such as headaches and stomach aches (Shetgiri, 2015). Some researchers suggest, however, that the poor health that is often experienced by victims of bullying may not be psychosomatic but may instead be linked to immune deficiencies (Vaillancourt et al., 2010). This may well be true since, as you may remember from Chapter 3, the vegetative vagus, the nerve system responsible for the freeze response to perceived threat, controls the immune system.

However, Shetgiri (2005) notes that, although bullied lesbian/gay/bisexual youth and children with learning disabilities are at higher risk of suicide than other victims, bully-victims tend to have the greatest risk for negative outcomes. Compared to all the other groups (bullies, victims, and children with no involvement in bullying), bully-victims are at the highest risk of social exclusion, school disengagement, depression, anxiety and somatic complaints, substance use and abuse, fighting, and weapons-carrying. In addition, they are at the highest risk of suicide, and they are the most likely to use weapons for the purpose of perpetrating mass school shootings, a subject that I will take up in Chapter 19.

Neurobiology and Bullying

The literature concerning the effects of bullying on the victim's brain tends to center on alterations in the HPA system. If you remember from Chapter 2, chronic stress is associated with high levels of cortisol in some individuals and low levels in others. Interestingly, Vaillancourt et al. (2010) note that boys who have been bullied by their peers tend to fall into the former category, while girls tend to fall onto the latter. To explain this difference, they suggest that peer rejection is experienced by girls as being much more stressful than it is by boys, given girls' higher valuation of relational inclusion.

Vaillancourt et al. (2010) liken the stress of being rejected by one's peers to that of being maltreated by one's caregivers, noting that research shows similar HPA dysregulation among both groups. At first glance, this might seem unlikely since relationships with parents and other attachment figures are a matter of life and death in infancy and toddlerhood while relationships with peers are not related to survival. However, they point out that the need for positive social affiliation is part of our evolutionary heritage as social animals, and social ostracism or rejection, whether during early and middle childhood or in later life stages, triggers stress responses. The psychological pain of social rejection is very like physical pain, and both are mediated by the same neurological system, the anterior cingulate and insula. The good news is that the psychological and physical distress caused by bullying and social rejection can be alleviated at least to some degree by oxytocin. You probably recall that oxytocin is the neurochemical associated with attachment. It is released during positive social experiences and when social support is available, and its presence is associated with reductions in anxiety. Therefore, if an individual who is being bullied or rejected by peers has a supportive friend, teacher or parent, the deleterious effects of stress may be reduced.

Attachment, Parenting, and Bullying

Kokkinos (2013) suggests that secure attachment acts as a protective factor against both bullying and peer rejection/victimization while insecure attachment is a risk factor for both. Specifically, his research has found that children with secure attachment are significantly less likely than their insecurely attached peers to be involved with either bullying or victimization. Importantly, they also tend to report significantly higher levels of parental warmth and acceptance. Moreover, he reports that while bullies tend to have an avoidant attachment style, victims tend to have an anxious attachment style. Unfortunately, Kokkinos' (2013) study does not use an instrument that identifies disorganized/disoriented attachment, so we cannot know how bullying and victimization are related to that attachment style.

These results concerning insecure attachment are not surprising given what we know about how attachment styles develop. As explained in Chapter 4, an avoidant style tends to develop when the parent punishes the child's manifestation of dependency needs, which results in the child using deactivation strategies to shut down his or her own emotions and avoid others' emotions (lack of compassion for self and others). The parents of an anxious/ambivalent child, on the other hand, tend to be inconsistent in their responses to their child's needs, leading the child to use hyperactivation strategies and displays of high emotionality that increase their chances of victimization by bullies who enjoy inflicting distress (Beduna & Perrone-Mc-Govern, 2019). At this time, there is no research on attachment disorganization and bullying/victimization. However, given the extreme insecurity that develops when a child cannot organize an effective proximity-seeking strategy, it seems likely that this style would place a child at heightened risk of both the externalizing and internalizing behaviors associated with bullying and victimization. I would be very interested in research exploring possible connections between disorganized attachment and bully-victims.

As might be expected, attachment is related to parenting styles, with the authoritative style being associated with secure attachment and insecure attachment related to the permissive and authoritarian styles. Not surprisingly, then, bullying is associated with authoritarian and punitive parenting, and in those families in which abuse, neglect, and hostility is common and in which violence of one parent against the other occurs (Kokkinos, 2013; Pontzer, 2010). Moreover, bully-victims report higher levels of parental rejection than either bullies or victims (Kokkinos, 2013). Other research has shown that "parents who interact with their children in a hostile, cold, indifferent, inconsistent, accusatory, and/or disappointed manner encourage their children to act" in similar ways (Pontzer, 2010, p. 271), resulting in increased likelihood of bullying. Other research shows that disciplinary slapping, even when it is employed only occasionally and even in a context of warm parenting, is associated with increased odds of youth being identified as either bullies or bully-victims (Fujikawa et al., 2018).

Charalampous et al. (2018) suggest that children may respond to authoritarian parenting by bullying others as a way of exerting freedom and gaining recognition. In addition, because their parents do not respond to them with sensitivity, they are likely to be insensitive to their victims' distress. Shetgiri (2013) notes that bullying is also predicted by both maternal and paternal depression, perhaps due to parents' increased irritability and hostility, as well as by poor parental monitoring. Lack of parental monitoring is especially problematic in the case of cyberbullying, since children can bully using their electronic devices so easily if parents aren't supervising them (Charalampous et al., 2018).

Charalampous et al. (2018) note that victimization is associated with both the authoritarian and permissive parenting style styles. Apparently, children who have grown up with authoritarian parenting (harsh, punitive, cold) tend to have lower self-esteem, which makes them more vulnerable to bullying. In contrast, children of overly protective permissive parents don't have the opportunity to learn conflict resolution skills that would protect them against bullying and thus may resort to maladaptive attempts at avoidance or develop a negative self-image, both of which place them at increased risk of future bullying (Charalampous et al., 2018; Stevens, De Bourdeaudhuij, & Van Oost, 2002). An authoritative parenting style, however, allows a child to disclose problems and ask for help when needed, and to use the parent as a source of support and comfort if the child experiences bullying (Charalampous et al., 2018).

Cyberbullying has become increasingly common with the ready availability of digital technology, especially mobile devices. However, a number of other issues are associated with cyber technology that I discuss in the next section.

Technology

Research indicates that smart phones, tablets and other devices are being given to younger and younger children, with a growing number of apps targeting even infants and toddlers (Levine, Waite, Bowman, & Kachinsky, 2019). Moreover, the number of children under the age of two who use electronic devices almost quadrupled over a two-year period (from 10% to 38% between 2011 and 2013) (Common Sense Media, 2013), and they now spend an average of 42 minutes a day watching television (29 minutes) and other media such as DVDs/video tapes or mobile devices (13 minutes) (Rideout, 2017).

The American Academy of Pediatrics Council of Communications and Media (AAP; 2016) argue that between birth and five years of age children's brains are growing rapidly and therefore are especially vulnerable. They emphasize that digital media use be avoided in children younger than about 18 months, though they make an exception for video chatting via media such as Skype. Levine et al. (2019) note that parents may justify allowing their children to use electronic media by saying that the programs they are watching are educational. However, the AAP (2016) note that in infancy and toddlerhood, young children simply can't learn from flat screens in the way they can from personal interactions in a three-dimensional environment (please see Table 16.2 for their recommendations). They suggest further that screen time should be limited, and parents should watch the program with the child and then reteach him or her the content rather allowing the child to watch alone. Furthermore, they warn that devices shouldn't be used as the primary way that a parent calms his or her child but note that limited use in particularly stressful times such as at the doctor's office or on airplane trips, they can be very useful. Lastly, they suggest that programming and apps should be closely monitored to screen out inappropriate or violent content, and that only high quality programs and apps should be given to the child.

TABLE 16.2   American Academy of Pediatrics Family Recommendations for Child Media Use

Don't
- Feel pressured to introduce technology early
- Leave the TV and other devices on when not in use
- Use digital media for children under age 18 months
- Allow toddlers to use media alone
- Allow more than one hour total screen time per day for children age two to five
- Allow fast-paced programming with a lot of distractions or violence
- Use media as the only way to calm the child
- Allow screen time from one hour before bedtime

Do
- Allow only high-quality programming such as *Sesame Street*
- Watch programs with the child, ask the child what he or she thinks of the program or app and reteach and apply content in the world around them
- Monitor programming content and downloaded apps, testing them before the child uses them
- Keep bedtimes, mealtimes, and parent-child playtimes screen-free for both child and parent
- Remove screens from bedrooms after bedtime

Source: AAP Council on Communications and Media (2016). Media and young minds. Pediatrics, 138(5), *1–6.*

Although these warnings by the AAP (2016) give clear indication of the possible negative effects of technology use among children, the use of technology is not necessarily a bad thing. In the sections below, I will identify both advantages and the dangers associated with use.

Advantages Offered by Technology

Although exposure of infants and toddlers to electronic media is discouraged as mentioned above, research indicates that kindergartners who have had access to digital learning resources come to the schoolroom door better prepared than those who have not had access to them (Lozano, Thai, & Ponciano, 2016). The use of electronic devices by children can have a positive impact on their learning in numerous ways, including by supporting letter name and sound learning and emerging writing skills (Neumann, 2018); increasing their understanding of the learning process, reinforcing persistence toward a learning goal, and encouraging independent learning; providing opportunities to develop creativity and to collaborate with peers; increasing literacy and numeracy skills, and second language development (Oliemat, Ihmeideh, & Alkhawaldeh, 2018). In addition, computer technology is even being used to increase social emotional learning and emotional intelligence in middle childhood (Amico, 2018), and virtual reality programs are showing promise in the treatment of physical disabilities and autism (Bailey & Bailenson, 2017). Of course, various forms of electronic media are also used for simple entertainment and relaxation, and parents may use it as a way to distract their children so that they, too, can relax or get things done (Levine et al., 2019).

Physical Health Issues and Technology Use

Although there are clear advantages to the availability of electronic media, it is also clear that there are problems associated with its use. For example, the more time a three- to five-year-old child spends in tablet use the more likely he or she is to have poor musculoskeletal development and risks associated with sedentary activities for brain development and physical health (Howie, Coenen, Campbell, Ranelli, & Straker, 2017). In addition, as children get older and spend more time out of the home and in the neighborhood, they become more vulnerable to accidents. If distracted by their mobile devices while walking, riding their bikes, or while driving (after they reach adolescence), they are at increased risk of being involved in a crash because of decreased attention to visual or auditory cues from the environment and/or cognitive distraction (Stavrinos, Pope, Shen, & Schwebel, 2018).

As discussed in Chapter 7, play is important for children of all ages (and adults, too, for that matter). Although children engage in non-technology play for about the same amount of time they spend in screen time, they spend the least amount of time in outdoor play where they would most likely be engaged in physical activity (Slutsky & DeShelter, 2017). Obesity is a major health concern in the United States and around the world, and lack of physical activity is associated with childhood obesity (Singh et al., 2010). In addition, research has shown that reducing the amount of time children spend in front of their televisions and on their devices during early and middle childhood can significantly reduce their BMI and improve their eating behaviors (Ma, et al., 2015).

Mental Health Issues and Technology Use

Sage and Burgio (2018) warn that wireless devices (e.g., cell phones, cordless phones, wireless laptop computers, and tablets) produce electromagnetic fields and pulsed radiofrequency radiation. They provide a review of studies suggesting that wireless emissions may be at least partially responsible for negative childhood outcomes, including problems with memory, learning, cognition, attention, and behavior. Moreover, other research has shown that regular frequent use of mobile devices such as smart phones and tablets is linked to clinical levels of behavioral problems such as conduct disorder and ADHD (Hosokawa & Katsura, 2018). Reduced social and emotional competencies that could promote bullying, especially cyberbullying are also associated with mobile device use (Nasaescu, Marin-Lopez, Llorent, Ortega-Ruiz, & Zych, 2018).

Other research suggests that children may be using their devices in such a way that they effectively block out the off-line world. If they do block others out, they may be undermining the availability of needed social support (Hadlington et al., 2019; Hosokawa & Katsura, 2018). Moreover, children may be using the devices in an effort to modify their mood much the same way that substances are used, and the language they use about how important their devices are to them sounds much like the language addicts use about their drugs (Sternberg, Luria, & Sheppes, 2018).

Davou and Sidiropoulou (2017) suggest that the growing frequency of use of electronic devices has fundamentally changed children's relationship with time and space and may affect their development of a sense of self, something that becomes particularly important as children move through middle childhood and enter adolescence. Today, it is possible for children to know what is going on anywhere in the world right as it is happening, and it is potentially possible for them to communicate with almost anyone at almost any time. They can see all kinds of life styles and ways of being, and they can see all kinds of real and potential global dangers. These researchers suggest that this unprecedented level of connectedness and relational availability has the capacity to influence a child's developing sense of self in the world as he or she looks for answers to the questions "who am I, and what do I want to do with my life?"

These researchers warn that human beings have traditionally obtained a sense of self that was based on "the givens around which everyday life was organized" (Davou & Sidiropoulou, 2017, p. 263), which was passed down from the older generation to the new and which provided a sense of cohesion to the developing sense of self. This is no longer the case. Instead, they argue that "Innumerable pathways seem now to be open to the individual, and the final choice appears as an 'as if' matter, a question of selecting between 'possible worlds'; a choice that can be continuously postponed" (p. 263). I, personally, do not know if this is a positive, negative, or neutral situation for children growing up today. However, Davou and Sidiropoulou paint a devastatingly bleak picture of the modern home and how technology may affect both the ability to be with others and the ability to be alone, saying that electronic devices

> exist in every room and are carried around as "body extensions." A T.V. set is almost permanently open somewhere around the family "dining table," and cell phones placed "on the table" keep family members connected with others during meals. It is a home crowded by potentially innumerable virtual others who intrude in face-to-face family interactions. As if family members have become more and more indifferent in communicating with one another, and as if individual users have never mastered—or have lost—the developmentally essential capacity for the experience of being alone and turned inwards, while some reliable other is present. (p. 263)

Given these possible negative outcomes, it is important that mental health professionals be aware of the technology use among the children we treat and provide guidance both to parents and to policy makers so that we give children the best opportunity to grow up healthy and happy.

> ### CLASS DISCUSSION
>
> What are the advantages and disadvantages you see with Macy's and Jet's use of digital devices and social media as presented in their case studies in the previous chapter?

Technology Use, Parenting, and Attachment

Parental attitudes and practices concerning the use of technology naturally influence their children's use of digital media. A considerable body of research addresses parental influences on the use of digital technology. This information will be presented first, followed by a discussion about the smaller number of studies exploring technology use and attachment.

Parental Influences

Research indicates that children are spending about the same amount of time at home as they did back in the early 2000s (Mullan & Chatzitheochari, 2019). However, because of the use of electronic devices by both parents and their children, the fact that they are both present in the same location does not mean that they are actually spending time in close interaction with each other. Instead, children report that they are spending more time "alone together," meaning that although they are in the same location as their parents, children are not necessarily interacting with them but are instead likely to be engaged in device use.

Parents may be complicit in this tendency toward isolation, preferring not to enforce boundaries in an effort to avoid conflict and keep peace in the home. However, it is clear that parents need to set, monitor, and enforce reasonable boundaries for their children's use of technology and to have open discussions with their children about safe and responsible use. Unfortunately, research has shown that most parents do not set clear boundaries regarding screen time, nor do they believe that content needs to be monitored for young children (Hadlington et al., 2019). However, even though children may balk at the rules parents' set around their use of technology, and even though they may argue vehemently and even sneak to use their devices, it is important that parents make their children aware of and accountable for how they prioritize their time (Koniski, 2018).

The boundaries that parents set on their children's access to and use of electronic media and mobile devices are influenced by practical considerations and parenting style. According to Coyne et al. (2017), parents of children who are intense criers, who are fussy, or who have particularly poor self-regulation are more likely to calm and soothe their children with mobile devices than those whose children are easier. In addition, they are more likely to exceed the AAP guideline for media use shown in Table 16.2. These researchers also note that permissive parents are most likely to let their children use screens excessively, while authoritative parents use screen time for behavior management and disciplinary purposes, allowing their children access to their devices as a reward or restrict it as a punishment.

Coyne et al. (2017) also note that parents who frequently view their own screens tend to allow their children higher levels of screen time and may use electronic devices to keep their children busy or to calm them before bedtime rather than interacting with them. Moreover, Levine et al. (2019) point out that parents who regularly use devices themselves often justify their children's use of devices by saying that they are watching educational programming. However, these researchers also note that children do not learn from devices as effectively as they learn from interaction with other people. Thus, they suggest that if parents want their children to use devices for educational purposes, their best bet would be to use the device *with* the child rather than letting the child use it alone. Levine's research shows clearly that children who use devices alone tend to have more self-regulation problems than those who use devices with their parents, prompting them to argue that

> When parents actively facilitate children's learning with [mobile devices] the children may be more likely to profit from potential educational aspects of [mobile device] use. When parents use [mobile devices] to distract or entertain their children, there might be greater risk that [mobile device] use will interfere with the development of children's ability to regulate their attention and emotions. (p. 98)

Lastly, Davou and Sidiropoulou (2017) note that devices can be used by both children and parents to cover up relational problems and emotional needs. Importantly, they emphasize that these devices should be used as "*instruments* for expanding experience and relationships and as *tools* for accessing sources of information, not as *substitutes* for experience and relationships or as sources of knowledge per se" (italics in the original) (p. 268).

Technology and Attachment

Little research has been conducted to date concerning how attachment is related to use of technology during childhood. One study, however, explores attachment and social skills among individuals who participate in online gaming (Kowert & Oldmeadow, 2015). Online gaming is a highly social environment, and because of growing concern that it might displace real-world social connection and interaction, these researchers wanted to know how gaming affects social interaction and if attachment styles are related to online gaming involvement. Contrary to their expectation, they discovered that individuals involved in online gaming do not differ significantly in social skills from those who do not join those communities. However, they also discovered that online gaming provides an effective space for individuals with avoidant attachment to meet their attachment and affiliation needs. The anonymity and reduced amount of social cues provided by the gaming sites apparently provides a sense of safety for self-disclosure for individuals who normally might avoid social contact.

CLASS DISCUSSION

Do you think Luke's involvement in online gaming is a good thing?

Social Media Use

The use of social networks has been both promoted and vilified. I will first discuss a small amount of research that suggests the positive influence of social media use and then discuss dangers associated with it. Lastly, I will identify how neurobiology and child maltreatment are related to problematic social media use.

Positive Aspects of Social Media Use

Some people see social media use as a useful means of promoting social connectedness and the development of social capital. For example, Coyne et al. (2018) note that social media has the capacity to strengthen family bonds and connectedness, and some adolescents use it to keep in touch with family. Lee and Horsely (2017) found that having a 4-H club Facebook page that could be accessed by youth members facilitated members' civic engagement and their development of positive youth development traits (competence, confidence, connection, character, caring, compassion, and contribution). Still other researchers have found that when social media provide avenues to humor, connectedness to peers, a broadened social network, and effective distraction, it can help to reduce anxiety and depression (Hoge, Bickham, & Cantor, 2017).

Negative Aspects of Social Media Use

In contrast to these positive outcomes of social media use, other research has linked social media use with increased depressive symptomatology and anxiety associated with social comparison, dysfunctional emotion regulation, bullying, and decreased life satisfaction directly associated with the frequency of use (Hoge et al., 2017). In addition, Alexander (2015) warns of the danger of sexual predation on social networking sites. This researcher canvassed a group of teachers and school counselors who had worked with teens who had been sexually assaulted by someone they met on the internet, asking them what factors they found to be most responsible for those assaults. The first theme they uncovered pointed to inadequate parental supervision and the lack of a caring home environment. Another factor frequently mentioned by the participants was the teens' desire for a relationship, a desire perhaps related to their lack of a caring family. Another theme provided by the teachers and counselors was the ready availability of chat rooms and venues such as Craigslist through which predators can easily make contact with teens. Instant gratification was a fourth theme, i.e., a desire by teens to relieve boredom instantly by talking to someone online. The majority of participants in the study believed that the first line of defense against internet predation is more parental support and supervision. However, they also cited a need for community education and awareness, as well as health education for teens that addresses this problem specifically.

Etiology of Mental Health Issues Associated with Social Media Use

Since the use of social networking sites is not uniformly linked to negative outcomes, researchers have begun looking for reasons why some individuals develop mental health issues associated with social media use and other don't. I will present the result of two interesting studies here, one exploring possible neurobiological causes and one exploring the effects of childhood maltreatment.

Neurobiological Differences

Sternberg et al. (2018) have explored the possibility that there are neurological differences between individuals who don't develop anxiety issues and those who do while using Facebook. They have found that those who report higher levels of anxiety show evidence of impaired neural filtering ability. That is, their brains do not allow them to filter out Facebook's icons for unread notifications, unread messages, and new friend requests from their working memory. Therefore, while working on a task given them by the researchers that requires their attention to other parts of the Facebook page, they are more likely to click on the icons and be taken off their task than are those who can effectively filter them out.

In addition, these researchers point out that anxiety among Facebook users is related to active (direct exchanges with others) rather than passive (simple monitoring of others' postings) use of Facebook and believe that those with low filtering capabilities are more likely to engage in active usage and develop anxiety. They go so far as to suggest that this reduced ability to filter out environmental cues for rewarding stimuli may be at the root of some individuals' addiction-like responses to Facebook and other social media. That is, impaired filtering abilities may result in the poor inhibitory control common to individuals who, even though they recognize the negative effects of their use, continue to abuse substances. Impulse control, as we have already learned, is a function of the OMPFC, and good functioning of the OMPFC is related to positive attachment experiences in infancy and toddlerhood. Therefore, research that addresses the connections between neural filtering capabilities and attachment anxiety and avoidance would be very valuable.

Childhood Maltreatment

Other research has focused on associations between maltreatment during childhood and problematic use of social media in young adulthood (Worsley, McIntyre, Bentall, & Corcoran, 2018). Problematic use of social media was measured in this study using a scale that reflected six components common to addiction—salience, mood modification, tolerance, withdrawal, conflict and relapse. Their findings show that maltreatment during childhood is positively associated with problematic social media use, but that the relationship between the two is complex. First, maltreatment is positively associated with problematic social media use. In addition, it is positively associated with both anxious and avoidant attachment. However, anxious attachment is *positively* associated with problematic social media use while avoidant attachment is *negatively* associated with it. This finding suggests that individuals with anxious attachment use social media as a means to get their needs for comfort and belongingness met. This would be an especially valuable outcome for individuals who have little or no access to face-to-face interaction (e.g., physical isolation in a rural environment) or who for some reason fear it.

In contrast, individuals with more attachment avoidance tend not to seek comfort from others and to have a reduced need for social contact. Therefore, they are less likely to develop problematic (i.e., addictive) social media use. However, when depression is added to the mix, even those with higher levels of attachment avoidance may develop problems. That is, avoidant individuals with more attachment-related depression are at an increased risk of problematic social media use because it allows them to avoid or reduce their negative emotions or to find a social network that doesn't involve distressing face-to-face interaction.

Summary

In summary, it is important to reiterate that the use of digital technology during childhood is not necessarily a bad thing. Technology is here, and it's not going away. Some researchers argue convincingly that children have a "right to an open future" (Sziron & Hildt, 2018, p. 1), i.e., a right to have future options open until they reach adulthood and can make decisions on their own. They suggest that adults have the duty to provide children with the opportunity to build a reasonably broad spectrum of capacities and skills that will support their functioning as adults. Therefore, from this perspective, providing even very young children with access to electronic media and opportunities to learn to use it effectively, efficiently, and responsibly is the duty of all the adults in a community. At the same time, it is also the duty of all the adults in the community, including not just parents, but also software and app manufacturers and marketers, as well as policy makers, to understand the implications of digital usage by this vulnerable age group and provide them with adequate protection. From a mental health perspective, it seems clear that practitioners need to be aware of the possible advantages and dangers of digital media use by children and their families so that we can provide them guidance and build effective interventions as they are needed.

We leave early and middle childhood behind now and move into adolescence and young adulthood. In the next three chapters, I will discuss expected neurobiological social changes generally experienced during this time of life. In addition, I will explore specific challenges that face individuals as they approach and enter adulthood.

CHAPTER 17

Brain Development and Attachment in Adolescence and Young Adulthood

LEARNING OBJECTIVES

After completing this chapter, readers should understand that:

- The identity established in adolescence is important to mental health and social functioning.
- Early attachment experiences affect the development of the four identity statuses.
- During adolescence and young adulthood there is a renewed period of blooming and pruning that both supports normal individuation processes and also directly affects risk-taking.
- Childhood attachment styles are related to adult states of mind regarding close relationships.
- There are two dimensions of attachment related to adult attachment styles—attachment anxiety and attachment avoidance.

KEY IDEAS

1. The brains of adolescents and young adults undergo a massive redevelopment that gradually improves their brains' efficiency and supports their emergence into adulthood.
2. The slow maturation of the prefrontal cortex and imbalances between neurochemicals in disparate parts of the brain can result in increased risky behavior in this age group.
3. The primary and secondary proximity-seeking strategies developed during infancy and early childhood are correlated with adolescent and adult attachment-related states of mind.
4. Attachment styles formed during childhood are somewhat open to change.
5. Attachment-related anxiety is associated with how worried the individual is about being abandoned in times of need.
6. Attachment-related avoidance is associated with how willing the individual is to depend on others and allowing others to depend on them.

Introduction

In this chapter, I will first discuss the phenomena related to development during adolescence and young adulthood—the establishment of a stable identity, changes in the brain that cause the increased vulnerability to accidents that we too often see in this age group, and adult attachment. Erikson (1968) indicated that the core developmental task of adolescence (*Identity vs. Role*

Diffusion) is to establish a relatively stable sense of individual identity. This involves the clarification and consolidation of personal values, goals, and beliefs, as well as growing expectations for how one is going to live one's life. Therefore, in the first part of this chapter, I will introduce the concepts of identity formation and identity status, and to help you see how identity manifests in behavior, I provide case studies that illustrate what each identity status looks like.

Adolescents don't suddenly become adults the day they turn 18 or 21. The transition into adulthood is a gradual process that takes place over a decade or longer during which who they are and what they are going to do with their lives begins to emerge through the process of life itself. Therefore, it is often called *emerging* adulthood (Arnett, 2000). Society has long known that adolescence is a time of great change in both body and brain. One of the most salient features of adolescence is puberty, a process that culminates in sexual maturity and the ability to reproduce. Less obvious, however, is the massive redevelopment of the brain that occurs during adolescence and young adulthood that sets the stage for individuals to move out into the world on their own. At the same time, however, these changes in the structure and function of the brain place individuals at increased risk. Therefore, in the second part of this chapter I will discuss the changes in the dopamine and oxytocin systems that explain some of the problems that occur during this time of life.

The core task during young adulthood (*Intimacy vs. Isolation*) is to begin to form deep associations with others. Failure to master these core tasks can result in social and vocational ineffectiveness and reduced quality of life. As individuals move through adolescence and transition into emerging adulthood, opportunities occur for close relationships to develop outside of the family, including friendships formed at school and at work, as well as romantic relationships. Thus, early attachment experiences begin to have powerful influences on social functioning and on how individuals decide with whom they will build relationships. This can be a rocky road for some, given that a host of genetic, biological, and environmental factors can influence the social engagement system. Indeed, Kessler et al. (2005) have shown that about 75% of mental health disorders originate before the age of 20. Thus, adolescents and emerging adults appear to be uniquely vulnerable to the development of psychological issues such as ADHD, depression, anxiety, and self-mutilation, as well as eating, substance use, and conduct disorders (Rossouw, 2018). Therefore, in the last section of this chapter I discuss how attachment styles that were formed early in life influence emotional and behavioral functioning and the establishment and maintenance of relationships in adolescence and young adulthood.

Identity

What is identity? Well, Kroger (2015) characterizes it as

> that entity which enables one to move with direction and effectiveness, to find meaningful outlets for the actualization of one's interests, talents, and values. Identity is shaped and reshaped by contextual forces as it mediates or is mediated by them. Identity's normative time of ascendance as an issue of primary concern is during adolescence and young adulthood, when decisions about the foundations on which one will enter adult life press for clarification and resolution. (p. 65)

Thus, identity formation is a central task during adolescence that may be complicated by early life experiences and that can either support or impair successful transition through later developmental stages.

As Erikson (1963) suggested, adolescence is a time of identity development in which young people look start looking for answers to the question, "Who am I as an individual, and where am I going in life?" In young adulthood, they begin to focus on establishing intimate relationships in the form of close friendships and working relationships as well as romantic relationships. Erikson argued that successfully developing a relatively clear identity during adolescence is important because genuine intimacy with another person requires the "ability to fuse your identity with somebody else's without fear that you're going to lose something of yourself" (p. 135). The discussion in this section concerning identity will explore how identity forms and how it manifests in an individual's goals, plans, and relationships.

Identity Formation

Identity formation starts in early adolescence as children begin to approach the time when they will take charge of their own lives and become who they are ultimately to become as adults. Erikson (1968) suggests that for individuals to move through this stage successfully, they must answer the fundamental question of "Who am I, and where am I going in my life?" and will base their identity on both personal and environmental factors. These factors could include what family they were born into and where they grew up, what kinds of talents and limitations they were born with or have developed during childhood, and what kinds of experiences they have had. Do they remember having support and acceptance, abuse or neglect, or trauma? How do these experiences define who they are? What can they expect as they enter the workplace and form close relationships? If they are unsuccessful in finding relatively clear answers to the question of who they are and where are they going, they will carry their confusion into the next stage, *Intimacy vs. Isolation*, with an increased likelihood that they will have difficulty forming and maintaining supportive and meaningful relationships in work, love, and play.

Marchetti et al. (2017) argue that people actually begin to develop a sense of self during infancy as their brains develop the capacity to recognize that they are separate from their mothers. As they go through life, they develop an autobiographical history based on their ongoing experiences and interpretations of events that have happened, their memory systems providing them with a sense of continuity and protecting them against fragmentation of their identity. When they reach adolescence, they actively begin to reflect on who they are for the first time, a capability determined by their capacity to mentalize (see Chapter 4 concerning the development of mentalization) and the maturation of their prefrontal cortex. These researchers emphasize that "the capacity to think about one's own mind so painstakingly built during infancy is now put to the test and, wherever specific deficiencies are present, they now come to light" (p. 3).

Crocetti (2017) suggests that when children enter adolescence "the many biological, cognitive, and social changes that occur stimulate young people to think about themselves, reflect on the kinds of people they want to become, and find their places in society" (p. 145). Erikson (1968) argued that as individuals mature, they have a need for both autonomy (individuality) and belongingness. Thus, identity formation involves the clarification of one's personal values, goals, and beliefs, one's expectation for one's roles and lifestyle, as well as clarification of where one belongs in one's culture and society. Erikson insisted that this process is necessary during adolescence so that truly intimate relationships can be established in young adulthood. He argued that genuine intimacy can occur only when there is "the capacity to commit to concrete affiliations and partnerships and to develop the ethical strength to abide by such commitments even though they may call for significant sacrifices and compromises" (p. 263).

Cheek and Cheek (2018) expanded on Erikson's ideas, arguing that identity includes four distinct aspects: personal, relational, public, and collective. Individuals' *personal identity* includes such factors as the sense of being a unique individual who remains essentially the same over time regardless of external changes; the knowledge of who one is and his or her evaluation and opinion of himself or herself; personal values, goals, hopes, and dreams; one's own emotions and thoughts as well as one's ways of managing them. A person's *relational identity* includes factors such as the quality of his or her relationship with family, good friends, and partner, and his or her willingness to connect with, share themselves with, and maintain interest in the thoughts and opinions of close others. One's *public identity* includes factors such as physical characteristics (attractiveness, height, weight, etc.), gestures, mannerisms, etc., and how popular one is, how others react to what the individual says and does, and how the individual reacts to others. Lastly, *collective identity* includes such factors as race/ethnicity, religion, or politics; where the person was raised and the culture(s) he or she was raised in and among; language(s) spoken and accent or dialect; and pride of family, community or country.

Erikson (1968) explains that identity formation involves two cognitive processes—exploration and commitment. *Exploration* involves the search for purpose and meaning in life by looking at and experimenting with alternative intellectual and social pursuits, lifestyles, hobbies, etc., and questioning existing values and beliefs (primarily gained from one's family). *Commitment* involves choosing between or combining the different possibilities that one finds in ways that fit one's personal strengths, preferences, and personality characteristics. It is the culmination of exploration in which the individual actually chooses a direction for his or her life that then informs decisions concerning his or her preparation for and entry into an occupation/career, suitable work/school and romantic relationships, and religious, political, and other memberships.

CLASS DISCUSSION

How do you think insecure attachment might affect the ability of individuals in adolescence and young adulthood to explore and commit to a particular direction in life?

Crocetti (2017) has expanded on Erikson's identity formation model by developing a three-factor model. In this model, she recognizes that individuals make commitments based on past exploration as Erikson did. However, she argues that they engage in on-going examination (through further in-depth exploration) of how those commitments are affecting their lives and then reconsider their commitments in light of what they find. Thus, identity formation is a dynamic process of initial exploration—initial commitment—further exploration—reconsideration—new or renewed and consolidated commitment. In addition, she argues that this process continues throughout the life span as individuals consider the choices they have made in the past as well as the choices they can make in the present.

Identity Status

The level of exploration and commitment individuals make regarding who they are and what direction they want their lives to take results in what is called an *identity status*. Kroger and Marcia (2011) identified four identity statuses:

1. ***Identity diffusion*** is characterized by little or no attempt at organized exploration of opportunities and alternatives and no commitment to a personal set of goals, values, and beliefs. Of course, in pre- or early adolescence, it could be expected that an individual will have explored or committed to a direction in life. However, by late adolescence, individuals who fall into this category tend to have discovered little purpose and meaning to their lives and have relatively low self-esteem, bouncing from one thing to another with no real sense of direction. They tend to have low self-esteem and an external locus of control, and they are likely to have relatively high levels of hopelessness. These individuals have relatively low levels of moral reasoning, are relatively easily influenced by peers, and are likely to assume their peers' social norms. Rather than using logic and analysis during decision-making, they tend to depend on others to decide for them, or they make decisions on their own for emotional reasons. Alternatively, they may procrastinate and avoid making a decision altogether. They tend to be relatively high in neuroticism, and may engage in grandiose (narcissistic) self-expression and manipulation. They often have difficulty getting along with others. Therefore, they may have few or no close friendships, and those relationships are likely to be superficial.

   Individuals in this category are likely to have had distant or rejecting parents who communicated with them inconsistently. Given these parenting practices, it is not surprising that research shows a correlation between this diffuse identity and insecure attachment (Arseth, Kroger, Martinussen & Marcia, 2009). Furthermore, of interest to mental health practitioners, individuals in this group are likely to end up in our offices presenting with both internalizing and externalizing disorders, especially borderline and other Cluster B personality disorders (Jung, Pick, Schluter-Muller, Schmeck, & Goth, 2013). For an example of this identity status, take a moment to read Case Study 17.1 concerning, you guessed it, Jet.

CASE STUDY 17.1. JET'S IDENTITY STATUS: DIFFUSED

Mrs. Dochterman, Jet's history teacher, is concerned about him because he has skipped several classes since the beginning of school and appears to be either sleepy or bored when he does come to class. Since he should graduate this year, she is concerned that he may either fail or drop out before graduation. She asks him to stay behind one day and tries to find out what is going on. When she asks him why he has missed classes, he says that he just hasn't felt like coming because he doesn't see how history relates to his life. When she asks him what he wants to do after graduation, he says, "I have no idea, probably get a job in construction or something." She suggests a vocational college if his grades would support it, but he just snorts a laugh and says, "Can I go now? I got things to do." Embarrassed and seething with rage at being singled out, he slouches

---

out of the room, reaching into his back pocket for the marijuana concealed there. Shaking her head, Mrs. Dochterman is glad to see him go; he is such a disagreeable boy!

2. ***Identity moratorium*** is characterized by active exploration of opportunities and possibilities but the person has not yet committed to a set of goals, values, or beliefs. As with identity diffusion, this lack of commitment can be expected during early adolescence. Later on, however, these individuals tend to exhibit a great deal of anxiety concerning what they are going to do with their lives and try to cope with that anxiety by using the psychological mechanisms of denial, projection, or identification so that they don't have to assume personal responsibility for their lack of direction. On the positive side, they tend have relatively good analytical skills and are able to look at issues from different perspectives. They may have established healthy close friendships but have probably not yet formed an intimate partnership with anyone. They report that earlier in life, their families tended to expect them to be independent, and they appear to be have relatively ambivalent attachment. Research by Arseth et al. (2009) reports that, similar to those in the diffuse category, those in moratorium also tend to report insecure attachments. Now take a moment to read about how Macy handles going to college in Case Study 17.2 as an example of this identity status.

CASE STUDY 17.2: MACY'S IDENTITY STATUS: MORATORIUM

When Macy graduated from high school, she didn't want to go to college right away. She had lots of ideas of what she might like to do with her life. Her mother had always assumed that she would go pre-med and then become a doctor. However, her grades were only mediocre, and more importantly, she couldn't imagine going to school for all those years. She liked the idea being a teacher, but she was also thinking how great it would be to be an interior designer. She and Tara decided that maybe it would be best for her to just take a year off before applying anywhere. She took a minimum wage job as a dishwasher at a popular restaurant but soon recognized she couldn't make enough money to live on at minimum wage, so she enrolled in a local state college and took courses without declaring a major. However, the college finally pressed her to declare, and so since she had been thinking about becoming a teacher, she chose education. She soon realized, though, that the jobs available for teachers where she lived didn't pay much and decided that maybe she should major in business and minor in interior design. Her first course, Accounting 101, was so boring to her that she found herself once again reconsidering her decision. After five years of bouncing from one discipline to another and never finishing anything, she finally realized that she really wanted was to be a nurse like her mother. She enrolled in nursing school and a year and a half later graduated with her degree. Although Macy had worried that her mother would be disappointed that she hadn't gone to medical school, Tara was beaming with pride and joy as her daughter crossed the stage on graduation day.

3. **Identity foreclosure** is characterized by a commitment to a set of *unquestioned* values, beliefs, and goals that often match those of their parents. Alternatively, in this identity status, the child may adamantly go against whatever the parents want, stubbornly committing to something that they disapprove of and thereby causing friction in the parent-child relationship. The commitment is made without active exploration of opportunities and alternatives. These individuals take on a ready-made identity. This identity may have been provided by parents, who they trust and admire, or it may be in direct opposition to what their parents want due to a lack of trust or admiration. Therefore, they tend to be less anxious than those in moratorium are because they have already decided what they are going to do with their lives. They tend to have higher levels of conformity to social norms, they bow easily to authority and depend on others to tell them what to do rather than make decisions on their own. They tend to have less developed analytic skills more difficulty integrating ideas. They tend to be somewhat rigid in their moral thinking and are more likely to endorse racial or homophobic prejudices than those in identity achievement. In addition, they are reluctant to try new experiences and they tend to make friends with those who are like themselves. These individuals tend to report having grown up in families in which parents actively discouraged individual opinions and expression. They have relatively high levels of attachment anxiety, though they are more secure than those in identity foreclosure or moratorium (Arseth et al., 2009). Now, see how Luke visualizes his possible study and career opportunities in Case Study 17.3.

CASE STUDY 17.3: LUKE'S IDENTITY STATUS: FORECLOSED

Luke's mother, Hazel, had long wanted him to study law. However, Luke had his sights set on becoming a computer game designer, and he and Hazel argued about this many times. When he got into online gaming a couple of years ago and started spending so much time on his tablet and computer, Hazel had become frustrated and dismayed. She tried rewarding him for improving his grades in the hopes that he would be stop playing and get serious about studying so that he would be able to get into a law program; he didn't care about the rewards, and he didn't stop playing. She tried taking his tablet and computer away; somehow he got another tablet and played on it after she went to bed. During the day, he would say he was going over to a friend's house but would hide out somewhere where he could play undistracted.

This all changed when Luke was 16 years old and his mother died a few months after being diagnosed with pancreatic cancer. Now living with an aunt and uncle, he is feeling terrible about the rift that their arguments had made between them and blames himself for it. Now he is trying to live out his mother's dream for him even though he has no real interest in law and even though he had resisted her meddling in his life for so many years. His aunt and uncle worry about him, though, since he is alone so much. They see that he hasn't made any friends at his new school, and he seems to them to be strangely unemotional, but they think that this is maybe just what happens when a teenager goes through what he has gone through. Luke is studying hard and no longer playing online games. He misses that community, but his aunt and uncle have already figured out the best law school for him to apply to, and he just doesn't seem to have the will to argue with them.

4. ***Identity achievement*** is characterized by commitment to a set of values, beliefs, and goals after active exploration of opportunities and alternatives. These individuals tend to have high levels of self-esteem and low levels of neuroticism. They like being around others and tend not to be shy. They have well-developed decision-making skills, are conscientious, and they work well under stress. They tend to have high levels of moral reasoning, empathize with others, and are interested in social justice. Being willing to share themselves with others, they are able to initiate and maintain genuinely intimate relationships with close friends and romantic partners. These individuals tend to report having had mothers who encouraged them to be free and independent in a context of connectedness and support, and they report the highest levels of secure attachment of any of the groups. Research indicates that the achieved identity status is positively related to secure attachment (Arseth et al., 2009). See how this works for Sophia in case Study 17.4.

CASE STUDY 17.4: SOPHIA'S IDENTITY STATUS: ACHIEVEMENT

Sophia's mom and dad had given her many opportunities to try out various activities: piano lessons, volleyball, chess, waterskiing, and horseback riding. However, her real love was ballet. She had taken lessons since the age of five, and she was very good at it. She danced almost daily, and her closest friends were the ones in her advanced classes. One day three years ago, she talked to her parents about going to a school for the arts about 45 minutes away rather than going to the high school near their home. It was a long discussion in which Sophia's parents brought up the many disadvantages of being a professional dancer, the most obvious ones being that she might not make it in such a competitive field, and that if she was injured, she would have nothing to fall back on if she didn't have a college degree. In addition, they worried that the rigor of her chosen career would make finding someone to love and have children with would be out of the question. However, they were enormously impressed by her mature responses to their questions and warnings. Concerning love and parenthood, she told them, "One thing at a time, please! I want to see how good I can be. You two have shown me how beautiful love can be, and I want to have my own children one day. Let's just take it one step at a time." They supported her in filling out the application and drove the 45 minutes each way to take her to school and bring her home every day. They accompanied her to competitions and held her close when she didn't always win. Today, at age 17, Sophia and her father signed a five-year contract for her with the Dutch Ballet in Amsterdam. She will leave for the Netherlands a week after graduation.

In summary, Mikulincer and Shaver (2016) suggest that identity formation "is a self-regulation task that involves information search, correction of one's values and beliefs, and implementation of decisions in pursuit of meaningful personal strivings" (p. 238). As you may recall from Chapter 6, good self-regulation is a product of secure attachment. In the case presentations associated with the identity statuses, it is possible to see how Jet and his brother Luke both show evidence of insecure attachment and self-regulation problems. In contrast, Macy and Sophia both seem to be relatively securely attached. However, while Sophia seems to be confident and mature, Macy appears to be somewhat anxious about keeping her mother's love, suggesting some level of insecurity.

Research by Arseth et al. (2009) shows that the identity achievement and moratorium identity statuses are significantly associated with higher levels of intimacy while the foreclosed and diffused statuses are associated with lower levels. They explain that "A genuinely intimate relationship involves sharing disclosure, responsiveness to another's needs, mutual acceptance, and respect, as well as a balance between emotional closeness and separation" (p. 698). For a successful transition through emerging adulthood to occur, the hard-won sense of an *independent* self-discovered in adolescence (when an individual may have the luxury of thinking primarily about his or her own wants and needs) must be balanced with a sense of an *interdependent* relationship (when both individuals have to take into consideration the other's wants and needs).

As you can see from the discussion of identity formation and from the case studies that exemplify the identity statuses, there is considerable variation in how easily an individual transitions through adolescence. Some of that variation can be explained by the changes that are occurring in the brains of individuals in this age group.

Changes in the Brain

As mentioned in Chapter 1, during the first few years of life the brain develops rapidly through a process of blooming. Then it goes through a process of pruning in which unused synaptic connections are sloughed off in an effort to make the brain more efficient. In adolescence, another round of blooming and pruning occurs that is apparently meant to help the individual move from the relative dependency of childhood to the relative independence of adulthood. This redevelopment of the brain results in an increase in the importance of peer relationships and a move toward relative independence from family.

Unfortunately, this redevelopment also tends to make adolescents and emerging adults more likely to engage in reckless behavior. These changes place them at risk for a variety of negative outcomes associated with impulsivity and sensation seeking, including accidents, suicide, and homicide. It is thought that this increased desire to seek out strong sensations and willingness to do risky things must have been adaptive for the developing human species, with the benefits of risking lives outweighing the costs. These risks have been defined as "engaging in behavior with potential rewarding outcomes, but also with significant potential negative consequences" (Victor & Hariri, 2018, p. 471). As Steinberg (2008) explains, there were probably times when *not* taking a risk may have had a worse outcome than taking one. In my own experience, older people tend to get set in their ways. (I am allowed to say this because I am one of those older people!) We are sure that how we do things is the way they should be done; after all, we have survived up to this point and must have done something right. Don't rock the boat! But what if there's a new way that will make life better for everyone? If the voice of caution and reason makes older, more experienced people want to stick to the tried and true, it's up to the younger people to go out there and try something new, even if it looks dangerous, unreasonable, or even pretty crazy. It must have worked often enough through the millennia that those who were willing to take a chance were able to pass that willingness on down to their children through their genes.

What might account for adolescents' and emerging adults' recklessness? Research shows that different parts of the brain develop adult capabilities at different rates. For example, Reyna & Farley (2006) show that by the age of 15, adolescents have developed logical-reasoning abilities comparable to those found in adults. However, the parts of the brain associated with decision-making, emotional control, impulse control and resistance to peer pressure don't reach adult levels until about the age of 25 (Steinberg, 2008). According to Johnson, Blum, and Giedd, (2009), society has long known that adolescents and young adults often show poor judgment and decision-making and thus may not be ready for the responsibilities of adulthood. For example, while an 18-year-old in the United States can join the military and can vote, he or she can't legally drink until age 21. Moreover, while some communities may allow a 16-year-old to be their mayor (and let him or her drive to work), we want a bit more maturity in our national leaders. Therefore, the minimum age for a member of the House of Representatives is 25, while the minimum age for a member of the Senate is 30, and for the President is 35.

While the cortex thickens throughout childhood and into adolescence due to continuing proliferation of neural connections, all parts of the brain do not mature at the same rate. Hormonal changes associated with sexual development in adolescence trigger a new round of blooming and pruning similar to that which occurred during infancy and early childhood when connections between brain regions were initially made (see Chapter 1). Synapses that are not being used are discarded, and those that remain are strengthened. In particular, neural circuitry in the prefrontal cortex is myelinated and grows stronger, faster connections with other parts of the brain, resulting in better functioning of memory, judgment, decision-making, impulse control, socialization, and interpretation of and reaction to emotions as the individual enters adulthood. However, this process takes place over a decade or more (think of the differences between an 11-year-old and a 21-year-old). During that time, imbalances between neurochemicals in disparate parts of the brain often result in increases in novelty- and sensation-seeking, and consequent increases in risky behavior (Victor & Hariri, 2018).

The final configuration that the adolescent's brain takes derives from the dynamic interaction of several factors, including genes, environment, levels of stress, and past experiences, as well as from individual personal decisions made throughout adolescence. Neural pathways associated with repeated experiences, patterns of behavior, and frequently experienced emotional states get myelinated, thus strengthening them and making them fast and efficient (Semper et al., 2016). This is good news if those experiences, behaviors, and moods are positive and prosocial, but bad news if they aren't.

It is commonly thought that the increased risk-taking apparent among adolescents may be due to one or a combination of the following: (1) they have deficits in their ability to process information; (2) they simply don't perceive risks in the same way that adults do and consequently have a sense of invulnerability; or (3) they are not as risk-averse as the younger children or adults around them. Research has shown, however, that *none* of these things is true. Indeed, research by Reyna and Farley (2006) has shown that adolescents process information as well as adults do; they feel just as vulnerable as adults do when faced with similar risks; and similar to adults, they even overestimate how dangerous a risk is. If none of that thinking is true, then what is going on in the adolescent and young adult brain?

Researchers think that successful transition from adolescence to adulthood requires that there be a balance in the functioning of three interrelated neurobiological constructs—threat sensitivity (mediated by the amygdala), reward sensitivity (mediated by the ventral striatum and mesolimbic dopamine pathway), and behavioral control (mediated by the prefrontal cortex) (Ernst & Fudge, 2010; Victor & Hariri, 2018). If you recall, the amygdala, which is functional at birth, is responsible for scanning the environment for danger. The reward system, which becomes fully functional during infancy, is where we experience pleasurable stimuli and are motivated to SEEK them out. The prefrontal cortex, which does not become fully functional until young adulthood, scans the memory to weigh the costs and benefits of our reactions to what the environment brings us and to determine if a given reward is worth the risk involved in attaining it. That is, it provides cortical top-down control over the bottom-up information being provided by the more primitive limbic structures (see Chapter 2). Thus, one of the important functions of the prefrontal cortex is to inhibit inappropriate/reflexive behaviors, allowing us to react rationally rather than automatically. You can probably see the problem here: the prefrontal cortex can't be counted on to provide rational decision-making consistently until *well after* adolescence.

Consistent with the risk behavior models mentioned above (Ernst & Fudge, 2010; Victor & Hariri, 2018), Steinberg (2008) argues that adolescents' willingness to engage in risky behavior stems from a developmental mismatch between what he calls the *socio-emotional* and *cognitive control* systems in which the cognitive control system matures more slowly than the socioemotional system. Specifically, there is an increase in the number of dopamine receptors in the prefrontal cortex and reward system that results in novelty seeking, and there is an increase in the number of oxytocin receptors in the limbic system that results in a willingness to engage in risky behavior with peers. The changes occur just when affiliation needs draw adolescents away from their families (who offer supervision and oversight) and toward their peers (who want to get away from supervision and oversight). Next, I will explain how these changes in the dopamine and oxytocin systems work.

Risk-Taking and Dopamine

According to Steinberg (2008), during early adolescence the pruning processes that are rearranging neural pathways cause changes in the ability of the OMPFC to manage the amount of dopamine produced in the mesolimbic dopamine reward pathway. The resultant higher levels of dopamine in the OMPFC make dopamine temporarily more rewarding than it was in the past and set off a SEEKING response, motivating the adolescent to seek sensation. In addition, researchers have found that among adolescents who are high sensation-seekers (as compared to low), there is evidence of a breakdown between the OMPFC and the amygdala such that the OMPFC doesn't pay attention to the danger messages the amygdala is sending (Cservenka, Herting, Seghete, Hudson, & Nagel, 2013). Therefore, the OMPFC will be less likely to balance the anticipation of reward against the possible negative consequences, and the adolescent will be more likely to engage in something risky. Unfortunately, there are many sensational things in the environment, such as relatively benign horror movies and the infinitely more dangerous fast cars, hood surfing, parkour, sex, drugs, and rock n' roll.

Interestingly, serotonin, a neurochemical that is released into many of the same parts of the reward system into which dopamine is released, acts to curb risk-taking. Unfortunately, it appears that (at least in animal models) serotonin receptors are not working efficiently during adolescence and thus do not control the effects of dopamine on reward learning, risk-taking behavior, aggression, and impulsivity (Boucher & Sandhu, 2013).

There is some good news. Steinberg (2008) found a curvilinear relationship between how old adolescents are and how rewarding they find risky behaviors to be. He showed that sensation-seeking, reward sensitivity, and risk preference (preference for short-term, lower rewards over longer-term, greater rewards) all peaked between the ages of 13 and 16 and then gradually declined. Could it be that this is why laws are written so that kids under the age of 16 don't get behind the wheel of a car, and why insurance companies place a high price on coverage for them up to age 25 when the prefrontal cortex at last matures?

Risk-Taking and Oxytocin

Steinberg (2008) notes that at the same time that changes are occurring in the dopamine system, changes are also occurring in the oxytocin system. While the increase in sex hormones (testosterone and estrogen) during early adolescence is not directly related to changes in the density of dopamine receptors, sex hormones are definitely related to changes in the number of oxytocin receptors in areas of the brain associated with memory for social information and the rewards of social bonding—the amygdala and the nucleus accumbens.

Recall that the nucleus accumbens is part of the reward system and that the oxytocin receptors there produce feelings of pleasure and wellbeing. The amygdala is responsible for determining at a very primitive level whether a given stimulus represents something that we should approach (pleasure) or something that we should avoid (pain). As we learned in Chapter 1, the oxytocin receptors in the amygdala are involved in positive social activities such as mother-child attachment but are also involved in our response to facial expressions and other social information mediated by the smart vagus. Thus, the increase in oxytocin receptors that occurs in response to the sudden influx of sex hormones makes adolescents acutely aware of feedback concerning their social acceptability (or lack thereof). Similar to the curvilinear relationship between age and sensation seeking, there is a curvilinear relationship between age and self-consciousness, which peaks at around the age of 15 and then slowly declines (Steinberg, 2008).

Steinberg (2008) emphasizes that, unlike dopamine, oxytocin does not influence risky SEEKING behaviors directly. Rather, research on adolescent substance use, criminal activity, sexual activity, and automobile accidents suggests that it is the indirect influence of the heightened awareness of social signals that causes adolescents to take chances, especially when they are with a group of their peers. Indeed, Steinberg's research (Gardner & Steinberg, 2005) found that in the presence of a group of peers, adolescents (ages 13–16) and young adults (ages 18–24) tend to focus more on the benefits of taking a risk than on the costs (when compared to adults). This difference in focus results in adolescents being twice as likely, and young adults being half again as likely, as adults are to take a risk. In addition, the study shows that both adolescents and young adults are more willing to engage in antisocial behavior when with a group of peers. Steinberg (2008) also reports similar results concerning risky driving and suggests that "peers may actually make potentially rewarding—and potentially risky—activities even more rewarding. In adolescence, then, "more might not only be merrier—more may also be riskier" (p. 92).

The research mentioned above suggests that the late development of adolescents' and young adults' prefrontal cortex makes them subject to poor decision making associated with *hot cognition*. Hot cognition occurs during times of high emotional arousal or conflict, while *cold cognition* occurs during times when emotional arousal is low (Steinberg, 2005). If interaction with peers is more emotionally arousing than interaction with, say, parents or teachers, an adolescent or young adult may well go for the intensity provided by novelty and risk made doubly delightful by the presence of peers. In addition, oxytocin is the neurochemical associated with trust. If a young person, for instance Macy (see Case Study 17.5) is under the influence of a highly activated oxytocin system, might she ask, "What could possibly go wrong?"

CASE STUDY 17.5 MACY'S BAD DECISION

Macy is 15 years old now and in the tenth grade. Her grandmother died last year after a brief illness, and now Macy comes home after school to an empty house, and it will be several hours before her mother gets home from work. The house echoes and creaks, and she is lonely and bored. She isn't allowed to have friends over when her mother isn't there, so she often spends time on social media. Two weeks ago, she went online and started chatting with a guy named Renee who lives in her town. He is so interesting and funny! He sent a picture of himself standing in front of the Eifel Tower in Paris. He is eighteen and adventurous. For example, he traveled through Europe last summer. Macy thinks he is so exotic and definitely cute.

Last week, Macy sent Renee a picture of herself, and he responded that he thought she was beautiful. She was thrilled, basking in the attention that he is giving her. Every afternoon since, she has texted him repeatedly throughout the day and rushed home so that she can chat with him online. Today, he says he wants to see her in person and asks her to meet him. She fixes her hair and make-up, puts on her sexiest outfit, and walks out the front door toward the car waiting down at the corner. Mom won't be back for a couple of hours, so she'll never know.

You may well ask, *What could Macy possibly be thinking?!* Well, her ADHD is making her impulsive, her sex hormones are making boys very interesting, her dopamine system is urging her to do something exciting, and her oxytocin system is making the possible rewards of doing that something even more exciting. Later, after her cognition has cooled, she may not even be able to say why she decided to walk down the street and get into that car.

Unfortunately, adolescents and young adults can make terrible mistakes sometimes, mistakes that they would not have made just a couple of years earlier and that they wouldn't dream of making after they reach full adulthood. Some of those mistakes may be due to the changes in brain functioning discussed above, but their behavior may also be influenced by their early attachment experiences, the subject that I will cover next.

Attachment in Adolescence and Emerging Adulthood

A broad range of correlational, experimental, and longitudinal research has shown a moderate correlation between the attachment style developed during infancy and early childhood and the style reported during adolescence and adulthood (Mikulincer & Shaver, 2016). This research indicates that, although many intervening factors can occur between childhood and adulthood, there's a pretty good chance that the style an individual develops in response to his or her primary caregiver's sensitivity and responsiveness (or lack thereof) will influence who he or she is able to initiate and maintain relationships with in adolescence and adulthood.

Mikulincer and Shaver (2016) explain that there is both good and bad news associated with the long-term effects of early attachment experiences. The bad news is that attachment insecurity can plague individuals throughout childhood and adolescence and then go on to produce insecurity in their adult relationships (which can then be passed on to their own children). At the same time, though, attachment security has the same lasting qualities but with positive outcomes. However, the early attachment bond is not set in stone. That is, it is possible (though not necessarily quick and easy) to change attachment styles and the working models of self and other associated with them. For example, a secure style can become more insecure (bad news) due to, say, protracted separation from a previously sensitive and responsive mother. Similarly, an insecure style may become more secure (good news) due to, say, removal from a violent and abusive home and placement in a foster home with sensitive and responsive foster parents. In my opinion, this last situation is particularly good news for mental health practitioners since if insecure attachment were indeed set in stone, we would pretty much be out of a job (bad news)!

As Mikulincer and Shaver (2016) explain, our early working models of self and other become a "prototype" (p.111) for later attachment patterns that are somewhat, but not completely, open to change. They argue that

> Current working models can be revised and updated across the lifespan by attachment-related experiences that deviate from previous experiences and existing knowledge. However, the prototype working models formed during the first few years of life continue to exist and exert a shaping influence on attachment patterns across the lifespan. (p. 111)

They explain that the persistence of attachment patterns over the long term results from the fact that working models are set into place during infancy and encoded into preverbal, procedural memory, thus becoming automatic responses to attachment-related triggers. Main (1995) argues that these nonconscious memories later become the adult's "state of mind with respect to attachment" (p. 437) that exert influence on close relationships. That is, unexamined assumptions and expectations (about self, others, and the world) drive decisions and behaviors.

Mental health professionals can see evidence of these nonconscious influences in our clients' (and our own) propensity to attract and form attachment relationships with people who fit their working models well. They then tend to behave the same way they did with their original attachment figures (Mikulincer & Shaver, 2016). Because they are nonconscious, the only way to recognize that they are at work is to notice patterns in "a person's proneness to seek out or recreate interpersonal experiences that fit with early prototype models and to appraise, interpret, and recall interactions in prototype-consistent ways" (p. 111).

We see this happening all the time as mental health practitioners, don't we? Take a moment to read Case Study 17.6 concerning Luke as he enters adulthood. Notice how his avoidant attachment formed in infancy and early childhood continues to affect his decisions concerning work and relationships even into young adulthood.

CASE STUDY 17.6 LUKE GROWN UP

After Luke graduated from college with a law degree, he landed a job with a local law firm. He found the work grueling and unsatisfying. He just couldn't work up any enthusiasm for trying to solve other people's problems, and his lack of social skills made it very difficult for him to bring in new business. He lasted three years before they fired him. He hadn't saved enough money to be able to last very long on his own, so he moved back in with his aunt and uncle as a temporary solution. However, a year later he still hadn't found another position as an attorney. To be truthful, he wasn't trying very hard. Instead, he had started online gaming again, and as he sat in front of the screen late one night, he began to hatch an idea; he would go back to school and get a degree in computer game design. He was excited about something for the first time in years. His aunt and uncle were not happy about this development, but they were also ready for him to get off his duff and move out of their house. If this would do it, they would support it.

Luke now has his degree and has started working with a team of video game designers. It was hard at first because he had to work with a group of people, something he was not at all comfortable with; he has always preferred to work on his own at his own pace. However, he has negotiated a deal in which he can work at home for most of the week and just show up for one or two team meetings. His boss and the other team members are happy with the arrangement because he always gets the work done and never asks for help. Often, he has to pull all-nighters to complete his part of the project, but he prefers not to have to depend on anyone else. The other team members sometimes ask him to go out and party with them. He goes occasionally but usually ducks out early. Although women are interested in him, he seldom goes out with anyone, usually having a one-night-stand with someone he picks up at the bar around the corner from his apartment. There was one woman who lasted three months, but when she said she wanted to have children one day, he stopped seeing her. Luke spends a lot of nights alone, working long hours, or drinking in front of the TV. He wakes up almost every day with a hangover. His best friend, the one who he can count on to lift his spirits, dull his loneliness, and put him to sleep at night is a bottle of scotch.

As this case study suggests, early attachment patterns can influence an individual's ability to form and maintain relationships later in life. In the next section, I will discuss adult attachment in detail.

Adult Attachment

Remember that the attachment style is, in essence, the answer to the critical survival question: *How do I have to be so that I can be with you?* If nothing changes during childhood, individuals will tend to continue to use the same attachment strategies and proximity-seeking behaviors that they employed in infancy, and their working models of self and other will also remain relatively unchanged (I am as I am treated). However, the language concerning the styles does change. Main (2000) explains the change in language as being necessary because a child's attachment status is fundamentally different from an adult's. Children's attachment style refers to the behaviors observed with a specific individual. That is, a child may be categorized as secure with her mother but anxious/ambivalent with her father. In contrast, an adult's attachment style refers to a more generalized concept based on how concerned they are that their close relational partners will abandon them and how willing they are to approach others in times of need. Thus, when we refer to an adult's attachment orientation, we are referring to his or her "*state of mind with respect to overall attachment history*" (p. 1079).

Based on Bowlby's (1969/1988) concepts of the internal working models of self and other, and on work by Hazan and Shaver (1987), Bartholomew and Horowitz (1991) developed a self-report instrument that asked young adults about their close relationships, placing them into one of four categories—secure, dismissing, preoccupied or fearful—according to how they described themselves. The adult secure style arises from the childhood secure style, and the adult dismissing, preoccupied, and fearful styles arise from the childhood avoidant, anxious/ambivalent, and disorganized/disoriented styles, respectively. Later research by Brennen, Clark, and Shaver (1998) uncovered two dimensions that underpin these categories— attachment anxiety and attachment avoidance. Please see Figure 17.1, which shows how Bowlby's, Bartholomew and Horowitz's, and Brennen's research fit together.

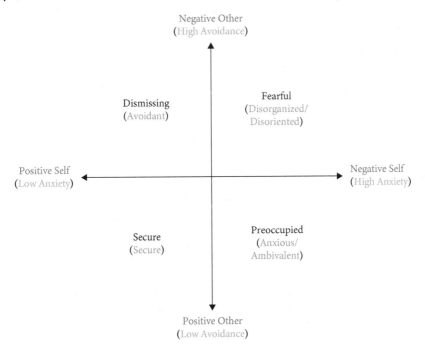

FIGURE 17.1 **Adult Attachment Dimensions and Styles**

Bartholomew and Horowitz (1991) determined respondents' attachment style by asking them to pick which of the descriptions below applied to them in their romantic relationships:

- *Secure*: "It is easy for me to become emotionally close to others. I am comfortable depending on them and having them depend on me. I don't worry about being alone or having others not accept me."
- *Preoccupied*: I want to be completely emotionally intimate with others, but I often find that others are reluctant to get as close as I would like. I am uncomfortable being without close relationships, but sometimes worry that others don't value me as much as I value them."
- *Dismissing*: "I am comfortable without close emotional relationships. It is very important to me to feel independent and self-sufficient, and I prefer not to depend on others or have them depend on me."
- *Fearful*: "I am uncomfortable getting close to others. I want emotionally close relationships, but I find it difficult to trust others completely, or to depend on them. I worry that I will be hurt if I allow myself to become too close to others.

As shown in Figure 17.1, the attachment dimensions identified by Brennen et al. (1998)—*attachment anxiety* and *attachment avoidance*—are depicted by the horizontal line representing attachment anxiety and the vertical line representing attachment avoidance. The two dimensions form the quadrants in which the Bartholomew and Horowitz styles are placed. Please note that the lines are two-way arrows, suggesting that an individual may be more or less anxious and more or less avoidant in their close relationships.

Attachment anxiety, not to be confused with an anxiety disorder (e.g., generalized anxiety disorder, panic disorder, etc.), refers to how concerned an individual is about a partner's availability in times of need, as well as how much the partner values him or her (i.e., how afraid they are of abandonment and how lovable they believe they are). Individuals who are relatively low level in attachment anxiety are not very worried that they are going to be abandoned and believe that their partner values them. Those high in attachment anxiety are intensely worried that their partner will not be there when needed and that their partner doesn't place much value on them or the relationship.

Attachment avoidance refers to how comfortable/uncomfortable an individual is being emotionally close to or dependent on a partner (or having the partner dependent on him or her). Individuals relatively low on attachment avoidance are willing to be emotionally close with their partner and are comfortable expressing need. Those relatively high in attachment avoidance tend to be highly self-reliant and to prefer emotional distance.

Effects of Early Internal Working Models on Later Attachment Styles and Dimensions

It can easily be seen how early internal working models of self and other later lead to the attachment styles seen in adolescence and adulthood. I will explain below the transition of each style from childhood to adolescence and adulthood.

Secure

As discussed in Chapter 6, secure infants and children tend to develop a positive internal working model of self that includes a view of self as loved, lovable, and deserving of love. In addition, they tend to develop a positive internal working model of other as being reasonably trustworthy, approachable, and helpful. As you can see in Figure 17.1, adolescents and emerging adults who have a positive view of self and a positive view of others fall into the *secure* quadrant.

For these individuals, the answer to the question, "How do I have to be so that I can be with you?" is that they can express distress through the normal social avenues. For example, if you remember Sophia Ramirez, you could assume that she can show her feelings, expressing them through vocal intonation, posture, gestures, or facial expressions. She can speak her feelings out loud, verbalizing that she is angry, sad, or afraid or that she wants or needs something. Since she has grown up believing "I am as I am treated," she is likely to believe that she is worthy of solicitous attention and can expect that her partner/friend will stand by her when she is distressed (or at least not attack her or run screaming). She is likely relatively unconcerned about being abandoned and sure that she is valued. She is probably willing to be emotionally close with others, is willing to depend on them in times of need, and will allow others to depend on her. A secure individual like Sophia, therefore, is likely to say: "I'm okay and you're okay, so we're okay."

Preoccupied

In contrast, those whose mothers were inconsistently sensitive, responsive, and available during infancy and childhood tend to be hypervigilent, always checking to see if mom is there, clinging to her, or angrily demanding her attention. They tend to develop an internal working model of self in which they are not sure that they are valued or worthy of love and attention. In addition, they tend to develop an internal working model of other in which they cannot trust that the other is going to be there for them in times of need. Later in life, this nonconscious fear of being abandoned makes them *preoccupied* with relationship.

Take Macy Oster, for example. For Macy, as she goes into young adulthood and begins to form intimate relationships, the answer to the question, "How do I have to be so that I can be with you?" is that she will probably try to keep tabs on her partner at all times, actively seeking attention even when there is no real danger or distress. If she perceives that her partner isn't attentive enough, she may become rageful. Since she has grown up believing "I am as I am treated," she will not be sure that she is worthy of solicitous attention and anxious that her partner/friend will not be there for her during times of trouble. Her clinginess, her constant demands, and/or her rage may backfire, resulting in her worst nightmare—the abandonment that she has always feared, and the evidence that shows that she is not lovable. A preoccupied individual like Macy, therefore, would be likely to say: "I'm not okay, and I don't know if I can count on you, so pay attention to me right now."

Dismissing

Those whose mothers punished their early dependency needs or rewarded independence tend to learn how to shut out their emotions either by distracting themselves or by dissociating. Their attachment behavioral and HPA systems are activated, but they learn how not to show it and/or how not even to feel it. They tend to develop an internal working model of self in which they do not feel valued by others as an individual or valued only under certain conditions. However, they are not worried about abandonment because they tend to view themselves as being able to take care of themselves without anyone else's help. Moreover, they do not want to experience negative affect and will avoid getting into a relationship with anyone who might expect them to be there in the bad times. Later in life, they tend to become *dismissing* of close relationships.

For someone like Luke, for example, the answer to the question, "How do I have to be so that I can be with you?" is probably, "I don't have to be with you!" Luke is likely to deny feelings of distress and avoid becoming dependent on anyone or having anyone depend on him. Since he has grown up believing "I am as I am treated," he may believe that he is not worthy of solicitous attention because he has always had to take care of himself. Alternatively, he may believe that he is better than other people are because he is not weak and needy. He will be reluctant or unwilling to ask for help and will assume that a partner/friend will be unavailable during time of trouble. Because he is isolated and lonely (emotions that he will probably deny but that his HPA system acknowledges), he may self-medicate with alcohol, drugs, work, sex, or other distractions. A relatively dismissing individual like Luke, therefore, would be likely to say: "I'm okay, and I don't need you for anything; don't ask me for anything; stay or go, I don't care."

Fearful

Lastly, children with the disorganized/disoriented style in infancy tend to become *fearful* as adults. These individuals had mothers who were either frightened by their children or frightening to them. These mothers may have engaged in outright abusive behavior (physical/sexual) or may have been highly intrusive and controlling. Alternatively, they may have reacted to their own unresolved experiences of trauma (e.g., dissociation or behavioral reactivity to intrusive memories) so that their child became overwhelmed with fright and unable to develop an organized proximity-seeking strategy that he or she could count on. In addition, development of the capacity to mentalize (see Chapter 4) may have been severely impaired, resulting in interpersonal relational difficulties, impulsivity, anger, and aggression.

Think about Jet's experiences from preconception through early and middle childhood. His answer to the question, "How do I have to be so that I can be with you?" as he reaches adolescence and adulthood is likely to be "I have no clue." Mikulincer and Shaver (2016) characterize individuals like Jet as being "the least secure, least trusting, and most troubled adolescents and adults, and their lives may have been scarred by physical and sexual abuse or other attachment-related traumas" (p. 40). They may shift between hyperactivation and deactivation strategies, both desperate for attention and terrified by it. In addition, they are more likely to become involved in criminal activity, substance abuse, and suicide attempts than are individuals with more secure attachment orientations (Bo et al., 2017). Since Jet has grown up believing "I am as I am treated," he is sure (at a nonconscious level) that he is neither loved nor deserving of love, and he has an expectation that others cannot be trusted not to hurt him. A fearful individual like Jet, therefore, would be likely to say: "I'm not okay, and you're not okay; the world is not okay."

Summary

In this chapter, we have learned about the normative process of identity formation that tends to occur during adolescence and what can happen if identity doesn't stabilize during this time. Adolescence is a life stage in which young people must explore their options and commit to a personal set of goals, values, and beliefs that provide them a sense of direction as they transition into young adulthood. Young adults, on the other hand, must begin to form deep associations, developing close relationships among friends, classmates, or colleagues at work, and/or with romantic partners. Some of the connections made during adolescence and young adulthood will provide social support for many years to come, thus facilitating successful transitions through middle to later adulthood.

In addition, we learned about the renewed blooming and pruning that begins around the time that puberty starts in adolescence and ends at around age 25. These changes appear to result in an increased interest in sensational experiences and a willingness to seek them out that is associated with changes in the production of dopamine and oxytocin specific to this age group. In addition, we have learned about the moderate correlation between childhood attachment styles and adult states of mind regarding attachment in which secure children tend to become secure adults and insecure children tend to become insecure adults. That is, the internal working models of self and other that developed in infancy and toddlerhood may be carried into adulthood where they will continue to influence social interactions and choices of friends and romantic partners, often for the remainder of life.

Because it is during adolescence and young adulthood that individuals reach sexual maturity, romantic relationships become increasingly important to them. In addition, other intimate relationships such as close friendships and work/school relationships also begin to become prominent. Therefore, in the next chapter, I will focus specifically on how attachment affects individuals' choices concerning their close relationships as well as how early family formation can impact the lives of individuals at this stage of life.

CHAPTER 18

Friendship, Sexuality, and Romance

LEARNING OBJECTIVES

After completing this chapter, readers should understand that:

- Attachment shapes sexual encounters and the functions that sex serves in close relationships as well as sexual risk-taking behaviors.
- There are multiple negative outcomes associated with teen pregnancy for both the mother and the child.
- The attachment dimensions affect both the initial choice of one's friendships, work relationships, and romantic relationships as well as on-going relationship interactions.

KEY IDEAS

1. Attachment anxiety and avoidance are related to young adults' social network characteristics and management.
2. Dysfunctions of the sexual system can follow from dysfunctional attachment patterns and the adoption of sexual hyperactivation or deactivation strategies.
3. The brain changes that occur during adolescence increase the likelihood of sexual risk-taking, though secure attachment may act as a protective factor against teens' decision to engage in sex.
4. Both anxiously- and avoidantly-attached individuals are more likely than secure individuals are to engage in unsafe sex.
5. Teen parenthood is associated with limited educational opportunities, poverty, unstable and conflictual relationships, and high levels of depression for the mother and developmental delays, poor cognitive and social development, and increased behavioral problems (both internalizing and externalizing) for the child.
6. Attachment anxiety and avoidance affect individuals' core wishes for relationships, the habitual behaviors used to pursue those goals, and individuals' ability to express their own needs and to recognize and respond to their partner's needs.
7. Unconscious attachment-related memories affect an individual's work relationships, friendships, and even his or her choice of mate.

Introduction

As children transition into adolescence and then into young adulthood, peer relationships begin to assume a growing importance as part of the drive toward individuation. Individuals begin to spend more time out in the community as they enter high school and the work environment, and their circle of friendships naturally tends to expand. In addition, with the advent of puberty, interest in sex tends to increase and the seeking out of romantic relationships often becomes a focus of attention. The transition into young adulthood comes with the need to form deep associations with others in order to avoid the negative physical and mental health consequences associated with isolation.

The friendship skills that adolescents develop as they make the transition to adulthood influence how successful they will be in establishing deep associations with others later. The formation of deep associations in young adulthood is considered to be a core task (Erikson, 1968), and failure to establish close relationships results in a host of physical and mental health problems (Ernst & Cacioppo, 1999). These deep associations include not just romantic/sexual relationships but close relationships with friends, classmates, colleagues at work, and perhaps teachers, mentors, and even a mental health provider. These nonsexual, nonromantic relationships are an extremely important form of social support. Not only do they fulfill our natural needs for affiliation, companionship, functional support and fun outside of the family environment, but they also can support us when relationships end for one reason or another.

One of the most salient features of adolescence is puberty, during which the sex drive ramps up and bodies become capable of reproduction. Research shows that up to 61% of adolescents have had sexual intercourse at least once by the end of high school, with 48% reporting being currently sexually active, and 20% reporting have had more than four sexual partners (Center for Disease Control and Prevention, 2018c). Although research has traditionally focused on the risks associated with adolescent sexual activity, more recent research has begun to view sexual development and the initiation of romantic relationships as normative (van de Bongardt, Yu, Dekovic, & Meeus, 2015). These researchers suggest that young people learn about their particular preferences concerning sexuality and intimacy, and they develop skills to manage intimate relationships through experimentation during adolescence. Victor and Hariri (2018) go so far as to suggest that adolescence is "the most critical phase in sexual development, as individuals begin to learn to associate stimuli such as bodily features, personality, and contextual cues with genitally induced sexual pleasure" (p. 478). Of course, what they learn during their early sexual development will lay down neural pathways that affect future sexual decision-making and behavior.

CLASS DISCUSSION

Thinking about the four case studies we have been following through the life stages, which of them do you think is the most likely to have become sexually active by the time they graduate from high school? Why do you think this? What kind of relationships do you think he or she will have with his or her sexual partner(s)?

In this chapter, I will discuss friendship, sex, and romance as they are influenced by attachment. Given that this period in life tends to include a greater likelihood of risk-taking than earlier or later in life because of the brain changes that occur at this time, I also discuss sexual risk-taking, a factor that can result in higher rates of teen pregnancy and early family formation. Then, because most individuals join the workforce during late adolescence and young adulthood, I will discuss how attachment influences relationships in the workplace.

Attachment and Friendship

Attachment clearly influences how successful an individual is in establishing both close friendships and romantic relationships. Sroufe (2002) states in no uncertain terms that his and his colleagues' research over a period of 26 years shows that

> nothing is more important for the child's development than the quality of the care received. This has been true for outcomes as diverse as competence with peers, behavior and emotional problems, successful completion of school, and adolescent risk behaviors such as promiscuity. … It is simply not the case that good parents pass along good genes to their children, resulting in good child behavior. What happens to children (and what happens to parents who care for them) matters deeply. Nor is it the case that peer experiences dwarf parenting experiences. Direct study shows that early quality of care strongly predicts peer experiences and that, subsequently, history with parents and history with peers interact in complex ways in shaping later child behavior (p. 187).

Thus, it is clear that attachment in infancy and early childhood affects an individual's ability to form friendships with peers later in life.

Recent research has examined how attachment anxiety and avoidance are related to young adults' social network characteristics and management (Gillith, Karantzas, & Selcuk, 2017). Social network characteristics include the strength of social ties and respondents' level of dependence on their network to fulfill social and emotional functions, characteristics that involve trust and closeness. Social network management refers to the ability to initiate, maintain, and dissolve relationships. The results of this research fall right in line with what attachment theory would predict. That is, these researchers found that insecure attachment is significantly related to respondents' perceptions of the strength (closeness) of their ties, how dependent they are on friends, and how they pursue, maintain, and end friendships. Individuals who are more attachment-anxious feel that their friends are not as close to them as they would like them to be. Their frantic efforts to increase closeness tend to be viewed by their friends as demanding and smothering, frequently resulting in distancing or withdrawal from the friendship. Attachment-avoidant individuals, on the other hand, also perceive their social ties as lacking closeness. However, the researchers suggest that this perception may be related to their own compulsive self-reliance and reluctance to become close to and depend on someone else. In contrast to more anxious individuals (who tend to try to maintain a relationship until their friend actively terminates it), more avoidant individuals tend to be the one to pull the plug.

Attachment and Sex

Mikulincer and Shaver (2016) emphasize that in the same way that evolution promoted the development of the *attachment* behavioral system to support survival through social interaction, it promoted the development of a *sexual* behavioral system to support survival through reproduction. Moreover, these two innate systems, though separate and distinct, interact with each other. Couch and Koeninger (2017) suggest that dopamine and norepinephrine are primarily responsible for the focus, energy, and animation that generally accompany the giddiness and euphoria associated with the physiological arousal (lust) of early love (usually lasting between 18 months and four years), while serotonin is associated with those butterflies you feel in your stomach. This early and intense passion tends over time to yield somewhat to a more companionate love that is based on oxytocin-fueled attachment that causes an increase in feelings of well-being and contentedness. In addition, the production of vasopressin is responsible for maintaining commitment in the relationship. Mikulincer and Shaver (2016) note that sex provides high levels of pleasure that support the attachment bond, while the attachment bond provides a sense of safety that supports sexual enjoyment. However, the relationship between sex and love is complex. Indeed, Birnbaum (2015), in his review of the literature concerning attachment and sexuality among adolescents, states that "past attachment experiences shape what people want out of sexual encounters, how they get their needs met, and what functions sex serves in their close relationships" (p. 270).

Mikulincer and Shaver (2016) explain that individuals with secure attachment have an internal working model of other that allows them to be comfortable being close to someone and willing to be vulnerable with them. At the same time, they have an internal working model of self that allows them to be confident of the sexual performance as well as attuned to and willing to communicate about their and their partner's interests and preferences. These authors go on to point out that, although attachment security is not closely associated with monogamy, it does facilitate healthy and realistic commitment to another. In addition, secure individuals are more likely to be comfortable abandoning themselves to deep sexual pleasure within or outside of marital bonds, and if they go outside of the marital bond for sex, they "would be expected to retain an accurate understanding of their own motives, the consequences for their relationship partners, and the consequences for themselves" (p. 376). The same cannot be said for those who are insecure.

Mikulincer and Shaver (2016) explain further that dysfunctions of the sexual system can follow from dysfunctional attachment patterns and the adoption of sexual hyperactivation or deactivation strategies. Hyperactivation may include "effortful, mentally preoccupying, sometimes intrusive, and occasionally even coercive attempts to persuade a partner to have sex or to acknowledge one's sexual value" (p. 374). Moreover, individuals with anxious attachment tend to have sex as a way gaining love, admiration, or acceptance and the possibility of a long-term relationship. They tend to equate sex with romantic love. Therefore, they may be willing to engage in unsafe sex or sex that is psychologically or physically painful. In contrast, deactivation may include denying desire and blocking sexual thoughts, arousal, and orgasmic pleasure, or avoiding or disparaging one's partner when he or she indicates a desire for sex. Individuals with avoidant attachment tend to lack perception of their partners' needs and preferences, and have sex as a way of gaining social prestige (bragging rights), self-esteem/affirmation, or power. They see sex and love as being two entirely different things, love being nonsensical fiction only depicted in the movies. They tend to prefer short-term relationships that require little emotional (or other) investment, and they engage in extradyadic relationships and "mate poaching" more often than do either secure or anxious individuals.

Interestingly, both anxious and avoidant individuals are more likely than secure individuals are to engage in unsafe sex, but for different reasons. Anxious individuals may be willing to engage in unwanted or unsafe sex due to a fear of rejection and abandonment, while avoidant individuals may have unwanted or unsafe sex because they don't want to disclose information about themselves or find out the intimate details of someone else's life. In addition, both anxious and avoidant individuals are more likely than secure individuals are to use alcohol or drugs before and during sex (Mikulincer & Shaver, 2016), reducing their inhibitions and affecting their ability to make considered judgments.

Sexual Risk-Taking

Although sexual activity may be normative during adolescence and young adulthood, it can also be risky, resulting in pregnancy, sexually transmitted diseases, and mental health issues. Indeed, early onset of sexual activity is considered to be a risk factor for negative physical and emotional outcomes (Zimmer-Gembeck & Helfand, 2008). Victor and Hariri (2018) emphasize that "sexual decision making involves uniquely powerful emotional and physiologic drives that may further accelerate subcortical [approach/avoidance] drives, which overwhelm the limited capacity of behavioral control through an immature PFC, ultimately resulting in significant risk for negative sexual health decisions" (p. 472). That is, the adolescent's dopamine and oxytocin systems may simply shout down the PFC's tiny little voice when he or she is in the heat of the moment (i.e., under the influence of hot cognition). However, secure attachment may act as a protective factor against teens' decision to engage in sex. For example, research shows that supportive parenting (characterized by high levels of connectedness, warmth, communication, and monitoring) is negatively correlated with endorsement of teens' favorable attitudes toward sex (Cox, Shreffler, Merten, Schwerdtfeger Gallus, & Dowdy, 2015).

As mentioned in Chapter 8, the use of digital devices has become the norm for children and adolescents in recent years, and the internet has become a resource that can promote both positive development (education, connectedness, etc.) and risky behavior. Collins et al. (2017) point out that the use of social networking sites has been shown to increase the risk of self-objectification and body shame, and can lead to reductions in sexual assertiveness. Moreover, it facilitates dating violence because of the ease with which an aggressor can use it to control a partner, disappear, and reunite. These authors also discuss the recent rise of sexting (the exchange of sexual messages or images) through cell phones or over the internet, which, according to Patchin (2017), approximately 12% of 12- to 17-year-olds report having sent at least once and almost 20% having received. Collins et al. (2016) suggest that, while sexting may be "an emerging aspect of natural adolescent sexual exploration and experimentation … [and] part of an existing or developing romantic relationship" (p. s164), it may also be the result of coercion or pressure, and there is the risk that it may be passed on to a broad audience for the purposes of revenge or humiliation. These authors also note that mobile devices make access to pornography extremely easy, anonymous, and hard for parents to monitor, with 42% of 10- to 17-year-olds reporting that they have seen pornography online and 27% indicating that they had intentionally sought the material out. They emphasize that traditional media (television, movies, music, video games) are also rife with sexual material that influence rates of teen sexual activity, acceptance of casual sex and unsafe sex practices, and promote gendered sexual scripts (e.g., female passivity, rejection of homosexuality, misogynistic attitudes).

Teen Parenting

Given the ubiquity of sexual messages in our society today, it is not surprising that many individuals start engaging in sexual activity during their teens and thus run the risk of becoming parents before they reach full adulthood. The good news is that teen pregnancy rates have been falling steadily since 2007 (Martin, Hamilton, Osterman, Driscoll, & Drake, 2018), though pregnancy rates among teens in the United States still outpace those of other developed countries (Sedgh, Finer, Bankole, Eilers, & Singh, 2015). Though the research is not clear at this point, these falling rates are thought to be the result of teens becoming less likely to engage in sex and more likely to use protection if they do have sex (Lindberg, Santelli, & Desai, 2016). Moreover, birth rates for teens vary widely by race/ethnicity, with the those for American Indian/Alaska Native teens (32.9/1000) being highest among all race/ethnicities, followed by Hispanic teens (28.9/1000), non-Hispanic black teens (27.5/1000), and non-Hispanic white teens (13.2/1000) (Martin, Hamilton, & Osterman, 2018). In addition, rates tend to be higher among teens who come from families with low income and low educational attainment (Penman-Aguilar, Carter, Snead, & Kourtis, 2013).

Having a baby during adolescence is associated with a host of negative outcomes. These teens tend to have limited education, to live in poverty, to have unstable and conflictual relationships, and high levels of depression (Lewin et al., 2015). Research has shown that, at least among African American teens, girls who give birth during their teen years are more likely than non-teenage mothers to report smoking, substance abuse, or delinquent behavior (Assini-Meytin & Green, 2015). Furthermore, these girls are more likely to live in poverty and be dependent on welfare, and this socioeconomic disadvantage tends to last well into their adulthood.

Important to the subject of this book, compared to adult mothers, teen mothers tend to have poorer parenting behaviors, are less sensitive and attuned to their babies, and are more likely to engage in psychological and physical aggression (Lewin et al., 2015). They are not as affectionate, show fewer positive facial expressions, and are less verbally and emotionally responsive to their infants compared to adult mothers (Chico, Gonzalez, Ali, Steiner, & Fleming, 2014). These researchers also note these young mothers also tend to have more unrealistic expectations for their infant's behavior, and they tend to prod, poke, and pinch their babies more than adult mothers do. Although having a baby is a major life transition regardless of age, it is especially difficult for teens.

Yoon et al. (2019) point out that teen mothers are not yet ready developmentally and cognitively for the challenges of motherhood and may resent the responsibilities associated with caring for an infant. Their ability to regulate their emotions may not have matured yet, and they may experience high levels of parenting stress. These factors may then prompt them to utilize harsh, punitive parenting practices that may, in turn, affect their baby's development. Chico et al. (2014) suggest that teen mothers' lack of sensitivity and attunement is associated with their underdeveloped executive function. You may remember from Chapter 8 that executive function has to do with the ability to organize and plan efficiently, to solve problems and make decisions, and to manage one's time. Deficits in these important abilities could easily lead to parenting stress and well as ineffective responses.

It should be no surprise, then, that children born to teen mothers are at increased risk of developmental delays, poor cognitive and social development and increased behavioral problems (both internalizing and externalizing) compare to children of adult mothers (Mollborn & Dennis, 2012; Pinzon, Jones, & Committee on Adolescence & Committee on Early Childhood, 2012; Ruedingera & Cox, 2012). Moreover, the children of teen mothers are at increased risk of adverse outcomes such as drug use, gang involvement, school dropout, and early pregnancy when they reach adolescence themselves (Pogarsky, Thornberry, & Lizotte, 2006).

The probability of negative outcomes among the babies of teen mothers is further increased if the mother was a victim of maltreatment during her own childhood (Pasalich, Cyr, Zheng, & McMahon, 2016; Yoon et al., 2019). Research by Yoon et al. (2019), for example, shows that among teen mothers with a history of childhood adversities, parenting stress, harsh physical punishment, and disagreements between the teen mother and her own mother concerning parenting are associated with increased rule-breaking and aggressiveness in the child at age 11. Furthermore, Pasalich et al. (2016) point out that a teen who was both physically and sexually abused during childhood is at an increased risk of becoming pregnant. Once the baby is born, he or she is at increased risk of exhibiting externalizing behaviors upon entry to the school system. Most likely, these externalizing behaviors develop through two pathways. First, the child tends to develop an insecure attachment style in infancy, which is related to externalizing behaviors in preschool. This early externalizing behavior is then associated with further externalizing behavior in third grade. Secondly, teen mothers tend to compound the problem by showing more hostility to their children in preschool, which is also associated with more externalizing behaviors in third grade. Then to close the circle, children with externalizing behaviors who grow up to have children of their own are at high risk of abusing them. Thus, it would appear that increasing attachment security in infants of teen mothers and decreasing their externalizing behaviors during the first few years of their schooling could go a long way toward curbing the intergenerational transmission of both teen pregnancy and abusive parenting.

Better outcomes among teen mothers and their children occur when the baby's father has positive contact with them for at least the first eight years (Lewin et al., 2015). Positive father involvement is most likely when there is a cooperative relationship with the mother in which they co-parent the child. Co-parenting has to do specifically with working together to care for the child, not with their romantic, legal, or financial relationship. Co-parenting can be complicated by the fact that many teen mothers do not live with the father of their baby, which often results in his having only limited access to the child. Moreover, the relationship between the mother and father may be relatively short-lived, and the introduction of a new love interest by either one can result in conflict. Because of their emotional immaturity, they may have relatively poor communication, interpersonal, and conflict management skills, and thus may have difficulty maintaining cooperative shared parenting responsibilities. However, Lewin and her colleagues argue that interventions targeting teen fathers and increasing cooperative co-parenting may help to interrupt the intergenerational transmission of insecurity and adversity and provide the babies of teen mothers with much-needed social support.

Attachment and Romantic Relationships

Sex is nature's way of making sure we have babies so that our species can survive. However, human babies take a long time to develop sufficiently to make it on their own, so we needed to develop a system to help us maximize our babies' survivability (Mikulincer & Shaver, 2016). Therefore, the sexual behavioral system "drives a person to want to have sex with *any* appropriate member of the species, whereas romantic attraction involves the choice of a specific partner with whom one already has or may be able to form an affectional bond that goes beyond merely having sex" (p. 373). However, sex among humans does not always result in pregnancy nor does it necessarily take place only in committed relationships. Indeed, sex can take the form of a casual one-night-stand with an anonymous partner, serial monogamy, or even rape. However, attachment (which is just as much of an innate drive as sex is) complements the sex drive by layering it with the desire for closeness and nurturing. The evolutionary development of the attachment behavioral system and the social engagement system provide mechanisms for sexual partners to form attachment bonds that will help promote survival of any children that result from their coupling (Birnbaum, 2015).

Romantic relationships become increasingly common as boys and girls transition through adolescence and into emerging adulthood, with approximately one in four 12-year-olds, half of 15-year-olds, and 70% of 18-year-olds reporting that they have had a special romantic relationship within the past year (Carver, Joyner, & Udry, 2003). According to Connolly et al. (2014), these relationships tend to be initiated in a predictable sequence, starting with relatively brief relationships in the context of mixed-gender groups and parties in early adolescence. They move into fairly casual and short-term relationships in dating groups during middle adolescence in which peer groups provide a place for fun and companionship with possible sexual overtones. In late adolescence, the relationships tend to become both more enduring and more serious. Then in young adulthood, romantic relationships may develop into committed, long-term relationships. However, it has become increasingly likely that young adults may postpone commitment in favor of development of school and career options, engaging in short-term relationships and casual sex.

The attachment dimensions and styles affect romantic relationships, both in the initial choice of one's partner and then in on-going relationship interactions. Mikulincer and Shaver (2016) explain that while sex comes out of the sexual behavior system, romantic attachment comes out of the attachment and caregiving systems. In romantic relationships, attachment has to do with using a partner as a safe haven during times of distress (as a baby does with his or her mother), while caregiving has to do with a partner's willingness and ability to provide needed support (as a mother does for her baby). They point out that for individuals to develop a deep romantic attachment to someone it takes about the same amount of time that it takes for babies to fully develop their bond with their mother—about two years—over which time both partners have time to experience how sensitive and responsive their partners are to their needs.

CLASS DISCUSSION

Have you ever been in love? What was it like when you first met? How did that change over time? How has your own attachment style affected your romantic relationships?

Relationship Goals and Behaviors

Mikulincer and Shaver (2016) explain that levels of attachment anxiety and attachment avoidance affect individuals' core wishes for relationship as well as the habitual behaviors they use to pursue those goals. In addition, they affect individuals' ability to express their own needs and to recognize and respond to their partner's needs. Take Macy, for example. She is relatively high in attachment anxiety. Therefore, when she falls in love, she may desperately want her partner to show her love and affection, and she may try to be as close as possible to him at all times, even when her life is going well and even when he may not want to be close to her for some reason. She may be afraid, however, that if she actually expresses her desire for closeness, he may get mad and leave. Or, she may be so focused on her own needs that she can't recognize that, say, watching football with his buddies on a Sunday afternoon doesn't constitute abandonment.

In contrast, think about Luke, who is high in attachment avoidance. In an intimate relationship, he probably will feel uncomfortable either giving or receiving signs of love and affection, and will try to put distance between himself and his partner even when he could really use help and even when she clearly is in need of his support. He may be unwilling to tell his partner that he needs help for fear that he will look weak and vulnerable. He may be so wrapped up in his own interests or have shut out his partner's expressions of need so that if he responds at all, his response may be completely off the mark.

Initiation, Consolidation, and Maintenance of Relationships

Research shows that the internal working models of self and other that are formed in early childhood tend to transfer over into romantic relationships even in the early flirtation and dating stages. Secure individuals are relatively free of the fear of either abandonment or intimacy and generally are able to regulate their own thoughts, feelings, and behaviors in the presence of the other's thoughts, feelings, and behaviors. Therefore, they are able to approach a possible partner in a relatively relaxed manner, explore the pros and cons of a possible relationship, allow the relationship to grow in intimacy at a rate and to a level that is reasonable for both, and end the relationship if it stops meeting their needs. Insecure individuals, on the other hand, may have trouble flirting and dating either because they jump in too fast or not fast enough. In addition, they may either reveal too much of themselves too soon, or they may not ever open up so that their partner can get to know them (Mikulincer & Shaver, 2016).

As the relationship progresses, consolidation may be difficult for insecure individuals (Mikulincer & Shaver, 2016). For example, individuals with high attachment anxiety may leap into relationships indiscriminately and find out only later that that their and their partners' goals and behaviors don't mesh. they may provide care and concern for their partners with the hope that it will show them in a good light, gain their partners' approval, and solidify their relationship. Because they are afraid to complain for fear of losing the relationship, they may fall into deep resentment that eventually explodes into conflict. Alternatively, they may complain incessantly, inadvertently causing conflict that only intensifies their anxiety about abandonment. They may try to dominate their partners aggressively, or may become submissive so that they avoid being rejected, setting them up for possible abuse (especially if there is a history of abuse during childhood). They may have trouble getting out of relationships, perhaps staying because of an overwhelming terror of being alone or because they believe they don't deserve better.

On the other hand, individuals who are high in avoidance may bolt at the first sign of a partner's expectations for closeness or interdependence. They may walk away from what could be a good relationship either because of unconscious fears of engulfment or assumptions that all relationships go bad, so better sooner than later. If they respond to a partner's expressed need, they may do so either out of a sense of obligation or because they think they will get something in return. They may stay in an unsatisfactory relationship because they want to avoid conflict and the emotions associated with it, perhaps even refusing to acknowledge that there is any conflict, minimizing the problem and denying a partner's legitimate concerns. If there is conflict anyway, they may try to dominate their partner, assuming that they are, of course, right, and their partner is wrong (Mikulincer & Shaver, 2016).

Mikulincer and Shaver (2016) would suggest that in contrast to insecure individuals, people who are secure are likely to have positive expectations for their own acceptability as well as their partners' trustworthiness and supportiveness. They may actively want a highly committed relationship, and they probably have the belief that deep and intimate associations can be maintained over the long term. They may recognize the inevitability of conflict between partners but have the skills to manage conflict in ways that result in a return to harmony. When their partners need them, they will probably be willingly do what they can without expectation for personal benefit, and they won't intrude care where it is not wanted or needed. If things go sour, although they may be sad and disappointed, they can let the relationship go, grieve as long as they need to, and eventually move on.

Choice of Mate

Mikulincer and Shaver (2016) explain that the research on mating preferences has found that, regardless of their attachment orientation, people generally are attracted to secure people. However, insecure people are more favorably drawn to others who are also insecure than are secure people. That is, secure people tend to be attracted only to others who are secure, while individuals with attachment anxiety may be attracted to others who are anxious, and individuals who have attachment avoidance may be drawn to other avoidants. However, some research suggests that opposites may attract, such that avoidants are drawn to anxious partners (Strauss, Morry & Kito, 2012). The propensity for insecure individuals to be attracted to other insecure individuals appears to be most likely among people who have experienced abuse during childhood. In any of these cases involving partnerships between insecure individuals, however, the relationships tend to be less stable than those involving at least one secure partner.

Work

As individuals move through adolescence and into young adulthood, it becomes more and more likely that they will enter the labor force. According to the U. S. Department of Labor (2018), just under one in four of high school students and about half of college students work. In contrast, about 63% of high school dropouts and 84% of young adults (ages 20–24) who are not in college work. Mortimer (2010) notes that there are both benefits and risks associated with working during this time of life. For example, adolescents often want the freedom to purchase things and participate in activities that their parents may not be willing or able to provide, or they may want to save money for college. In addition, having a job and earning money can make them feel more like adults. Working can also encourage the development of values such as personal responsibility and a good work ethic, and can be a place in which to learn important social skills. However, if too much emphasis is placed on work, academic performance (which provides information and skills needed for success in the workplace) may be adversely affected, possibly resulting in dropout and consequent loss of earning potential.

Both the work environment and the type and quality of the work being performed can affect a person's experience of work (Mortimer, 2010). However, of interest to the subject matter addressed in this book, the work experience can also be influenced by attachment. A review of the literature concerning attachment dynamics and work relationships shows that relationships with organizational leaders, colleagues, and mentors, as well as with the organization itself, are influenced by the unconscious expectations/assumptions and habitual behaviors associated with an individual's early attachment experiences (Yip, Ehrhardt, Black & Walker, 2015). Since many of you who are reading this book may be students, I will use you as an example of how attachment issues may affect your job satisfaction and performance:

Just for a moment, imagine that you have recently graduated with your MSW and are working at a mental health agency as a therapist. As you imagine the scenarios below, remember first that everybody has an attachment style, so you, your supervisor, his or her supervisor, and the CEO or owner of your agency all come into the workplace with attachment histories. Now, imagine that your direct supervisor has a relatively secure attachment style. You can expect that she will be able to delegate work effectively and, though offering you support if needed, will allow you considerable autonomy to do your work. She will have a relational leadership style in which she is interested in you and provides ways for you to develop your skills. If for some reason you are not able to do the job required of you, she will tell you what is wrong and give you chances to correct your performance. However, she will let you go if she has to in a professional manner.

In contrast, what if you have a direct supervisor who has attachment avoidance? He is likely to want to be in control of everything, unwilling to delegate, and insensitive or oblivious to your needs. He may close his door so that he doesn't have to interact with his workers, and he may work long hours so that he doesn't have to interact with anyone at home either. Rather than motivating you by praising and supporting you, he may try to motivate you through threat or through monetary rewards. He will assume that you have no loyalty to the agency, and he has no loyalty to you. If you mess up, he will have no qualms about letting you go and may not want to tell you that you are fired face to face.

If your supervisor has a more anxious attachment style, there is likely to be considerable chaos in the workplace. You may never know what to expect from her. One day she may try to be your friend and another day treat you with disdain. This supervisor will likely be preoccupied with what her boss thinks of her work. She may say yes to anything her boss suggests, afraid that her boss will get mad if she points out that something won't work. As she passes the boss's demands on down to you, her self-regulation problems may cause her to overreact to any distress you voice. If you ask for clarification about new procedures, she may make an answer up because she doesn't want either you or her boss to know that she doesn't know. If you mess up, this supervisor would probably rather keep you than let you go, if only so you will be more firmly under her control because of her beneficence. However, if she does let you go, she may vilify you so that she can justify her decision to herself and to others.

Now, to complicate matters further, you have an attachment style, too, and that style is going to interact with your supervisor's style. If you're both secure, great. However, if you are avoidant, you are probably going to have doubts about your supervisor's trustworthiness, and you may have an increased risk for burnout because you won't ask for help from your boss or from your colleagues. If your boss is avoidant, too, you may like each other but keep a lot of distance. If your boss is anxious, you may not like each other much, your boss saying that you are cold and a loner, and you saying that your boss is intrusive and unreasonably reactive. If you are anxious, you may pester your supervisor and your colleagues for advice and attention and be afraid to do anything on your own. If your boss is also anxious, you may get along well. However, there may be boundary issues in which you become overly friendly and then disappointed and angry when either of you thinks the other isn't sufficiently responsive. If your boss is avoidant, your demands for feedback and attention may be perceived as inappropriate at best and maddening at worst, either of which sets you up for your worst nightmare, termination.

Lastly, I need to point out that, as mentioned in Chapter 4, attachment styles can change. Therefore, it is possible that you can become more secure (or more insecure) in response to working in an environment in which you are surrounded by secure (or insecure) coworkers. If you are a leader in your organization, you might want to consider your workers' attachment styles when structuring the workplace. Yip et al. (2015) suggest that attachment-anxious and avoidant workers may benefit from being placed in situations where interdependence is simply part of the structure so that avoidant individuals can receive social support without having to ask for it and anxious individuals can get an increased sense of belonging.

In summary, it is likely that mental health professionals will find attachment issues cropping up in their own workplace. The more secure practitioners and administrators are, the better off everybody is—one more reason for everyone to do their own work. If you find that the same issues are coming up again and again in different places where you work, you may want to check out your attachment patterns. Are you reacting to your supervisor the same way you reacted to you alcoholic father or your bipolar mother? Is that coworker down the hall acting the way your sister did when you were five years old? Are you terrified when your boss calls that he is about to fire you even though you are in reality doing a great job? Are you holing up in your office? Are you working sixty or eighty hours a week and have no other life to speak of? If so, it may be time to find a good therapist!

CLASS DISCUSSION

How do your early life experiences and attachment style affect your relationship with your co-workers or classmates? Your boss or teachers?

Summary

Adolescence and young adulthood are life stages that include an enormous amount of change both in neurological and social terms. Sexual maturity and relative independence from family encourage the development of close relationships that meet our need for affiliation, companionship, and social support. Attachment anxiety and attachment avoidance that are prompted by early attachment experiences can interfere with an individual's ability to form and maintain mutually satisfying relationships and result in many of the psychological issues that mental health practitioners address. Moreover, insecure attachment can interact with the neurological changes that occur during this stage resulting in increases in sexual risk-taking and consequent early family formation and sexually transmitted diseases.

Attachment issues can also affect an individual's ability to establish satisfactory relationships in home, school, and/or work environments. That is, individuals tend to act out their unconscious attachment patterns in their relationships wherever they may be. Because attachment-related assumptions about self and others are held in the right-brain, non-conscious memory, they are hard to recognize and tend to be repeated again and again. Our job as mental health practitioners is often to help the individual bring unconscious patterns into consciousness where they can be verbalized and addressed. Unfortunately, the patterns can be so deeply entrenched that the individual may come to identify himself or herself with their patterns—"I just can't get along with other people," or "Nobody is ever going to love me," for example—and act out their pain in violence and/or addiction, issues that will be discussed in the next chapter.

CHAPTER 19

Special Challenges in Adolescence and Young Adulthood

LEARNING OBJECTIVES

After completing this chapter, readers should understand:

- Which brain systems and neurochemicals are involved in substance use and abuse.
- How attachment affects the probability that an individual will develop problematic use of substances.
- How attachment is related to the perpetration of violence in adolescence and young adulthood.

KEY IDEAS

1. Adolescent and young adult brains are especially vulnerable to the toxic effects of psychoactive substances.
2. Secure attachment is a protective factor against self-harm and suicidal ideation.
3. There are attachment-related differences between individuals who commit street violence and those who commit mass shootings.
4. Early attachment insecurity is associated with violence among adolescents and young adults and may be the root of mass school shootings.

Introduction

Secure attachment sets the stage for adequate regulation of thoughts, emotions, and behaviors throughout life. Insecure attachment, on the other hand, sets the stage for a wide range of problems in self-regulation that can result in many of the issues that mental health professions deal with. Mikulincer and Shaver (2016) explain that in general, clients with attachment-related anxiety tend to hyperactivate their attachment behavioral system by up-regulating the intensity and persistence of their negative emotions. Therefore, these clients "experience an unmanageable stream of negative thoughts and feelings, which contribute to cognitive disorganization and, in some cases, culminate in psychopathology" (Mikulincer & Shaver, 2016, p. 396). However, they caution that, except for specific attachment disorders (e.g., reactive attachment disorder), attachment anxiety and avoidance alone are not directly responsible for psychopathology. They argue instead that "attachment insecurities act as catalysts of other pathogenic processes by reducing psychological and social resources and weakening a person's resilience" (p. 397). Having reviewed literally hundreds of studies concerning links between attachment and various mental health diagnoses, they found that secure attachment has been shown consistently to be related to lower levels of a wide variety of psychopathologies. Table 19.1 provides a summary of mental health disorders associated with attachment anxiety and avoidance commonly treated by mental health professionals.

TABLE 19.1   Mental Health Disorders Associated with the Attachment Dimensions

Avoidant Attachment:
- Suicidality
- PTSD (avoidant symptoms)
- Eating disorder
- Conduct disorder
- Addiction (substance and behavioral)

Anxious Attachment:
- Suicidality
- Obsessive-compulsive disorder
- Hoarding
- Eating disorder
- Conduct disorder
- Addiction (substance and behavioral)

Fearful (both anxious and avoidant):
- Dissociative symptoms and dissociative identity disorder
- Schizotypy and schizophrenia
- Psychosis
- Substance abuse

Source: Mikulincer, M. & Shaver, P. R. (2016). Attachment in adulthood: Structure, dynamics, and change (2nd ed.). New York, NY: Guilford Press.

You may notice that several problems appear in more than one dimension. This is because the same behavior can arise in response to different thoughts, emotions, and behaviors. For example, Mikulincer and Shaver (2016) point out that some research suggests that a person may attempt suicide in a desperate effort to get attention, a hyperactivation strategy associated with anxious attachment. Another person, however, may attempt suicide because of deep despair, exercising an extreme form of deactivation. Someone may commit crimes in a maladaptive cry for help (hyperactivation) similar to attempting suicide. An avoidant individual, on the other hand, may use antisocial behavior "as a means of denying the importance of attachment relationships and gaining distance from unresponsive parents" (p. 433), or they may have a lack of trust in social norms (deactivation). Anorexia may be associated with "the suppressive, need-denying nature of deactivating strategies [or with] the chaotic, self-gratifying, and uncontrollable nature of hyperactivating strategies" (p. 430). Substance abuse and behavioral addictions, such as gambling, sex, and Internet addictions, may afford individuals with attachment anxiety release from anxiety, tension, and stress while affording individuals with attachment avoidance a way to avoid emotional dependency (Schindler et al., 2005).

In addition, Mikulincer and Shaver (2016) suggest that when attachment insecurities are coupled with trauma, abuse, loss and/or adversity, practitioners are likely to be faced with "extreme, disorganized, or especially dysfunctional attempts to hyperactivate or deactivate the attachment system" (p. 436) in the form of personality disorders. They suggest that personality disorders are related to attachment insecurity such that attachment avoidance is associated with Cluster A (paranoid, schizoid, and schizotypal) symptoms while attachment anxiety is associated with Cluster B (antisocial, borderline, histrionic, and narcissistic) and Cluster B C (avoidant, dependent, and obsessive-compulsive) symptoms. Interestingly, the symptoms associated with many of the personality disorders appear to decline (though they do not disappear entirely) between the ages of 20 and 50, with the greatest changes seen among individuals with borderline and antisocial symptoms (Gutierrez et al., 2012).

In summary, insecure attachment is related to psychopathology among the adolescents and young adults that mental health practitioners treat. Although attachment may not be the primary cause of a disorder, it appears to be a major contributing factor that a practitioner may want to address through direct attachment-based interventions. However, whatever kinds of interventions we utilize, it may be advisable to keep attachment (our own as well as our clients') in mind and do our best to provide a safe haven for our clients to reveal themselves and create a secure base from which they can explore their issues. Two particularly troubling mental health issues plague society currently: addiction and violence, especially the mass violence we are experiencing today in the form of school shootings. I would like to address both of these in some detail here in an effort to raise awareness about how they are rooted in insecure attachment.

Addiction

One of the risky behaviors that adolescents and young adults are likely to engage in due to their heightened desire for sensation seeking is alcohol and drug use. The use of these substances has been shown to have serious negative consequences, including sleep deprivation or disruption, impaired academic engagement and performance, and reduced emotional regulation and increased interpersonal conflict (Lisdahl, Schollenbarger, Sagar, & Gruber, 2018).

According to the Monitoring the Future Study (Schulenberg et al., 2018), alcohol is the most commonly used substance in adolescence and young adulthood, with 85% of individuals age 19–28, 62% of high school seniors, 42% of tenth graders, and 23% of eighth graders having used it at least once in their lives. Unfortunately, a significant portion of individuals in these age groups report having used large amounts of alcohol (five or more drinks at one sitting) in the past two weeks—32% of 19–28 year olds, 17% of high school seniors, 10% of tenth graders and 4% of eighth graders. Furthermore, among 19–28 year olds, 41% had used an illicit drug at least once in the past year while 40%, 18%, and 13% of high school seniors, tenth graders and eighth graders, respectively, reported past-year use. The most commonly used illicit drug by far was marijuana, which about 1 in 13 19–28 year-olds and 1 in 17 high school seniors report smoking daily or near daily. Thus, it can be seen that many adolescents and young adults are putting powerful psychoactive substances in their bodies that can and do affect brain functioning and development.

Since adolescence and young adulthood is a time of increased risk taking, it is the time that most people experiment with alcohol and other drugs (Degenhardt et al., 2008). Because peer relationships become increasingly important during adolescence, individuals may use substances in an effort to appear socially competent and, upon entry into the university environment, to gain acceptance among new acquaintances (Angelone, Marcantonio, & Melillo, 2018). Schindler et al. (2005) point out that, although adolescents and young adults who use substances most often do so with their peers, these relationships generally are not stable and long lasting and cannot be considered close friendships. Rather, they argue that substance use, especially use that results in frequent and repeated intoxication, tends to disrupt relationships, thus interfering with the development of intimacy. Moreover, Angelone et al. (2018) point out that the increase of alcohol use during adolescence and young adulthood can result in serious negative impacts on self-esteem, body image, and levels of depression. In addition, substance use is associated with sexual victimization among young women. Those who have been victimized are likely to try to numb their emotions with more substances, thus placing themselves at increased risk of further victimization.

Although not every youth who tries a psychoactive substance will go on to develop problematic use, some portion who experiment will go on to use more regularly and to develop substance-related problems. Age of initiation is one of the important factors determining the transition from experimentation to use to abuse and dependency. For example, research has shown that while less than 3% of adults who report having tried marijuana *after* age 17 developed a cannabis-use disorder, more than 11% who report having tried it *before* the age of 17 developed a disorder (Substance Abuse and Mental Health Services Administration, 2014). Other research shows that the odds of developing alcohol-use disorder drops by 14% for each added year before use onset (Grant & Dawson, 1997).

Currently, addiction is thought of as both a disease of the brain (Ersche et al., 2012; Volkaw, 2005) and as an attachment disorder (e.g., Flores, 2001/2004; Unterrainer et al., 2017). I will start this section with a discussion of how the use of psychoactive substances affects the brain during adolescence and young adulthood. Then I will discuss how attachment is related to substance abuse in this age group.

Addiction and the Brain

As discussed in the previous chapter, there is a major reorganization of the brain during adolescence that improves its efficiency. In addition, the prefrontal areas of brain associated with judgment, impulse control, problem-solving, and decision-making do not completely mature until around the age of 25. Although it may be that young people do not suffer as much from alcohol hangovers and other negative social and physical effects as adults do, they definitely are at higher risk of substance-related neurocognitive impairment and development of substance-use disorders than either children or adults (Lisdahl et al., 2018; Unterrainer et al, 2017). That is, it appears that, for reasons that are yet unclear, adolescents are especially vulnerable to the toxic effects of both alcohol and marijuana (and probably other drugs as well) right at the time when they are most likely to experiment with them. The good news is, however, that it appears that the damage may be minimized if the individual can be motivated to maintain extended abstinence (Lisdahl et al., 2017).

Addiction and Attachment

Unterrainer et al. (2017) have shown that individuals who are addicted to multiple drugs show clear evidence of disordered attachment associated with diminished white matter in several areas of the brain. In addition, a meta-analysis of the literature concerning adolescent substance use and abuse shows that insecure attachment is a risk factor for the development of a substance-use disorder (Schindler & Broning, 2015). Interestingly, this review shows that secure attachment is positively associated with experimentation, suggesting that the *use* of substances during this life stage may be "related to the developmental task of learning to handle culturally accepted substances" (p. 307). However, the risk for developing substance *abuse* is about one third lower among securely attached adolescents compared to those who are insecurely attached.

Regarding relationships between specific attachment styles/dimensions and substance abuse, Schindler and Broning's (2015) meta-analysis shows that the dismissing attachment style is the one most frequently found among substance abusers in this age group, though both preoccupied and disorganized are not uncommon. An earlier study shows that among a sample of individuals in treatment for substance-use disorder, 61% reported that they were avoidant, while 27% and 12% reported being secure and anxious/ambivalent, respectively (Schindler et al., 2005). In addition, youths who were drug dependent tended to have a fearful attachment style, and both the severity of their addiction and the likelihood of their having a co-morbid psychiatric disorder were positively related to how fearful they were.

Schindler et al. (2009) also show that different attachment dimensions and styles are related to individuals' choice of substances, their choices being driven by the specific emotional effect desired and the emotional effect desired being driven by attachment strategies. For example, dismissing attachment is associated with both alcohol and cannabis use, while fearful attachment is associated with heroin use. In regards to opiates such as heroin, they suggest that these substances may be "the most efficient 'attachment substitutes' and the most attractive substances for individuals with very insecure patterns of attachment" (Schindler & Broning, 2015, p. 306) because their euphoric and sedating effects mimic the soothing effects associated with a mother's provision of a safe haven. Indeed, a study by Schindler et al. (2009) found that three quarters of the opioid abusers in their sample reported a fearful attachment style (with the remaining 25% having a preoccupied style). Given that opioid addiction is currently a topic of extreme interest in communities across the United States, substance abuse practitioners may be interested in treating opiate abuse from an attachment perspective.

Schindler and Broning (2015) argue that since the majority of individuals with substance-use issues report attachment avoidance, it is likely that they are using substances in an effort to self-medicate the emotional distress associated with childhood sexual abuse, maltreatment, neglect, loss, or parental mental illness. Lacking other coping skills, substance use may help those who have suffered trauma manage the symptoms of PTSD. Similarly, Mikulincer and Shaver (2016) suggest that individuals with attachment avoidance may use substances to help them detach from emotional and psychological distress while those with attachment anxiety may use them to "pacify or tranquilize their distress and block the uncontrollable spread of anxious ruminations and memories" (p. 433). Unfortunately, however, although substances may help individuals to avoid negative thoughts and affects, they also keep the individual from doing the work needed to resolve their trauma (Schindler et al., 2005).

In summary, substance abuse and behavioral addictions are likely to have their start during adolescence and to be rooted in early attachment insecurity. As mentioned in Chapter 17, adolescence is Erikson's (1963) *Identity vs. Role Diffusion* developmental stage in which teens who do not discover who they are and where they are going tend to drift into problematic behavioral patterns that do not support success in forming close relationships in emerging adulthood. Therefore, it is clearly important for mental health practitioners and researchers to find effective prevention and early intervention programs that can work to minimize the damage caused by substance use and abuse and maximize the probability that youths will develop to their full potential.

Violence Against Self and Others

Research shows that violence is highly prevalent among adolescents and young adults. Although the leading cause of death among adolescents is accidents (Minino, 2010), suicide is the third-leading cause of death among children 10 to 14 years old and the second-leading cause among those 15 to 25 years old (Stone et al., 2017). Moreover, homicide is the third-leading cause of death among individuals age 10 to 24 (David-Ferdon et al., 2016). Almost one in four youths in grades 9 through 12 reported having been in a physical fight within the past year (males, 28.4%; females, 16.5%). Over 16% reported having carried a weapon (gun, knife, or club) on one or more days in the past month (males, 24.3%; females, 7.5%), while 5% reported specifically having carried a gun (males, 8.7%; females, 1.6%). These authors also reported that the leading cause of death (48.2 per 100,000) among African American adolescents (ages 10–24) was homicide, and that homicide was the second-leading cause of death (9.6 per 100,000) for Hispanic youths. In comparison, only 2.6 per 100,000 white youths died by homicide. In addition, over a half a million youths ended up in the emergency room due to injuries sustained from physical assault. It is clear, then, that violence is a serious issue among adolescents and young adults (Center for Disease Control and Prevention, 2016).

Although there appears to be a rise in incidents of violence during adolescence followed by a continuing decrease from later young adulthood through middle and late adulthood, the vast majority of adolescents never engage in any antisocial behavior or commit a violent act (Loeber & Farrington, 2012). Duke, Pettingell, McMorris, and Borowsky (2010) have shown that the adolescents most likely to become violent are those who have suffered one or more adverse incidents during childhood (most commonly, physical or sexual abuse, or alcohol or drug use by a household family member). In addition, the more adverse incidents a youth has suffered, the more likely he or she is (an increase of 35% to 144% with each added adversity) to engage in delinquent behavior, bullying, physical fighting, dating violence, weapon carrying, self-harm, and suicidal ideation or attempts.

The antecedents to youth violence include a broad array of individual, family, and social factors (see Table 19.2). French (2008) points out that there is a genetic component to antisocial behaviors in which certain differences in gene characteristics are associated with increased risk of violent behavior. However, he emphasizes that among individuals with this gene characteristic, *only* those growing up in particular environmental conditions (esp. maltreatment) go on to develop antisocial behaviors. Thus, violence appears to be inextricably linked to the social environment.

Duke et al. (2010) found that youths living in poverty with low parental supervision and responsiveness, family mental health issues, or family conflict were more likely to have suffered adverse incidents than children in better circumstances did. Moreover, harsh physical punishment, residential transience, or neighborhood violence were also associated with more adverse incidents. In addition, they noted that children who suffer physical or sexual abuse are at high risk of developing insecure attachment, hopelessness and depression, anger, and a perceived need for self-protection. One group of researchers has suggested that violence among

TABLE 19.2   Risk Factors Associated with Youth Violence

Family Factors:
- Harsh, rejection parents
- Parental domestic violence
- Child abuse/neglect
- Chaotic family environment
- Inconsistent discipline
- Poor parental monitoring of child aggression
- History of traumatic separation from caretakers

Neurobiological Factors:
- Neurocognitive deficits
- Perinatal complication
- Genetic risks
- Low resting heart rate
- Up-regulated HPA system

Academic Achievement:
- Poor school readiness
- Poor school attachment
- Low GPA

Individual Characteristics:
- History of aggressiveness or impulse control issues
- Psychopathy
- Narcissism; entitlement
- Need for power and control
- Lack of empathy

Social Rejection
- Exclusion
- Devaluation
- Disrespect
- Bullying

Other Factors:
- Media violence
- Access to guns
- Substance use and abuse
- Poverty and social distrust

Source: Bushman, B. J., Newman, K., Calvert, S. L., Downey, G., Dredze, M., Gottfredson, M., . . Webster, D. W. (2016). Youth violence: What we know and what we need to know. American Psychologist, 71(1), 17-39.

adolescents results from a cascade of negative circumstances starting with social disadvantage in childhood (e.g., low socioeconomic status, maternal depression) that would make harsh or inconsistent parenting more likely. This kind of parenting would then lead to deficits in cognitive and social functioning that would result in academic failure and the development of behavioral/conduct problems and violence (Dodge, Greenberg, Malone, & Conduct Problems Prevention Research Group, 2008).

CLASS DISCUSSION

Are there experiences in Jet's life that might predispose him to develop violent behavior in adolescence or young adulthood? What about Luke?

According to Bushman et al. (2016), the vast majority of youth violence occurs among individuals who live in urban areas rife with crime and poverty. Many of these youths are members of street gangs, and the violent acts that they commit either target specific individuals in an effort to protect their "turf" or are attempts at self- or group-protection. Knives and clubs are, of course, easy to come by, but guns are also surprisingly easy to find, even for youths under the age of 18, obtained through the black market, a gift from a friend or family member, or theft.

Self-Harm

Research indicates that most people who intentionally hurt themselves do so between the ages of 11 and 25 (Rossouw, 2018). Children in out-of-home placements and those in the juvenile justice system are at increased risk of self-harm, and girls are at much higher (three times) risk than boys. It is important for mental health practitioners to have their eyes wide open to the possibility of self-harm among the adolescents who come to them because research has shown that clinically depressed adolescents who engage in non-suicidal self-injury are at increased risk of subsequent suicide attempts (Asarnow et al., 2011; Wilkinson, Kelvin, Roberts, Dubocka, & Goodyer, 2011).

Yurgulen-Todd (2007) show that the limbic areas become active in adolescents who read emotionally arousing material, suggesting that they are having a subjective emotional experience; the same activation does not occur in adults. Rossouw (2018) suggests that this emotional reaction to news about another adolescent's extreme behavior (e.g., suicide, homicide) may be responsible for self-harm or copycat reactions. She notes that adolescents who get caught up in this ripple effect are not simply attention-seeking but may have an overwhelming need to discharge intolerable levels of emotional discomfort by acting out. She notes that these adolescents are often unable to explain why they have acted out because they don't understand it themselves. Rossouw argues that when an adolescent's capacity to mentalize has been compromised,

> self-related negative cognitions are experienced with great intensity, leading to both intense depression and an urgent need for distraction. Furthermore, when nonmentalizing leads to social isolation … engaging in self-harm and manipulative behavior may restore reconnection. … When mentalization of social experience fails, impulsive (poorly regulated) behaviors and subjective states triggering self-harm become prominent. (p. 423)

Recall that the development of the capacity to mentalize is dependent on the healthy functioning of the smart vagus. Healthy functioning of the smart vagus is, in turn, dependent on adequate parenting that includes the sensitivity, responsiveness, and contingent communication associated with secure attachment (see Chapter 4). Nunes and Mota (2017) have shown that adolescents whose parents are either permissive (overly indulgent, poor limit setting and discipline) or authoritarian (harsh punishment, low communication, low warmth) tend to have relatively low quality emotional bonds with their parents. Thus, it is thought that they are more likely to have suicidal ideation than those whose emotional bonds are strengthened by an authoritative parenting style (emotionally supportive, flexible, rewarding rather than punishing).

School Shooters

There is a subset of violent youths that is of particular interest to researchers, mental health providers, educators, and the general public right now—school shooters. The number of mass shootings in schools almost doubled between 1981 and 2010 (Agnich, 2015). School shooters have killed 138 people and injured another 438 just since the 2012 mass shooting at Sandy Hook Elementary School (Patel, 2018).

French (2008) has pointed out that there are two subcategories of aggression, "hot" and "cold." "Hot" aggression generally arises in response to real or perceived threat or frustration. It is often driven by a fearful (fight/flight) overreaction to adults or peers the individual believes have hostile intentions towards them. These individuals tend to be highly impulsive and have a history of physical abuse, social instability, or early mental health problems. In contrast, individuals who engage in "cold" aggression tend to have little or no sympathetic arousal, do not act impulsively, and may show no evidence of fear, frustration, or anger when they act. Instead, they act aggressively "in order to obtain a desired goal or favorable outcome whether for food, property or social status … [and their actions are] organized, patterned, goal-directed and controlled" (p. 43). School shooters' actions would appear to fall into this "cold" aggression category.

Bushman et al. (2016) suggest that there are significant differences between adolescents and young adults who commit mass violence on school campuses and those who commit street violence (See Table 19.3). Other researchers who have explored factors associated with school shooters have discovered an array of personal, family, and school/societal factors (See Table 19.4). Of particular interest to the subjects being addressed in this book are the personal and family factors associated with school shooters. A recent review of the literature concerning school shooters shows that no studies to date have explored relationships between infant/early childhood attachment and school shootings during adolescence/young adulthood (Horton, unpublished manuscript). This gap in the literature is surprising given the number of victims involved, the pain and suffering of their families, friends, and associates, and the fear generated among the public at large. However, given the list of personal and family factors shown in Table 19.4, it can be seen that many of the personal mental health issues found among school shooters can be directly related to failed attachment. Furthermore, the family factors presented in that table showing unresponsive, insensitive, or inconsistent parenting can easily be seen as responsible for that attachment failure.

TABLE 19.3   Violence Among School Shooters vs. Street Shooters

STREET SHOOTERS	SCHOOL SHOOTERS
Lower SES	Middle class
Urban	Suburban or rural
Minority	White
Male	Male
Social inclusion; many friends (gangs)	Social exclusion; few friends (wannabe, goth, geek, etc.)
No suicidal ideation	Suicidal ideation and attempts
Self- or group protection	Revenge, fame/notoriety
Know their victims personally	Don't know their victims personally
Alcohol/drugs before violence	No alcohol/drugs before violence

Source: Bushman, B. J., Newman, K., Calvert, S. L., Downey, G., Dredze, M., Gottfredson, M., . . Webster, D. W. (2016). Youth violence: What we know and what we need to know. American Psychologist, 71(1), 17–39.

TABLE 19.4 Personal, Family and School/Societal Risk Factors for School Shooters

Personal:
- Depressive symptomatology[1, 5, 6, 7, 8]
- Anger management[6, 8]
- Anxiety[1]
- Abuse/neglect[2]
- Narcissism, lack of empathy, need for power/fame[2, 5, 8]
- Victim of bullying, teasing, humiliation[5, 6, 7]
- Rejection/marginalization, disrespect[1, 3, 6]
- Paranoia (sensitivity, shame)[3]
- Psychosis[1, 4]
- Trauma[2, 4]
- Developmental disorder[1]
- Personality disorder[1]
- Low self-esteem[1, 6]
- Moving from a small school to larger school with fewer student resources[10]

Family:
- Turbulent parent/child relationship[8]
- Permissive parenting style; parent accepts child's pathology or misconduct[8]
- Lack of imtimacy[8]
- Low supervision[2, 8]
- Divorce or other broken family[6]
- Parental mental health issues, substance abuse, incarceration[6]

School/Societal:
- School size and student support[10]
- Perceived favoritism of others by school administrators and teachers[9]
- Problems with teachers resulting in suspensions/expulsions[2]
- Culture of masculine violence[7, 9]
- Availability of guns[2, 7]
- Failure of school/community to identify and address problems[7]

Sources: [1]Bondu & Scheithauer (2014/2015); [2]Bushman et al. (2016); [3]Dutton, D. G., White, K. R., & Fogarty, D. (2013); [4]Langman (2013); [5]Leary, M. R., Kowalski, R. M., Smith, L., & Phillips, S. (2003); [6]Nader, K. & Nader, W. (2012); [7]Newman, K. S., Foz, C., Harding, D., Mehta, J., & Froth, W. (2004); [8]O'Toole (2000); [9]Tonso (2009); [10]Baird, Roellke, & Zeifman (2017)

For example, Sitnick et al. (2017) have found in their research comparing adolescents arrested for violent crimes to adolescents arrested for nonviolent crimes that the violent youths were significantly more likely to have had harsh parenting and low self-regulation during childhood. In addition, behavioral problems identified among children as young as six years old have been shown to be related to violent behavior in adolescence (Brody, et al., 2001; Kokko, Tremblay, Lacourse, Nagin, & Vitar, 2006). It is logical to assume that problematic behavior at age six did not just suddenly appear among children in this age group. However, researchers have not yet conducted the needed longitudinal research to show that attachment problems in infancy could be related to extreme violence such as mass school shootings in adolescence. As Sroufe (2005) argues, the quality of the attachment relationship formed in infancy is the foundation for the development of emotional regulation, and dysregulation arises directly out of those earliest experiences. It might well be that school shooters haven't received a foundation for adequate self-regulation during infancy and early childhood so that they can weather the trials and tribulations of school life. Madfis (2017) notes that, although "school rampage perpetrators lack any single profile. … It is simply not the case that everyone in the population is equally likely to become a rampage shooter" (p. 26). There is apparently some combination of genetic and environmental factors that cause a "perfect storm" of conditions that push a young person to make the tragic decision to kill as many people as he can. Take a moment to read the on-going story of Jet in Case Study 19.1 to see how this situation might arise in a young man's life.

CASE STUDY 19.1: JET COMES UNDONE

Jet has just entered high school and is attending a school that has many more students than the middle school he attended before. He was hoping that things would go better for him at the new school, that he would make some friends, maybe play on the football team. However, several of the kids from his old middle school have moved over into the high school with him, and they are again teasing him, calling him or "Susie" or some other girl's name. This is particularly humiliating since he is interested in a girl in his math class named Susie and becomes enraged when he sees that she hears what those boys are saying. However, he keeps his rage to himself, gets on his bicycle, and skips school for the rest of the day. When Luke comes home that afternoon, Jet beats him up and tells him that if he tells their mom, he'll kill him. Luke doesn't tell.

The next day, he approaches Susie to say hello, but she turns her back on him, giggling with her girlfriends. He thinks he hears one of them say "gay." Later that day, he finds out that he had not made the football team and watches as two of his tormentors celebrate that they have made it onto the team. Depressed and angry, he goes to his English class where he thinks his teacher is smirking at him when he can't answer a question. Jumping up, he throws his desk against the wall and curses and threatens the teacher. He is suspended from school for a week.

Jet feels that this suspension is unfair since he has seen football players get away with worse. When his mother asks him what happened, he takes a butcher knife out of a kitchen drawer and says he's going to carve her heart out. She runs from the house and drives away, returning two hours later. She says nothing to him on her return, closing the door to her bedroom and locking it. Every time he goes past it to the bathroom during the night, he bangs on it just to wake her up. The next morning, there's a note on the kitchen table saying that she's going to the doctor's and will see him later. She wishes him a happy day.

Over the course of the school year, Jet starts hanging out with several boys who like to skip school and smoke weed. The boys who had teased him now avoid him. Girls look away when he passes. His teachers are uneasy about him but too busy to try to find out what is going on with him. He does enough schoolwork to get by but spends most of his time at home on the computer playing violent video games and roaming the internet. The day he turns 18, he buys a semi-automatic pistol and boxes of ammunition and hides them in his closet.

Three days later, his mother dies from pancreatic cancer.

He and his brother move in with a family friend. He lasts a month there before being told to leave after he threatened to rape the friend's 10-year-old daughter because she had laughed at him. Leaving his brother behind, he moves in with one of his friends who lets him sleep on his sofa. He is boiling with grief and anger. He feels powerless and invisible. It is all so unfair! Three weeks before graduation, he takes his gun, rides his bicycle to school, walks into the football locker room and opens fire. He kills 12 members of the football team, the coach, and a custodian who happened to be cleaning the room. Then he gets on his bicycle and rides away in the chaos. Later, the police would see that he had spent months researching how the Columbine killers had planned their 1999 mass assault on classmates and teachers. Asked why he did it, he says, "They deserved it, and I hope they burn in hell."

What a sad ending to such a sad case. Had Jet's adoptive parents, teachers, and school administrators, and others who came in contact with him out in the community been able to recognize and address his disturbed behaviors early on, his and his victims' life trajectories may have been entirely different. Jet was not a "bad" boy; he simply had neurological pathways laid down in the first two years of life that set him up for a profoundly dysfunctional response this "perfect storm" of events. Yes, Jet is ultimately responsible for his behavior, and the court system will determine what happens from this point on. However, as mental health professionals working in communities in which individuals who are faced with circumstances similar to those of Jet, it might be valuable for us to think about which individuals and systems could have intervened over the 18 or so years that it took to get him to the point that he acted in the way he did.

Summary

In this chapter, two very problematic challenges that face adolescents and young adults were discussed—addiction and violence. Addiction has been characterized as both a brain disorder and an attachment disorder, and substance use and abuse is common in these age groups. As discussed in earlier sections of this book, early attachment insecurity can result in the formation of an inadequate reward system, an over-reactive HPA system, and/or an underactive emotion regulation system, which can then set the individual up for substance abuse and co-morbid disorders. These effects are exacerbated by the normative redevelopment of brain circuitry that occurs during adolescence that promotes sensation-seeking and poor decision-making. In addition, addiction causes disruptions in the formation of new attachments as the individual enters adulthood, a time during which it is important to establish close romantic and work relationships and friendships that will provide needed social support. Therefore, preventing the adolescents' initiation of substance use as much as possible until after the brain has matured is a worthy goal for mental health professionals.

Violence is also common among adolescents and young adults. Homicide is the second-leading cause of death among adolescents, and suicide is the third-leading cause. Numerous factors influence rates of violence, including individual, family, school, and social factors. Of course, attachment insecurity is an important influence in violence against both self and others. Moreover, although mass shootings are relatively rare, they are stark reminders of how badly things can go wrong. The research discussed above suggests that, although no longitudinal evidence yet exists for a connection between early attachment problems and later extreme violence, the suspicion is that there is such a connection. If mental health practitioners can intervene in dysfunctional families in the first few years of a child's life so that secure attachment and a good social engagement system are allowed to form, it might go a long way toward minimizing violence and maximizing healthy functioning.

Epilogue

Human beings are profoundly social animals. We are creatures of longing—longing for both differentiation and linkage, aloneness and togetherness. We need to be ourselves at the same time that we need to be with others. We have a right brain that needs to be linked with our left brain so that we can understand and respond to the world we find ourselves in. These linked but differentiated hemispheres let us see the new as new and the old as old so that we can see the present as the present, the past as the past, and the future as what may or may not come next. Our brains are like a set of nesting dolls. The innermost doll is our extremely ancient brain that reacts to the world reflexively by freezing, running, fighting, or approaching with no need for thought or feeling. Surrounding that brain, and linked to it, is our emotional brain that lets us connect with others and read their feelings, and to work together to survive. Surrounding both of those brains, and linked to them, is the newest and still evolving brain that makes us human. Now we can think and compare and reflect and decide and know, and know that we know.

Our brain's basic architecture is determined by a template that nature has provided in our genes. However, its ultimate functioning is determined by the dynamic interaction between the individual and his or her physical and social environments. Speaking about Darwin's idea of survival of the fittest, Cozolino (2008) says, "For Darwin, fitness isn't a matter of physical fitness, but the goodness of fit between an animal and its environment" (p. 23). As social animals, how we fit with others in our environment is of primary importance to individual survival and to the survival of the species. As mental health practitioners, then, finding ways to help people to find and sustain better relationships is at the root of our effectiveness.

The very earliest, and therefore the primary, influence within the social environment is the relationship between a mother and her baby. This relationship is the foundation upon which all future relationships will be built, and it promotes the fundamental linkages between the enskulled and the embodied brains, between the left and the right hemispheres, between thought, emotion, and reaction. Thus, it is fundamental to individual human behavior within society, and it remains of central importance to both mental and physical health throughout the lifespan.

This book has provided an overview of how the developing brain and early attachment experiences affect human behavior during the time before a baby is born until he or she reaches adulthood. Taking a person-in-environment perspective, I have identified important brain regions and systems and explained how early relationships, even those relationships that occur before a baby is conceived (perhaps even *generations* before he or she is conceived) determine the structure and functioning of his or her brain. The majority of the connections in the brain occur in the context of early attachment experiences and are in place by age three. Because of the brain's ability to change in response to the demands of the environment (i.e., neuroplasticity), the attachment style developed in these first few years is not etched in stone. That is, later experiences can form new neural pathways. However, because these earliest patterns are laid down in implicit memory, they can be difficult to change and are likely to persist into adulthood, either providing integration and resiliency or blocking healthy and mutually satisfying connectedness and support.

As this book has hopefully made clear, secure attachment builds a brain that works efficiently and promotes adaptive responses to stress. In essence, securely attached children use the adults close to them to manage their stress until they are capable of doing this on their own reliably as they mature through childhood and into adulthood. In contrast, insecure attachment builds a brain that performs at less-than-optimal levels and decreases adaptive self-regulation and creativity; insecurely attached children are, basically, in a state of chronic arousal and therefore are likely to react to stress in maladaptive ways. Without corrective attachment experiences, this situation is likely to last for the remainder of the individual's life. Therefore, it is important for mental health practitioners to understand the pervasive effects of attachment, both their own and their clients', and to use this understanding to inform their interventions and to strengthen their compassion for their clients and themselves.

If my own experience of learning about attachment and neurobiology is any indication, the information in this book can transform your understanding of why clients with mental health problems have those problems and act them out how they act them out. Moreover, it can point the way for appropriate and effective prevention and intervention modalities and techniques. I hope that my efforts to assemble and make sense of the literature on neurobiology, its relationship to attachment, and the mental health issues that arise out of inadequate neural integration will inspire you just as I have been inspired.

References

AAP Council on Communications and Media (2016). Media and young minds. *Pediatrics, 138*(5), 1–6.

Agnich, L. (2015). A comparative analysis of attempted and completed school-based mass murder attacks. *American Journal of Criminal Justice, 40*, 1–22. Doi: https://doi.org/10.1007/s12103-014-9239-5

Aimone, J. B., Deng, W., & Gage, F. H. (2010). Adult neurogenesis: integrating theories and separating functions. *Trends in Cognitive Sciences, 14*(7), 325–337. Doi: https://doi.org/10.1016/j.tics.2010.04.003

Ainsworth, M. D. S. (1963). The development of infant-mother interaction among the Ganda. In B. M. Foss (Ed.), *Determinants of infant behavior* (Vol. 2, pp. 67–112). New York, NY: Wiley.

Ainsworth, M. D. S., Blehar, M. C., Waters, E., & Wall, S. (1978). *Patterns of attachment: A psychological study of the Strange Situation.* Hillsdale, NJ: Lawrence Erlbaum.

Alexander, R. (2015). How to protect children from internet predators: A phenomenological study. *Annual Review of Cybertherapy and Telemedicine, 13*, 82–88.

Alexander, S. A., Fusco, C., & Frolich K. L. (2015). 'You have to do 60 minutes of physical activity per day ... I saw it on TV': Children's constructions of play in the context of Canadian public health discourse of playing for health. *Sociology of Health & Illness, 37*(2), 227–240. Doi: https://doi.org/10.1111/1467-9566.12179

Alhusen, J. L. (2008). A literature update on maternal-fetal attachment. *Journal of Obstetric, Gynecologic, & Neonatal Nursing: Clinical Scholarship for the Care of Women, Childbearing Families, & Newborns, 37*(3), 315–328. Doi: https://doi.org/10.1111/j.1552-6909.2008.00241.x

Allen, J. G. (2004). *Coping with trauma: Hope through understanding* (2nd ed.). Washington, DC: American Psychiatric Publishing.

American Psychiatric Association (2013). *Diagnostic and statistical manual of mental disorders* (5th ed.). Washington, DC: Author.

Amico, A. D. (2018). The use of technology in the promotion of childhood emotional intelligence: The multimedia program "Developing Emotional Intelligence." *International Journal of Emotional Education, Special Issue, 10*(1), 47–67.

Ammaniti, M. & Gallese, V. (2014). *The birth of intersubjectivity: Psychodynamics, neurobiology and the self.* New York, NY: W. W. Norton & Co.

Anderson, C. & Cacola, P. (2017). Implications of preterm birth for maternal mental health and infant development. *MCN: The American Journal of Maternal/Child Nursing, 42*(2), 108–114. Doi: https://doi.org/10.1097/nmc.0000000000000311

Angelone, D. J., Marcantonio, T., & Millilo, J. (2018). An evaluation of adolescent and young adult (re) victimization experiences: Problematic substance use and negative consequences. *Violence Against Women, 24*(5), 586–602. Doi: https://doi.org/10.1177/1077801217710001

Ardell, J. L. (2004). Intrathoracic neuronal regulation of cardiac function. In J. A. Armour and J. L. Ardell (Eds.), *Basic and clinical neurocardiology* (pp. 118–152). New York, NY: Oxford University Press.

Arnett, J. J. (2000). Emerging adulthood: A theory of development from the late teens through the twenties. *American Psychologist, 55*(5), 469–480. Doi: https://doi.org/10.1037//0003-066x.55.5.469

Arseth, A. K., Kroger, J., Martinussen, M., & Marcia, J. E. (2009). Meta-analytic studies of identity status and the relational issues of attachment and intimacy. *Identity: An International Journal of Theory and Research, 9*(1), 1–32, DOI: 10.1080/15283480802579532

Asarnow, J. R., Porta, G. Spirito, A., Emslie, G., Clarke, G. Wagner, K. D., ... Brent, D. (2011). Suicide attempts and nonsuicidal self-injury in the treatment of resistant depression in adolescents: Findings from the TORDIA study. *Journal of the American Academy of Child and Adolescent Psychiatry, 50*(8), 772–781. Doi: https://doi.org/10.1016/j.jaac.2011.04.003

Assini-Meytin, L. C. & Green, K. M. (2015). Long-term consequences of adolescent parenthood among African-American Urban youth: A propensity score matching approach. *Journal of Adolescent Health, 56*, 529–535. Doi: https://doi.org/10.1016/j.jadohealth.2015.01.005

Arseth, A. K., Kroger, J., Martinussen, M., & Marcia, J. E. (2007). Meta-analytic studies of identity status and the relational issues of attachment and intimacy. *Identity: An International Journal of Theory and Research, 9*(1), 1–32. Doi: https://doi.org/10.1080/15283480802579532

Babenko, O., Kovalchuk, I., & Metz, A. S. (2015). Stress induced perinatal and transgenerational epigenetic programming of brain development and mental health. *Neuroscience and Biobehavioral Reviews, 48*, 70–91. Doi: https://doi.org/10.1016/j.neubiorev.2014.11.013

Badenoch, B. (2008). *Being a brainwise therapist: A practical guide to interpersonal neurobiology.* New York, NY: W. W. Norton & Co.

Badenoch, B. & Kestly, T. (2015). Exploring the neuroscience of healing play at every age. In D. A. Crenshaw and A. L. Stewart (Eds.), *Play therapy: A comprehensive guide to theory and practice* (pp. 524–538). New York, NY: Guilford Press.

Bailey, J. O. & Bailenson, J. N. (2017). Considering virtual reality in children's lives. *Journal of Children and Media, 11*(1), 107–113. Doi: https://doi.org/10.1080/17482798.2016.1268779

Baird, A. A., Roellke, E. V., & Zeifman, D. M. (2017). Alone and adrift: The association between mass school shootings, school size, and student support. *The Social Science Journal, 54*, 261–270. Doi: https://doi.org/10.1016/j.soscij.2017.01.009

Barrasso-Catanzaro, C. & Eslinger, P. J. (2016). Neurological bases of executive function and socio-emotional development: Typical and atypical brain changes. *Family Relations, 65*(February), 108–119. Doi: https://doi.org/10.1111/fare.12175

Bartholomew, K. & Horowitz, L. M. (1991). Attachment styles among young adults: A test of a four-category model. *Journal of Personality and Social Psychology, 61*(2) 224–244. Doi: https://doi.org/10.1037//0022-3514.61.2.226

Bassett, D. R., John, D., Conger, S. A., Fitzhugh, E. C., & Coe, D. P. (2015). *Journal of Physical Activity and Health, 12*, 1102–1111. Doi: https://doi.org/10.1123/jpah.2014-0050

Bastian, A. (2018). Children's brains are different. In D. J. Linden (Ed.), *Think tank: Forty neuroscientists explore the biological roots of human experience.* (pp. 40–44). New Haven, CT: Yale University Press.

Beduna, K. N. & Perrone-McGovern, K. M. (2019). Recalled childhood bullying victimization and shame in adulthood: The influence of attachment security, self-compassion, and emotion regulation. *Traumatology, 25*(1), 21–32. Doi: https://doi.org/10.1037/trm0000162

Benoit, D. (2004). Infant-parent attachment: Definition, types, antecedents, measurement and outcome. *Paediatric and Child Health, 9*(8), 541–545. Doi: https://doi.org/10.1093/pch/9.8.541

Berridge, K. C. & Robinson, T. E. (2016). Linking, wanting and the incentive-sensitization theory of addiction. *American Psychologist, 71*(8), 670–679. Doi: https://doi.org/10.1037/amp0000059

Birnbaum, G. E. (2015). Like a horse and carriage? The dynamic interplay of attachment and sexuality during relationship development. *European Psychologist, 20*(4), 265–274. Doi: https://doi.org/10.1027/1016-9040/a000237

Blair, C. (2002). School readiness: Integrating cognition and emotion in a neurological conceptualization of children's functioning at school entry. *American Psychologist, 57*(2), 111–127. Doi: https://doi.org/10.1037//0003-066x.57.2.111

Bo, S., Sharp, C., Fonagy, P., & Kongerslev, M. (2017). Hypermentalizing, attachment, and epistemic trust in adolescent BPD: Clinical illustrations. *Personality Disorders: Theory, Research and Treatment, 8*(2), 172–182. Doi: https://doi.org/10.1037/per0000161

Bollas, C. (1987). *The shadow of the object: Psychoanalysis of the unthought known.* New York, NY: Columbia University Press.

Bondu, R. & Scheithauer, H. (2015). Narcissistic symptoms in German school shooters. *International Journal of Offender Therapy and Comparative Criminology, 59*(4), 1520–1535. Doi: https://doi.org/10.1177/0306624X14544155

Booth, P. B., Lender, D., & Lindaman, S. (2018). Playing with someone who loves you: Creating safety and joyful parent-child connection with theraplay. In T. Marks-Tarlow, M. Solomon, and D. Siegel (Eds.), *Play and creativity in psychotherapy.* New York, NY: W. W. Norton & Co.

Born, J. (2010). Slow-wave sleep and the consolidation of long-term memory. *World Journal of Biological Psychiatry, 11*(1), 16–21. Doi: https://doi.org/10.3109/15622971003637637

Boucher, M. & Sandhu, P. (2013). The neurobiology of adolescent addiction. In, R. Rosner (Ed.), *Clinical handbook of adolescent addiction*. (pp. 78–87). Hoboken, NJ: John Wiley & Sons.

Bowlby, J. (1969/1982). *Attachment and loss: Vol. 1, Attachment*. New York, NY: Basic Books.

Bowlby, J. (1973). *Attachment and loss: Vol. 2, Separation: Anxiety and anger*. New York, NY: Basic Books.

Bowlby, J. (1980). *Attachment and loss*. New York, NY: Basic Books.

Bowlby, J. (1988). *A secure base: Parent-child attachment and healthy human development*. New York, NY: Basic Books.

Brack, K. E. (2015). The heart's "little brain" controlling cardiac function in the rabbit. *Experimental Physiology, 100*(4), 348–353. Doi: https://doi.org/10.1113/expphysiol.2014.080168

Brannigan, R., Cannon, M., Tanskanen, A., Huttonen, M. O., Leacy, F. P., & Clarke, M. C. (2019). The association between maternal stress during pregnancy and offspring clinically diagnosed psychiatric disorders. *Acta Psychiatrica Scandinavica, Jan. 4*, no pagination specified. Doi: https://doi.org/10.1111/acps.12996

Bravo, J. A., Forsythe, P. Chew, M. V., Escaravage, E., Savignac H. M., Dinan, T. G., Bienenstock, J., & Cryan, J. F. (2011). Ingestion of lactobacillus strain regulates emotional behavior and central GABA receptor expression in a mouse via the vagus nerve. *PNAS Proceedings from the National Academy of Sciences of the United States of America, 108*(38), 16050–16055. Doi: https://doi.org/10.1073/pnas.1102999108

Brennen, K. A., Clark, C. L., & Shaver, P. R. (1998). Self-report measurement of adult attachment: An integrative overview. In, J. A. Simpson and W. S. Rholes (Eds.), *Attachment theory and close relationships*. (pp. 46–76). New York, NY: Guilford Press.

Brez, C. & Sheets, V. (2017). Classroom benefits of recess. *Learning Environments Research, 20*, 433–445. Doi: https://doi.org/10.1007/s10984-017-9237-x

Brisch, K. & Hollerbach, J. (2018). B.A.S.E.—Babywatching: An attachment-based program to promote sensitivity and empathy and counter fear and aggression. In H. Steele and M. Steele (Eds.), *Handbook of attachment-based interventions* (pp. 339–359). New York, NY: Guilford Press.

Brody, G. H., Ge, X., Conger, R. D., Gibbons, F. X., Murry, M. V., Gerrard, M., & Simmons, R. L. (2001). The influence of neighborhood disadvantage, collective socialization, and parenting on African American children's affiliation with deviant peers. *Child Development, 72*(4), 1231–1246. Doi: https://doi.org/10.1111/1467-8624.00344

Brown, S. & Eberle, M. (2018). A closer look at play. In T. Marks-Tarlow, M. Solomon, and D. J. Siegel (Eds.), *Play & creativity in psychotherapy*. (pp. 21–38). New York, NY: W. W. Norton & Co.

Brummelte, S. & Galea, L. A. M. (2016). Postpartum depression: Etiology, treatment and consequences for maternal care. *Hormones and Behavior, 77*, 153–166. Doi: https://doi.org/10.1016/j.yhbeh.2015.08.008

Budell, L., Jackson, P., & Rainville, P. (2010). Brain responses to facial expressions of pain: Emotional or motor mirroring? *NeuroImage, 53*, 355–363. Doi: https://doi.org/10.1016/j.neuroimage.2010.05.037

Bushman, B. J., Newman, K., Calvert, S. L., Downey, G., Dredze, M., Gottfredson, M., . . Webster, D. W. (2016). Youth violence: What we know and what we need to know. *American Psychologist, 71*(1), 17–39. Doi: https://doi.org/10.1037/a0039687

Campbell, S. B., Halperin, J. M., & Sonuga-Barke, E. J. S. (2014). A developmental perspective on attention-deficit/hyperactivity disorder (ADHD. In M. Lewis and K. D. Rudolph (Eds.), *Handbook of developmental psychopathology* (pp. 427–448). New York, NY: Springer Science+Business Media. Doi: https://doi.org/10.1007/978-1-4614-9608-3_22

Cantle, A. (2013). Alleviating the impact of stress and trauma in the neonatal unit and beyond. *Infant Observation, 16*(3), 257–269. Doi: https://doi.org/10.1080/13698036.2013.852723

Carter, C. S. & Porges, S. W. (2011). The neurobiology of social bonding and attachment. In J. Decety and J. T. Cacioppo (Eds.), *The Oxford handbook of social neuroscience* (pp. 151–163). New York, NY: Oxford University Press.

Carver, K., Joyner, K., & Udry, J. R. (2003). National estimates of adolescent romantic relationships. In P. Florsheim (Ed.), *Adolescent romantic relations and sexual behavior: Theory, research and practical applications* (pp. 23–56). Mahwah, NJ: Lawrence Erlbaum Associates.

Cassidy, J., Erlich, K. B., & Sherman, L. J. (2014). Child-parent attachment and response to threat: A move from the level of representation. In M. Mikulincer and P. Shaver (Eds.), *Mechanisms of social connection: From brain to group* (pp. 125–143). Washington, DC: American Psychological Association.

Center for Disease Control and Prevention (2016). *Youth violence: Facts at a Glance*. Retrieved from https://www.cdc.gov/violenceprevention/pdf/yv-datasheet.pdf

Center for Disease Control and Prevention (2018a). *Data and statistics on children's mental health*. Retrieved from https://www.cdc.gov/childrensmentalhealth/data.html

Center for Disease Control and Prevention (2018b). *Developmental disabilities*. Retrieved from https://www.cdc.gov/ncbddd/developmentaldisabilities/facts.html

Center for Disease Control and Prevention (2018c). *Infertility*. Retrieved from https://www.cdc.gov/nchs/fastats/infertility.htm

Center for Disease Control and Prevention (2018d). *Violence prevention*. Retrieved from https://www.cdc.gov/violenceprevention/childabuseandneglect/fastfact.html

Center for Disease Control and Prevention (2019). *Premature birth*. Retrieved from https://www.cdc.gov/reproductivehealth/features/premature-birth/index.html

Chambers, J. (2017). The neurobiology of attachment: From infancy to clinical outcomes. *Psychodynamic Psychiatry, 45*(4), 542–563. Doi: https://doi.org/10.1521/pdps.2017.45.4.542

Charalampous, K., Demetriou, C., Tricha, L., Ioannou, M., Georgiou, S., Nikiforou, M., & Stavrinmides, P. (2018). The effect of parenting style on bullying behaviors and the mediating role of peer attachment relationships: A longitudinal study. *Journal of Adolescence, 64*, 109–123. Doi: https://doi.org/10.1016/j.adolescence.2018.02.003

Cheek, N. N. & Cheek, J. M (2018). Aspects of identity: From the inner-outer metaphor to a tetrapartite model of the self. *Self and Identity, 17*(4), 467–482. Doi: https://doi.org/10.1080/15298868.2017.1412347

Chen, C., Martinez, R. M., & Cheng, Y. (2018). The developmental origins of the social brain: Empathy, morality, and justice. *Frontiers in Psychology, December*(9), article 2584, no pagination specified. Doi: https://doi.org/10.3389/fpsyg.2018.02584

Chen, F. S., Heinrichs, M., & Johnson, S. C. (2017). Oxytocin and the emergence of individual differences in the social regulation of stress. *Social and Personality Psychology Compass, 11*(8), 1–9. Doi: https://doi.org/10.1111/spc3.12332

Cheng, S. & Delville, Y. (2009). Vasopressin facilitates play fighting in juvenile golden hamsters. *Physiology and Behavior, 98*(1–2), 242–246. Doi: https://doi.org/10.1016/j.physbeh.2009.04.019

Chico, E., Gonzalez, A., Ali, N., Steiner, M., & Fleming, A. S. (2014). Executive function and mothering: Challenges faced by teenage mothers. *Developmental Psychobiology, 56*(5), 1027–1035. Doi: https://doi.org/10.1002/dev.21185

Childre, D. & Rozman, D. (2007). *Transforming depression: The Heartmath solution to feeling overwhelmed, sad and distressed*. Oakland, CA: New Harbinger Publications.

Churchland, P. S. (2014). The neurobiological platform for moral values. *Behaviour, 151*, 283–296.

Cicchetti, D. & Tucker, D. (1994). Development and self-regulatory structures of the mind. *Development and Psychopathology, 6*, 533–549. Doi: https://doi.org/10.1017/s0954579400004673

Clark, G., Grenham, S., Scully, P., Fitzgerald, P., Moloney, R. D., Shanahan, F., Dinan, T. G., & Cryan, J. F. (2013). The microbiome-gut-brain axis during early life regulates the hippocampal serotonergic system in a sex-dependent manner. *Molecular Psychiatry, 18*, 666–673. Doi: https://doi.org/10.1038/mp.2012.77

Collins, R. L., Strasburger, V. C., Brown, J. D., Donnerstein, E., Lenhart, A., & Ward, L. M. (2017). Sexual media and childhood well-being and health. *Pediatrics, 140*(s2), S162–S166. Doi: https://doi.org/10.1542/peds.2016-1758x

Combs-Orme, T. (2013). Epigenetics and the social work imperative. *Social Work, 58*(1), 23–30. Doi: https://doi.org/10.1093/sw/sws052

Common Sense Media (2013). Zero to eight: Children's media use in America 2013. Retrieved from https://www.commonsensemedia.org/research/zero-to-eight-childrens-media-use-in-america-2013/key-finding-2%3A-kids%27-time-on-mobile-devices-triples

Condon, J. T., Corkindale, C. J., & Boyce, P. (2008). Assessment of postnatal paternal-infant attachment: Development of a questionnaire instrument. *Journal of Reproductive and Infant Psychology, 26*(3), 195–210. Doi: https://doi.org/10.1080/02646830701691335

Condon, J., Corkindale, C., Boyce, P., & Gamble, E. (2013). A longitudinal study of father-to-infant attachment: Antecedents and correlates. *Journal of Reproductive and Infant Psychology, 31*(1), 15–30. Doi: https://doi.org/10.1080/02646838.2012.757694

Condon, P. & DeSteno, D. (2017). Enhancing compassion: Social psychological perspectives. In E. M. Seppala, E. Simon-Thomas, S. Brown, M. C. Worline, C. C. Daryl, and J. R. Doty (Eds.), *The Oxford handbook of compassion science* (pp. 287–298). New York, NY: Oxford University Press.

Connolly, J., McIsaac, C., Shulman, S., Wincentak, K., Joly, L., Heifetz, M., and Bravo, V. (2014). Development of romantic relationships in adolescence and emerging adulthood: Implications for community mental health. *Canadian Journal of Community Mental Health, 33*(1), 7–19. Doi: https://doi.org/10.7870/cjcmh-2014-002

Couch, L. L & Koeninger, A. L. (2017). Attraction: The many factors that draw us to like, lust and love. In R. W. Summers (Ed.), *Social psychology: How other people influence our thoughts and actions*, (pp. 299–314). Santa Barbara, CA: Greenwood.

Coughlin, C., Lyons, K. E., & Ghetti, S. (2014). Remembering the past to envision the future in middle childhood: Developmental linkages between prospection and episodic memory. *Cognitive Development, 30*, 96–110. Doi: https://doi.org/10.1016/j.cogdev.2014.02.001

Courtney, J. A. & Nowakowski-Sims, E. (2019). Technology's impact on the parent-infant attachment relationship: Intervening through FirstPlayTM therapy. *International Journal of Play Therapy, 28*(2), 57–68. Doi: https://doi.org/10.1037/pla0000090

Cox, R. B., Shreffler, K. M., Merten, M. J., Schwerdtfeger Gallus, K., & Dowdy, J. L. (2015). Parenting, peers and perceived norms: What predicts attitudes toward sex among early adolescents? *Journal of Early Adolescence, 35*(1), 30–53. Doi: https://doi.org/10.1177/0272431614523131

Coyne, S. M., Radesky, J., Collier, K. M., Gentile, D. A., Linder, J. R., Nathanson, A. I., Rasmussen, E. E., Reich, S. M., & Rogers, J. (2018). Parenting and digital media. *Pediatrics, 140*(s2), S112–S116. Doi: https://doi.org/10.1542/peds.2016-1758n

Cozolino, L. (2008). *The healthy aging brain: Sustaining attachment, attaining wisdom*. New York, NY: W. W. Norton & Co.

Cozolino, L. (2010). *The neuroscience of psychotherapy: Healing the social brain*. (2nd ed.). New York, NY: W. W. Norton & Co.

Cozolino, L. (2014). *The neuroscience of human relationships: Attachment and the social brain*. (2nd ed.). New York, NY: W. W. Norton & Co.

Craig, W. M. & Pepler, D. J. (2007). Understanding bullying: From research to practice. *Canadian Psychology, 48*(2), 86–93.

Creeley, C. E. & Olney, J. W. (2013). Drug-induced apoptosis: Mechanism by which alcohol and many other drugs can disrupt brain development. *Brain Science, 3*, 1153–1181. Doi: https://doi.org/10.3390/brainsci3031153

Crenshaw, J. T. (2007). Healthy birth practice # 6: Keep mother and baby together—it's best for mother, baby and breastfeeding. *Journal of Perinatal Education, 23*(4), 211–217. Doi: https://doi.org/10.1891/1058-1243.23.4.211

Crocetti, E. (2017). Identity formation in adolescence: The dynamic of forming and consolidating identity commitments. *Child Development Perspectives, 11*(2), 145–150. Doi: https://doi.org/10.1111/cdep.12226

Cross, D., Fani, N., Powers, A., & Bradley, B. (2017). Neurobiological development in the context of childhood trauma. *Clinical Psychology: Science and Practice, 24*(2), 111–124. Doi: https://doi.org/10.1111/cpsp.12198

Cservenka, A., Herting, M. M., Mackiewicz Seghete, K. L., Hudson, K. A., & Nagel, B. J. (2013). High and low sensation seeking adolescents show distinct patterns of brain activity during reward processing. *NeuroImage, 66*(1 February), 184–193. Doi: https://doi.org/10.1016/j.neuroimage.2012.11.003

Cyr, C., Euser, E. M., Bakersman-Kranenburg, M. J., van IJzendorn, M. H. (2010). Attachment security and disorganization in maltreating and high-risk families: A series of meta-analyses. *Developmental Psychopathology, 22*, 87–108. Doi: https://doi.org/10.1017/s0954579409990289

Dahmen, B., Putz, V., Herpertz-Dahlman, B., & Konrad, K. (2012). Early pathogenic care and the development of ADHD-like symptoms. *Journal of Neural Transmission, 119*, 1023–1036. Doi: https://doi.org/10.1007/s00702-012-0809-8

Damasio, A. (1999). *The feeling of what happens: body, and emotions in the making of consciousness*. Orlando, FL: Harcourt.

Damasio, A. (2010). *Self comes to mind: Constructing the conscious brain*. New York, NY: Pantheon Books.

Damasio, A. (2018). *The strange order of things: Life, feeling and the making of cultures*. New York, NY: Pantheon Books.

David-Ferdon, C., Vivolo-Kantor, A. M., Dahlberg, L. L., Marshall, K. J., Rainford, N. & Hall, J. E. (2016). *A comprehensive technical package for the prevention of youth violence and associated risk behaviors*. Atlanta, GA: National Center for Injury Prevention and Control, Centers for Disease Control and Prevention. Doi: https://doi.org/10.15620/cdc.43085

Davidson, R. J. (2000). Affective style, psychopathology, and resilience: Brain mechanisms and plasticity. *American Psychologist, 55*, 1196–1214. Doi: https://doi.org/10.1037//0003-066x.55.11.1196

Davidson, R. J. (2012). The neurobiology of compassion. In C. K. Germer and R. D. Siegel (Eds.) *Wisdom and compassion in psychotherapy: Deepening mindfulness on clinical practice* (pp. 111–118). New York, NY: Guilford Press.

Davis, K., Desrocher, M., Moore, T. (2011). Fetal alcohol spectrum disorder: A review of neurodevelopmental findings and interventions. *Journal of Developmental and Physical Disabilities, 23*, 143–167. Doi: https://doi.org/10.1007/s10882-010-9204-2

Davou, B. & Sidiropoulou, A. (2017). Family life around screens: Some thoughts on the impact of ICTs on physiological development and the development of relationships. *Contemporary Family Therapy, 39*, 261–270. Doi: https://doi.org/10.1007/s10591-017-9435-9

Degenhardt, L., Chiu, W. T., Sampson, N., Kessler, R. C., Anthony, J. C., Angermeyer, M. Wells, J. E. (2008). Toward a global view of alcohol, tobacco, cannabis, and cocaine use: Findings from the WHO World Mental Health Surveys. *PLoS Medicine, 5*(7), 1053–1076. Doi: https://doi.org/10.1371/journal.pmed.0050141

Diamond, G., Russon, J., & Levy, S. (2016). Attachment-based family therapy: A review of the empirical support. *Family Process, 55*(3), 595–610. Doi: https://doi.org/10.1111/famp.12241

Diaz, A., Blankenship, T. L., & Bell, M. A. (2018). Episodic memory in middle childhood: Age, brain electrical activity, and self-reported attention. *Cognitive Development, 47*, 63–70. Doi: https://doi.org/10.1016/j.cogdev.2018.03.003

Diaz, N., Horton, E. G., & Malloy, T. (2014). Attachment style, spirituality, and depressive symptoms among individuals in substance abuse treatment. *Journal of Social Service Research, 40*(3), 313–324. Doi: 10.1080/01488376.2014.896851

Diaz, N., Horton, E. G., Green, D. McIlveen, J., Weiner, M., & Mullaney, D. (2011). Relationship between spirituality and depressive symptoms among individuals who abuse substances. *Counseling and Values, 56*(1), 43–56. Doi: 10.1002/j.2161-007X.2011.tb01030.x

Diego, M. A., Dieter, J. N. I., Field, T., Lecanuet, J. P., Hernandez-Reif, M., Beutler, J., Largie, S. … Fawwaz, S. (2002). Fetal activity following stimulation of the mother's abdomen, feet and hands. *Developmental Psychobiology, 41*(4), 396–406. Doi: https://doi.org/10.1002/dev.10071

Dirix, C. E. H., Nijhuis, J. G., Jongsma, H. W., & Hornstra, G. (2009). Aspects of fetal learning and memory. *Child Development, 80*(4), 1251–1258. Doi: https://doi.org/10.1111/j.1467-8624.2009.01329.x

Dissanayake, E. (2017). Ethology, interpersonal neurobiology, and play: Insights into the evolutionary origins of the arts. *American Journal of Play, 9*(2), 143–168.

Doan, H. M. & Zimerman, A. (2003). Conceptualizing prenatal attachment: Toward a multidimensional view. *Journal of Prenatal and Perinatal Psychology and Health, 18*(2), 109–129.

Dodge, K. A., Greenberg, M. T., Malone, P. S. & Conduct Problems Prevention Research Group (2008). Testing an idealized dynamic cascade model of development of serious violence in adolescence. *Child Development, 79*(6), 1907–1927. Doi: https://doi.org/10.1111/j.1467-8624.2008.01233.x

Donelan-McCall, N. & Olds, D. (2018). In H. Steele and M. Steele (Eds.), *Handbook of attachment-based interventions* (pp. 79–103). New York, NY: Guilford Press.

Dozier, M., Bernard, K., & Roben, C. (2018). Attachment and biobehavioral catch-up. In H. Steele and M. Steele (Eds.), *Handbook of attachment-based interventions* (pp. 27–49). New York, NY: Guilford Press.

Duschinsky, R. (2018). Disorganization, fear, and attachment: Working toward clarification. *Infant Mental Health Journal, 39*(1), 17–29. Doi: https://doi.org/10.1002/imhj.21689

Duke, N. N., Pettingell, S. L., McMorris, B. J., Borowsky, I. W. (2010). Adolescent violence perpetration: Associations with multiple types of adverse childhood experiences. *Pediatrics, 125*(4), e778–e786. Doi: https://doi.org/10.1542/peds.2009-0597

Dunbar, R. I. M. (2010). The social role of touch in humans and primates: Behavioural function and neurobiological mechanisms. *Neuroscience and Biobehavioral Review, 34*, 260–268. Doi: https://doi.org/10.1016/j.neubiorev.2008.07.001

Dutton, D. G., White, K. R., & Fogarty, D. (2013). Paranoid thinking in mass shooters. *Aggression and Violent Behavior, 18*, 548–553. Doi: https://doi.org/10.1016/j.avb.2013.07.012

Entringer, S., Buss, C., & Wadhwa, P. D. (2010). Prenatal stress and developmental programming of human health and disease risk: Concepts and integration of empirical findings. *Current opinions in Endocrinology, Diabetes and Obesity, 17*(6), 507–516. Doi: https://doi.org/10.1097/med.0b013e3283405921

Erikson, E. (1963). *Childhood and society* (2nd ed.). New York, NY: W. W. Norton.

Erikson, E. (1968). *Identity: Youth and crisis*. New York: W. W. Norton and Co.

Ernst, J. M. & Cacioppo, J. T. (1999). Lonely hearts: Psychological perspectives on loneliness. *Applied and Preventive Psychology, 8*, 1–22. Doi: https://doi.org/10.1016/s0962-1849(99)80008-0

Ernst, M. E. & Fudge, J. L. (2010). Adolescence: On the neural path to adulthood. In J. E. Grant and M. N. Potenza (Eds.), *Young adult mental health* (pp. 19–39). New York, NY: Oxford University Press. Doi: https://doi.org/10.1093/med:psych/9780195332711.003.0002

Ersche, K. D., Jones, P. S., Williams, G. B., Turton, A., J., Robbins, T. W., & Bullmore, E. T. (2012). Abnormal brain structure implicated in stimulant drug addiction. *Science, 335*, 601–604. Doi: https://doi.org/10.1126/science.1214463

Evrensel, A. & Ceylan, M. E. (2015). The gut-brain axis: The missing link in depression. *Clinical Pharmacology and Neuroscience, 13*(3), 239–244. Doi: https://doi.org/10.9758/cpn.2015.13.3.239

Fabbri-Destro, M. & Rizzolatti, G. (2008). Mirror neurons and mirror systems in monkeys and humans. *Physiology, 23*, 171–179. Doi: https://doi.org/10.1152/physiol.00004.2008

Felitti, V. J., Anda, R. F., Nordenberg, D., Williamson, D. F., Spitz, A. M., Edwards, V., Koss, M. P., & Marks, J. S. (1998). Relationship of childhood abuse and household dysfunction to many of the leading causes of death in adults: The Adverse Childhood Experiences (ACE) study. *American Journal of Preventive Medicine, 14*(4), 245–258. Doi: https://doi.org/10.1016/j.amepre.2019.04.001

Fifer, W. P., Monk, C. E., & Grose-Fifer, J. (2001). Prenatal development and risk. In G. Bremner and A. Fogel (Eds.), *Blackwell handbook of infant development* (pp. 505–542). Malden, MA: Blackwell Publishers. Doi: https://doi.org/10.1002/9780470996348.ch18

Finch, C. E. & Loehlin, J. C. (1998). Environmental influences that may precede fertilization: A first examination of the prezygotic hypothesis from maternal age influences on twins. *Behavioral Genetics, 28*(2), 101–106.

Fishbane, M. D. (2013). *Loving with the brain in mind: Neurobiology and couples therapy*. New York, NY: W. W. Norton & Co.

Fisher, J., Cabral de Mello, M., Patel, V., Rahman, A., Trach, T., Holton, S., & Holmes, W. (2012). Prevalence and determinants of common perinatal mental disorders in women in low- and lower-middle income countries: A systematic review. *Bulletin of the World Health Organization, 90*, 139G-149G. Doi: https://doi.org/10.2471/blt.11.091850

Fisher, H. E., Xu, X., Aron, A., & Brown, L. L. (2016). Intense, passionate, romantic love: A natural addiction? How the fields that investigate romance and substance abuse can inform each other. *Frontiers in Psychology, 7*(article 687), 1–10. Doi: https://doi.org/10.3389/fpsyg.2016.00687

Fisher, S. F. (2014). *Neurofeedback in the treatment of developmental trauma*. New York, NY: W. W. Norton & Co.

Flaherty, E., Thompson, R., Litrownik, A., Zolotor, A., Dubowitz, H., Runyan, D., English, D., & Everson, M. (2009). Adverse childhood exposures and reported child health at age 12. *Academic Pediatrics, 9*, 150–156. Doi: https://doi.org/10.1016/j.acap.2008.11.003

Flores, P. J. (2001). Addiction as an attachment disorder: Implications for group therapy. *International Journal of Group Therapy, 51*(1), 63–81. Doi: https://doi.org/10.1521/ijgp.51.1.63.49730

Flores, P. J. (2004). *Addiction as an attachment disorder*. Lanham, MD: Jason Aaronson.

Fonagy, P., Gergely, G., Jurist, E. J., & Target, M. I. (2002). *Affect regulation, mentalization, and the development of self*. New York, NY: Other Press. Doi: https://doi.org/10.1037/e515962006-012

Fonzo, G. A., Ramsawh, H. J., Flagan, T. M., Simmons, A. N., Sullivan, S. G., Allard, C. B., Paulus, M. P., & Stein, M. B. (2016). Early life stress and the anxious brain: Evidence for a neural mechanism linking childhood emotional maltreatment to anxiety in adulthood. *Psychological Medicine, 46*, 1037–1054. Doi: https://doi.org/10.1017/s0033291715002603

Fraley, R. C., Waller, N. G., & Brennen, K. A. (2000). An item response theory analysis of self-report measures of adult attachment. *Journal of Personality and Social Psychology, 78*(2), 350–365. Doi: https://doi.org/10.1037//0022-3514.78.2.350

Franklin, T. B., Russig, H., Weiss, I. C., Graff, J., Linder, N., Michalon, A., Vizi, S., & Mansuy, I. M. (2010). Epigenetic transmission of the impact of early stress across generations. *Biological Psychiatry, 68*(5), 408–415. Doi: https://doi.org/10.1016/j.biopsych.2010.05.036

Fredrickson, B. L. & Siegel, D. (2017). Broaden-and-build theory meets interpersonal neurobiology as a lens on compassion and positivity resonance. In P. Gilbert (Ed.), *Compassion: Concepts, research, and applications* (pp. 203–217). New York, NY: Routledge/Taylor and Francis. Doi: https://doi.org/10.4324/9781315564296-12

French, W. P. (2008). The neurobiology of violence and victimization. In T. W. Miller (Ed.), *School violence and primary prevention* (pp. 25–58). New York, NY: Springer Publishing. Doi: https://doi.org/10.1007/978-0-387-77119-9_3

Fuchs, P. N., Peng, Y. B., Boyette-Davis, Y. A., Uhelski, M. L. (2014). The anterior cingulate and pain processing. *Frontiers in Integrative Neuroscience, 8*, article 35. Doi: https://doi.org/10.3389/fnint.2014.00035

Fujikawa, S., Ando, S., Nishida, A., Usami, S., Koike, S., Yamasaki, S., Morimoto, Y., … Kasai, K. (2018). Disciplinary slapping is associated with bullying involvement regardless of warm parenting in early adolescence. *Journal of Adolescence, 68*, 207–216. Doi: https://doi.org/10.1016/j.adolescence.2018.07.018

Galland, L. (2014). The gut microbiome and the brain. *Journal of Medicinal Food, 17*(12), 1261–1272. Doi: https://doi.org/10.1089/jmf.2014.7000

Gao, W., Grewen, K., Knickmeyer, R. C., Qui, A., Salzwedel, A., Weili, W., & Gilmore, J. H. (2019). *Neuroimage, 185*, 802–812. Doi: https://doi.org/10.1016/j.neuroimage.2018.04.032

Gardner, M. & Steinberg, L. (2005). Peer influence on risk-taking, risk preference, and risky decision making in adolescence and adulthood: An experimental study. *Developmental Psychology, 41*(4), 625–635. Doi: https://doi.org/10.1037/0012-1649.41.4.625

Gazzillo, F., Fimiani, R., De Luca, E., Dazzi, N., Curtins, J. T., & Bush, M. (2019). New developments in understanding morality: Between evolutionary psychology, development psychology, and control-mastery theory. *Psychoanalytic Psychology, March 11*, no pagination specified. Doi: https://doi.org/10.1037/pap0000235

Gendron, M., Roberson, D., van der Vyver, J. M., & Barrett, L. F. (2014). Perceptions of emotions from facial expressions are not culturally universal: Evidence from a remote culture. *Emotion, 14*(2), 251–262. Doi: https://doi.org/10.1037/a0036052

Gerdes, K. E., Segal, E. A., & Harmon, K. K. (2014). *Your brain on empathy: Implications for social work practice.* In H. C. Matto, J. Strolin-Goltzman and M. S. Ballan (Eds.), *Neuroscience for social work: Current research and practice* (pp.9–36). New York, NY: Springer Publishing. Doi: https://doi.org/10.1891/9780826108777

Gilbert, P. (2014). Attachment theory and attachment-focused therapy for depression. In A. N. Danqua and K. Berry (Eds.), *Attachment theory in adult mental health: A guide to clinical practice* (pp. 35–47). New York, NY: Routledge/Taylor & Francis. Doi: https://doi.org/10.4324/9781315883496

Gillath, O., Karantzas, G. C., & Selcuk, E. (2017). A net of friends: Investigating friendship by integrating attachment theory and social network analysis. *Personality and Social Psychology, 43*(11), 1546–1565. Doi: https://doi.org/10.1177/0146167217719731

Gilligan, C. (1977). In a different voice: Women's conceptions of self and of morality. *Harvard Educational Review, 47*(4), 481–517. Doi: https://doi.org/10.17763/haer.47.4.g6167429416hg5l0

Ginsburg, K. R. & the Committee on Communications and the Committee on Psychosocial Aspects of Child and Family Health (2007). The importance of play in promoting healthy child development and maintaining strong parent-child bonds. *Pediatrics, 119*(1), 182–191. Doi: https://doi.org/10.1542/peds.2006-2697

Glenn, M. (2015). Prenatal and perinatal psychology: Vital foundations of body psychotherapy. In G. Matlock and H. Weiss (Eds.), *Handbook of body psychotherapy and somatic psychology* (pp. 332–344). Berkley, CA: North Atlantic Books.

Glover, V. (2014). Maternal depression, anxiety and stress during pregnancy and child outcome: what needs to be done? *Best Practice & Research Clinical Obstetrics and Gynecology, 28*, 25–35. Doi: https://doi.org/10.1016/j.bpobgyn.2013.08.017

Glynn, L. M. & Sandman, C. A. (2011). Prenatal origins of neurological development: A critical period for fetus and mother. *Current Directions in Psychological Science, 20*(6), 384–389. Doi: https://doi.org/10.1177/0963721411422056

Goetz, J. L. & Simon-Thomas, E. (2017). The landscape of compassion: Definitions and scientific approaches. In E. M. Seppala, E. Simon-Thomas, S. Brown, M. C. Worline, C. C. Daryl, and J. R. Doty (Eds.), *The Oxford handbook of compassion science* (pp. 3–15). New York, NY: Oxford University Press. Doi: https://doi.org/10.1093/oxfordhb/9780190464684.013.1

Goleman, D. (2013). *Focus: The hidden driver of excellence.* New York, NY: Harper Collins.

Gordon, G. (2014). Well played: The origins and future of playfulness. *American Journal of Play, 6*(2), 234–266.

Govrin, A. (2014). The ABC of moral development: An attachment approach to moral judgment. *Frontiers in Psychology, 5*(Jan 24), Article 6, no pagination specified. Doi: https://doi.org/10.3389/fpsyg.2014.00006

Grandqvist, P., Sroufe, L. A., Dozier, M., Hesse, E., Steele, M., van IJzendoorn, Solomon, J., ... Duschinsky, R. (2017). Disorganized attachment in infancy: A review of the phenomenon and its implications for clinicians and policy makers. *Attachment and Human Development, 19*(6), 534–558. Doi: 10.1080/14616734.2017.1354040

Grant, B. F. & Dawson, D. A. (1997). Age at onset of alcohol use and its association with DSM-IV alcohol abuse and dependence: Results from the National Longitudinal Alcohol Epidemiologic Survey. *Journal of Substance Abuse, 9*, 103–110. Doi: https://doi.org/10.1016/s0899-3289(97)90009-2

Grzadzinski, R. L., Luyster, R., Spencer, A. G., & Lord, C. (2014). Attachment in young children with autism spectrum disorders: An examination of separation and reunion behaviors with both mothers and fathers. *Autism, 18*(2), 85–96. Doi: https://doi.org/10.1177/1362361312467235

Guo, G. & Stearns, E. (2002). The social influences on the realization of genetic potential for intellectual development. *Social Forces, 80*(3), 881–910. Doi: https://doi.org/10.1353/sof.2002.0007

Gutierrez, F., Vall, G., Peri, J. P., Bailles, E., Ferraz, L., Garriz, M., & Caseras, X. (2012). Personality disorder features through the life course. *Journal of Personality Disorders, 26*(5), 763–774. Doi: https://doi.org/10.1521/pedi.2012.26.5.763

Guyer, A. E., Perez-Edgar, K., & Crone, E. A. (2018). Opportunities for neurodevelopmental plasticity from infancy through early adulthood. *Child Development, 89*(3), 687–697. Doi: https://doi.org/10.1111/cdev.13073

Hackett, J. A., Sengupta, R., Zylicz, J. J., Murakami, K., Lee, C., & Down, T. A. (2013). Germline DNA demethylation dynamics and imprint erasure through 5-hydroximethyl cytosine. *Science, 339*(Jan. 25), 448–452. Doi: https://doi.org/10.1126/science.1229277

Hadlington, L., White, H., & Curtis, S. (2019). "I cannot live without my [tablet]": Children's experiences of using tablet technology within the home. *Computers in Human Behavior, 94*, 19–24. Doi: https://doi.org/10.1016/j.chb.2018.12.043

Hallin, A. -L., Bengtsson, H., Frostell, A. S., Stjernqvist, K. (2011). The effect of extremely preterm birth on attachment organization in later adolescence. *Child: Care, Health, and Development, 38*(2), 196–203. Doi: https://doi.org/10.1111/j.1365-2214.2011.01236.x

Hanson, J. L., Albert, D., Iselin, A.-M. R., Carree, J. M., Dodge, K. A., & Hariri, A. R. (2015). Cumulative stress in childhood is associated with blunted reward-related brain activity in adulthood. *Social Cognitive and Affective Neuroscience, 11*(3), 405–412. Doi: https://doi.org/10.1093/scan/nsv124

Harlow, H. (1958). The nature of love. *American Psychiatry, 13*, 673–685.

Harlow, H. (1959). Love in infant monkeys. *Scientific American, 200*(6), 68–74. Doi: https://doi.org/10.1038/scientificamerican0659-68

Hart, S. (2018). *Brain, attachment, personality: An introduction to neuroaffective development.* New York, NY: Routledge.

Hastings, P., Miller, J. G., Kahle, S., & Zahn-Waxler, C. (2014). The neurobiological bases of empathic concern for others. In M. Killen and J. G. Smetana (Eds.), *Handbook of moral development* (2nd ed.), pp. 411–434. New York, NY: Psychology Press. Doi: https://doi.org/10.4324/9780203581957.ch19

Hawkins, J. (2005). *On intelligence: How a new understanding of the brain will lead to the creation of truly intelligent machines.* New York, NY: Owl Books/Holt.

Hazan, C. & Shaver, P. (1987). Conceptualizing romantic love as an attachment process. *Journal of Personality and Social Psychology, 52*, 511–524. Doi: https://doi.org/10.1037//0022-3514.52.3.511

Hebb, D. O. (1949). *The organization of behavior.* New York, NY: Wiley & Sons.

Hennig, K. H. (2004). Care gone awry: The role of attachment and reflective functioning. In T. A. Thorkildsen and H. J. Walberg (Eds.), *Nurturing morality* (pp. 61–76). New York, NY: Kluwer Academic/Plenum Publishers. Doi: https://doi.org/10.1007/978-1-4757-4163-6_4

Heshmati, M. (2009). Cocaine-induced LTP in the ventral tegmental area: New insights into mechanism and time course illuminate the cellular substrates of addiction. *Journal of Neurophysiology, 101*, 2735–2737. Doi: https://doi.org/10.1152/jn.00127.2009

Hesse, E. & Main, M. (1999). Second-generation effects of unresolved trauma in nonmaltreating parents: Dissociated, frightened, and threatening parental behavior. *Psychoanalytic Inquiry, 19*(4), 481–540. Doi: https://doi.org/10.1080/07351699909534265

Hesse, E. & Main, M. (2006). Frightened, threatening, and dissociative parental behavior in low-risk samples: Description, discussion, and interpretations. *Development and Psychopathology, 18*(2), 309–343. Doi: https://doi.org/10.1017/s0954579406060172

Hickok, G. (2014). *The myth of mirror neurons: The real neuroscience of communication and cognition*. New York, NY: W. W. Norton & Co.

Hill, C. E., Satterwhite, D. B., Larrimore, M. I., Mann, A. R., Johnson, V. C., Simon, R. E. & Knox, S. (2012). Attitudes about psychotherapy: A qualitative study of introductory psychology students who have never been in psychotherapy and the influence of attachment style. *Counseling and Psychology Research, 12*(1), 13–24. Doi: https://doi.org/10.1080/14733145.2011.629732

Hoge, E., Bickham, D., & Cantor, J. (2017). Digital media, anxiety, and depression in children. *Pediatrics, 140*(s2), s76–s80. Doi: https://doi.org/10.1542/peds.2016-1758g

Holroyd, C. B. & Umemoto, A. (2016). The research domain criteria framework: The case for the anterior cingulate. *Neuroscience and Biobehavioral Reviews, 71*, 418–443. Doi: https://doi.org/10.1016/j.neubiorev.2016.09.021

Horton, E. G. (2018). Unpublished manuscript. How Little We Know: A Literature Review of Attachment and Parenting Styles Associated with School Shooters.

Horton, E. G., Diaz, N., Weiner, M., & Malloy, T. (2012). Adult attachment style, spirituality, and religiosity among individuals in treatment for substance use disorders. *Florida Public Health Review, 9*, 121–131. Doi: https://doi.org/10.1007/s11469-015-9596-4

Horton, E. G., Luna, N., & Malloy, T. (2015). Exploring the relationships between spirituality and personality disorder traits among a sample of in-patients in treatment for substance use disorder. *International Journal of Mental Health, 13*(5), No Pagination.

Horton, E. G., Luna, N., and Malloy, T. (2016). Exploring relationships between adult attachment, spirituality and personality disorder traits among individuals in in-patient treatment for substance use disorders. *International Journal of Social Work, 3*(1), 16–41. doi: 10.5296/ijsw.v3i1.8384

Horvath, A. O., Del Re, A. C., Fluckiger, C., & Symonds, D. (2011). Alliance in individual psychotherapy. *Psychotherapy, 48*(4), 9–16. Doi: https://doi.org/10.1037/a0022186

Hosokawa, R. & Katsura, T. (2018). Association between mobile technology use and child adjustment in early elementary school age. *PLoS ONE, 13*(12), Dec 14, Article e0208844. Doi: https://doi.org/10.1371/journal.pone.0208844

Howard, L. M., Molyneaux, E. Dennis, C.-L., Rochat, T., Stein, A., & Milgrom, J. (2015). Non-psychotic disorders in the perinatal period. *Lancet, 384*, 1775–1788. Doi: https://doi.org/10.1016/s0140-6736(14)61276-9

Howie, E. K., Coenen, P., Campbell, A. C., Ranelli, S., & Straker, L. M. (2017). Head, trunk, and arm posture amplitude and variation, muscle activity, sedentariness and physical activity of 3 to 5 year-old children during tablet computer use compared to television watching and toy play. *Applied ergonomics, 65*, 41–50. Doi: https://doi.org/10.1016/j.apergo.2017.05.011

Hughes, F. P. (2010). *Children, play, and development* (4th ed.). Thousand Oaks, CA: Sage Publications.

Huttenlocher P. (2002). Neural plasticity: The effects of the environment on the development of the cerebral cortex. Cambridge, MA: Harvard University Press.

Jacobs, M. B., Boynton-Jarrett, R. D., & Harville, E. W. (2015). Adverse childhood event experiences, fertility difficulties and menstrual cycle characteristics. *Journal of Psychosomatic Obstetrics and Gynecology, 36*(2), 46–57. Doi: https://doi.org/10.3109/0167482x.2015.1026892

Johnson, S. B., Blum, R. W., & Giedd, J. N. (2009). Adolescent maturity and the brain: The promise and pitfalls of neuroscience research in adolescent health policy. *Journal of Adolescent Health, 45*, 216–221. Doi: https://doi.org/10.1016/j.jadohealth.2009.05.016

Jubinville, J., Newburn-Cook, C., Hegadoren, K., & Lacaze-Masonteil, T. (2012). Symptoms of acute stress disorder in mothers of premature infants. *Advances in Neonatal Care, 12*(4), 246–253. Doi: https://doi.org/10.1097/anc.0b013e31826090ac

Juffer, F., Bakermans-Kranenburg, M. J., & van IJzendoorn, M. H. (2018). Video-feedback intervention to promote positive parenting and sensitive discipline. In H. Steele and M. Steele (Eds.), *Handbook of attachment-based interventions* (pp. 1–26). New York, NY: Guilford Press. Doi: https://doi.org/10.1016/j.copsyc.2017.03.012

Jung, E., Pick, O., Schluter-Muller, S., Schmeck, K., & Goth, K. (2013). Identity development in adolescence with mental problems. *Child and Adolescent Psychiatry and Mental Health, 7*(26), no pagination specified. Doi: https://doi.org/10.1186/1753-2000-7-26

Kandel, E. R., Schwartz, J. H., & Jessell, T. M. (2000). *Principles of neural science* (4th ed.). Columbus, OH: McGraw-Hill.

Kelly, R., Zatzick, D., & Anders, T. (2001). The detection and treatment of psychiatric disorders and substance use among pregnant women cared for in obstetrics. *American Journal of Psychiatry, 158*(2), 213–219. Doi: https://doi.org/10.1176/appi.ajp.158.2.213

Keltner, D., Oakley, K, & Jenkins, J. (2014). *Understanding emotions* (3rd ed.). Hoboken, NJ: John Wiley & Sons.

Kern, J. K., Geier, D. A., Sykes, L. K., Geier, M. R., & Deth, R. C. (2015). Are ASD and ADHD a continuum? A comparison of pathophysiological similarities between the disorders. *Journal of Attention Disorders, 19*(9), 805–827. Doi: https://doi.org/10.1177/1087054712459886

Kessler, R. C., Berglund, P., Demler, O., Jin, R., Merikangas, K. R., & Walters, E. E. (2005). Lifetime prevalence and age-of-onset distributions of DSM-IV disorders in the National Co-morbidity Survey Replication. *Archives of General Psychiatry, 62*(6), 593–602. Doi: https://doi.org/10.1001/archpsyc.62.6.593

Kestly, T. (2018). A cross-cultural and cross-disciplinary perspective of play. In T. Marks-Tarlow, M. Solomon, and D. J. Siegel (Eds.), *Play & creativity in psychotherapy* (pp. 110–127). New York, NY: W. W. Norton & Co.

Kinney, D. K., Munir, K. M., Crowley, D. J., & Miller, A. M. (2008). Prenatal stress and risk for autism. *Neuroscience and Biobehavioral Reviews, 32*, 1519–1532. Doi: https://doi.org/10.1016/j.neubiorev.2008.06.004

Knickmeyer, R. C., Goutard, S., Kang, C., Evans, D., Wilber, K., Smith, J. K., Hamer, R. M. ... Gilmore, J. H. (2008). A structural MRI study of human brain development from birth to 2 years. *Journal of Neuroscience, 28*(47), 12176–12182. Doi: https://doi.org/10.1523/jneurosci.3479-08.2008

Knudsen, E. I. (2004). Sensitive periods in the development of the brain and behavior. *Journal of Cognitive Neuroscience, 16*(8), 1412–1425.

Kohlberg, L. (1969). Stage and sequence: the cognitive developmental approach to socialization. In D. A. Goslin (Ed.), *Handbook of socialization theory and research* (pp. 347–480). Chicago, IL: Rand McNally.

Kohlberg, L. (1976). Moral stages and moralization: The cognitive developmental approach. In T. Lickona (Ed.), *Moral development and behavior: Theory, research, and social issues* (pp. 31–53). New York, NY: Holt.

Kokkinos, C. M. (2013). Bullying and victimization in early adolescence: Associations with attachment style and perceived parenting. *Journal of School Violence, 12*, 174–192. Doi: https://doi.org/10.1080/15388220.2013.766134

Kokkinos, C. M. & Panayiotou, G. (2004). Predicting bullying and victimization among early adolescents: Associations with disruptive behavior disorders. *Aggressive Behavior, 30*, 520–533. Doi: https://doi.org/10.1002/ab.20055

Kokko, K., Tremblay, R. E., Lacourse, E., Nagin, D., & Vitaro, F. (2006). Trajectories of prosocial behavior and physical aggression in middle childhood: Links to adolescent school dropout and physical violence. *Journal of Research on Adolescence, 16*(3), 403–428. Doi: https://doi.org/10.1111/j.1532-7795.2006.00500.x

Koniski, E. (2018). 'Please turn it off': Negotiations and morality around children's media use at home. *Discourse & Society, 29*(2), 142–159. Doi: https://doi.org/10.1177/0957926517734349

Korb, S., Malsert, J., Strathearn, L., Vuilleumier, P., & Niedenthal, P. (2016). Sniff and mimic—Intranasal oxytocin increases facial mimicry in a sample of men. *Hormones and Behavior*, *84*, 64–74. DOI: 10.1016/j.yhbeh.2016.06.003

Kowart, R. & Oldmeadow, J. A. (2015). Playing for social comfort: Online video game play as a social accommodator for the insecurely attached. *Computers in Human Behavior, 53*, 556–566. Doi: https://doi.org/10.1016/j.chb.2014.05.004

Kringelbach, M. L. & Berridge, K. C. (2015). Motivation and pleasure in the brain. In W. Hoffman and L. F. Nordgren (Eds.), *The psychology of desire* (pp. 129–145). New York, NY: Guilford Press.

Kroger, J. (2015). Identity development through adulthood: The move toward "wholeness". In K. C. McLean and M. Syed (Eds.), *The Oxford handbook of identity development* (pp. 65–80). New York, NY: Oxford University Press. Doi: https://doi.org/10.1093/oxfordhb/9780199936564.013.004

Kroger, J. & Marcia, J. (2011). The identity statuses: Origins, meaning and interpretations. In S. J. Schwartz, K. Luyckx, and V. L. Vignoles (Eds.), *Handbook of identity theory and research* (pp. 31–53). New York, NY. Springer. Doi: https://doi.org/10.1007/978-1-4419-7988-9_2

Kuntoro, I. A., Dwiputri, G., & Adams, P. (2018). The contributions of parenting style and theory of mind to the understanding of morally relevant theory of mind in Indonesian children. In A. Ariyanto, H. Mulak, P. Newcombe, F. Piercy, E. K. Poerwandari, and S. H. R. Suradijonon (Eds.), *Diversity in unity: Perspectives from psychology and behavioral sciences* (pp. 83–89). New York, NY: Routledge/Taylor & Francis Group. Doi: https://doi.org/10.1201/9781315225302-11

LaBianca, S., Pagsberg, A. K., Jakobsen, K. D., Demur, A. B., Bartalan, M., LaBianca, J., & Werge, T. (2018). Brief report: Clusters and trajectories across the autism and/or ADHD spectrum. *Journal of Autism and Developmental Disorders, 48*, 3629–3636. Doi: https://doi.org/10.1007/s10803-018-3618-6

Landers, M. S. & Sullivan, R. M. (2012). The development and neurobiology of infant attachment and fear. *Developmental Neuroscience, 34*(2–3), 101–114.

Langman, P. (2013). Thirty-five rampage school shooters: Trends, patterns, and typology. In N. Bockler, T. Seeger, P. Sitzer and W. Heitmeyer (Eds.), *School shootings* (pp. 131–156). New York, NY: Springer Science+Business Media. Doi: https://doi.org/10.1007/978-1-4614-5526-4_6

Lanius, U. F. (2014). Attachment, neuropeptides, and autonomic regulation: A vagal shift hypothesis. In U. F. Lanius, S. F. Paulson, and F. M. Corrigan (Eds.), *Neurobiology and treatment of traumatic dissociation: Towards an embodied self* (pp. 105–129). New York, NY: Springer Publishing. Doi: https://doi.org/10.1891/9780826106322.0006

Lau-Zhu, A., Fritz, A., & McLoughlin, G. (2019). Overlaps and distinctions between attention deficit/hyperactivity disorder and autism spectrum disorder in young adulthood: Systematic review and guiding framework for EEG-imaging research. *Neuroscience and Biobehavioral Review, 96*, 93–115. Doi: https://doi.org/10.1016/j.neubiorev.2018.10.009

Lavin, C., Melis, C., Mikulan, E., Gelormini, C., Huepe, D., & Ibanez, A. (2013). The anterior cingulate cortex: A integrative hub for human social-driven interaction. *Frontiers in Neuroscience, 7*(64), 1–4. Doi: https://doi.org/10.3389/fnins.2013.00064

Leary, M. R., Kowalski, R. M., Smith, L., & Phillips, S. (2003). Teasing, rejection, and violence: Case studies of the school shootings. *Aggressive Behavior, 29*, 202–214. Doi: https://doi.org/10.1002/ab.10061

LeDoux, J. (2002). *Synaptic self: How our brains become who we are.* New York, NY: Penguin Books.

Lee, A. R. & Horsely, J. S. (2017). The role of social media on positive youth development: An analysis of 4-H Facebook page and 4-H'ers' positive development. *Children and Youth Services Review, 77*, 127–138. Doi: https://doi.org/10.1016/j.childyouth.2017.04.014

Leech, R., Braga, R., & Sharp, D. J. (2012). Echoes of the brain within the posterior cingulate cortex. *Journal of Neuroscience, 32*(1), 215–222. Doi: https://doi.org/10.1523/jneurosci.3689-11.2012

Le Merrer, J., Becker, J. J., Befort, K., & Kieffer, B. L. (2015). Reward processing by the opioid system in the brain. *Physiological Reviews, 89*(4), 1379–1412. Doi: https://doi.org/10.1152/physrev.00005.2009

Lenzi, D., Trentini, C., Tambelli, R., & Pantana, P. (2015). Neural basis of attachment-caregiving systems interaction: Insights from neuroimaging studies. *Frontiers in Psychology, 6*, Article 1241, no pagination specified. Doi: https://doi.org/10.3389/fpsyg.2015.01241

Levine, L.E., Waite, B. M., Bowman, L. L., & Kachinsky, K. (2019). Mobile media use by infants and toddlers. *Computers in Human Behavior, 94*, 92–99. Doi: https://doi.org/10.1016/j.chb.2018.12.045

Lewin, A., Hodgkinson, S., Waters, D. M., Premphe, H. A., Beers, L. S., & Feinberg, M. E. (2015). Strengthening positive coparenting in teen parents: A cultural adaptation of an evidence-based intervention. *Journal of Primary Prevention, 36*, 139–154. Doi: https://doi.org/10.1007/s10935-015-0388-1

Li, X. & Zheng, X. (2014). Adult attachment orientations and subjective well-being: Emotional intelligence and self-esteem as moderators. *Social Behavior and Personality, 42*(8), 1257–1266. Doi: https://doi.org/10.2224/sbp.2014.42.8.1257

Liljenfors, R. & Lundh, L-G. (2015). Mentalization and intersubjectivity towards a theoretical integration. *Psychoanalytic Psychology, 12*(1), 36–60. Doi: https://doi.org/10.1037/a0037129

Lindberg, L. D., Santelli, J. S., & Desai, S. (2016). Understanding the decline in adolescent fertility in the United States, 2007–2012. Journal of Adolescent Health, 59(5), 577–583. Doi: https://doi.org/10.1016/j.jadohealth.2016.06.024

Lisdahl, K. M., Shollenbarger, S., Sagar, K. A., & Gruber, S. A. (2018). The neurocognitive impact of alcohol and marijuana use on the developing adolescent and young adult brain. In P. M. Monti, S. M. Colby, and T. O., Tevyaw (Eds.), *Brief interventions for adolescent alcohol and substance abuse* (pp. 50–82). New York, NY: Guilford Press. Doi: https://doi.org/10.1080/07317107.2019.1599265

Littrell, J. (2015). *Neuroscience for psychologists and other mental health professionals: Promoting wellbeing and treating mental illness.* New York, NY: Springer Publishing. Doi: https://doi.org/10.1891/9780826122797

Loeber, R. & Farrington, D. P. (2012). From juvenile delinquency to adult crime: Criminal careers, justice policies, and prevention. New York, NY: Oxford University Press. Doi: https://doi.org/10.1093/acprof:oso/9780199828166.001.0001

Lozano, P., Thai, K. P., & Ponciano, L., (2016). Using early learning technology to prepare Head Start families for kindergarten. Age of Learning and ABCmouse.com. Available at https://www.ageoflearning.com/case_studies/ABCmouse_CaseStudy_Albina_Head_Start.pdf.

Luna, N., Horton, E. G., & Malloy, T. (2016). Examining protective factors for dysthymia among individuals attending substance abuse treatment. *Journal of Social Service Research, March 13.* No pagination. Doi: https://doi.org/10.1080/01488376.2016.1147518

Luna, N., Horton, E. G., Newman, D., and Malloy, T. (2015). An empirical study of attachment dimensions and mood disorders in inpatient substance abuse clients: The mediating role of spirituality. *Addiction Research and Theory, Dec. 29,* No Pagination. Doi: https://doi.org/10.3109/16066359.2015.1119267

Lupien, S. J., McEwen, B. S., Gunnar, M. R., & Heim, C. (2009). Effects of stress throughout the lifespan on the brain, behavior and cognition. *Nature Reviews Neuroscience, 10*(6), 434–445. Doi: https://doi.org/10.1038/nrn2639

Lyons-Ruth, K. & Jacobvitz, D. (2017). Attachment disorganization from infancy to adulthood: Neurobiological correlates, parenting contexts, and pathways to disorder. In J. R. Cassidy and P. R. Shaver (Eds.), *Handbook of attachment: Theory, research and clinical applications,* (3rd ed.) (pp.667–695). New York, NY: Guilford Press.

Ma, A. M., Frick, K. D., Crawford, A., & Guyer, B. (2015). Early childhood health promotion and its life course health consequences. In A. J. Reynolds, A. J. Rolnick, and J. A. Temple (Eds.), *Health and education in early childhood: Predictors, interventions and policies* (pp. 113–144). New York, NY: Cambridge University Press. Doi: https://doi.org/10.1017/cbo9781139814805.010

MacKinnon, A. L., Carter, C. S., Feeley, N., Gold, I., Hayton, B., Santhakumaran, S., & Zelkowitz, P. (2018). Theory of mind as a link between oxytocin and maternal behavior. *Psychoendocrinology, 92,* 87–94. Doi: https://doi.org/10.1016/j.psyneuen.2018.03.018

Madfis, E. (2016). In search of meaning: Are school rampage shootings random and senseless violence? *Journal of Psychology, 151*(1), 21–35. Doi: https://doi.org/10.1080/00223980.2016.1196161

Main, M. (1995). Attachment: Overview, with implications for clinical work. In S. Goldberg, R. Muir and J. Kerr (Eds.), *Attachment theory: Social, developmental and clinical perspectives* (pp. 127–159). Hillsdale, NJ: Analytic Press. Doi: https://doi.org/10.1177/00030651990470010403

Main, M. (2000). The organized categories of infant, child, adolescent and adult attachment: Flexible vs. inflexible attention under attachment-related stress. *Journal of the American Psychoanalytic Association, 48*(4), 1055–1096. Doi: https://doi.org/10.1177/00030651000480041801

Main, M., Kaplan, N., & Cassidy, J. (1985). Security in infancy, childhood and adulthood: A move to the level of representation. *Monographs of the Society for Research in Child Development, 50*(1–2), 66–104. Doi: https://doi.org/10.2307/3333827

Main, M. & Solomon, J. (1990). Procedures for identifying infants as disorganized/disoriented during the Ainsworth Strange Situation. In M. T. Greenberg, D. Ciccheti, and M. Cummings (Eds.), *Attachment in the preschool years: Theory, research and intervention* (pp. 121–160). Chicago, IL: University of Chicago Press.

Marchetti, A. Massaro, D., & Di Dio, C. (2017). The bodies "at the forefront": Mentalization, memory, and construction of the self during adolescence. *Frontiers in Psychology, 8*(article 1502), pp. 1–4. Doi: https://doi.org/10.3389/fpsyg.2017.01502

Marks, A. D. G., Horrocks, K. A., & Schutte, N. S. (2016). Emotional intelligence mediates the relationship between insecure attachment and subjective health outcomes. *Personality and Individual Differences, 98,* 188–192. Doi: https://doi.org/10.1016/j.paid.2016.03.038

Marks-Tarlow, T., Solomon, M. & Siegel, D. J. (2018). Introduction. In T. Marks-Tarlow, M. Solomon, and D. J. Siegel (Eds.), *Play & creativity in psychotherapy* (pp. 1–12). New York, NY: W. W. Norton & Co.

Marmarosh, C., Gelso, C., Markin, R., Majors, R., Mallery, C., & Choi, J. (2009). The real relationship in psychotherapy: Relationships to adult attachments, working alliance, transference, and therapy outcome. *Journal of Counseling Psychology, 56*(3), 337–350. Doi: https://doi.org/10.1037/a0015169

Martin, J. A., Hamilton, B. E., & Osterman, M. J. K. (2018). Births in the United States, 2017. *NCHS Data Brief* (318), 1–8.

Martin, J. A., Hamilton, B. E., Osterman M. J. K., Driscoll, A. K., & Drake. P. (2018). Births: Final data for 2017. *National Vital Statistics Reports, 67*(8). Hyattsville, MD: National Center for Health Statistics.

Martin, J. A. & Osterman, M. J. K. (2018). Describing the increase of preterm births in the United States, 2014-2106. *NCHS Data Brief (312).* Hyattsville, MD: National Center for Health Statistics.

Maslow, A. H., (1943). A theory of human motivation. *Psychological Review, 50*(4), 370–396. Doi: https://doi.org/10.1037/h0054346

Matto, H., Strolin-Goltzman, J., & Ballan, M. (2014). *Neuroscience for social work: Current research and practice.* New York, NY: Springer Publishing. Doi: https://doi.org/10.1891/9780826108777

May, P. A., Chambers, C. D., Kalberg, W. O., Zellner, J., Fledman, H., Buckley, D., Kopald, D. … Hoyme, H. E. (2018). Prevalence of fetal alcohol syndrome disorders in 4 US communities. *Journal of the American Medical Association, 319*(5), 474–482.

Mayer, E. A. (2011). Gut feelings: The emerging biology of gut-brain communication. *Nature Reviews Neuroscience, 12*(8), 453–456. Doi: https://doi.org/10.1038/nrn3071

Mayer, E. A. & Hsiao, E. Y. (2017). The gut and its microbiome as related to central nervous system functioning and psychological well-being: Introduction to the special issue of Psychosomatic Medicine. *Psychosomatic Medicine, 79*, 844–846. Doi: https://doi.org/10.1097/psy.0000000000000525

Mayer, J. D., Salovey, P., & Caruso, D. R. (2004). Emotional intelligence: Theory, findings and implications. *Psychological Inquiry, 15*(3), 197–215. Doi: https://doi.org/10.1207/s15327965pli1503_02

McCarty, W. A. & Glenn, M. (2008). Investing in human potential from the beginning of life: Keystone to maximizing human capital. *Journal of Prenatal and Perinatal Psychology and Health, 23*(2), 117–135.

McCraty, R. (2015a). Heart rate variability: New perspectives on physiological mechanisms, assessment of self-regulatory capacity, and health risk. *Global Advances in Health and Medicine, 4*(1), 46–61. Doi: https://doi.org/10.7453/gahmj.2014.073

McCraty, R. (2015b). *Science of the heart: Exploring the role of the heart in human performance, Vol. 2.* Boulder Creek, CA: HeartMathTM Institute.

McCrimmon, A. W., Climie, E. A., & Huynh, S. (2018). The relation between emotional intelligence and resilience in at-risk populations. *Developmental Neurorehabilitation, 21*(5), 326–335. Doi: https://doi.org/10.1080/17518423.2017.1387873

McGilchrist, I. (2009). *The master and his emissary: The divided brain and the making of the western world.* New Haven, CT: Yale University Press. Doi: https://doi.org/10.2307/j.ctvcb5c0t

McKenzie, R. & Dallos, R. (2017). Autism and attachment difficulties: Overlap of symptoms, implications and innovative solutions. *Clinical Child Psychology, 22*(4), 632–648. Doi: https://doi.org/10.1177/1359104517707323

McLaughlin, K. A., Sheridan, M. A., & Nelson, C. A. (2017). Neglect as a violation of species-expectant experience: Neurodevelopmental consequences. *Biological Psychiatry, 82*(October 1), 462–471. Doi: https://doi.org/10.1016/j.biopsych.2017.02.1096

McRae, E. M., Stoppelbein, L., O'Kelley, S. E., Fite, P., & Greening, L. (2019). Predicting child behavior: A comparative analysis between autism spectrum disorder and attention deficit/hyperactivity disorder. (2019). *Journal of Child and Family Studies, 28*, 668–683. Doi: https://doi.org/10.1007/s10826-018-1299-6

Medford, N. & Critchley, H. D. (2010). Conjoint activity of anterior insular and cingulate cortex: Awareness and response. *Brain Structure and Function, 214*, 535–549. Doi: https://doi.org/10.1007/s00429-010-0265-x

Meuti, V., Aceti, F., Giacchetti, N., Carluccio, G. M., Zaccagni, M., Marini, I., Giancola, O. & Biondi, M. (2015). Perinatal depression and patterns of attachment: A critical risk factor? *Depression Research and Treatment, 2015*(Article ID 105012), 1–9. Doi: https://doi.org/10.1155/2015/105012

Mikami, A. Y., Miller, M., & Lerner, M. D. (2019). Social functioning in youth with attention-deficit/hyperactivity disorder and autism spectrum disorder: Transdiagnostic commonalities and differences. *Clinical Psychology Review, 68*, 54–70. Doi: https://doi.org/10.1016/j.cpr.2018.12.005

Mikulincer, M. & Shaver, P. R. (2016). *Attachment in adulthood: Structure, dynamics, and change* (2nd ed.). New York, NY: Guilford Press.

Milteer, R. M., Ginsburg, K. R., the Council on Communications and Media, & Committee on Psychosocial Aspects of Child and Family Health (2012). The importance of play in promoting healthy child development and maintaining strong parent-child bond: Focus on child in poverty. *Pediatrics, 129*(1), e204–e213. Doi: https://doi.org/10.1542/peds.2011-2953

Minino, A. M., (2010). Mortality among teenagers aged 12–19: United States, 1999–2006. NCHS data brief, no. 37. Hyattsville, MD: National Center for Health Statistics. Doi: https://doi.org/10.1037/e665432010-001

Mollborn, A. & Dennis, J. A. (2012). Explaining the early development and health of teen mothers' children. *Sociological Forum, 27*, 1010–1036. Doi: https://doi.org/10.1111/j.1573-7861.2012.01366.x

Monk, C., Spicer, J., & Champagne, F. A. (2012). Linking prenatal adversity to developmental outcomes in infants: The role of epigenetic pathways. *Development and Psychopathology, 24*, 1361–1376. Doi: https://doi.org/10.1017/s0954579412000764

Monks, C. P., Ortega Ruiz, R., & Torrado, V. E. (2002). Unjustified aggression in preschool. *Aggressive Behavior, 28*(6), 458–476. Doi: https://doi.org/10.1002/ab.10032

Montgomery, A. (2013). *Neurobiology essentials for clinicians: What every therapist needs to know.* New York, NY: W. W. Norton & Co.

Mortimer, J. T. (2010). The benefits and risks of adolescent employment. *Prevention Researcher, 17*(2), 8–11.

Mosier, W. A. (2013). Addressing the affective domain: What neuroscience says about social/emotional development in early childhood. In L. H. Wasserman and D. Zambo (Eds.), *Early childhood and neuroscience—Links to development and learning, educating the young child* (pp. 77–103). New York, NY: Springer Science+Business Media Dordrecht. Doi: https://doi.org/10.1007/978-94-007-6671-6_6

Mullan, K. & Chatzitheochari, S. (2019). Changing times together? A time-diary analysis of family time in the digital age in the United Kingdom. *Journal of Marriage and Family, March 11*, no pagination specified. Doi: https://doi.org/10.1111/jomf.12564

Munich, R. L. & Munich, M. A. (2009). Overparenting and the narcissistic pursuit of attachment. *Psychiatric Annals, 39*(4), 227–235. Doi: https://doi.org/10.3928/00485713-20090401-04

Nader, K. & Nader, W. (2012). Youth at risk: Targeted shootings, other school violence and suicide. In K. Nader (Ed.) *School rampage shootings and other youth disturbances: Early preventative interventions* (pp. 33–70). New York, NY: Routledge. Doi: https://doi.org/10.4324/9780203855454

Nam, S. K. & Lee, S. M. (2015). The role of attachment and stigma in the relationship between stress and attitudes toward counseling in S. Korea. *Journal of Counseling and Development, 93*(2), 212–224. Doi: https://doi.org/10.1002/j.1556-6676.2015.00197.x

Narvaez, D. & Lapsley, D. K. (2005). The psychological foundations of everyday morality and moral expertise, In D. Lapsley and C. Power (Eds.), *Character psychology and character education* (pp. 140–165). Notre Dame, IN: University of Notre Dame Press. Doi: https://doi.org/10.1017/cbo9780511627125.008

Narvaez, D. & Vaydich, J. L. (2008). Moral development and behavior under the spotlight of the neurobiological sciences. *Journal of Moral Education, 37*(3), 289–312. Doi: https://doi.org/10.1080/03057240802227478

Nasaescu, E., Marin-Lopez, I., Llorent, V. J., Ortega-Ruiz, R., & Zych, I. (2018). Abuse of technology in adolescence and its relation to social and emotional competencies, emotions in online communication, and bullying. *Computers in Human Behavior, 88*, 114–120. Doi: https://doi.org/10.1016/j.chb.2018.06.036

National Association of Social Workers (2017). *Code of Ethics.* Available at https://www.socialworkers.org/About/Ethics/Code-of-Ethics

Navarro, R., Larranaga, E., & Yubero, S. (2018). Differences between preadolescent victims and non-victims of cyberbullying in cyber-relationship motives and coping strategies for handling problems with peers. *Current Psychology, 37*, 116–127. Doi: https://doi.org/10.1007/s12144-016-9495-2

Nephew, B. C., Byrnes, E. M., & Bridges, R. S. (2010). Vasopressin mediates enhanced offspring protection in multiparous rats. *Neuropharmacology, 58*(1), 102–106. Doi: https://doi.org/10.1016/j.neuropharm.2009.06.032

Neumann, M. M. (2018). Using tablets and apps to enhance emerging literacy skills in young children. *Early Childhood Research Quarterly, 42*, 239–246. Doi: https://doi.org/10.1016/j.ecresq.2017.10.006

Newland, L. A., & Coyl, D. D. (2010). Fathers' role as attachment figures: An interview with Sir Richard Bowlby. *Early Child Development and Care, 180*(1–2), 25–32. Doi: https://doi.org/10.1080/03004430903414679

Newman, K. S., Foz, C., Harding, D., Mehta, J., & Froth, W. (2004). *Rampage: The social roots of school shootings.* New York, NY: Basic Books.

Noorhasan, D. (2014). Does psychiatric diagnosis affect fertility outcomes? In D. L. Barnes (Ed.), *Women's reproductive health across the lifespan.* (pp. 141–158). Cham, Switzerland: Springer International Publishing. Doi: https://doi.org/10.1007/978-3-319-05116-1_8

Nowakowski, R. S. (2006). Stable neuron numbers from cradle to grave. *Proceedings of the National Academy of Sciences of the United States of America, 103*(33), 12219–12220. Doi: https://doi.org/10.1073/pnas.0605605103

Nuccini, F., Paterlini, M., Gargano, G., & Landini, A. (2015). The attachment of prematurely born children at school age: A pilot study. *Clinical Child Psychology and Psychiatry, 20*(3), 381–394. Doi: https://doi.org/10.1177/1359104515589640

Nunes, F. & Mota, C. P. (2017). Parenting styles and suicidal ideation in adolescents: Mediating effect of attachment. *Journal of Child and Family Studies, 26*, 734–747. Doi: https://doi.org/10.1007/s10826-016-0611-6

Ogden, P. (2018). Play, creativity, and movement vocabulary. In T. Marks-Tarlow, M. Solomon, and D. J. Siegel (Eds.), *Play & creativity in psychotherapy* (pp. 92–109). New York, NY: W. W. Norton & Co.

Oliemat, E., Ihmeideh, F., & Alkhawaldeh, M. (2018). The use of touchscreen tablets in early childhood: Children's knowledge, skills, and attitudes toward tablet technology. *Children and Youth Services Review, 88*, 591–597. Doi: https://doi.org/10.1016/j.childyouth.2018.03.028

Oliveira, P. S., Fearon, R. M. P., Belsky, J., Fachada, I., & Soares, I. (2015). Quality of institutional care and early childhood development. *International Journal of Behavioral Development, 39*(2), 161–170. Doi: https://doi.org/10.1177/0165025414552302

Olweus, D. & Limber, S. P. (2010). Bullying in school: Evaluation and dissemination of the Olweus Prevention Program. American Journal of Orthopsychiatry, 80(1), 124–134. Doi: https://doi.org/10.1111/j.1939-0025.2010.01015.x

O'Rahilly, R. & Muller, F. (2006). *The embryonic human brain: An atlas of development stages* (3rd ed.). Hoboken, NJ: John Wiley & Sons.

O'Toole, M. E. (2000). *The school shooter: A threat assessment perspective.* Quantico, VA: National Center for the Analysis of Violent Crime, FBI Academy.

Padron, E., Carlson, E. A., & Sroufe, L. A. (2014). Frightened vs. not frightened disorganized infant attachment. *American journal of Orthopsychiatry, 84*(2), 201–208. Doi: https://doi.org/10.1037/h0099390

Panksepp, J. (2009). Brain emotional systems and qualities of mental life: From animal models of affect to implications for psychotherapies. In D. Fosha, D. Siegel, and M. Solomon (Eds.), The healing power of emotion: Affective neuroscience, development, and clinical practice (pp. 1–26). New York, NY: W. W. Norton & Co.

Panksepp, J. (2010). Affective neuroscience of the emotional BrainMind: Evolutionary perspectives and implications for understanding depression. *Dialogues in Clinical Neuroscience, 12*(4), 533–545.

Panksepp, J. & Watt, D. (2011). What is basic about basic emotions? Lasting lessons from affective neuroscience. *Emotion Review, 3*(4), 387–296. Doi: https://doi.org/10.1177/1754073911410741

Panksepp, J. (2012a). What is an emotional feeling: Lessons about the affective origins from cross-species neuroscience. *Motivation and Emotion, 36*, 4–15. Doi; https://doi.org/10.1007/s11031-011-9232-y

Panksepp, J. (2012b). *The archeology of the mind: Neuroevolutionary origins of human emotions.* New York, NY: W. W. Norton.

Panksepp, J. (2018). PLAY and the construction of creativity, cleverness, and reversal of ADHD in our social brains. In T. Marks-Tarlow, M. Solomon, and D. J. Siegel (Eds.), *Play & creativity in psychotherapy* (pp. 242–270). New York, NY: W. W. Norton & Co.

Papousek, M. (2016). Disinterest in play in infancy: Problems in the regulation of attention and play. In M. Cierpka (Ed.) *Regulatory disorders in infants.* (pp. 161–180). Cham, Switzerland: Springer International Publishing. Doi: https://doi.org/10.1007/978-3-319-43556-5_8

Pasalich, D. S., Cyr, M., Zheng, Y., & McMahon, R. J. (2016). Child abuse history in teen mothers and parent-child risk processes for offspring externalizing problems. *Child Abuse and Neglect, 56*, 89–98. Doi: https://doi.org/10.1016/j.chiabu.2016.04.011

Patchin, J. W. (2017). New teen sexting data. Available at https://cyberbullying.org/new-teen-sexting-data.

Patel, J. K. (2018). After Sandy Hook more than 400 people have been shot in over 200 school shootings. New York Times, Feb. 15. Available at https://www.nytimes.com/interactive/2018/02/15/us/school-shootings-sandy-hook-parkland.html?utm_source=newsletter&utm_medium=email&utm_campaign=&stream=top-stories Doi: https://doi.org/10.4337/9781781002124.00027

Pawluski, J. L., Lonstein, J. S., & Fleming, A. S. (2017). The neurobiology of postpartum anxiety and depression. *Trends in Neurosciences, 40*(2), 106–120. Doi: https://doi.org/10.1016/j.tins.2016.11.009

Pelligrini, A. D. & Smith, P. K. (1998). Physical activity play: The nature and function of a neglected aspect of play. *Child Development, 69*(3), 577–598. Doi: https://doi.org/10.1111/j.1467-8624.1998.00577.x

Penman-Aguilar, A., Carter, M., Snead, M. C., & Kourtis, A. P. (2013). Socioeconomic disadvantage as a social determinant of teen childbearing in the U.S. Public Health Report, 128(suppl 1), 5–22. Doi: https://doi.org/10.1177/00333549131282s102

Pennestri, M., Gaudreau, H., Bouvette-Turcot, A., Moss, E., Lecompte, V., Atkinson, L., Lydon, J., Steiner, M., & Meany, M. J., on behalf of the Mavan Research Team (2015). Attachment disorganization among children in the Neonatal Intensive Care Unit: Preliminary results. *Early Human Development, 91,* 601–606. Doi: https://doi.org/10.1016/j.earlhumdev.2015.07.005

Perry, B. D. (2002). Childhood experience and the expression of genetic potential: What childhood neglect tell us about nature and nurture. *Brain and Mind, 3,* 79–100.

Perry, E. & Flood, A. (2016). Autism spectrum disorder and attachment: A clinician's perspective. In H. K. Fletcher, A. Flood, and D. J. Hare (Eds.), Attachment and intellectual and developmental disability: A clinician's guide to practice and research (pp. 79–103). Hoboken, NJ: Wiley-Blackwell Publishing. Doi: https://doi.org/10.1002/9781118938119.ch5

Pessoa, L. (2008). On the relationship between emotion and cognition. *Nature Reviews Neuroscience, 9*(2), 148–158.

Petrides, K. V. & Furnham, A. (2003). Trait emotional intelligence: Behavioural validation in two studies of emotion recognition and reactivity to mood induction. *European Journal of Personality, 17,* 39–75. Doi: https://doi.org/10.1002/per.466

Petrowski, K., Pokorny, D., Nowacki, K., & Buckheim, A. (2013). The therapist's attachment representation and the patient's attachment to the therapist. *Psychotherapy Research, 23*(1), 25–34. Doi: https://doi.org/10.1080/10503307.2012.717307

Pfeifer, J. H., Dapretto, M., & Lieberman, M. D. (2010). Neural foundations of evaluative self-knowledge in middle childhood, early adolescence and adulthood. In P. D. Zelazo, M. Chandler, and E. Crone (Eds.), *Developmental social cognitive neuroscience* (pp. 141–164). New York, NY: Taylor & Francis.

Piaget, J. (1936/1952). *The origins of intelligence in children.* New York, NY: International Universities Press.

Pinzon, J. L., Jones, V. F., & Committee on Adolescence and Committee on Early Childhood (2012). Care of adolescent parents and their children. *Pediatrics, 130,* 1743–1756. Doi: https://doi.org/10.1542/peds.2012-2879

Plessis, M. P., Smeekens, S., Cillessen, A. H. N., Whittle, S., & Guroglu, B. (2019). Bullying the brain? Longitudinal links between childhood peer victimization, cortisol, and adolescent brain structure. *Frontiers in Psychology, 9*(article 2706), 1–9. Doi: https://doi.org/10.3389/fpsyg.2018.02706

Pogarsky, G., Thornberry, T. P., & Lizotte, A. J., (2006). Developmental outcomes for children of young mothers. *Journal of Marriage and Family, 68*(2), 332–344. Doi: https://doi.org/10.1111/j.1741-3737.2006.00256.x

Pontzer, D. (2010). A theoretical test of bullying behavior: Parenting, personality, and the bully/victim relationship. *Journal of Family Violence, 25,* 259–273. Doi: https://doi.org/10.1007/s10896-009-9289-5

Porges, S. (2011). *The polyvagal theory: Neurophysiological foundations of emotions, attachment, communication, self-regulation.* New York, NY: W. W. Norton & Co.

Porges, S. (2017). *The pocket guide to the polyvagal theory: The transformative power of feeling safe.* New York, NY: W. W. Norton.

Porges, S. W. & Furman, S. A. (2011). The early development of the autonomic nervous system provides a neural platform for social behavior: A polyvagal perspective. *Infant and Child Development, 20,* 106–118. Doi: https://doi.org/10.1002/icd.688

Prehn, K. & Heerkeren, H. R. (2014). Moral brains—possibilities and limits of the neuroscience of ethics. In M. Christen, C. van Shaik, J. Fischer, M. Huppenbauer, and C. Tanner (Eds.), *Empirically informed ethics: Morality between facts and norms* (pp. 137–157). Cham, Switzerland: Springer International Publishing. Doi: https://doi.org/10.1007/978-3-319-01369-5_8

Premack, D. & Woodruff, G. (1978). Does the chimpanzee have a theory of mind? *Behavioral and Brain Sciences, 25,* 1–72.

Price, S. A. & Brosnan, S. F. (2012). To each according to his need? Variability in the responses to inequity in non-human primates. *Social Justice Research, 25,* 140–169. Doi: https://doi.org/10.1007/s11211-012-0153-z

Rakic, P. (2006). No more cortical neurons for you. *Science, 313,* 928–929.

Rash, J. A. & Prkachin, K. M. (2013). Cardiac vagal reactivity during relived sadness is predicted by affect intensity and emotional intelligence. *Biological Psychology, 92*(2), 106–113. Doi: https://doi.org/10.1016/j.biopsycho.2012.11.009

Raz, S. & Zysberg, L. (2015). Neural correlates of emotional intelligence: A review. In L. Zysberg and S. Raz (Eds.), *Emotional intelligence: Current evidence from psychophysiological, education and organizational perspectives* (pp. 3–18). Haupauge, NY: Nova Science Publishers. Doi: https://doi.org/10.1016/j.bandc.2014.09.003

Reck, C., Tietz, A., Muller, M., Seibold, K., & Tronick, E. (2018). The impact of maternal anxiety disorder on mother-infant interaction in the postpartum period. *PLoS ONE, 13*(5): e0194763, no pagination specified. Doi: https://doi.org/10.1371/journal.pone.0194763

Reyna, V. & Farley, E. (2006). Risk and rationality in adolescent decision-making: Implications for theory, practice and public policy. *Psychological Science in the Public Interest, 37*, 1–44. Doi: https://doi.org/10.1111/j.1529-1006.2006.00026.x

Richards, K. V. (2016). Safe & Sound: Experiences of caregivers in an attachment-based parenting group. *Dissertation Abstracts International: Section B: The Sciences and Engineering, Vol 76*(10B[E]), no pagination specified.

Rideout, V. (2017). *The Common Sense census: Media use by kids age zero to eight*. San Francisco, CA: Common Sense Media.

Rogers, L. J. (2000). Evolution of hemispheric specialization: Advantages and disadvantages. *Brain and Language, 73*, 236–253. Doi: https://doi.org/10.1006/brln.2000.2305

Rommelse, N. N., van der Meer, J. M., Hartman, C. A., & Buitelaar, J. K. (2016). Cognitive profiling useful for unraveling cross-disorder mechanisms: Support for a step-function endophenotype model. *Clinical Psychological Science, 4*, 957–970. Doi: https://doi.org/10.1177/2167702616638826

Rosenberg, S. (2017). *Accessing the power of the vagus nerve: Self-help exercises for anxiety, depression, and autism*. Berkeley, CA: North Atlantic Books.

Roskam, I., Stievenart, M., Tessier, R., Muntean, A., Escobar, M. J., Santalices, M. P., Juffer, F., van IJzendoorn, M. H., & Poerrehumbert, B. (2014). Another way of thinking about ADHD: The predictive role of early attachment deprivation in adolescents' level of symptoms. *Social Psychiatry and Psychiatric Epidemiology, 49*, 133–144. Doi: https://doi.org/10.1007/s00127-013-0685-z

Ross, E. J., Graham, D. L., Money, K. M., & Stanwood, G. D. (2015). Developmental consequences of fetal exposure to drugs: What we know and what we still must still learn. *Neuropsychopharmacology Reviews, 40*, 61–87. Doi: https://doi.org/10.1038/npp.2014.147

Rossen, L., Hutchinson, D., Wilson, J., Burns, L., Olsson, C., Allsop, S., Elliot, E., ... & Mattick, R. P. (2016). Predictors of postnatal mother-infant bonding: The role of antenatal bonding, maternal substance use and mental health. *Archives of Women's Mental Health, 19*(4), 609–622. Doi: https://doi.org/10.1007/s00737-016-0602-z

Rossouw, T. (2018). Mentalization-based therapy for adolescents: Managing storms in youth presenting with self-harm and suicidal states. In H. Steele and M. Steele (Eds.), *Handbook of attachment-based interventions* (pp. 419–440). New York, NY: Guilford Press.

Ruedingera, E. & Cox, J. (2012). Adolescent childbearing: Consequences and intervention. *Current Opinion in Pediatrics, 24*, 446–452.

Sage, C. & Burgio, E. (2018). Electromagnetic fields, pulse radiofrequency radiation, and epigenetics: how wireless technologies may affect childhood development. *Child Development, 89*(1), 129–16. Doi: https://doi.org/10.1111/cdev.12824

Saleeby, D. (1992). Biology's challenge to social work: Embodying the person-in-environment perspective. *Social Work, 37*(2), 112–118. Doi: https://doi.org/10.1093/sw/37.2.112

Sasselli, V., Pachnis, V., & Burns, A. J. (2012). The enteric nervous system. *Developmental Biology, 366*(1), 64–73. Doi: https://doi.org/10.1016/j.ydbio.2012.01.012

Schindler, A. & Broning, S. (2015). A review on attachment and adolescent substance abuse: Empirical evidence and implications for prevention and treatment. *Substance Abuse, 36*, 304–313. Doi: https://doi.org/10.1080/08897077.2014.983586

Schindler A., Thomasius, R., Peterson, K., & Sack, P. (2009). Heroin as an attachment substitute? Differences in attachment representations between opioid, ecstasy and cannabis abusers. *Attachment and Human Development, 11*(3), 307–330. Doi: https://doi.org/10.1080/14616730902815009

Schindler, A., Thomasius, R., Sack, P., Gemeinhardt, B., Kustner, U., & Eckert. J. (2005). Attachment and substance use disorders: A review of the literature and a study in drug dependent adolescents. *Attachment and Human Development, 7*(3), 207–228. Doi: https://doi.org/10.1080/14616730500173918

Schoppe-Sullivan, S. J., Kotila, L. E., Jia, R., Lang, S. N., & Bower, D. J. (2013). Comparisons of levels and predictors of mothers' and fathers' engagement with their preschool-age children. *Early Childhood Development and Care, 183*(3–4), 498–514. Doi: https://doi.org/10.1080/03004430.2012.711596

Schore, A. N. (1994). *Affect regulation and the origin of the self: The neurobiology of emotional development*. New York, NY: Taylor & Francis.

Schore, A. N. (2000). Attachment and regulation of the right brain. *Attachment and Human Development, 2*, 23–47. Doi: https://doi.org/10.1080/146167300361309

Schore, A. N. (2001). Effects of a secure attachment relationship on right brain development, affect regulation, and infant mental health. *Infant Mental Health Journal, 22*(1–2), 7–66. Doi: https://doi.org/10.1002/1097-0355(200101/04)22:1<7::aid-imhj2>3.0.co;2-n

Schore, A. N. (2002a). Advances in neuropsychoanalysis, attachment theory, and trauma research: Implications for self psychology. *Psychoanalytic Inquiry, 22*, 433–484. Doi: https://doi.org/10.1080/07351692209348996

Schore, A. N. (2002b). The neurobiology of attachment and early personality organization. *Journal of Prenatal and Perinatal Psychology & Health, 16*(3), 249–263.

Schore, A. N. (2005). Attachment, affect regulation, and the developing right brain: Linking development neuroscience to pediatrics. *Pediatrics in Review, 28*(8), 204–217. Doi: https://doi.org/10.1542/pir.26-6-204

Schore, A. & Marks-Tarlow, T. (2018). How love opens creativity, play, and the arts through early right-brain development. In T. Marks-Tarlow, M. Solomon, and D. J. Siegel (Eds.), *Play & creativity in psychotherapy* (pp. 64–91). New York, NY: W. W. Norton & Co.

Schuder, S. E. (2005). Stress-induced hypocortisolemia diagnosed as psychiatric disorders responsive to hydrocortisone replacement. Annals of the New York Academy of Science, 1057, 466–478. Doi: https://doi.org/10.1196/annals.1356.036

Schulenberg, J. E., Johnston, L. D., O'Malley, P. M., Bachman, J. G., Miech, R. A. & Patrick, M. E. (2018). Monitoring the Future national survey results on drug use, 1975–2017: Volume II, College students and adults ages 19–55. Ann Arbor: Institute for Social Research, The University of Michigan. Available at http://monitoringthefuture.org/pubs.html#monographs. Doi: https://doi.org/10.3998/2027.42/146531

Schwerdtfeger, K. L. & Goff, B. S. (2007). Intergenerational transmission of trauma: Exploring mother-infant prenatal attachment. *Journal of Traumatic Stress, 20*(1), 39–51. Doi: https://doi.org/10.1002/jts.20179

Sciaraffa, M. A., Zeneah, P. D., & Zeneah, C. H. (2018). Understanding and promoting resilience in the context of adverse childhood experiences. *Early Childhood Education Journal, 46*, 343–353. Doi: https://doi.org/10.1007/s10643-017-0869-3

Sedgh, G., Finer, L. B., Bankole, A., Eilers, M. A., & Singh, S. (2015). Adolescent pregnancy, birth, and abortion rates across countries: Levels and recent trends. *Journal of Adolescent Health, 56*(2), 223–230. Doi: https://doi.org/10.1016/j.jadohealth.2014.09.007

Segrin, C., Woszidlo, A., Givertz, M., & Montgomery, N. (2013). Parent and child traits associated with overparenting. *Journal of Social and Clinical Psychology, 32*(6), 569–595. Doi: https://doi.org/10.1521/jscp.2013.32.6.569

Semper, J. V. O., Murillo, J. I., & Bernacer, J. (2016). Adolescent emotional maturation through divergent models of brain organization. *Frontiers in Psychology, 7*(Article 1263), 1–12. Doi: https://doi.org/10.3389/fpsyg.2016.01263

Sempio, O. L., Fabio, R. A., Tiezzi, P., & Cedro, C. (2016). Parental and teacher attachment in children at risk of ADHD and with ADHD. *Lifespan and Disability, XIX*(1), 57–77.

Seng, J. S., D'Andrea, W., & Ford, J. D. (2014). Complex mental health sequelae of psychological trauma among women in prenatal care. *Psychological Trauma, Theory, Research, Practice and Policy, 6*(1), 41–49. Doi: https://doi.org/10.1037/a0031467

Seng, J. S., Low, L., Sperlich, M., Ronis, D., Liberzon, I. (2011). Post-traumatic stress disorder, child abuse history, birthweight, and gestational age: A prospective cohort study. *British Journal of Obstetrics and Gynecology, 118*, 1329–1339. Doi: https://doi.org/10.1111/j.1471-0528.2011.03071.x

Shaver, P. R. & Mikulincer, M. (2002). Attachment-related psychodynamics. *Attachment & Human Development, 4*, 133–161. Doi: https://doi.org/10.1080/14616730210154171

Shaver, P. & Mikulincer, M. (2012). An attachment perspective on morality: Strengthening authentic forms of moral decision making. In M. Mikulincer and P. Shaver (Eds.), *The social psychology of morality: Exploring the causes of good and evil* (pp. 257–274). Washington, DC: American Psychological Association. Doi: https://doi.org/10.1037/13091-014

Shechtman, Z. & Dvir, V. (2006). Attachment style as a predictor of behavior in group counseling with preadolescents. *Group Dynamics, 10*(1), 29–42. Doi: https://doi.org/10.1037/1089-2699.10.1.29

Sheikh, M. A., Abelsen, B., & Olsen, J. A. (2016). Clarifying associations between childhood adversity, social support, behavioral factors, and mental health, health, and well-being in adulthood: a population-based study. *Frontiers in Psychology, 7*, 1–24. Doi: https://doi.org/10.3389/fpsyg.2016.00727

Sheina, E., Smirnova, E., & Ryabkova, I. (2017). The developmental potential of toys and games. In T. Bruce, P. Hakkararainen, and M. Bredikyte (Eds.), The Routledge international handbook of early childhood play (pp. 305–312). New York, NY: Routledge/Taylor and Francis Group. Doi: https://doi.org/10.4324/9781315735290-28

Sheridan, M. A. & McLaughlin, K. A. (2016). Neurobiological models of the impact of adversity on education. *Current Opinions in Behavioral Sciences, 10*, 108–113. Doi: https://doi.org/10.1016/j.cobeha.2016.05.013

Shetgiri, R. (2013). Bullying and victimization among children. *Advances in Pediatrics, 60*, 33–51. Doi: https://doi.org/10.1016/j.yapd.2013.04.004

Shonkoff, J. P. & Garner, A. S., and the Committee on Psychosocial Aspects of Child and Family Health (2012). The lifelong effects of early life adversity and toxic stress. *Pediatrics, 129*(1), E232–E246. Doi: https://doi.org/10.1542/peds.2011-2663

Sibcy, G. A. & Knight, A. M. (2017). Emotional intelligence and the attachment behavioral system. In R. W. Summers (Ed.), *Social psychology: How other people influence our thought and actions* (Vol 1), (pp. 59–86). Santa Barbara, CA: Greenwood Press/ABC-CLIO.

Siegel, D. (2001). Toward an interpersonal neurobiology of the developing mind: Attachment relationships, "mindsight" and neural integration. *Infant Mental Health Journal, 22*(1–2), 67–94. Doi: https://doi.org/10.1002/1097-0355(200101/04)22:1<67::aid-imhj3>3.0.co;2-g

Siegel, D. (2003). An interpersonal neurobiology of psychotherapy. In M. F. Solomon and D. Siegel (Eds.), *Healing trauma: Attachment, mind, body and brain*. New York: NY: W. W. Norton. Doi: https://doi.org/10.1080/00029157.2005.10403641

Siegel, D. (2004). Attachment and self-understanding: Parenting with the brain in mind. *Journal of Prenatal and Perinatal Psychology and Health, 18*(4), 273–285.

Siegel, D. (2006). An interpersonal neurobiology approach to psychotherapy. *Psychiatric Annals, 36*(4), 248–256.

Siegel, D. (2010). *The mindful therapist: A clinician's guide to mindsight and neural integration*. New York, NY: W. W. Norton & Co.

Siegel, D. (2012a). *The developing mind: How relationships and the brain interact to shape who we are*. New York, NY: Guilford Press.

Siegel, D. (2012b). *Pocket guide to interpersonal neurobiology: An integrative handbook of the mind*. New York, NY: W. W. Norton & Co.

Siegel D. & Bryson, T. (2011). *The whole-brain child: 12 revolutionary strategies to nurture your child's developing mind*. New York, NY: Delacourt Press.

Siegel, D. & Hartzell, M. (2003). *Parenting from the inside out: How a deeper self-understanding can help you raise children who thrive*. New York, NY: Penguin. Doi: https://doi.org/10.1007/s10615-009-0226-0

Siegel, D., Siegel, M. W., & Shah, A. V. (2010). Brain, mind and behavior. In D. Wedding and M. L. Stuber (Eds.), *Behavior and medicine* (5th ed.), (p. 3–21). Cambridge, MA: Hogrefe Publishing.

Singh, G. K., Siahposh, M., & Kogan, M. D. (2010). Neighborhood socioeconomic conditions, built environments, and childhood obesity. *Health Affairs, 29*, 503–512. Doi: https://doi.org/10.1377/hlthaff.2009.0730

Sitnick, S. L., Shaw, D. S., Weaver, C. M., Shelleby, E. C., Choe, D. E., Reuben, J. D., Gilliam, M., Winslow, E. B., & Taraban, L. (2017). Early childhood predictors of severe youth violence in low-income male adolescents. *Child Development, 88*(1), 27–40. Doi: https://doi.org/10.1111/cdev.12680

Slutsky, R. & DeShelter, L. M. (2017). How technology is transforming the ways in which children play. *Early Child Development and Care, 187*(7), 1138–1146. Doi: https://doi.org/10.1080/03004430.2016.1157790

Sroufe, L. A. (2002). From infant attachment to promotion of adolescent autonomy: Prospective longitudinal data on the role of parents in development. In J. G. Borkowski, S. L. Ramey, and M. Bristol-Power (Eds.), *Parenting and the child's world: Influences on academic, intellectual, and social-emotional development* (pp. 187–202). Mahwah, NJ: Psychology Press. Doi: https://doi.org/10.4324/9781410603616-10

Sroufe, L. A. (2005). Attachment and development: A prospective, longitudinal study from birth to adulthood. *Attachment and Human Development, 7*(4), 349–367. Doi: 10.1080/14616730500365928

Sroufe, L.A., Carlson, E.A., Levy, A.K., & Egeland, B. (1999). Implications of attachment theory for developmental psychopathology. *Development & Psychopathology, 11*, 1–13. Doi: https://doi.org/10.1017/s0954579499001923

Sroufe, L. A., Egeland, B., Carlson, E., & Collins, W. A. (2005). Placing early attachment experiences in developmental context: The Minnesota Longitudinal Study. In K. E. Grossman, K. Grossman and E. Waters (Eds.), *Attachment from infancy to adulthood: The major longitudinal studies* (pp. 48–70). New York, NY: Guilford Press. Doi: https://doi.org/10.1017/s0033291706237346

Stagnitti, K. (2017). A growing brain – a growing imagination. In E. Prendiville and J. Howard (Eds.), *Creative psychotherapy: Applying the principles of neurobiology to play and expressive-arts-based practice* (pp. 185–200). New York, NY: Routledge/Taylor and Francis Group. Doi: https://doi.org/10.4324/9781315680507

Stanescu, A. D., Balalau, D. O., Ples, L., Paunica, S., & Balalau, C. (2018). Postpartum depression: Prevention and multimodal therapy. *Journal of Mind and Medical Sciences, 5*(2), 163–168. Doi: https://doi.org/10.22543/7674.52.p163168

Stavrinos, D., Pope, C. N., Shen, J., & Schwebel, D. C. (2018). Distracted walking, bicycling, and driving: Systematic review and meta-analysis of mobile technology and youth crash risk. *Child Development, 89*(2), 118–128. Doi: https://doi.org/10.1111/cdev.12827

Steinberg, L. (2005). Cognitive and affective development in adolescence. *Trends in Cognitive Sciences, 9*(2), 69–74. Doi: https://doi.org/10.1016/j.tics.2004.12.005

Steinberg, L. (2008). A social neuroperspective on adolescent risk-taking. *Developmental Review, 28*, 78–106.

Stern, D. N. (1985). *The interpersonal world of infants*. New York, NY: Basic Books.

Stern, D. N. (2004). *The present moment in psychotherapy and everyday life*. New York, NY: W. W. Norton & Co.

Sternberg, N., Luria, R., & Scheppes, G. (2018). For whom is social-networking usage associated with anxiety? The moderating role of neural working-memory filtering of Facebook information. *Cognitive, Affective, & Behavioral Neuroscience, 18*, 1145–1158. Doi: https://doi.org/10.3758/s13415-018-0627-z

Stevens, V., De Bourdeaudhuij, I., & Van Oost, P. (2002). Relationship of the family environment to children's involvement in bully/victim problems at school. *Journal of Youth and Adolescence, 31*, 419–428. Doi: https://doi.org/10.1023/a:1020207003027

Stiles, J. & Jernigan, T. L. (2010). The basics of brain development. *Neuropsychology Review*, 20, 327–348.

Stone, D.M., Holland, K.M., Bartholow, B., Crosby, A. E., Davis, S., and Wilkins, N. (2017). Preventing suicide: A technical package of policies, programs, and practices. Atlanta, GA: National Center for Injury Prevention and Control, Centers for Disease Control and Prevention. Doi: https://doi.org/10.15620/cdc.44275

Stopbullying.gov (2018). Facts about bullying. Available at https://www.stopbullying.gov/media/facts/index.html#stats.

Storebo, O. J., Rasmussen, P. D., & Simonsen, E. (2016). Associations between insecure attachment and ADHD: Environmental mediating factors. *Journal of Attention Disorders, 20*(2), 187–196. Doi: https://doi.org/10.1177/1087054713501079

Storebo, O. J. & Simonsen, E. (2014). Is ADHD an early stage in the development of borderline personality disorder? *Nordic Journal of Psychiatry, 68*(5), 289–295. Doi: https://doi.org/10.3109/08039488.2013.841992

Strathearn, L. (2017). Maternal neglect: Oxytocin, dopamine and the neurobiology of attachment. *Journal of Neuroendocrinology, 23*, 1054–1065. Doi: https://doi.org/10.1111/j.1365-2826.2011.02228.x

Strauss, C., Morry, M. M., & Kito, M. (2012). Attachment styles and relationship quality: Actual, perceived, and ideal partner matching. *Personal Relationships, 19*, 14–36. Doi: https://doi.org/10.1111/j.1475-6811.2010.01333.x

Substance Abuse and Mental Health Services Association (2014). Results from the 2013 National Survey on Drug Use and Health: Summary of National Findings, NSDUH Series H-48, HHS Publication No. (SMA) 14-4863. Rockville, MD: Substance Abuse and Mental Health Services Administration. Doi: https://doi.org/10.1037/e380242004-001

Suddendorf, T. & Corballis, M. C. (2007). The evolution of foresight: What is mental time travel, and is it unique to humans? *Behavioral and Brain Sciences* 30, 299–351. Doi: https://doi.org/10.1017/s0140525x07001975

Suna, K. K., Ilay, G., Aysenur, A., Han, G. K., Ulku, U. E., Pasa, U., & Fatma, C. (2016). Effects of infertility etiology and depression on female sexual function. *Journal of Sex and Marital Therapy, 42*(1), 27–35. Doi: https://doi.org/10.1080/0092623x.2015.1010673

Swanson, K., Beckwith, L., & Howard, J. (2000). Intrusive caregiving and quality of attachment in prenatally drug-exposed toddlers and their primary caregivers. *Attachment and Human Development, 2*(2), 130–148. Doi: https://doi.org/10.1080/14616730050085527

Sziron, M. & HGildt, E. (2018). Digital media: The right to an open future and children 0–5. *Frontiers in Psychology*, 9(Nov 6), Article 2137, no pagination specified.

Szalavitz, M. & Perry, B. D. (2011). *Born for love*. New York, NY: Harper Collins Publishers.

Taddei, S. & Contena, B. (2017). Cognitive processes in ADHD and Asperger's disorder: Overlap and differences in PASS profiles. *Journal of Attention Disorders, 21*(13), 1087–1093. Doi: https://doi.org/10.1177/1087054713510350

Tarasuik, J. C., Ciorciari, J., & Stough, C. (2009). Understanding the neurobiology of emotional intelligence: A review. In C. Stough, D. H. Saklofske, and J. D. A. Parker, *Assessing emotional intelligence: Theory, research, and applications*. (pp. 307–320). New York, NY: Springer Science + Business Media. Doi: https://doi.org/10.1007/978-0-387-88370-0_16

Tareen, R. S. & Tareen, A. N. (2014). Attachment disorders and mental health issues in the newborn. In D. E. Greydanus, A. N. Feinberg, and J. Merrick (Eds.), *Caring for the newborn: A comprehensive guide for the clinician* (pp. 109–124). Hauppauge, NY: Nova Biomedical Books.

Tasimi, A. & Young, L. (2016). Memories of good deeds past: The reinforcing power of prosocial behavior in children. *Journal of Experimental Child Psychology, 147*, 159–166. Doi: https://doi.org/10.1016/j.jecp.2016.03.001

Teague, S. J., Gray, K. M., Tonge, B. J., & Newman, L. K. (2017). Attachment in children with autism spectrum disorder: A systematic review. *Research in Autism Spectrum Disorders, 35*, 35–50. Doi: https://doi.org/10.1016/j.rasd.2016.12.002

Teague, S. J., Newman, L. K., Tonge, B. J., Gray, K. M., & The MHYPeDD team (2018). Caregiver mental health, parenting practices, and perceptions of child attachment in children with autism spectrum disorder. *Journal of Autism and Developmental Disorders, 48*, 2642–2652. Doi: https://doi.org/10.1007/s10803-018-3517-x

Teicher, M. H. & Samson, J.A. (2016). Annual research review: Enduring neurobiological effects of childhood abuse and neglect. *Journal of Child Psychology and Psychiatry, 57*, 241–266. Doi: https://doi.org/10.1111/jcpp.12507

Thapar, A. (2018). Discoveries on the genetics of ADHD in the 21st century: New findings and their implications. *American Journal of Psychiatry, 175*(1), 943–950. Doi: https://doi.org/10.1176/appi.ajp.2018.18040383

Thijssen, S., Van 't Veer, A. E., Witteman, J., Meijer, W. M., van IJzendoorn, M. H., & Bakersman-Kranenburg, M. J. (2018). Effects of vasopressin on neural processing of infant crying in expectant fathers. *Hormones and Behavior, 103*, 19–27. Doi: https://doi.org/10.1016/j.yhbeh.2018.05.014

Thompson, R. A. (2001). Sensitive periods in attachment? In D. B. Bailey, Bruer, J. T., & Symons, F. J. (Eds.), *Critical thinking about critical periods* (pp. 83–106). Baltimore, MD: Paul H. Brookes Publishing. Doi: https://doi.org/10.1177/027112140102100306

Thomson, P. (2012). Shared experiences: The prenatal relational model and group process. In I. Harwood, W. Stone, and M. Pines (Eds.), *Self experiences in group, revisited: Affective attachments, intersubjective regulations, and human understanding* (pp. 11–33). New York, NY: Routledge. Doi: https://doi.org/10.4324/9780203119341

Tonso, K. L. (2009). Violent masculinities as tropes for school shooters. *American Behavioral Scientist, 52*(9), 1266–1285. Doi: https://doi.org/10.1177/0002764209332545

Tremlow, S. T., Fonagy, P., Campbell, C., & Sacco, F. C. (2018). Creating a peaceful school learning environment: Attachment and mentalization efforts to promote creative learning in kindergarten through fifth-grade elementary school students with broad extension to all grades and some organizations. In H. Steele and M. Steele (Eds.), *Handbook of attachment-based interventions* (pp. 360–374). New York, NY: Guilford Press.

Tse, W. S., Siu, A. F. Y., & Wong, T. K. Y. (2017). How does maternal oxytocin influence children's mental health problem and maternal mental health problem? *Psychiatry Research, 258*, 124–129. Doi: https://doi.org/10.1016/j.psychres.2017.09.068

Tuhkanen, H., Pajulo, M., Jussila, H., & Ekholm, E. (2019). Infants born to women with substance use: Exploring early neurobehavior with the Dubowitz neurological examination. *Early Human Development, 130*, 51–56. Doi: https://doi.org/10.1016/j.earlhumdev.2018.12.019

Tyrka, A. R., Burgers, D. E., Phillip, N. S., Price, L. H., Carpenter, L. L. (2013). The neurobiological correlates of childhood adversity and implications for treatment. *Acta Scandinavica, 128*, 434–447. Doi: https://doi.org/10.1111/acps.12143

Unterrainer, H., Hiebler-Ragger, M., Koschutnig, K., Fuchshuber, J., Tscheschner, S., Url, M., Wagner-Skacel, J. Fink, A. (2017). Addiction as an attachment disorder: White matter impairment is linked to increased negative affective states in poly-drug use. *Frontiers in Human Neuroscience, 11*(April), Article, 208. Doi: https://doi.org/10.3389/fnhum.2017.00208

U.S. Department of Health and Human Services (2018). *Physical activity guidelines for Americans* (2nd ed.). Washington, DC: Author.

U. S. Department of Labor, Bureau of Labor Statistics (2018). *College enrollment and work activity of high school graduates*. Available at: https://www.bis.gov/news.release/hsgec.nr0.htm.

Vaillancourt, T., Clinton, J., McDougall, P., Schmidt, L. A., & Hymel, S. (2010). The neurobiology of peer victimization and rejection. In S. R. Jimerson, S. M. Swearer, and D. L. Espelage (Eds.), *Handbook of bullying in schools: An international perspective* (pp. 293–304). New York, NY: Routledge/Taylor & Francis Group.

Van den Bergh, B. R. H., van den Heuvel, M. I., Lahti, M., Braeken, M., de Rooij, S. R., Entringer, S., Hoyer, D., Roseboom, T. Schwab, M. (2017). Prenatal developmental origins of behavior and mental health: Influence of maternal stress in pregnancy. *Neuroscience and Biobehavioral Reviews.* Doi: https://doi.org/10.1016/j.neubiorev.2017.07.003

Van de Bongardt, D., Yu, R., Dekovic, M., & Meeus, W. H. J. (2015). Romantic relationships and sexuality in adolescence and young adulthood: The role of parents, peers, and partners. *European Journal of Developmental Psychology, 12*(5), 497–515. Doi: https://doi.org/10.1080/17405629.2015.1068689

Van der Kolk, B. A. (2005). Developmental trauma disorder: Toward a rational diagnosis for children with complex trauma. *Psychiatric Annals, 35*(5), 401–408. Doi: https://doi.org/10.3928/00485713-20050501-06

Van der Meer, L., Costafreda, S., Aleman, A., & David, A. S. (2010). Self-reflection and the brain: A theoretical review and meta-analysis of neuroimaging studies with implications for schizophrenia. *Neuroscience and Biobehavioral Reviews, 34*, 935–946. Doi: https://doi.org/10.1016/j.neubiorev.2009.12.004

Vanderschuren, L., Achterberg, E. J. M., & Trezza, V. (2016). The neurobiology of social play and its rewarding value in rats. *Neuroscience and Biobehavioral Reviews, 70*, 86–105. Doi: https://doi.org/10.1016/j.neubiorev.2016.07.025

Van IJzendoorn, M. H. & Bakermans-Kranenburg, M. J. (2006). DRD4 7-repeat polymorphism moderates the association between maternal unresolved loss or trauma and infant disorganization. *Attachment and Human Development, 8*(4), 291–307. Doi: https://doi.org/10.1080/14616730601048159

Van IJzendoorn, M. H. & Kroonenberg, P. M. (1988). Cross-cultural patterns of attachment: A meta-analysis of the Strange Situation. *Child Development, 59*, 147–156. Doi: https://doi.org/10.1111/j.1467-8624.1988.tb03202.x

Van IJzendoorn, M. H., Rutgers, A. H., Bakermans-Kranenburg, M. J., van Daalen, E., Dietz, C., Buitelaar, J. K., Swinkels, S. H. N., Naber, F. B. A., & van Engeland, H. (2007). *Child Development, 78*(2), 597–608. Doi: https://doi.org/10.1111/j.1467-8624.2007.01016.x

Van IJzendoorn, M. H., Schuengel, C., & Bakermans-Kranenburg, M. J. (1999). Disorganized attachment in early childhood: Meta-analysis of precursors, concomitants and sequelae. *Development and Psychopathology, 11*, 225–249. Doi: https://doi.org/10.1017/s0954579499002035

Verny, T. R. & Weintraub, P. (2002). *Tomorrow's baby: The art and science of parenting from conception to infancy.* New York, NY: Simon & Schuster.

Victor, E. C. & Hariri, A. R. (2016). A neuroscience perspective on sexual risk behavior in adolescence and emerging adulthood. *Development and Psychopathology, 28*, 471–487. Doi: https://doi.org/10.1017/s0954579415001042

Vivanti, G. & Nuske, H. J. (2017). Autism, attachment, and social learning: Three challenges and a way forward. *Behavioural Brain Research, 325*, 251–259. Doi: https://doi.org/10.1016/j.bbr.2016.10.025

Volkaw, N. (2005). What do we know about drug addiction? *The American Journal of Psychiatry, 162*(8), 1401–1402. Doi: https://doi.org/10.1176/appi.ajp.162.8.1401

Wade, P. A. & Archer, T. K. (2006). Epigenetics: Environmental instructions for the genome. *Environmental Health Perspectives, 114*(3), A140–A141. Doi: https://doi.org/10.1289/ehp.114-a140

Walker, S. C. & McGlone, F. P. (2013). The social brain: Neurobiological basis of affiliative behavioural and psychological well-being. *Neuropeptides, 47*, 379–393. Doi: https://doi.org/10.1016/j.npep.2013.10.008

Wallin, D. J. (2007). *Attachment in psychotherapy.* New York, NY: Guilford Press.

Ward, L. M. (2016). Media and sexualization. State of empirical research, 1995–2105. *Journal of Sex Research, 53*(4–5), 560–577. Doi: https://doi.org/10.1080/00224499.2016.1142496

Watson, J. C. (2016). The role of empathy in psychotherapy: Theory, research and practice. In D. J. Cain, K. Keenan and S. Rubin (Eds.), *Humanistic psychotherapies: Handbook of research and practice* (p. 115–145). Washington, DC: American Psychological Association. Doi: https://doi.org/10.1037/14775-005

Weinfield, N. S., Sroufe, L., & Egeland, B. (2000). Attachment from infancy to early adulthood in a high-risk sample: Continuity, discontinuity, and their correlates. *Child Development, 71*, 695–702. Doi: https://doi.org/10.1111/1467-8624.00178

Weinstein, A. D. (2016). *Prenatal development and parents' lived experiences: How early events shape our psychophysiology and relationships.* New York, NY: W. W. Norton & Co. Doi: https://doi.org/10.7812/tpp/16-186

Wilkinson, P., Kelvin, R., Roberts, C., Dubicka, B., & Goodyer, I. (2011). Clinical and psychosocial predictors of suicide attempts and nonsuicidal self-injury in the Adolescent Depression Antidepressants and Psychotherapy Trial (ADAPT). *American Journal of Psychiatry, 168*(5) 495–501. Doi: https://doi.org/10.1176/appi.ajp.2010.10050718

Williams, A. J., Smith, D., & Winters, R. (2016). Applying Olweus' conceptualization of bullying to early childhood. *Contemporary perspectives on research on bullying and victimization in early childhood education* (pp. 87–104). Charlotte, NC: IAP Information Age Publishing.

Wolfe, P. (2010). *Brain matters: Translating research into classroom practice*, (2nd ed.). Alexandria, VA: ASCD.

Wolke, D., Eryigit-Madzwamuse, S., & Gutbrod, T. Very preterm/very low birthweight infants' attachment: Infant and maternal characteristics. *Archives of Disease in Childhood. Fetal and Neonatal Edition, 99*(1), F70–F75. Doi: https://doi.org/10.1136/archdischild-2013-303788

Wolynn, M. (2016). *It didn't start with you: How inherited family trauma shapes who we are and how to end the cycle.* New York, NY: Penguin Books.

Worsley, J. D., McIntyre, J. C., Bentall, R. P., & Corcoran, R. (2018). Childhood maltreatment and problematic social media use: The role of attachment and depression. *Psychiatry Research, 267*, 88–93. Doi: https://doi.org/10.1016/j.psychres.2018.05.023

Yehuda, R., Cai, G., Golier, J. A., Sarapas, C., Galea, S., Ising, M., Rein, T., ... Buxbaum, J. D. (2009). Gene expression patterns associated with posttraumatic stress disorder following exposure to the World Trade Center attacks. *Biological Psychiatry, 66*(7), 708–711. Doi: https://doi.org/10.1016/j.biopsych.2009.02.034

Yehuda, R., Daskalakis, N. P., Bierer, L. M., Bader, H. M. Klengel, T., Holsbor, F., & Binder, E. B. (2016). Holocaust exposure induced intergenerational effects on FKBP5 methylation. *Biological Psychiatry, 80*(5), 372–380. Doi: https://doi.org/10.1016/j.biopsych.2015.08.005

Yehuda, R., Engel, S. M., Brand, S. R., Seckl, J., Marcus, S. M., Berkowitz, G. S. (2005). Transgenerational effects of posttraumatic stress disorder in babies of mothers exposed to the World Trade Center attacks during pregnancy. *Journal of Endocrinology & Metabolism, 90*(7), 4115–4118. Doi: https://doi.org/10.1210/jc.2005-0550

Yip, J., Ehrhardt, K., Black, H., & Walker, D. O. (2015). *Journal of Organizational Behavior, 39*, 185–198.

Yoon, Y., Cederbaum, J. A., Mennen, F. E., Traube, D. E., Chou, C-P., Lee, J. O. (2019). Linkage between teen mother's childhood adversity and externalizing behaviors in their children at age 11: Three aspects of parenting. *Child Abuse and Neglect*, 88, 326–336. Doi: https://doi.org/10.1016/j.chiabu.2018.12.005

Young, K. C., Kashdan, T. D., McKnight, P. E., Blalock, D. V., Yuen, M., Richberg, J. B., (2015). Happy and unhappy adolescent bullies: Evidence of theoretically meaningful subgroups. *Personality and Individual Differences, 75*, 224–228. Doi: https://doi.org/10.1016/j.paid.2014.11.024

Yuill, N., Henske, S., Williams, S. E., & Leith, G. (2014). How getting noticed helps getting on: Successful attention capture doubles children's cooperative play. *Frontiers in Psychology, 5*, Article 419, no pagination specified. Doi: https://doi.org/10.3389/fpsyg.2014.00418

Zeanah, C., Cheser, T., Boris, N., & the American Academy of Child and Adolescent Psychiatry (AACAP) Committee on Quality Issues (CQI) (2016). Practice parameters for the assessment and treatment of children and adolescents with reactive attachment disorder and disinhibited social engagement disorder. *Journal of the American Academy of Child and Adolescent Psychiatry, 55*(11), 990–1003. Doi: https://doi.org/10.1016/j.jaac.2016.08.004

Zeanah, C., Smykes, A., Koga, S., Carlson, E., & the Bucharest Early Intervention Project Core Group (2005). Attachment in institutionalized and community children in Romania. *Child Development, 76*, 1015–1028. Doi: https://doi.org/10.1111/j.1467-8624.2005.00894.x

Zelenko, M., Kraemer, H., Huffman, L., Gschwendt, M., Pageler, N., & Steiner, H. (2005). Heart rate correlates of attachment status in young mothers and their infants. *Journal of the American Academy of Child and Adolescent Psychiatry, 44*(5), 470–476. Doi: https://doi.org/10.1097/01.chi.0000157325.10232.b1

Zimmer-Gembeck, M. J. & Helfand, M. (2008). Ten years of longitudinal research on U. S. adolescent sexual behavior: Developmental correlates of sexual intercourse, and the importance of age, gender, and ethnic background. *Developmental Review, 28*(2), 153–224. Doi: https://doi.org/10.1016/j.dr.2007.06.001

Index

Burgio, E., 239
Bushman, B. J., 285

C

cannabis, 160
caregiving, 136–139, 174
care/nurturance system, 48
care/nurturing system.
    See nurturing system
care seeking, 136–139
Carter, C. S., 155
Centers for Disease Control and
    Prevention (CDC), 178, 217
central nervous system (CNS),
    14–15, 157
cerebellum, 20, 161. *See also* brain
cerebral cortex, 19, 24–27
    attachment and, 91–93
    description, 24
    divisions, 25, 25–27
    frontal lobe, 26–27
    occipital lobe, 25
    parietal lobe, 25
    structure, 24–25
    temporal lobes, 25–26
cerebral hemorrhage, 158
challenges
    abuse, 215–221
    mental health, 214–231
    neglect, 215–221
    to conception, 155
    to prenatal brain development,
        156–162
    trauma, 215–221
Chambers, J., 147
chaos, 215
Charalampous, K., 237
Chico, E., 271
childcare practices, 137
child protective services (CPS),
    154–155
children/childhood. *See also* early
    childhood; middle
    childhood
    abuse, 159
    adult attachment styles and,
        167
    brain development, 180–191
    developmental task, 152
    expectations, 199
    maltreatment, 244
    media use, 238
    neglect, 173–175
    obesity, 200, 239
chronic stress, 155
Churchland, P. S., 209
Cicchetti, D., 141
cingulate cortex, 22–23
clear-cut attachment, 103
clinical work, attachment theory

in, 111–116
    client and, 112
    overview, 111–112
    practitioner and, 113–116
    therapeutic processes, 112–113
cocaine, 153
    during pregnancy, 159
cognition, 177
cognitive control system, 256
cognitive development, 158
cognitive empathy, 67
cognitive skills, 200
coherent narratives, 146, 148–149
cold aggression, 287
cold cognition, 258
collaboration, 146, 147
collective identity, 249
collective morality, 210
Combs-Orme, T., 2, 3, 81
commitment, 249
communication
    collaborative, 147
    emotions, 142
    nonverbal, 147
compassion, 68–69
complex trauma, 218
conception, 125, 155
conditioned fear, 52
conditioning memory, 35–36
conduct disorder, 240
conflict resolution skills, 237
conformity-oriented parenting
    style, 212
confusion, 171
Connolly, J., 273
consciousness, integration of,
    71–72
Contena, B., 222
contingent communication, 89
cooperative play, 203
Corballis, M. C., 121, 189
corpus callosum, 28, 162, 220
cortical consolidation, 42
cortisol, 11–12
Couch, L. L., 269
countertransference, 41, 114
Coyne, S. M., 241–243
Cozolino, L., 8, 19, 22–24, 28, 29,
    31, 47, 50–51, 55–58, 65, 66,
    69, 74, 76, 89–92, 291
Craigslist, 243
crying, 138–139
C-section, 176
cultural influences, emotions on,
    49
cyberbullying, 234, 237
cytoplasm, 7

D

Dallos, R., 230–231
Damasio, A., 44–46, 49, 210

Dapretto, M., 188
Davis, K., 161
Davou, B., 240, 242
delayed recall, 42
dendrites, 7
depression, 156, 215, 243–244. *See
    also* postpartum depression
    diagnoses of, 174
    during pregnancy, 156–160
    maternal prenatal stress, 157
developmental stage
    Industry vs. Inferiority, 215
    Initiative vs. Guilt, 214
diffusion of identity, 250–251
digital devices, 270
disengagement, 142–143
disinhibited social engagement
    disorder (DSED), 174–175
dismissing attachment style, 167
dismissing behavior, 263–264
disorganized/disoriented
    attachment, 85, 108, 165,
        167, 171, 173
    behaviors, 165, 166
    children, 200
    vs. avoidant attachment, 171
Dissanayake, E., 201
dissociation, 168–169
dissociative behaviors, 168–169
dissociative disorders, 169
distorted memories, 167
distractibility, 157
DLPFC. *See* dorso-lateral
    prefrontal cortex (DLPFC)
DNA, 7
Doan, H. M., 140
domestic violence, 156
dopamine, 10, 138–139, 196
    attachment and, 95
    risk-taking and, 256–257
dorso-lateral prefrontal cortex
    (DLPFC), 26
drug abuse, 160, 281–283
DSM5, 174, 222
Duke, N. N., 284
Duschinsky, R., 171
Dwiputri, G., 212

E

early childhood. *See also* middle
    childhood
    brain development, 180–191
    challenges to mental health,
        214–231
    peer relationships, 189
    physical play, 202–203
    prefrontal cortex, 183–188
    social environment. *See* social
        environment of early and
        middle childhood

mammals, 16
managing emotions, 205, 207
marijuana, 159
Marks-Tarlow, T., 193, 198
maternal behaviors, 137
maternal history of trauma, 159
maternal prenatal drug abuse, 160
maternal prenatal stress, 157
maternal prenatal substance
    abuse, 156
maternal prenatal substance use,
    156
maternal psychological issues,
    175–178
maternal psychology
    anxiety, 176–177
    attachment and, 178
    postpartum depression,
        176–177
    prematurity and, 178
    substance abuse, 175–176
    substance use, 175–176
maternal stress, 156–157
mating preferences, 275
maturation of prefrontal cortex,
    183–188
    executive functions, 185–187
    self-evaluation, 187–188
McCarty, W. A., 152–153
McCraty, R., 19, 64
McGilchrist, I., 27–28, 29, 43,
    50, 73
McKenzie, R., 230–231
McLaughlin, K. A., 219–220
McMorris, B. J., 284
medial forebrain bundle (MFB),
    57
memory, 33–43
    attachment and, 101–102
    characteristics, 33
    description, 33
    emotions and, 39
    explicit, 36–43
    formation and access, 33–34
    implicit, 34–36
    integration, 75
    long-term. See long-term
        memory
    working, 37
mental health, 158, 179
    case study, 216
    challenges, 214–231
    consequences, 217–219
    etiology of, 243–244
    issues/disorders, 280, 280–281
    practitioners, 152, 157, 160,
        166, 233
    technology, 239–241
    timing, 159

mentalization, 67, 210
mental models, 36
mental time travel, 189
mesolimbic dopamine pathway, 57
mesolimbic dopamine system, 51
metaphor and attachment style,
    199
methamphetamine, 153
    during pregnancy, 159
methylation, 2, 3, 225
Meuti, V., 177
microbiome, 18
microbiota-gut-brain axis, 18
microglia, 7
micromanaging, 170
middle childhood, 190. See
        also early childhood
    brain development, 180–191
    challenges to mental health,
        214–231
    peer relationships, 189
    prefrontal cortex, 183–188
Mikami, A. Y., 224
Mikulincer, M., 84, 86, 88, 100,
    103, 104, 105, 114, 115, 167,
    211–212, 253–254, 264, 269,
    273–275, 279–280, 283
mind, 4. See also brain
mirror-resonance system, 65–69
    compassion, 68–69
    empathy, 67–68
    imitation, 66
    intersubjectivity, 66–67
mobilization without fear, 60
Money, K. M., 159
Monitoring the Future Study, 281
monoamines, 10–12. See
        also neurotransmitter
    dopamine, 10
    serotonin, 11
    stress hormones, 11–12
moral development, 209–211
    neurobiology of, 209–210
morality, 193, 209
    attachment and, 211–213
    defined, 209
moratorium of identity, 251
Mortimer, J. T., 275
Mota, C. P., 286
mother-child interactions, 165
mother-child relationship
    care seeking, 136
    coherent narratives, 146,
        148–149
    collaboration, 146, 147
    emotional communication,
        142, 146, 149
    infancy and toddlerhood, 143
    reflective dialogue, 146,
        147–148

repair, 146, 148
mother-infant relationship, 145
motor cortex, 26
motor skills, 152
Munich, M. A., 170
Munich, R. L., 170
mutually regulated
    communication, 67
myelin, 7
myelination, 13, 161

N

narrative integration, 76, 148
Narvaez, D., 210–212
nature and nurture, 1–2
negative emotions, 50
neglect, 155, 179, 215–221. See
        also mental health
    consequences of, 217–221
    educational effects of
        childhood, 219
    emotional, 216
    neurodevelopmental effects of,
        219–220
    physical, 216
    prevalence of, 216–217
neonate intensive care unit
    (NICU), 178
nervous system, 14–15, 15, 196
neural integration. See integration
neural networks, 7–8
neuro-behavioral disorder
    associated with prenatal
    alcohol exposure (ND-
    PAE), 161
neurobiological consequences,
    219–221
neurobiological functioning,
    225–231
neurobiology
    bullying and, 236
    emotional intelligence (EI),
        206–207
    moral development, 209–210
    play, 196–198
neuroception, 46
neurochemicals, 93–95
neuro-clusters, 182
neurodevelopment, 159
neurodevelopmental disorders,
    215
neurodevelopmental effects
    of neglect, 219–220
    of trauma and abuse, 220–221
neuroinflammation, 157
neurological differences, 244
neurological dysfunction, 165
neurological functioning, 175
neurons, 7
neuroplasticity, 12–13, 139
neuroticism, 253

Printed in the USA
CPSIA information can be obtained
at www.ICGtesting.com
LVHW081559110824
787958LV00016B/1118